The Emergence of the Modern Middle East

The Moshe Dayan Center for Middle Eastern and African Studies seeks to contribute by research, documentation, and publication to the study and understanding of the modern history and current affairs of the Middle East and Africa. The Center is part of the School of History and the Lester and Sally Entin Faculty of Humanities at Tel Aviv University.

The Tami Steinmetz Center for Peace Research which was established in 1992 is an interdisciplinary academic unit at Tel Aviv University. Its mandate is to promote academic activity related to conflict resolution and peace-making, with special reference to the Arab-Israeli conflict.

Within this framework, the center:

- Initiates, encourages and supports research projects on subjects related to its mandate both in the Middle East and in other regions of the world.
- Holds research workshops and local and international conferences dealing with relevant subjects.
- Fosters academic collaboration with similarly oriented institutions in Israel and abroad.

The S. Daniel Abraham Center for International and Regional Studies which was established in 2004 by Tel Aviv University, promotes collaborative, interdisciplinary scholarship and teaching on issues of global importance. Combining the activities and strengths of Tel Aviv University's professors and researchers in various disciplines, the Abraham Center aims to integrate international and regional studies at the University into informed and coherent perspectives on global affairs. Its special focus is inter-ethnic and inter-religious conflicts around the world, with particular emphasis on possible lessons for the Israeli-Palestinian conflict.

The Center's founding director is Prof. Raanan Rein. Rein is Professor of Spanish and Latin American History and the Vice President of Tel Aviv University.

www.tau.ac.il/humanities/abraham

The Emergence of the Modern Middle East

Asher Susser and Duygu Atlas

Companion Volume for Parts I and II of the Massive Open Online Course (MOOC)

Conducted by Tel Aviv University in collaboration with Coursera

ISBN: 978-965-224-107-8

Production and cover design: Elena Kuznetsov, The Moshe Dayan Center

Printed in Israel by Tel Aviv University Press

Acknowledgments

This companion volume is an edited version of the lectures that we prepared and delivered during the first and second runs of Parts One and Two of the course on "The Emergence of the Modern Middle East" as a Massive Open Online Course (MOOC) presented through Coursera.

The first PDF files of transcripts were prepared with important input from one of our outstanding students in the first run of the course, Ms. Kathleen Cook, from Phoenix, Arizona in the US. The initial transcripts have been corrected and edited by the authors for this book format and we have added a detailed Table of Contents and an Index. Any remaining flaws or errors are, of course, entirely ours.

None of this would have come to fruition without the extraordinary team effort of all those involved with the various phases of the MOOC production at Tel Aviv University (TAU): Prof. Raanan Rein, the Vice President of the University; Yaniv Abramson, Administrative Director for Enrichment Courses at TAU; Yuval Shraibman, the CEO of "TAU Online – innovating Education" a subsidiary of the university for MOOC production; and TAU Online's instructional designers: Alon Gurevich and Nadav Stark. We could not have managed without the efforts of Dr. Esther Webman, a senior fellow at the Moshe Dayan Center at TAU, who patiently and painstakingly reviewed the entire manuscript and made many useful suggestions and improvements, and Elena Kuznetsov, also of the Dayan Center, who invested much time and effort, expertise and diligence in preparing the text for publication. Last, but by no means least, we would like to make special mention of Prof. Uzi Rabi, the Director of the Moshe Dayan Center, for his assistance and support in placing the facilities of the Center at our disposal for the publication of this project. To all we express our sincerest gratitude.

Asher Susser
Duygu Atlas

Tel Aviv, February 2017

About the Authors

Asher Susser is Professor Emeritus of Middle Eastern History at Tel Aviv University (TAU); the Stanley and Ilene Gold Senior Fellow at the Moshe Dayan Center for Middle Eastern and African Studies at TAU; and the Stein Family Professor of Modern Israel Studies at the University of Arizona. He was the Director of the Dayan Center for twelve years and taught for over thirty five years in TAU's Department of Middle Eastern History. He has been a Fulbright Fellow; a visiting professor at Cornell University, the University of Chicago, Brandeis University, and the University of Arizona. His most recent book is on ***Israel, Jordan and Palestine; The Two-State Imperative*** (2012). He also wrote *inter alia* ***Jordan: Case Study of a Pivotal State*** (2000); ***A Political Biography of Jordan's Prime Minister Wasfi al-Tall*** (1994); and a monograph on ***The Rise of Hamas in Palestine and the Crisis of Secularism in the Arab World*** (2010).

Duygu Atlas has an MA degree in Middle Eastern History from Tel Aviv University (TAU) and is presently a PhD candidate in TAU's School of History writing on Turkey's Jewish minority and its identity formation. She is also a researcher at the Moshe Dayan Center for Middle Eastern and African Studies. In 2016, she was awarded the Dan David Prize for Young Researchers. In her research, she focuses on minorities in Turkey. Her published articles include "The Role of Language in the Evolution of Kurdish National Identity in Turkey" (2014); "Turkey, Its Kurds and the Gezi Park Protests" (2014); and "The Jews of Mardin" (2016, in Turkish).

Table of Contents

Chapter One

The Middle East in the Modern Era

What is the Middle East?

This course on the Emergence of the Modern Middle East will expand upon the history of the Middle East of the last 200 years or so, from the early 19th century until the Arab Spring of the early 21st century. Speaking of the Middle East in the modern era requires a definition of both the Middle East and the modern era. The term Middle East is hardly self-evident. Looking at this region from the main cities of the Middle East, from Istanbul, Cairo or Tel Aviv, it would not be the "middle" nor the "east" of anywhere. The term Middle East is a term created by people who looked at the region from somewhere else. It was the Middle East if one was looking at the region from Paris, London or Washington, that is, from outside. From the vantage point of the Western outside, it was that "Middle East," which was on the way to the "Far East."

Yet, even though it was created by foreigners, all the peoples of the Middle East use this term to describe the region in which they themselves live. In Arabic, Turkish, Persian and Hebrew, this region is called the Middle East by the various peoples of the Middle East despite the term's foreign origins.

The term was originally used by an American naval historian, Alfred Thayer Mahan, in an article which popularized the term in 1902. The fact that a term created by a foreigner has been adopted by the local peoples, is an indication of the enormous effect that foreign powers have had in the creation of this modern Middle East.

The term "Middle East" was coined in 1902 by

Alfred Thayer Mahan

Time is defined in this region, according to the Gregorian Western calendar. There are Muslim and Jewish calendars, yet day to day life in the countries of the Middle East is not governed by them, but rather by a Western Christian calendar. Thus, both time and space in the Middle East have been defined by outsiders.

therefore not called into question until the very end of the 19th and the early 20th century, with the emergence of Arab nationalism, and even then only partially, and not by all the Arabs as one.

With the fall of the Ottoman Empire and the creation of new states on the ruins of the Empire, the state structure of the region served Western imperial interests, especially those of France and Britain. Therefore, even though these states were created when Arab nationalism was already a factor in the Middle East, not much respect was shown towards the ideas of Arab nationalism, which spoke of the unification of the Arabic-speaking peoples. As a result, the Arab state order, as created after the First World War, did not enjoy much legitimacy in the eyes of the Arab peoples.

The Rise and Fall of Arab Nationalism

Arab nationalism fought against this imperial state order and was a very popular movement throughout much of the 20th century. Arabism, though essentially secular, always contained a certain Islamic religious component, and Arab nationalism thereby offered a more acceptable transition from traditional Islamic identity to the more secular idea of nationalism. Arab nationalism provided an appealing compromise between purely secularist national ideas and the more traditional Islamic identity.

But as popular as Arab nationalism was, it was a dismal failure in political practice. Most notably, Arab nationalism failed in the conflict with Israel. Israel, smaller and less populous than the Arab countries, defeated the Arabs twice, first in 1948, and then, perhaps even more humiliatingly, in 1967. These wars with Israel and the defeat of the Arabs served as a monument to Arab failure to effectively meet the Western challenge. As a monument to Arab failure, Israel, needless to say, faces great difficulty to being accepted by the Arab world around it.

In the aftermath of the 1967 War, politics in the Middle East were governed by two dominant, albeit contradictory trends. The one was the final acquiescence of the Arab states in the colonial state order. The Arab states, realizing the failure of Arab nationalism, came to terms with the Arab state structure. It became more legitimate to speak about the Egyptian state, for example, and Egyptian state interest, *raison d'état* as the French call it. As did other Arab states like Jordan and Syria, and the Palestinians too. Less was said about Arab nationalism, and more was said about the need to unabashedly pursue state interest.

Challenging this acquiescence in the colonial state order and the political status quo was the radical Islamic revival, which filled much of the vacuum left by Arab nationalism. On the one hand, there was the radical Islamic revival and on the other, the territorial states and the existing regimes. The regimes and the

Islamists were in conflict with each other in many of the Arab states, from the far west of North Africa all the way to the Gulf. This radical Islamic revival was essentially at loggerheads with the Westernizing modernization process of the last 150–200 years, as it sought to promote an alternative route to modernity. It would be mistaken to see the Islamic revival as opposed to modernity, which it was not. It was, rather, an Islamic effort to find an avenue to modernity within the framework of an Islamic cultural, moral and legal framework.

Defining the Modern Era

It has been common in the writing of Middle Eastern history to start the modern era in 1798. In 1798 Napoleon invaded Egypt, and ushered in through his invasion, a long period of rapid and radical change. Though reasonable, this determination of the Napoleonic invasion as the beginning of the modern era, is problematic. It rests on the hidden assumption that the modern era in the Middle East was created solely through European influence and supremacy in an area which was in decline, stagnant and moving nowhere. There is a historiographical debate about whether it was ever really correct to begin the modern era with Napoleon's invasion of Egypt.

Napoleon's Invasion of Egypt, 1798

Jean-Léon Gérôme [Public domain or Public domain], via Wikimedia Commons

The Italian historian and philosopher Benedetto Croce (1866–1952) has noted that all history was contemporary history. All history was written from the point of view of the present, and as the present changed constantly so did our views about the past. Our ideas about the past and the ways in which we write about the past, are in constant flux. Therefore, not surprisingly, the portrayal of the Napoleonic invasion as the sole impetus for change and modernization in the region was challenged in later years.

First let us look at the so called thesis of decline. The thesis of decline argues that since its peak in the mid-16th century, in the period of the Sultan Süleyman the Magnificent (who died in 1566), the Ottoman Empire entered into a 350-year linear decline. Thus, over half of the Empire's existence was this linear decline that continued for centuries. The Middle East had become a dormant, stagnant society resurrected by the Western encroachment and it was Western enlightenment and vitality that brought about the modernization of the Middle East.

Istanbul (Late 19th and Early 20th Century)

But this was not really so. In the Middle East, well after the 17th century, there were vibrant cities with centers of government and courts of law, centers of learning and arts and crafts, and trade with the West and the East. It was not a stagnant, rotting entity. It is true that the Empire did not expand and from 1683, the failure of the siege of Vienna, the Ottoman Empire was in constant retreat in terms of territory. It did weaken in comparison to parts of Europe, certainly to northern and western Europe, but far less in comparison to southern Europe or Russia. This was more a matter of relative retreat in comparison to the Empire's former greatness, rather than a uniform linear decline.

On the one hand, it is true that the defeat at the gates of Vienna in 1683 was the beginning of a period of territorial contraction. But, on the other hand, there were very handsome defeats dealt by the Ottomans to the Russians, for example in 1711, in the war fought between them in what is presently the country of Moldavia. On the one hand, the Ottoman Empire was the "sick man of Europe." But on the other, it enjoyed unquestioned Islamic legitimacy. Even when rebellions in the Empire brought down the ruling Sultan, the legitimacy of the Empire remained intact.

This remained true until the rise of new ideas like nationalism in the late 19th and early 20th century. It was only then that the Empire was seriously challenged by new ideas from Europe, and that the legal system was questioned. Until then, the legal system was seen as fair and reasonable. But when European style legal and educational reforms were introduced, these had a dramatic impact on issues such as collective identity. These did not improve matters, but quite the opposite. During the 19th century, the difficulties of the Empire became more obvious, clearly seen from the Napoleonic invasion of Egypt, as one example. But other examples throughout the 19th century were the nationalist uprisings against the Ottoman Empire, amongst the Christians in the Balkans. In these nationalist uprisings the Christian nations of the Balkans, such as the Greeks, the Serbs and the Bulgarians gradually broke away from the Ottoman Empire and succeeded in obtaining their independence. It is also true that in the 19th century, the Western advance and advantage in science and technology and power projection was very clear. But then again, on the other hand, the Empire strengthened its hold in much of the Arabic-speaking provinces, and controlled a huge domain, all the way from Yemen to Libya, all still part of the Ottoman Empire.

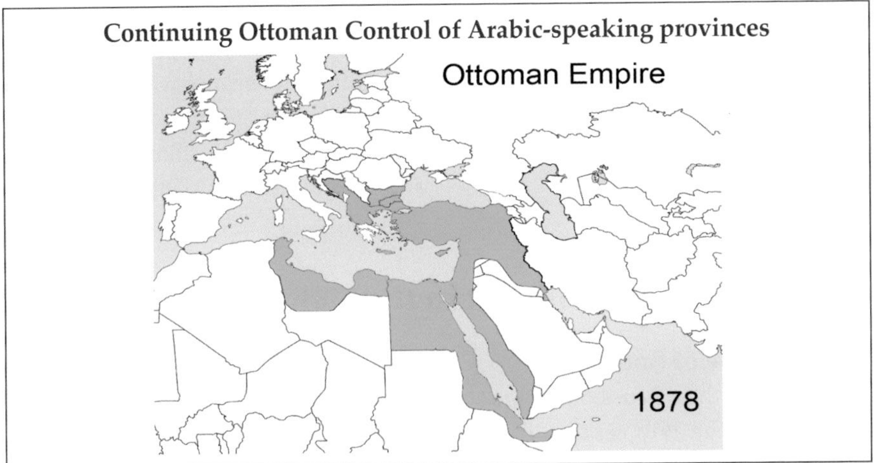

Continuing Ottoman Control of Arabic-speaking provinces

There were indeed frequent rebellions against the Ottomans since the end of the 16th century. This was a sign of weakness. But the fact that the Empire survived these rebellions time and time again was another sign of Ottoman resilience. The 17th century was a period of growing decentralization and empowerment of local potentates and rising urban social classes. Some historians argue that this was a negative force, that it was an indication of the decline of the Ottoman Empire. But others would argue quite the opposite, that it enabled an often effective, albeit indirect form of control, and that it was not a sign of decline at all. Hugh Nolan, a non-academic Irish historian, not writing about the Ottoman Empire, made a general comment: "Aye," he said, "the two things happen at one time. Things get better, and they get worse."

So what difference does this discussion make? Did it all begin with Napoleon or not? What is the correct periodization of this modern era? Was change initiated entirely from outside by the enlightened, progressive West, on a dormant, stagnant, and backward society? Did nothing change in the Middle East until Napoleon? The answer to all these questions is that it was obviously not so. The picture was much more complex. The European input added great momentum to a process that had already begun. Some go even as far as to argue that Napoleon interrupted a local process of modernization, which could have been a successful alternative to the Western model. Had it not been for the Western impact, they say, the Middle East would have established its own model of modernity. Maybe, but equally, maybe not.

Historians have questioned whether it does all begin with Napoleon, but no one has actually offered an alternative periodization. The bottom line of the debate could be the balanced conclusion that Dror Ze'evi has drawn: "The Napoleonic phase was a key to a new period of rapid change, but one that added a quantum leap forward to an ongoing process."[1]

The colonial interaction, with all its obvious negatives, created an unprecedented measure of rapid change in politics, the economy, and perhaps, most importantly, in the sphere of ideas and the erosion of tradition. And ideas, one ought to note, can be more subversive and dangerous than occupation. Ideas tend to erode fundamental beliefs and traditions. Occupations come and go.

The Middle East in the 19th Century

The Structure of Society

Moving on to the discussion on the structure of society in the Middle East at the beginning of the 19th century it is important to recognize that, in comparison to Europe, the emphasis in the Middle East was on the structure of society by groups as the basic components of society, rather than societies composed of individuals. The British historian Malcolm Yapp described Middle Eastern society in the following terms: Middle Eastern society "was composed ... of various groups whose relationship to each other was like that of pieces in a mosaic. Governments recognized the existence of these groups and dealt with them in different ways. There was no assumption that society was composed of numbers of individuals who should be treated in a uniform fashion; rather different groups had different rights and interests and required to be governed in different ways."[2] Indeed, the different groups in Middle Eastern society were based on birth — family, extended family and tribe, and most importantly, religious denomination. People in the Middle East defined themselves, first and foremost, by their religious association.

In 1800, the great majority of the Middle Eastern population were Muslims. There were various minorities, such as, Orthodox Christians and Jews. In Egypt, there was a significant Coptic Christian population. In the European parts of the

---

1. Dror Ze'evi, "Back to Napoleon? Thoughts on the Beginning of the Modern Era in the Middle East," *Mediterranean Historical Review*, Vol. 19, No. 1 (June 2004), pp. 73–94.
2. MalcomYapp, *The Making of the Modern Near East, 1792–1923* (London: Longman, 1987), p. 36.

Ottoman Empire, there was a Christian majority that outnumbered the Muslims by two to one.

Some Middle Eastern minorities are referred to in the professional literature as "compact minorities." Compact minorities are so defined since they are located in one single particular territory, like the Maronite Christians in Mount Lebanon, the Alawis in northwestern Syria, or the Druze who are concentrated in the Druze mountain area, which is in southern Syria, and partly in Lebanon. Compact minorities, located in a specific territory, had a tendency to develop a very strong communal identity. Whereas the Orthodox Christians, who were dispersed throughout the Ottoman Empire, for example, and were not a compact minority, had a much greater tendency to support Arab nationalism than did the Maronite Christians of Mount Lebanon. Thus, political affiliations of minorities were influenced by their geographical location and situation.

The Ottomans governed these minorities through their own autonomous institutions. This was called the *millet* system. The minorities were known as millets, or autonomous peoples. The minorities were governed by laws of their own, as not all peoples of the Ottoman Empire were subject to the same legal authority. Non-Muslims paid taxes that Muslims did not pay. This was known as the *jizyah*, a poll tax, although the Ottomans were not very strict about it, and only about one third of the non-Muslims actually paid *jizyah*. In theory, Muslims followed their law, and Christians and Jews followed theirs. The non-Muslim communities were not only concerned with religion. They administered their own courts of law and their own schools for the education of their particular communities.

The Muslim community was not uniform either, and was divided between Sunni Muslims and Shi'ite Muslims. The original difference between Sunnis and Shi'is was not really about dogma, but much more about politics. The division between Sunnis and Shi'is goes back to the 7th century and was part of a political struggle over the succession to the Caliphate after the passing of the Prophet. In the eyes of his supporters, the fourth Caliph was supposed to have been Ali, the son-in-law of the Prophet. His supporters were known as the Ali faction, Shi'at Ali. Shi'a means faction, and it was from their support of Ali that the name Shi'a derived. Other minorities, like the Alawis and the Druze, were sects that broke away from the Shi'a in the 10th and 11th centuries and were not part of the community of Muslim believers.

Official establishment Islam was represented by the chief of the religious establishment in the Ottoman Empire, the Sheikh al-Islam, the chief religious authority appointed by the Sultan, who was the chief religious authority for the Muslims in the Empire. But there was also popular and not only establishment Islam. These were the Sufi mystical orders, to which large portions of the Muslim population belonged.

In the social hierarchy in the Ottoman Empire of the 19th century, the government composed of the military and the bureaucracy, staffed almost entirely by Muslims, was at the top. It was not customary for Jews and Christians to be part of either the military or the bureaucracy, although in the bureaucracy, there were Jews and Christians, particularly as translators. Second to government was the religious establishment and the religious functionaries; the judges and those who interpreted religious law for the general population. Then there were those who were outside government, the merchants, the peasants, the tribesmen, the townsmen, the members of the professional guilds and the notables in the provincial parts of the Empire who were bridges between the rulers and the ruled, and were also very often the tax collectors and the landowners.

There were deep divisions between town and village. The town was the center of government, commerce, education and the bureaucracy. Peasants, in the eyes of the townsmen, were regarded as illiterate, uncultured, and ignorant of the outside world. There was a great deal of tension between landowners in the towns and the peasantry. These tensions between landowners and the peasantry were to be an integral part of the revolutionary politics of the Middle East of the 20th century.

In the 19th century Middle Eastern society underwent a major transformation. Government became more centralized, and thus, more powerful. Landowners grew even stronger, and the tensions between them and the peasantry were exacerbated. A new education system that was introduced into the Empire under the impact of European influence engendered a new educated secular class of the modernizing Empire that weakened the status of the religious establishment. All the same, association with religious community, tribe and family, remained the core organizing principle of society. The issue of new ideas led to the increased importance of the religious minorities because of their knowledge of languages, their relative openness to Europe, and their improved status as a result of the reforms that were introduced in the Ottoman Empire during the 19th century.

The Economy

As for the economy of the Middle East at the beginning of the 19th century, there are few reliable statistics. It is estimated that the Middle Eastern population at that time was about 30 million: 6 million in Iran, 24 million in the various Ottoman territories, and some 3.5 million in Egypt, counted separately because of the independent route that Egypt took in the 19th century. That figure of 3.5 million in Egypt is an interesting point to note at present. Since the beginning of the 19th century, until today, the beginning of the 21st century, Egypt's population has increased 25 times over. The Middle East in the early 19th century was relatively underpopulated, whereas now the great problem of the Middle East, and a major reason for the outbreak of the so called "Arab Spring," is that the region is very overpopulated.

In the early 19th century, things were different and population was kept low because of the wars that broke out between the Ottomans and the Persians, and especially between the Ottomans and various European powers. Famine was frequent and disease was very common. There was also birth control, mainly through abortion. There were losses of life due to famine in countries like Egypt and Iraq, which were completely dependent on the flow of the great rivers, the Nile in Egypt and the Tigris and the Euphrates in Iraq. When rainfall was low, populations suffered from famine, causing huge loss of life. Plague was another cause of tragic loss of life. One sixth of the population of Egypt succumbed to the plague in 1785. Over 300,000 people died in Istanbul because of the plague in 1812.

During the 19th century, there was a revolutionary increase of population. Western medicine, public health measures, better communications and transportation, increased security, reduced internal violence, all led to an ever increasing population in the 19th century. The same was true at an even faster rate in the 20th century.

The Nile, Euphrates and Tigris Rivers

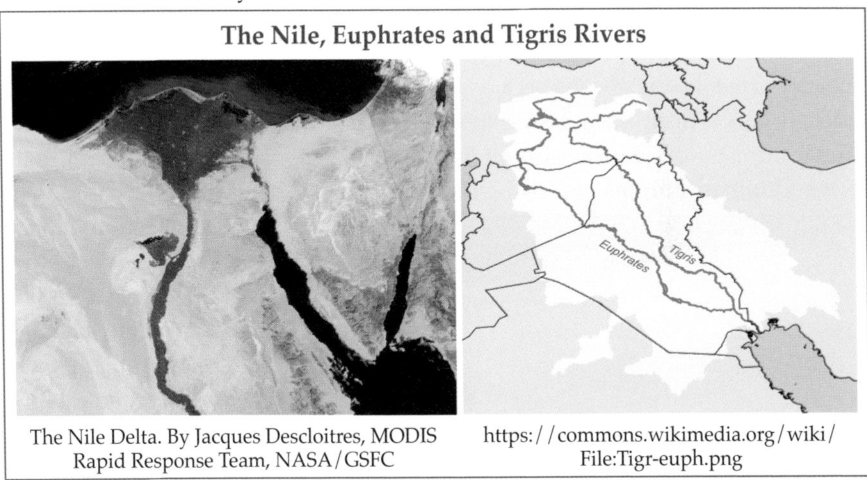

The Nile Delta. By Jacques Descloitres, MODIS Rapid Response Team, NASA/GSFC

https://commons.wikimedia.org/wiki/File:Tigr-euph.png

There were also changes in the composition of the population. The fact that the Ottoman Empire was gradually losing its European provinces also meant that the Ottoman Empire was gradually losing much of its Christian population. Provinces that were lost to Christian powers led to the immigration of Muslims from these areas into the Ottoman Empire. The Ottoman Empire, therefore, became ever more Muslim and ever less Christian during the 19th century.

In the period between 1912 and 1923, there was a demographic disaster in the Middle East. Twenty percent of the population of Anatolia, which is the major land mass of Turkey, died in that period due to wars and other inflictions, and 10 percent of them emigrated.

During the 19th century with the emergence of the nationalist idea, there was a trend towards the "territorialization" of identity. It was no longer enough for indigenous communities to live in their various particular locations. Under the impact of European ideas, these religious minorities sought a territorial identity and contiguity in the form of a state. The creation of these territorial identities led to bloody clashes between different religious and national groups. The most tragic of all and the most well-known was the terrible tragedy of the Armenians in Turkey of the First World War. "Territorialization" of identity had some very nasty, unintended consequences.

Because the growth of population in the Middle East in the 19th century, on the eve of the First World War, the Middle East was no longer self-sufficient in food. This was a problem that was only aggravated as time went by and it has become even more of a problem in the Middle East of today, which is both overpopulated and incapable of feeding itself.

In the economic relations between the Middle East and the West during the 19th century Britain surpassed France as the leading commercial super power in the region. At the end of the 19th century, most of the Middle East's commerce was with Europe. Middle East exports of raw materials and food items went to Europe, while the Europeans, as a result of their Industrial Revolution, exported finished goods from Europe to the Middle East. There was a massive flow of capital from Europe to the Middle East, and the creation of a huge debt, both in the Ottoman Empire and in Egypt, to European countries and banks. The connection with Europe and the attendant economic changes were much slower in Iran. Being much further away from Europe, Iran had far less direct contact with Europe, than either the Ottoman Empire or Egypt.

Politics

On politics in the Middle East of the 19th century, one may refer again to the British historian Malcolm Yapp, who spoke about politics being governed by two main characteristics. Government was diverse and minimal, he observed.[3] The governments, as already noted, recognized the existence of groups and not individuals. Muslims and non-Muslim subjects were governed in different ways and by different laws. Muslims followed the Shari'a, and Christians and Jews followed their own ecclesiastical or legal frameworks. Tribesmen had their own modes of settling disputes and foreigners were also granted special legal privileges which were called the capitulations. The capitulations allowed foreigners to be governed by the laws of their own countries, implemented by their respective consular representatives. Government was minimal, as was taxation. Services like law and education were not supplied by the central government, but by the various communities.

To outside observers, this often gave the impression of a decentralized and even ineffective government in decline. But as another British historian, Albert Hourani, has noted, these were actually adaptations in the style of governance according to changing circumstances that actually remained quite effective. The locus of power shifted from the Sultan to the higher echelons of the bureaucracy in the office of the Grand Vizier, the chief minister. Provinces were often controlled by local potentates as was the case in Egypt and in other parts of the Empire.

In the Arab cities of the Empire, there were notable families, some Arab, some Turkish that assumed positions of wealth and power. Because of the importance of religion, notable families tended to send their children to obtain religious education and to become functionaries in the religious and legal establishment. Through this kind of employment, they gained control of religious endowments, *awqaf* as they are known in Arabic, which were sources of great wealth and political control. Boys but not girls, were schooled in the traditional schools, the *Kuttab* and the *Madrasas*, where they learned the Qur'an and religious jurisprudence, as well as some secular subjects like mathematics and astronomy.[4]

The Changing Balance of Power with Europe

During the 19th century, there was a dramatic change in the balance of power with Europe. Up until the middle of the 18th century, the Ottomans saw

3. Yapp, *The Making of the Modern Near East*, p. 36.
4. Albert Hourani, *A History of the Arab Peoples* (New York: Warner Books, 1991), pp. 249–255.

themselves on an equal footing with Europe, and before this period, even superior to Europe. But in the last quarter of the 18th century, it was becoming increasingly apparent that the gap between the Ottoman Empire and Western Europe, in science, technology, military and economic power was growing in favor of the Europeans. Important advances in medicine led to dramatic population growth in Europe. Technology enabled modern shipbuilding, and therefore also economic growth. The wealth of the West enabled the creation of powerful navies and armies, and all of this served the expansion of Europe ever more at the expense of the Ottomans.

The Russian-Ottoman War of 1768 to 1774 was a critical turning point. The Russians emerged victorious in this confrontation, and conquered Crimea. This great victory brought the Russians onto the shores of the Black Sea, which from then onwards ceased to be an enclosed Ottoman lake. The Russians were getting ever closer to the Straits, the Bosphorus and the Dardanelles, that lead into the Mediterranean. The loss of Crimea did not only mean the loss of complete Ottoman control of the Black Sea. It also meant the first serious loss of a territory populated by Muslim subjects.

The Loss of Crimea: Formally Annexed to Russia in 1783

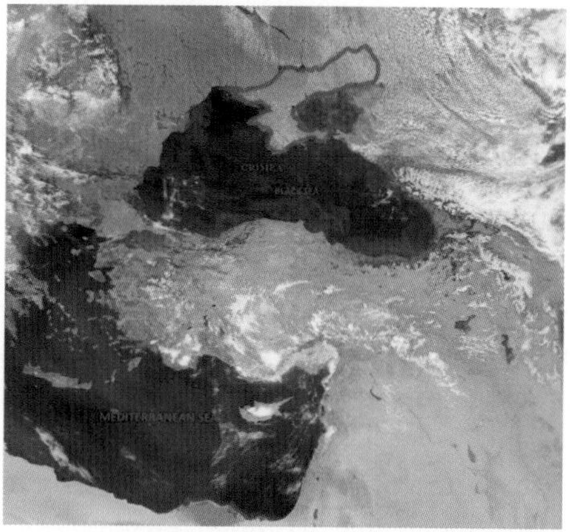

https://commons.wikimedia.org/wiki/File:The_Danube_Spills_into_the_Black_Sea.jpg

The loss of Ottoman control of Muslim peoples was a historical reversal of great symbolic meaning. It undermined the critically important religious legitimacy of the Ottoman Empire as the sovereign ruler and protector of the Muslim believers. As such, the Empire was committed to the protection of Muslim peoples from domination by hostile Christian powers.

In the 19th century European empires seemed to rule the world. This led to the realization of the peoples in the Middle East, and the Ottoman government too, that something had gone awfully wrong in the cosmic order of things. The belief in the historical supremacy of Islam over all other religions and peoples, was in need of an update. A fundamental change in thinking was required. It was already at the end of the 18th century, when Sultan Selim III initiated the first serious efforts at modernizing the Ottoman army.

The British and French Empires (1920)

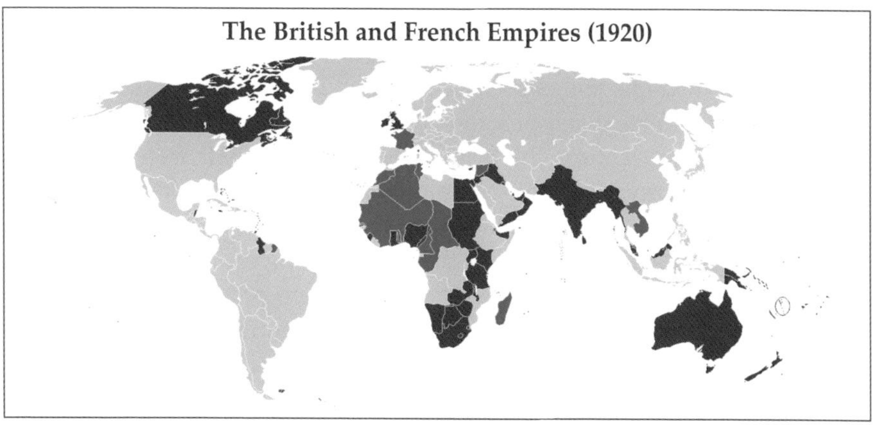

Selim III (reign 1789–1807)

By John Young (1755-1825) [Public domain], via Wikimedia Commons

Selim's reforms began in the 1790s, actually prior to the Napoleonic invasion of Egypt. The fact that the reforms began in the military was very important in and of itself. It meant that the military was to become the vanguard of Western-style modernizing reform, which had great effect on politics in the Middle East in later years. Military officers were amongst the most westernized in Middle Eastern societies and were often the leaders of revolutionary change.

Revolutionary change in the military led to revolutionary change in other spheres too. Modernizing the military required the learning of foreign languages, such as French, English, and German. The learning of foreign languages in order to modernize the military led eventually to the influx of foreign ideas and foreign ideas were the most important in creating what one could call the cultural shock for the Muslim world in its recognition that Islam was no longer a superior civilization. The Muslims could no longer trust in their own self-sufficiency. New ideas, such as equality before the law, individual rights, and nationalism gave rise to new forms of identity and to new forms of organization of the political community.

The most dramatic foreign intrusion was Napoleon's invasion of Egypt in the summer of 1798. The French stayed for three years until they were forced out by the British and the Ottomans. But this was the first intrusion into the very heartland of the Ottoman Empire and it was not only an intrusion, but also an eye-opening exposure to the enormity of European power at that time.

Moreover, this was not only military power but also an exhibition of the prowess of Western science. The French came to Egypt not only with their armies, but with scientific missions that exposed the Middle East to this whole new world of scientific advancement and progress.

During the 19th century, the people of the Middle East were exposed to an explosion of European energy. The population of Europe increased by 50 percent from 1800 to 1850. Britain's population grew in this period from 16 million to 27 million. London became the largest city on earth with a population of 2.5 million. There was much available manpower needed both for industry and the development of large modern armies. Between 1815 and 1850, Britain's exports to the countries of the Eastern Mediterranean increased by 800 percent. Europe's need for raw materials meant olive oil from Tunisia, silk from Lebanon and cotton from Egypt.

The European merchants had the power of their home countries behind them. The Russians and the French interfered regularly in the affairs of the Christians in the Ottoman Empire, the Russians supporting their fellow co-religionists, Orthodox Christians like the Serbs and the Greeks, and the French protecting Catholics. At a later stage, Britain tried to play this minority game by supporting the Jews and the Zionist idea in Palestine. Support for nationalist aspirations of the Christian communities of the Ottoman Empire came very regularly from the Europeans. The Christians were also the first to be affected by Western ideas. By the nature of things, the Christians of the Middle East had a greater openness to the Christian West.

The "Eastern Question"

These were the years in which the so-called "Eastern Question" developed. The Eastern Question preoccupied the European powers but it was really a question about the fate of the Ottoman Empire, which had a very critical impact on the European balance of power. The fear of the European powers was that a decline or collapse of the Ottoman Empire, could lead to a European struggle for the remnants of the Empire that would upset the balance of power in Europe and set the stage for an awfully destructive European war. Seeking to prevent such an outcome the European powers, generally speaking, shared the collective interest to preserve the integrity of the Ottoman Empire, despite its weakness, to forestall the disintegration of the Empire and thereby to avoid the destabilization of the power relations in Europe.

At the end of the 18th and at the beginning of the 19th century, Russia posed the greatest challenge to the Ottoman Empire. There were two components of this Russian challenge: The religious factor, Russia's support for Orthodox

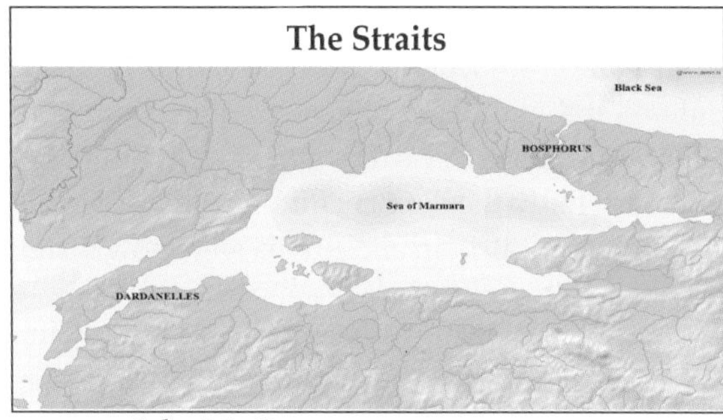

The Straits

Christians in the Middle East, and the strategic factor, Russia's desire to advance southwards to the Black Sea, and beyond, advancing towards the Straits, the Bosphorus and the Dardanelles, in order to eventually reach the warm waters of the Mediterranean.

Britain also became an interested party in the affairs of the Middle East as a result of her acquisition of India, the so-called "jewel in the crown" of the British Empire. To maintain the connection with India, Britain obviously required safe

The Route to India

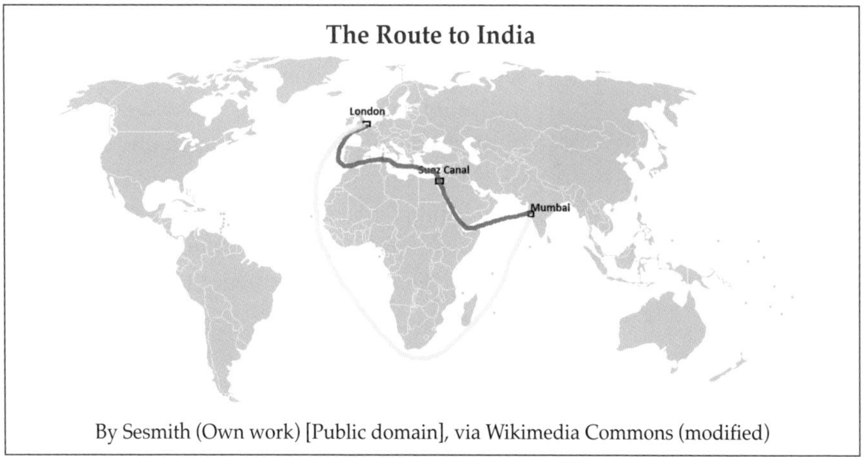

By Sesmith (Own work) [Public domain], via Wikimedia Commons (modified)

passage which went through the Mediterranean and the Middle East. Britain therefore acquired a strategic interest in the preservation of Middle Eastern stability.

But things were not always managed so easily. Bonaparte's expedition to Egypt in 1798 was a typical example of such destabilizing difficulties. Napoleon occupied Cairo in July 1798. A month later, in August,

Thomas Whitcombe [Public domain], via Wikimedia Commons

the French fleet was destroyed by the British in the Battle of the Nile, severing Napoleon's communications with France. In September of 1798, the Ottomans declared war on France and entered into an alliance against France with both Britain and Russia. Bonaparte set off for Syria but was stopped at Acre in May 1799, and he returned to France. In 1801, the French force in Egypt finally surrendered to a British expeditionary force. Britain and Russia were now firmly allied to preserve the integrity of the Ottoman Empire.

Muhammad Ali

Auguste Couder [Public domain], via Wikimedia Commons

But a new reality had emerged in Egypt in the meantime. In the aftermath of the French occupation, Muhammad Ali, an Ottoman officer of Albanian origin, was dispatched by the Ottomans to govern Egypt on their behalf. But instead he gradually assumed control of Egypt as the de facto local ruler. Muhammad Ali became the creator of modern Egypt, essentially separating Egypt from the Ottoman Empire. He instituted military reforms, followed by a host of reforms in other spheres, actually advancing in reform ahead of the Ottoman Empire. By establishing his own autonomous control of Egypt in the early 19th century, Muhammad Ali and Egypt also became part of the famous "Eastern Question."

A core component of this "Eastern Question" during the 19th century was the conflict between the Ottoman Empire and its Christian subjects in the Balkans. Christians in the Balkan provinces of the Ottoman Empire eagerly debated and adopted modern European ideas like nationalism and it was with European support that they were eventually successful in their struggles for independence. The Greeks were the first, in the 1820s, followed by others like the Serbs, the Romanians and the Bulgarians. There was a dominant religious element in these nationalist movements. It was, after all, always Christians fighting against Muslims, and thus, the virtually natural support of the Europeans for these newly emerging

Theodoros Vryzakis [Public domain], via Wikimedia Commons

independence movements of Christian nations versus the Ottomans. European support for Greek independence was also motivated by a romanticized image of ancient Greece that was linked to this new struggle of the Greeks for their independence.

As the Ottomans seemed to be losing in their struggle with the Greeks, Muhammad Ali, now the de facto ruler in Egypt, was called upon by the Ottomans to help suppress the Greek uprising. But the Turco-Egyptian fleets were defeated in Navarino by a combined British-French force in 1827. Muhammad Ali was promised Syria in return for his assistance, but the Ottomans did not keep their word. Muhammad Ali then invaded Palestine and Syria in 1831 and defeated the Ottomans in Konya, which is deep inside Anatolia, in 1832. He was now a very real threat to the integrity of the Ottoman Empire. In their despair, the Ottomans sought help from their erstwhile enemies, the Russians, with whom they signed a defense pact in 1833.

The Russians were interested in preserving the integrity of the Ottoman Empire against other threats, but this gave the impression to some of the European powers that Russia was acquiring a form of protectorate over the Ottoman Empire. Britain therefore became committed to removing Muhammad Ali from Syria, not because she cared that much about the Middle East, but because of Britain's concerns for the balance of power in Europe.

Muhammad Ali defeated the Ottomans again in 1839. Britain and Russia cooperated to remove the threat posed by Muhammad Ali, and forced him out of Syria and back to Egypt. But Muhammad Ali was now given the hereditary possession of Egypt in exchange for his removal from Syria. That meant that Egypt was no longer only under the rule of Muhammad Ali, but it was promised as an inheritance to Muhammad Ali's sons and their sons thereafter, thus creating a dynasty which ruled in Egypt all along until 1952, when it was overthrown by the Egyptian officers under General Nagib and Colonel Nasser.

Matters were destabilized again between the powers in 1854 with the outbreak of the Crimean War. This was a war fought by the Russians against the Ottomans, who were backed by Britain and France. The trouble was ignited at first by a conflict between France and Russia over the protection of Christian holy places in Palestine. The Russians demanded concessions from the Ottomans, who refused, resulting in

Treaty of Paris, 1856
Territorial integrity of the Ottoman Empire guaranteed by the European powers.

By Édouard-Louis Dubufe [Public domain], via Wikimedia Commons

the war that was eventually brought to an end by the Treaty of Paris in 1856. The Treaty of Paris guaranteed the territorial integrity of the Ottoman Empire by the European powers. But in return for this European guarantee, the Sultan promised reforms and better treatment of Christian minorities.

What this meant, in conclusion, was growing European interest and interference in the lands of the Ottoman Empire, which also led to the promotion of nationalist movements that threatened the Empire and made it absolutely crucial for the Sultan to engage in urgent reform to avert defeat. The reforms did not save the Empire in the end, but they did eventually help to create the modern Middle East as we know it.

Key Sources and Suggested Further Reading

- Hourani, Albert, *A History of the Arab Peoples* (New York: Warner Books, 1991).
- Hourani, Albert, Khoury, Philip and Wilson, Mary (Eds.), *The Modern Middle East: A Reader* (London: I.B. Tauris, 2011).
- Lewis, Bernard, *Islam and the West* (Oxford University Press, 1993).
- Lewis, Bernard, *The Middle East: 2000 Years of History From the Rise of Christianity to the Present Day* (London: Weidenfeld and Nicolson, 1995).
- Yapp, Malcolm, *The Making of the Modern Near East, 1792-1923* (London: Longman, 1987).
- Ze'evi, Dror, "Back to Napoleon? Thoughts on the Modern Era in the Middle East," *Mediterranean Historical Review*, Vol. 19, No. 1, June 2004.

Chapter Two

Modernity, Tradition and the Age of Reform

The impact of Europe at the end of the 18th and the early 19th century inspired an extended period of reform that continued throughout the 19th century. Though reforms related, initially, to the military in the main, reform in the military led very rapidly to reforms that affected all spheres of life. Reforms altered the lifestyle and the economy and impacted upon the world of ideas. The age of reform, therefore, was an ongoing struggle between the forces of continuity and change, between the forces of modernity and tradition.

There were two centers of reform: The Ottoman Empire and Egypt. The Ottoman Empire and Egypt are discussed separately, even though they were essentially parts of the same political entity, mainly because Egypt from the Napoleonic era onwards, under Muhammad Ali, gradually emerged as an independent political unit. Moreover, these were two very different territories in geo-strategic and geographical terms, and these affected the extent and the pace of reform in the Ottoman Empire, on the one hand, and in Egypt, on the other.

Egypt is the very unique land of the Nile Valley. The people of Egypt have lived for thousands of years along the River. They are the people of the Nile Valley, which by its very nature tended to be a highly centralized political entity, with the River as the artery of effective governmental control, for centuries upon centuries. The Ottoman Empire, on the other hand, was not very centralized. As a huge and very diverse territorial entity, it had many local potentates who wielded a great deal of influence. Reform in the Ottoman Empire was much more difficult to implement, and was generally less consistent than in Egypt with its highly centralized structure. The Ottomans were also preoccupied mainly by military needs and were engaged in the development of a huge modernized military force because of the Empire's repeated engagement in war throughout the 19th century. This was not true of Egypt, and reforms, therefore, had varying results, moving further and faster in Egypt than they did in the Ottoman Empire.

The Beginning of Reform in the Ottoman Empire

The age of reform in the Ottoman Empire began with Sultan Selim III, who reigned from 1789 to 1807. This was a period of accelerated reform and it is interesting to note that Selim III came to power in the same year of the French Revolution. During the last quarter of the 18th century, the Ottoman Empire's decline was becoming ever more obvious. While, on the other hand, in Europe of the French Revolution the great power of Europe was expressing itself against the background of Ottoman lethargy, as revealed by the Napoleonic invasion of Egypt in 1798. Prior to this period, the Ottomans could still cling to the belief in the inherent superiority of Islam, and assume that minor reforms in the domain of the military and the methods of war would suffice.

The French Revolution

But by the end of the 18th century, it was very clear that this would not be enough. In 1783, the Ottomans finally lost Crimea to the Russians. As already noted, great historical importance was attached to this defeat. It was the first surrender of a Muslim populated territory to a Christian power. This loss of Muslim territory called the legitimacy of the Ottoman Empire as an Islamic empire into question. After all, the legitimacy of the Empire was grounded in its protection of the Muslim peoples. This loss of the Crimea, therefore, was an indication of the comprehensive failure of the Ottoman system, no more and no less.

In order to engage in reform the traditional world view that included a considerable resistance to the very idea of reform had to be overcome. As Bernard Lewis has noted, in the Islamic state and community, it was believed that they "were the sole repositories of enlightenment and truth, surrounded by an outer darkness of barbarism and unbelief."[1] There was nothing to learn from the outside world. There was, therefore, great difficulty in making the transition into a world where this was no longer true and where the Islamic state was no longer "the sole repository of enlightenment and truth," and one depended not only upon learning from the Christian world, but also upon becoming more dependent on the goodwill of Christian powers.

1. Bernard Lewis, *The Middle East; A Brief History of the last 2000 Years* (New York: Touchstone Books, 1997), p. 305.

Christoph Weigel the Elder [Public domain], via Wikimedia Commons

There were two main opponents to reform in the Ottoman Empire, the *ulama,* that is the religious establishment, the men of religion, and the Janissaries. The Janissaries were the elite military force of the Ottoman Empire. Both of these were extremely resistant to any idea of reform. The opposition of the *ulama* was based on opposition, in principle, to any innovation, particularly to the adoption of infidel practices, which was what reform actually meant.

The Devshirme System: Recruitment of Christian Boys

By Matrakci Nasuh (http://warfare.atwebpages.com/Ottoman/Ottoman.htm) [Public domain], via Wikimedia Commons

The Janissary corps, the one-time elite Ottoman infantry, had lost much of its quality and had become exceptionally corrupt. The Janissaries, *Yeniçeri* in Turkish, which means "new soldier," were originally Christian boys abducted from their families to be raised as Muslims, elite soldiers and loyal servants of the Sultan. But with time, positions in the force were inherited or sold to non-professionals. The Janissaries gradually declined and became an ineffective and weak military force. In the end, they turned into a troublesome lot, at the disposal of the enemies of reform.

In his program of reform, Selim III employed foreign advisors, many of whom were French. He also established permanent embassies in Western Europe, and Ottoman officials who served in these embassies, became the future architects of reform in the later years of the Ottoman Empire. The focus of reform, as already mentioned, was on the military. This was a factor of great importance not only then, but all the way through to modern times. Military officers in the Middle East, having been at the center of the process of reform,

Example: Mustafa Kemal Atatürk, the founder of the Republic of Turkey

By Presidency of Republic of Turkey (http://www.tccb.gov.tr/sayfa/ata_ozel/fotograf/). [Public domain] via Wikimedia Commons

became the standard bearers of modernization and secularization. Throughout the history of the Middle East of the last two centuries military officers have been at the core of revolutionary movements and of the clashes between the forces of modernity and the forces of tradition.

The most important reform of Selim III in the field of the military was the establishment of a "new corps" known as *Nizam-i Jedid*. The force was established in 1791 and the ranks of the *Nizam-i Jedid* were filled by conscription, following the example of European conscript armies. In 1805, the Janissaries, obviously opposed to this kind of competition, revolted against the general conscription and defeated the new troops.

Other auxiliary troops of the Ottoman army rebelled in 1807 because they were required to wear European-style uniforms. It is particularly interesting to note that just the change of uniforms was enough to arouse a rebellion. Dress touched on the very sensitive issue of collective identity. It was not just about the changing of clothing. The problem of European-style uniforms meant abandoning the external appearance that distinguished between Muslims and infidels. For Muslims it was important to make such distinctions in conformity with the Islamic tradition requiring believers to "distinguish yourselves" from the infidels.[2]

The mutiny of the auxiliaries was supported by both the Janissaries and the *ulama*, the religious establishment. The Janissaries and the *ulama* had either ideological reasons or motives of self-interest to oppose the reforms. For the *ulama* it was both ideology and self-interest. After all, the reforms meant the erosion of the place of religion and the men of religion in the state. For the Janissaries, it was mainly an issue of self-interest. The creation of new military forces would turn them, within time, into a superfluous, outdated military order. But it was their opposition that led to the overthrow of the reforming Sultan Selim III, who was deposed in 1807. The main reason for his failure to implement reform was simply that the opponents of reform outnumbered those who supported it. The fact that the reforms were carried out with foreign advice made it much easier to discredit them as infidel innovations.

What was required to continue the pace of reform was to remove the Janissaries as a force of consequence. Sultan Mahmud II did exactly that.

Mahmud II (r. 1808–1839)

https://commons.wikimedia.org/wiki/File:Sultan_Mahmud_II.jpg

2. Bernard Lewis, *The Emergence of Modern Turkey*, Second Edition (Oxford University Press, 1968), p. 100.

Mahmud II, who ruled from 1808 to 1839, abolished the Janissary corps in 1826 and was consequently often described as the Ottoman version of the Russian Peter the Great in terms of his contribution to modernization and reform in the Ottoman Empire.

In the Greek Revolt of the 1820s the Janissaries as a military force revealed their total incompetence. Mahmud II renewed his attempt at forming a new army in 1826. This time, however, he was careful in formulating the reforms within an Islamic framework in order to forestall accusations of infidel innovations. There were Muslim instructors and a *fatwa*, religious ruling, was issued to the effect that the reforms were in line with the Shari'a, Islamic law.

Mahmud II's New Army: Asakir-i Mansure-i Muhammediye (Muhammad's Victorious Soldiers)

Fausto Zonaro [Public domain], via Wikimedia Commons

However, the Janissaries, as Mahmud had expected, revolted yet again in rejection of the reforms. The Sultan, this time, was well prepared and he crushed the Janissaries with great force. They no longer enjoyed popular support as the protectors of the faith. By then they were seen for what they really were: an unruly, self-interested rabble. Thousands of Janissaries were killed in the uprising and the Janissary corps was finally abolished. Ottoman historians refer to this as "the Auspicious Event," and in terms of reform and modernization, indeed it was. The road to the creation of a European-style army and for comprehensive reform was now wide open.

The religious establishment and the provincial notables who had hitherto enjoyed a great deal of political power, suffered from a steady reduction in their influence as a result of the strengthening of state power with the advent of reform. European-style reforms even with the assistance of European advisors were openly carried out. New schools were established mainly to support the military reforms: a medical school for army doctors and a school of military sciences. It is important to note that the language of instruction in these schools was French and the exposure to foreign languages laid the intellectual groundwork for the exposure to the world of foreign ideas.

But in the meantime, the focus was on the reform of the military, and it took a long time for the new army to prove itself in the battlefield. It did so, very successfully, in the initial phases of the First World War, but that was a long time ahead. The reform of the military was a very important tool in maintaining the power of the central government. Mahmud II also reformed the bureaucracy and officials became ministers with European titles, and Ottoman Muslims were encouraged to learn foreign languages. Student missions were sent abroad from 1827 onwards and from 1833 a translation bureau was in operation too. The spread of a growing body of translations, by means of the printing press obviously meant, with time, the spread of foreign ideas. The reopening of overseas embassies in 1834, which had been shut down after the fall of Selim III in 1807, was another important form of exposure to the windows of the West.

Reforms definitely strengthened the position of the central government at the expense of competing agents of power that existed in the Ottoman Empire such as the *ulama*, the Janissaries, the professional guilds or the provincial notables. The persistent reforms of Mahmud II regularized and legitimized change. It was now more acceptable to engage in reform and change, overcoming the initial, traditional opposition to this kind of innovation. In order to legitimize his reforms, Mahmud II concealed the extent of change by presenting reform as the abolition of harmful innovations to protect Islam, thereby presenting the reforms as if they were part of a project not to weaken the hold of Islam on society, but actually to reinforce it. Yet, it was this initiation of modest reform that eventually opened the floodgates of Western-style modernization.

It is especially noteworthy that this was not a revolution of the masses and the reforms were not implemented as a result of popular protest, but a top-down process which often encountered opposition from below rather than receiving the encouragement of the population at large. The driving force behind the reforms was the need to preserve the Empire rather than answering to public pressure. The mass of the population was indifferent to the reforms or even hostile to change. The impact of reform on the masses was actually very partial.

This is important to remember when discussing later periods in the 20th or the 21st century. In more recent years, the revival of tradition, through Islamic movements had very many takers amongst the general population. The reform was top-down and when changes of leadership took place in the Ottoman Empire, reforms were often set back, if the Sultan coming to power happened to be less interested in change than his predecessors.

The *Tanzimat*

In 1839 Sultan Abdülmecid succeeded Mahmud II. This was the beginning of the period known in Ottoman history as the *Tanzimat*, the reforms. The reform of the Empire was guided from now on by official policy statements and was an organized process that continued for decades. The goals of the *Tanzimat* were set out in two reforming edicts. The first was the Hatt-i Sherif of Gulhane, the Noble Edict of the Rose Garden (of the Sultan's Palace) as it is known, that was issued in 1839. The second edict, issued in 1856, proclaiming more or less the same reforms, but in greater detail, was the Hatt-i Humayun, the Imperial Edict, that was followed by the promulgation of the Ottoman constitution in 1876.

Abdülmecid I (r. 1839–1861)

See page for author [Public domain], via Wikimedia Commons

If the reforms were meant to create a more liberal form of government, they failed to do so. The Ottoman Empire did not become more liberal or democratic. But if they were designed to strengthen the central government and prolong the life of the Empire they succeeded. The Empire lasted for another 80 years, which was an impressive achievement in and of itself.

The first priority with these new reforms, as before, was the army. Between one half and two thirds of all expenditure on the reforms went to the building of various military forces. Funds to pay for the army required a change in the method of taxation. The method of taxation was therefore modernized, and the old system of tax farming (*iltizam* in Turkish), whereby notables were given the right to collect taxes from the populace, was abolished. These notables often pocketed much of the taxes, and the system became corrupt and ineffective.

There was a need for wide-scale administrative reform in order to carry out the reforms. This led to the development of a modern system of education to supply the much needed skilled manpower for the execution of the reforms in the army and the administration.

The system of provincial government was remodeled by the passing of a new provincial administration law, the Vilayet Law of 1864, which established a much more centralized government run from Istanbul, which allowed for a more effective collection of taxes and a more efficient administration of the provinces by the government in the capital. The provinces were tied more directly to the center, at least to a certain degree, thanks to the *Tanzimat*. The *vilayets* (the provinces) were placed under a governor, and a structured system of sub-districts, all run by appointees from Istanbul. Local councils were also created in the various provinces. The councils included some appointed officials and some elected members, and these operated alongside the governors as a form of representation of local opinion.

A Ministry of Education was established in 1847, thereby removing education from the control of the religious establishment where it had been until then, weakening ever more the status and the stature of the *ulama* in the Ottoman Empire. The establishment of the Ministry of Education and the creation of the new schools was in recognition of the need for the acquisition of the skills for the advancement of the Empire in this world, based on the understanding that religion was far more valuable for the next world than it was for this one. There was a need to keep up not only with the advances that were taking place in Europe, but also in the Christian schools within the Empire itself.

During the *Tanzimat* the education system was not entirely revolutionized. It was much more difficult to change schools and education in the villages than it was in the towns and the cities. All the same, the *Tanzimat* did succeed in creating a number of excellent high schools in the main cities of Turkey which educated the bureaucrats who would carry on with the reforms until the very end of the Empire.

Reforms in administration and the military led necessarily to reform in the legal system. Indeed, the reforms in the legal system were the most revolutionary of all, since they had to mean the undermining of religious law, the Shari'a. It also affected collective identity as there was nothing that weakened the hold of Islam on society more than legal reform. Perhaps the most important legal reform of all was the decision to grant all subjects of the Empire equality before the law. This was not the case until the *Tanzimat*. As already noted, religious minorities such as Jews and Christians enjoyed religious autonomy but they were never equal before the law. Islam in the eyes of the believers was a superior civilization with a superior legal system. The granting of equality before the law essentially meant that Muslims, Jews and Christians were all equal before a law, which could no longer be the Shari'a. Granting equality eroded one of the very basic principles of the Shari'a, according to which Muslims were believed to be superior to Jews, Christians and other minorities. Equality before the law was also a revolutionary change in the sense that now the same law would apply to all the subjects of the Ottoman Empire, as opposed to the former system whereby different laws applied to the different communities.

This could also be seen as the territorialization of the legal system. For the first time ever, there was one legal system that applied to all subjects of the Empire as equals, no longer communities governed by their particular legal codes, but individuals who were equal before a law that applied to all. This was an important step towards territorial nationalism. If the law applied territorially to all subjects of the Empire, and not to communities as communities, it was also a step towards the territorialization of collective identity.

The Edict of 1839, in which equality before the law was proclaimed, was justified as a need to correct the deviation from the Shari'a of the last 150 years, making the argument that countries that did not follow the Shari'a could not survive. Thus, the erosion of the Shari'a was explained and justified as if it were an upholding of the Shari'a, which it was not. The deviation from the Shari'a that had to be corrected, according to the edict of the Sultan, required new legislation. New legislation suggested that the Shari'a was no longer sufficient, and that new legislation would have to be taken from other, external, legal systems.

The 1839 Edict introduced principles such as the security of life and property, the abolition of tax farming, organized enlistment to the army, and, of course, justice and equality for all subjects regardless of their religion. The deviation from the Shari'a meant that God's law was no longer good enough. This was the beginning of the secularization of law and an emulation of European models. Such new laws also required the training of lawyers and judges to apply them and thereby amplified the blow to the religious establishment, the *ulama* and their authority.

The guaranteeing of equality to the minorities was meant to preserve their loyalty to the Empire. But, in fact, the opposite was achieved. Equality for the minorities was intended to offer the Christians of the Empire, who were gradually breaking away (as in the uprising of the Greeks in the 1820s), equal participation within the Empire as Ottoman subjects. But the Christians drew a totally different conclusion. If equality, then they sought equality in states of their own outside the Empire. Thus, the reforms only accelerated the Christian desire to break away, which most of them indeed did.

For many Muslims, the idea of the equality of all before the law was a cause for considerable consternation. In their mind this was an incorporation of the practices of the infidels and an undermining of the Shari'a that not all Muslim subjects of the Empire could accept without complaint. A major outburst occurred in Damascus in 1860 where thousands of Christians were massacred in a protest against the new reforms of the *Tanzimat*.

Damascus 1860

Jan-Baptist Huysmans [Public domain], via Wikimedia Commons

Interestingly, the Jews of Damascus were not affected by

the outbreak of violence. It was not the Jews against whom the Muslims protested. Their complaint was against the increasing influence of the Christian powers and of the local Christians and their schools. The Jews of the Empire did not represent foreign powers, nor were there any external Jewish powers that threatened the Empire. As a result, the Jews were not seen as partners or agents of foreign influence. On the contrary, the Jews were seen for what they really were, loyal Ottoman subjects.

Jews in Jerusalem, 19th century

By w:Detroit Photographic Company [Public domain], via Wikimedia Commons

The Christians in the Empire had a desire to secede wherever this was territorially feasible. It was not territorially feasible everywhere, but in places where it was, as in the Balkans, this was the preferred option for the Christian minorities. What made matters more difficult for the Empire in the new circumstances was that it was no longer possible to suppress the Christians who sought to break away, because of European pressure. As the British historian Malcolm Yapp has pointed out, there was an inherent contradiction in the new reality. The state was becoming more powerful and more centralized as a result of the reforms, but its ability to exploit these new advantages was limited by increasing external influence.[3]

A Jewish woman in Istanbul, 17th century

By G. la Chapelle [Public domain], via Wikimedia Commons

An Ottoman Jew, 18th century

Painting of a Jewish man from the Ottoman Empire, 1779 [Public domain], via Wikimedia Commons

Increasing foreign influence was also evident in the timing of the various edicts of reform. They were invariably published at times when the Ottomans needed to create a more liberal and progressive impression on the

3. MalcomYapp, *The Making of the Modern Near East, 1792-1923* (London: Longman, 1987), p. 114.

European powers. It would be wrong, however, to conclude that the reforms were just window dressing for the Europeans. There was a genuine desire for reform from within the Ottoman Empire out of recognition that the Empire had to be reformed and strengthened in its own self-interest. At the same time, the Ottomans also understood their need for European assistance.

Thus, the reforms in 1839 were introduced when the Ottomans desperately needed help against Muhammad Ali who was threatening Istanbul. In 1856, the reforms were issued at the end of the Crimean War, when the Ottomans were again in need of European support against Russian designs. In 1876, the constitution was ratified in an effort to avoid European intervention as the Empire was going bankrupt. It was at that time also, the mid-1870s, that the financial problems of the Empire were compounded by the possible intervention of the Europeans on behalf of the Christians in their struggles against the Ottomans in the Balkans.

Yet, it should also be noted that the constitution was passed in 1876 for real domestic reasons too. There was a movement known as the Young Ottomans, the most famous spokesperson of which was Namik Kemal. Namik Kemal made the convincing and factually correct argument that the *Tanzimat* reforms had disempowered the forces which had traditionally restrained the power of the Sultan and the government, the *ulama* and the Janissaries.

The Young Ottomans

Namik Kemal
https://commons.wikimedia.org/wiki/File:Kemalbey.jpg

In order to exercise influence over the Sultan and in order to maintain the momentum of reform, when the Sultans in power were reluctant to do so, there was a need for greater control over the Sultan. This was to be obtained through the vehicle of *shura*, the Islamic injunction for consultation, which was the formal justification for the creation of a parliament and for the passing of a constitution.

The Ottoman Parliament

By The Graphic (en:The Graphic, April 7, 1877) [Public domain], via Wikimedia Commons

These ideas of constitutionalism and parliament were part of a broader movement (discussed below) of Islamic reform, which spoke of the need for a synthesis between Western ideas and Islamic values so as

Russo-Turkish War (1877–1878)

The Repulsion of the Bajazet Fortress Assault, June 8, 1877
Lev Feliksovich Lagorio, 1891 [Public domain], via Wikimedia Commons

not to abandon society's Islamic identity in the process of Westernizing reforms. Reform of the Empire was essential, but so was the preservation of the Empire's Islamic character.

The issue of the Empire's Islamic identity was highlighted further by the troubles of the 1870s. The Empire was bankrupted by the expense of the reforms. Due to the loss of Christian territories in the Balkans and the consequent migration of Muslims from these lost territories into the Empire, the Empire was becoming ever more Muslim and ever less Christian. After the 1878 war with the Serbs and the Bulgarians that led to further Christian gains and to another war with Russia, which also ended in Ottoman defeat, there were increasingly vocal critics of reform and expressions of resentment for the concessions that were being made to Christians and to Christian powers.

Ottoman Constitution of 1876

قانون اساسی

قانون اساسی‌یه دائر شرف‌صدور ایدن خط همایون
عدالت مشحون شاهانه‌نك صورت
منیفه‌سیدر

استانبول — مطبعهٔ احمد کامل

Published by Ahmed Kamil Printing House, Istanbul [Public domain], via Wikimedia Commons

Sultan Abdülhamid II, who reigned from 1876 to 1909, dissolved the newly formed parliament in 1878. The constitution remained in place but was not acted upon. Pan-Islamism became a feature that the new Sultan emphasized as a common front of Muslim peoples against the European Christian powers. Muslim solidarity, in this phase, was still much easier to mobilize amongst the masses than more secular notions of nationalism.

If the *Tanzimat* reforms were supposed to have been a process of liberalization, then the suspension of the constitution in 1878 marked its failure. But it was never really intended as a process of liberalization. The reforms of the institutions of government and the military served the Empire and its long term survival. With all their shortcomings and limitations, the *Tanzimat* laid the foundations of modern Turkey. As Bernard Lewis has put it: The greatest achievement of the *Tanzimat* was in the field of education. A new group of educated elites graduated from the new schools. At the same time, there was also widespread hostility towards the reforms as a form of foreign intrusion. In reality there was only one option, and that was to move forward towards more reform and more change. For Turkey there was no turning back.[4]

Muhammad Ali and Reform in Egypt

At the end of the 18th century, Egypt was in a state of anarchy as conflicts raged between various Mamluk factions. Although the Mamluks were originally slave soldiers they were eventually to become the masters of Egypt. It was they who controlled Egypt for very many years, long before the invasion of Napoleon.

The 1798 French invasion, however, ushered in a new era in Egypt's history. The struggle for power between the French and the Ottomans was followed by another round of struggle between the Ottomans and the Mamluks that came in the wake of the ouster of the French. Muhammad Ali, who arrived in Egypt in 1801 as second in command of the Albanian troops that had been sent by the

The Mamluks

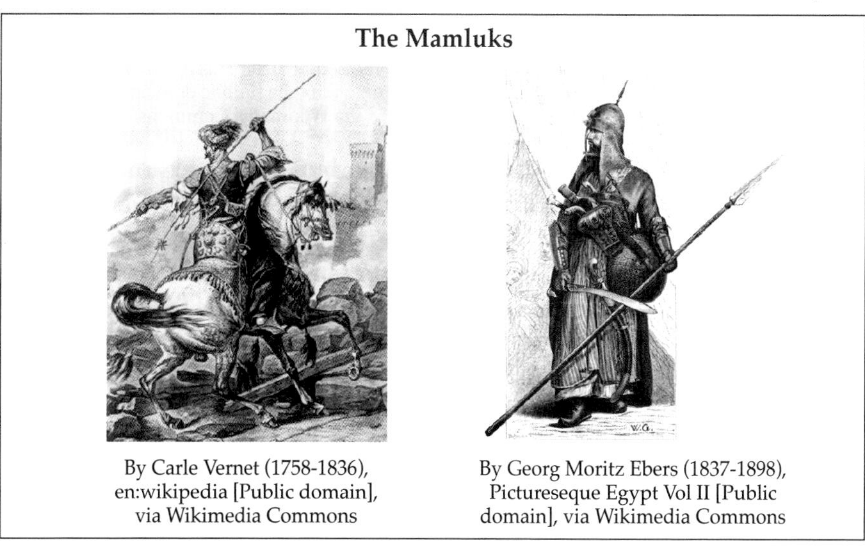

By Carle Vernet (1758-1836), en:wikipedia [Public domain], via Wikimedia Commons

By Georg Moritz Ebers (1837-1898), Pictureseque Egypt Vol II [Public domain], via Wikimedia Commons

Ottomans to take control of Egypt from the French, took Egypt over for himself and forced the Ottomans to recognize him as its governor. Between 1809 and 1812, Muhammad Ali went about destroying the power of the Mamluks, who still remained an important military force in Egypt. A massacre of Mamluks was organized by Muhammad Ali in Cairo in 1811, and their power in Egypt was finally broken.

4. Bernard Lewis, *The Emergence of Modern Turkey*, p. 128.

The population of Alexandria rose from 15,000 in 1805 to 150,000 in 1847 including a large number of foreigners. Egypt was transformed from a state of anarchy, as it had been before the Napoleonic invasion, when Egypt was still under the reign of the Mamluks, into a strong centralized state which possessed unprecedented power and control over its people.

During the period from 1811 until 1841, Muhammad Ali was engaged in a series of foreign military adventures. From 1811 to 1813, he waged a successful campaign in the Hijaz to subjugate the Wahhabis, the Islamic fundamentalists, on the Sultan's behalf, in order to strengthen the Ottoman hold on the region. In 1818, he destroyed the Wahhabi base in Central Arabia, in the Najd. In 1839, he was once again occupied with the Arabian Peninsula. From 1820 to 1826, he brought the Sudan under Egyptian control, which did not prove to be a very profitable conquest. During the 1820s, he assisted the Sultan against the Greeks. But then, as already noted, in 1831, he invaded Syria to fight against the Ottomans. He might even have considered advancing on Istanbul if it were not for his fear of the Russians, the British and other European powers. In 1840, he was eventually forced to settle only for Egypt, and its hereditary governorship in his family, no mean feat in and of itself.

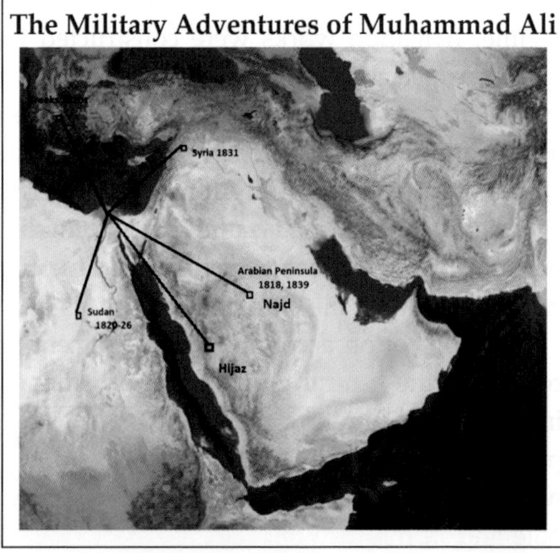

The Military Adventures of Muhammad Ali

Malcolm Yapp discussed the possible reasons for these adventurous undertakings of Muhammad Ali.[5] One explanation given was that he was an Arab nationalist, and that he sought the establishment of a great Arab state. But this theory does not hold much water as Muhammad Ali didn't even speak Arabic but Turkish, and he was even said to regard Egyptian-Arabs with a measure of contempt. Arab nationalism in the 1830s or 1840s was hardly spoken of and Arabism as a nationalist identity was expressed seriously only at the very end of the 19th century.

Another theory claimed that he was an Egyptian nationalist and that Muhammad Ali's expansionist ambitions were in pursuit of Egyptian national goals. It is true that Egypt was his base, but Muhammad Ali did not have any

5. MalcomYapp, *The Making of the Modern Near East*, p. 154.

notion of Egyptian nationalism. Egyptian nationalism was also an identity which came to the fore only at the end of the 19th century, way beyond Muhammad Ali's time. A third theory sees Muhammad Ali acting in a Muslim and Ottoman context, seeking advancement within the Ottoman system, that is, increasing his power as a local potentate within the Ottoman Empire. A fourth theory sees Muhammad Ali simply as a military adventurer.

The answer to this query would appear to be in a combination of the third and the fourth explanations. That is, Muhammad Ali was acting in the Muslim and Ottoman context, seeking to advance his own power as an autonomous ruler within the Ottoman system, and as a military adventurer. The ideas of nationalism that some people wish to associate with him are just a figment of their imagination.

Khedive Ismail (r. 1863–1879)

[Public domain], via Wikimedia Commons

After Muhammad Ali, there was a certain slowdown in the process of reform, which picked up again under Muhammad Ali's grandson, Khedive Ismail. Khedive was a title Ismail bestowed upon himself. He did so in order to emphasize the independence of Egypt from the Ottoman Empire, Khedive being the title of a ruler that suggested that he was more than just another governor under the Ottomans, but rather the autonomous ruler of Egypt.

Khedive Ismail, who ruled from 1863 to 1879, was described by the historian P.J. Vatikiotis as the "impatient Europeaniser."[6] Indeed he was. Khedive Ismail was one who saw Egypt as part of Europe and he provided the means for the great advancement of the country and the emergence of a Westernized intellectual elite in government, education and letters. Unfortunately, however, his impatient Europeanising bankrupted the country, leading eventually to the British occupation of Egypt.

One of the more important developments and with the most lasting influence during Khedive Ismail's reign was the opening of the Suez Canal in 1869. Ismail, however, was lavish and at times reckless in his spending, bringing Egypt to its knees. In 1875, Britain bought the Khedive's shares in the Suez Canal and became the major shareholder in this key artery to India, a factor which played very importantly in the development of Britain's imperial role in Egypt and in the Middle East as a whole. Great advances were made during Ismail's time,

6. P. J. Vatikiotis, *The Modern History of Egypt* (London: Weidenfeld and Nicolson, 1969), Chapter 5.

in agriculture, especially in cotton for export and he expanded the cotton and sugar industries as well.

During Ismail's reign there was an impressive construction spree of canals, bridges, telegraph, railway lines and the modernization of Egyptian cities. The immigration of Europeans in great numbers, who were needed for their expertise, was also an impressive feature of Khedive Ismail's rule. From a few thousand Europeans in Egypt in 1860, there were more than 100,000 in 1876. Many Egyptians were in daily contact with Europeans in business and in European modelled schools. Khedive Ismail founded specialized schools for lawyers, administrators, engineers, technicians, linguists, teachers and craftsmen, and even religious sheikhs. He was the first ruler in Egypt to bring education to girls. Ismail encouraged Western habits, Western dress and a Western lifestyle in general. This was all a huge step forward towards the creation of modern Egypt.

But at the same time, there were mounting troubles, financial bankruptcy, first and foremost, and increasing foreign control of Egyptian finances as a result. There was mounting disaffection of the fledgling nationalist movement in Egypt with the increasing foreign control. Eventually this all led to the invasion of Egypt by Britain in 1882 (see Chapter Three), initially to ensure the repayment of Egypt's debts. The British stayed, however, for 70 years.

From the advent of Muhammad Ali's rule at the beginning of the 19th century, Egypt was set on a different path from the rest of the Ottoman Empire, gradually becoming a separate political entity. This trend only increased after the British occupation, and the development rather rapidly thereafter, of an Egyptian nationalist movement, well before the evolution of Arab nationalism.

Islamic Reform or Modernism

The prolonged period of reform throughout the 19th century, gave rise to a unique and historically important debate in the sphere of ideas on the Islamic response to this challenge of modernity. Benedict Anderson observed that "in Western Europe, the eighteenth century marked not only the dawn of the age of nationalism but the dusk of religious modes of thought," which were superseded by rationalist secularism.[7] But in the Middle East, this was not so. The late 19th and early 20th centuries, were an era of profound ideological ferment and Islamic reform, as Western ideas such as secularism and nationalism dominated the local intellectual discourse. But in the Middle East, as opposed to

7. Benedict Anderson, *Imagined Communities; Reflections on the Origin and Spread of Nationalism* (London: Verso, 1991), p. 11.

Europe, the dawn of nationalism was never quite the dusk of religious modes of thought. Rather, the two continued to compete with each other, experiencing different periods of relative success in the marketplace of ideas.

There was, of course, an inherent tension between faith, religious belief and secularism. For centuries, it was believed amongst Muslims that society was legitimate only in as much as it behaved in accordance with Muslim religious law, the Shari'a. But the essence of secularism, in addition to the separation of religion and state, accepted the assumption that no one person or group had a monopoly over the absolute truth. Secularism meant tolerance of difference and disagreement, and of different perceptions regarding the desired political order.

This was completely at variance with religious belief in a divine political order. The divine political order, as understood in the world of Islam, was a political order that could not be shared with others who did not belong to the same community of believers. There was a distinction between the divine order and the man-made order, shaped in accordance with man's will and not God's revelation. There was in Islam the clear-cut distinction between the House of Islam, *Dar al-Islam*, that part of the world ruled by religious Islamic law and by Muslims, and *Dar al-Harb*, the House of War, that part of the world outside the world of Islam. In this distinction between *Dar al-Islam* and *Dar al-Harb*, the House of Islam was self-contained, in possession of its own legal and ideological system. But in the new modern era, there was a growing recognition of the inability to remain self-contained within the ideological content of *Dar al-Islam*. There was an understanding of the fact that Western superiority was not only about knowledge and technology. This superiority had a theoretical and philosophical foundation that had to be penetrated by the Muslims to grasp the real sources of Western power.

The movement of Islamic Reform or Islamic Modernism was an effort by Muslim thinkers to find a compromise between these obvious tensions between faith and human reason, between tradition and modernity. These Islamic reformers attempted to show the compatibility of Islam and modern ideas and institutions, reason, science, technology, democracy, constitutionalism and representative government. All these did not conflict with Islam, if Islam would only be correctly interpreted. There was also a need to answer the European offensive against Islam, the attack made by Europeans on Islamic culture arguing that Islam itself was the cause for the stagnation of the Muslims. This ideological offensive launched by Europeans against Islam was, in the eyes of the Muslim reformers, more dangerous than invasion or occupation, and an answer had to be found.

Ernest Renan (1823–1892)

By J.M. Lopez – Rue Condorcet Paris (Carte de Visite). [Public domain], via Wikimedia Commons

The French philosopher Ernest Renan, who was also a Middle Eastern scholar, was famous for his critique of Islam as being incompatible with modern civilization. This was part of a European sense of superiority which was expressed in many ways, such as in Rudyard Kipling's "The White Man's Burden" or in the French belief in what they called their *mission civilisatrice,* their mission to civilize other peoples.

In the Middle East significant openings were made to Western influence and Western cultural impact. The new education systems that were created in the Ottoman Empire and in Egypt gave a new status to those who had received a Western education. The spread of foreign languages, printing in Arabic, newspapers and journals in Arabic, all carried new ideas into the local discourse. The impressions gained by those who visited Europe as part of the student missions, that were sent from the Ottoman Empire or from Egypt, were instrumental in fomenting critical debate on Islam and Western-style modernity.

Rifa'a al-Tahtawi (1801–1873)

Imam or spiritual mentor of Egyptian student delegation who became the most avid student of them all
By Zerida at English Wikipedia (Transferred from en.wikipedia) [Public domain], via Wikimedia Commons

One such student who visited Europe was the Egyptian Rifa'a al-Tahtawi, who traveled to Paris during Muhammad Ali's reign and returned to Egypt with some very important impressions. Tahtawi noted that in France, "even the common people know how to read and write." But "among their ugly beliefs," he observed, was "that the intellect and virtue of their wise men are greater than the intelligence of the prophets."[8] Against this kind of intellectual background the question was to what extent was it possible to adopt the sources of European power in order

8. Albert Hourani, *A History of the Arab Peoples* (New York: Warner Books, 1991), p. 305.

to become a part of the modern world? Would it be possible to learn Western ways without dissolving the Islamic identity of the community? Could Muslims accept the ideas of the modern West without betraying their own past and their own identity? Of course, the Christians in the Middle East did not have such problems and it was much easier for them to adopt and incorporate ideas from the West than it was for their Muslim neighbors.

First in line of modern Muslim reformers was Jamal al-Din al-Afghani. Afghani lived from 1838 to 1897, and was actually a Shi'i of Persian origin. He took the name Afghani in order to appear to Egyptians and to others as a Sunni. Afghani operated, in the main, from Egypt and his teachings were an important catalyst for Islamic reform. Afghani was an ardent advocate of modern science and one who presented Islam as a religion of progress and change. Afghani argued that modernity posed no threat to an Islam that was correctly interpreted and understood.

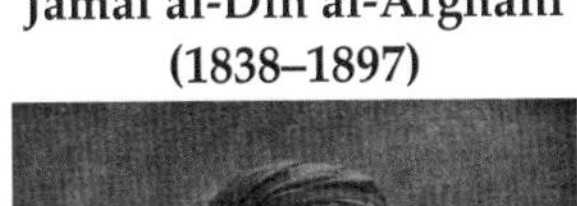

Jamal al-Din al-Afghani (1838–1897)

By Yacquub cAbd al-cAziiz Abul Ala Maududi. [Public domain], via Wikimedia Commons

Such reform required the reopening of the gates of *ijtihad* (independent interpretation of Islamic law and jurisprudence). The gates of *ijtihad* in the Sunni tradition had been closed in the 10th century and Afghani was critical of the resultant stagnation and imitation of the past that had become so customary. Reopening the gates of *ijtihad* would allow for a more liberal and flexible interpretation of Islamic religion. For Afghani, Islam was a religion of reason and action. Muslims ought to reclaim the sources of Western power such as reason, science and technology as their own. As he argued, they were in fact part and parcel of the original Islamic heritage.

From the mid-8th to the 13th century, Islamic thinkers and scientists made important contributions in a variety of fields: medicine, mathematics, science, philosophy, astronomy...

In earlier times Islamic civilization had made contributions to philosophy, medicine, science and mathematics that had been critically important for the evolution of these fields of modern knowledge. Belonging to their own glorious past, Afghani argued, the Muslims should simply reclaim what had been originally their own and transmitted by them to the West.

For Afghani, there was a pan-Islamic identity and duty. Pan-Islam was a form of national solidarity that united Muslim believers in their competition with the West. But speaking of pan-Islam as a form of national solidarity was actually a deviation from the traditional view of the Muslim belief. Afghani was suggesting that being a Muslim was more than just their belief in divine revelation and life in accordance with the Shari'a. In Afghani's thinking, Islam was a kind of nationalist ideology, one of active solidarity and a basis for the unity of the Muslims against the European threat.

Albert Hourani, the British historian, writes the following of Afghani[9]: "In Afghani's mind, Islam meant activity. The true attitude of the Muslim," Afghani argued, "is not one of passive resignation to whatever might come, as coming directly from God; it is one of responsible activity in doing the will of God," which was something very different. Man's decisions were his own according to Afghani, but God had given man, through reason and the revelation of the prophets, the indication of how these decisions ought to be made. Believing in predestination meant that God would be with man if he acted rightly. This interpretation encouraged activism and initiative and not passivity, and was Afghani's main message to the Islamic world to which he belonged.

This was true not only for activities geared towards attaining happiness in the next world, which is what traditional believers tended to emphasize, but also for success in this world, which was really what concerned Afghani. The laws of Islam, Afghani contended, were also the laws of human nature. Therefore if man obeyed the teachings of Islam, he abided by the rules of nature, and achieved happiness and success in this world.

What was true for individuals was also true for society as a whole. When societies followed the rules of Islam they became stronger. When they disobeyed, they got weaker. Islam, Afghani argued, required solidarity and mutual responsibility and these were the foundation for the strength of nations.

The importance of Afghani was not that he was a secular nationalist himself, which he was not, but the fact that he laid the ideological foundations for the penetration of secular nationalist ideas.

There was an inherent problem in Afghani's line of argument: If the laws of Islam and the laws of nature were essentially one and the same, why not adopt the laws of nature in their entirety, become a secularist and abandon Islam altogether? Afghani and others like him opened the floodgates to just such questions.

---

9. Albert Hourani, *Arabic Thought in the Liberal Age, 1798-1939* (Cambridge University Press, 1984), pp. 128–129.

Muhammad Abduh (1849–1905)

By Zerida at English Wikipedia (Transferred from en.wikipedia) [Public domain], via Wikimedia Commons

Afghani's most enthusiastic and important disciple was the Egyptian Muhammad Abduh, who lived from 1849 to 1905. Abduh's emphasis was constantly on human reason and the contention that there was no inherent conflict between religion and reason or between religion and modern science. The adoption of the sources of Western power, rationalism, science and technology were all possible without really being in conflict with Islam, so he argued. Abduh's Islamic reformism meant the penetration of the belief in the rational activity of man. This was a dramatic shift in attitude because it meant the legitimization of change and innovation, not only in the military or in administration, but the legitimization of change and innovation in the especially sensitive sphere of ideas.

This emphasis on the compatibility of Islam and modernity was not an attempt to curb the process of modernization but an attempt to control it, to have a process of modernization that would be placed within an Islamic framework that would tolerate Westernization and modernization without disrupting or dissolving the Islamic identity of the community. For those who received Western style education in the new schools, Abduh's perception of Islam enabled them to adopt Western secular ideas without any sense of betraying their past or their collective identity. The renewal of Islam based on the selective integration of modern ideas rather than a wholesale unrestricted Western secular modernization was the objective that Afghani and Abduh sought to achieve, thereby encouraging progress while preserving the Islamic identity and values of society.

Abduh himself was not an Arab nationalist, but the ideas he promoted provided the foundations for the emergence of Arab nationalism. Abduh, in his desire for reform, tended to emphasize human wisdom and human reason as well as the importance of reviving the original Arabic Islamic ideal. Islam of the Arabs, in the days of the Prophet and shortly thereafter, was the ideal form of Islam to which modern Muslims should aspire. The emphasis on the Arab nature of early Islam was to contribute later on to the emergence of Arab nationalism.

A student and disciple of Abduh was a Syrian by the name of Rashid Rida who lived from 1865 to 1935. Rida, though born in Syria, was active in Egypt like many others in his time. Egypt under the British occupation allowed for greater intellectual freedom than was customary under the Ottomans.

Rashid Rida (1865–1935)

https://commons.wikimedia.org/wiki/File:Rashid_rida.jpg

Rida was a devoted disciple of Abduh, but he followed a more Islamic fundamentalist course. In his later years, Rida was deeply disturbed by what began to look like the overwhelming Westernization and secularization of Muslim society. Rida established a movement called the *Salafiyya*, named after the Prophet and his close circle in the early years of Islam, known as the *Salaf*. The *Salafiyya* movement was devoted to the return of Islamic society to the original values of the early period of the Prophet. Rida tended to glorify Arab Islam of the early years. God's revelation, as Rida pointed out, was in Arabic. It was the Arabs who were the vanguard of the *umma*, the Islamic community of believers. It was the fault of the Turks, people like Rida argued, that the Islamic *umma* had entered a period of decline. The revitalization of Islam in the modern era, therefore, depended on the re-establishment of Arab Muslim leadership of the *umma*.

Abd al-Rahman al-Kawakibi (1849–1902)

http://commons.wikimedia.org/wiki/File%3AAl-Kawakibi.jpg

This kind of thinking, placing the emphasis on the Arab nature of early Islam, was an argument in favor of the centrality of the Arabs to the greater effort of strengthening the Muslim *umma* in the present. This was not quite Arab nationalism. After all, Rida was speaking about the revival of Islam, in which the Arabs had an indispensable role. Rida, therefore, did not call for breaking away from the Empire or for undermining the Ottomans, although after the Young Turk Revolution of 1908 and their growing criticism of religion, Rida's tendency towards Arab nationalism became more visible. But Rida still emphasized the restoration of the Caliphate governed by religious law, as the ultimate objective. So in Rida's mind, the revival of the Islamic community was the main thrust, in which the Arabs had a key role to play, but this was not Arab nationalism, *per se*.

In this line of reformers, after Rida, perhaps the most important of them all was Abd al-Rahman al-Kawakibi. Kawakibi lived from 1849–1902 and, like Rida, was born in Syria. But he too ended up in Cairo because of the relative freedom under the British occupation. Kawakibi was more radical than Rida on the centrality, if not to say the superiority of the Arabs. The Caliphate should return to the Arabs, he argued, as the Ottomans were incapable of retrieving its former glory. Kawakibi also had some rather vague ideas about a spiritual Caliphate, something akin to the Papacy, thereby, adopting this more Christian notion of separation of religion and state. But his main contribution was in his emphasis on the centrality of the Arabs to any kind of Muslim reform.

In conclusion, one should stress the following: The reformers contributed to the spread of the idea that politics was more about the will of man than the will of God. The centrality of the will of man and the sovereignty of man and ideas like self-determination were either directly or indirectly promoted by these Islamic reformers.

The British historian Elie Kedourie wrote a book about Afghani and Abduh that was entitled *An Essay on Religious Unbelief and Political Activism in Modern Islam*. Kedourie argued that Afghani and Abduh were not dedicated Islamic reformers at all, but were actually engaged in subversive unbelief under a false religious cover. After all, their ideas stood in complete contrast to traditional Islam. However religious they may or may not have been, they were definitely breaking down the walls of Islamic self-sufficiency in the realm of ideas. Intentionally or not, they set the stage for the secular and secularizing platform of nationalism. Nationalism, after all, was an idea that believed in the actions of man, and was based on the collective identity of people defined by their language and the territory they inhabited, rather than their religious belief.

The disciples of Afghani and Abduh went in very different directions. If, as they said, there was no contradiction between reason and religion, one could draw two very different conclusions. On the one hand, if Islam was reason, why take the Western road to modernity? Alternatively one could argue, if Islam was reason, why not Westernize completely? Thus, amongst their successors there were some ultra-secularists, on the one hand, and traditionalists, on the other, who reasserted a self-sufficient Islamic alternative to the West. Rashid Rida eventually became one of those, and emerged as the mentor of the organization of Muslim Brethren that was founded in Egypt in the late 1920s.

The struggle between modernity and tradition is a constant theme throughout the history of the modern Middle East. The "Arab Spring" and its aftermath is just the latest chapter in this intriguing saga of this fascinating part of the world.

Key Sources and Suggested Further Reading

- Esposito, John, *Islam and Politics* (Syracuse University Press, 1991).
- Hourani, Albert, *A History of the Arab Peoples* (New York: Warner Books, 1991).
- Hourani, Albert, *Arabic Thought in the Liberal Age, 1798-1939* (Cambridge University Press, 1984).
- Kedourie, Elie, *Afghani and 'Abduh: An Essay on Religious Unbelief and Political Activism in Modern Islam* (London: Frank Cass, 1966).
- Lewis, Bernard, *Islam and the West* (New York: Oxford University Press, 1993).
- Lewis, Bernard, *The Middle East: 2000 Years of History From the Rise of Christianity to the Present Day* (London: Weidenfeld and Nicolson, 1995).
- Lewis, Bernard, *The Emergence of Modern Turkey* (New York: Oxford University Press, 2002).
- Vatikiotis, P.J., *The Modern History of Egypt* (London: Weidenfeld and Nicolson, 1969).
- Yapp, Malcolm, *The Making of the Modern Near East, 1792-1923* (London: Longman, 1987).

Chapter Three

The Rise of Nationalism; the Demise of Empire

The Dominance of Religious Identity

https://www.flickr.com/photos/cool-art/7414678540/sizes/l/

Muslims did not traditionally make a connection between collective identity and territory. Collective identity for Muslims was a matter of religious belief and not of territorial affiliation. But under the impact of European ideas during the 19th century, the idea of territorial nationalism became more acceptable. Concepts began to change, and in the generation of Islamic Reform in the late 19th and early 20th century, nationalism became a much more acceptable idea.

The Ottoman Imperial School of Military Engineering

See page for author [Public domain], via Wikimedia Commons

The Ottoman Imperial School of Civil Administration

See page for author [Public domain], via Wikimedia Commons

There were three main forms of nationalism in this period: Turkish, Arab and Egyptian. These nationalisms were the property, for the most part, of an intellectual, Westernizing, urban elite. Nationalism was usually not the province of the masses. Nationalists were often the graduates of the new schools, those who had been exposed more intensively to Western ideas. The new schools produced new social classes and new professions. Teachers in the new schools who were teaching new subjects, and lawyers and judges who were administering new European inspired legal systems, were the most supportive of the new nationalist ideas.

Abdülhamid II

See page for author [Public domain], via Wikimedia Commons

Most of the population remained deeply embedded in Islamic tradition, though, what exactly tradition meant was beginning to change too. Religious leaders still wielded considerable authority. The Ottoman Sultan at the end of the 19th century, Abdülhamid II, claimed to be the Caliph of all Muslims, mobilizing popular support for the Ottoman Empire on the basis of their Islamic identity. Nevertheless, nationalist movements did arise and in response to a variety of different challenges.

Turkish Nationalism

The challenges that led to the emergence of Turkish nationalism were mainly European political pressures and the problems arising from the secession of Christian populated territories in the European provinces of the Empire. During the *Tanzimat* the enactment of legislation establishing equality before the law that included Christians and Muslims was intended also to create a shared Ottoman identity. But it did not, and "Ottomanism" failed to keep the Christians in the Empire. In the wake of Christian secession, Sultan Abdülhamid II turned to pan-Islam to strengthen the bonds between the peoples of the Empire, which was becoming ever more Muslim, as the Christians seceded.

However, pan-Islam and the uniting of the people on the basis of their religion was becoming less acceptable to the new Westernizing Turkish elite. They believed in a European-styled Turkish national solidarity based on their common language, Turkish. The Empire now was almost entirely Turkish and Arab. Therefore, the emphasis on Turkishness was a potential cause of tension with the Arabs, especially after 1908 when the Young Turks came to power.

Though Turkish nationalists, the Young Turks were reluctant to push too far for Turkish nationalism so as not to create a rupture with the very large Arab Muslim population.

The Young Turks were young military officers and bureaucrats, graduates of the *Tanzimat* and not the usual opponents of the Sultan, such as the local potentates, the unruly tribes or the Christians. It was the Young Turks who staged a revolution in July 1908, deposed the Sultan in April of 1909, and continued with the process of reform in the military with German advisers. As their predecessors, they continued building new schools and adding to legal reform. The Young Turks also continued building a modern infrastructure, telegraph, roads and railways, generally modernizing the Empire. Government became ever more centralized, including even the development of an effective secret police.

1908 Young Turk Revolution

By Anonymous [Public domain], via Wikimedia Commons

Many of those who carried out the Revolution of 1908 were military officers organized in the Committee of Union and Progress (CUP). They sought the salvation of the Empire, believed in Turkish nationalism, in Westernized education and in the restoration of the 1876 constitution.

Ottoman Parliament in 1908

See page for author [Public domain], via Wikimedia Commons

The defeat of Russia in 1905 by the Japanese made an impressive impact on the Young Turks and on many others in the Muslim Middle East. This was a historic defeat of a European power by an Asian power. In looking for the success of the Japanese against the Russians, many in the Middle East focused on the fact that Japan had gone in the direction of constitutionalism, whereas the Russians had not. The idea of a constitutional government as a source of collective power was gaining ground.

Russo-Japanese War of 1905

By Tōjō Shōtarō [Public domain], via Wikimedia Commons

For the Young Turks, however, constitutionalism also meant the steady shift of power into the hands of the army at the expense of both the Sultan and the bureaucracy. They also believed that the resumption of parliamentary life would ease European pressure. But it did not. In 1911 the Italians took Tripoli in Libya. In the Balkans, the Ottomans continued to lose ground and in 1912–1913, they lost nearly all the territory they had left in Europe.

The Italo-Turkish War of 1911

Photograph by API (Lombardi Historical Collection) [Public domain], via Wikimedia Commons

By Nzeemin [CC-BY-SA-3.0 (http://creativecommons.org/licenses/by- sa/3.0)], via Wikimedia Commons

The Balkan Wars of 1912–13

By Esemono (https://commons.wikimedia.org/wiki/File:Territorial_changes_of_the_Ottoman_Empire_1913.jpg)

In 1913, the CUP assumed complete control, which they had not enjoyed until then. But they

1913 Coup d'état

By Behaeddin Rahmizadé [Public domain], via Wikimedia Commons

did not manage to do much before the outbreak of the First World War, and that changed a great deal.

Since the second half of the 19th century, there was a steadily increasing interest in the history of the Turkish people, the Turkish language and Turkish literature. Ziya Gökalp, who lived from 1876 to 1924, was the most prominent ideologue of Turkish nationalism. He rejected Ottomanism and made the Turkish nation the basis of his vision. But as long as the Empire continued to exist, Turkish nationalism as a practical political program, had little appeal to the leadership and to the general public. The CUP, though sympathetic and supportive of Turkish nationalism, continued like their predecessors with Ottomanism, centralization and modernization. It would take the end of Empire for Gökalp's ideology to become the policy of the new Turkish Republic.

Ziya Gökalp (1876–1924)

See page for author [Public domain], via Wikimedia Commons

This rise of Turkishness and Turkish nationalism begs the question of its relationship to the notorious Armenian genocide. Since the Empire was losing territory continuously, it faced increasing nationalist challenges by others that served to reinforce Turkish identity and nationalist passions. With the loss of the European

Armenian Presence in Eastern Anatolia in the Early 17th century

By Yerevanci (Own work) [CC-BY-SA-3.0 (http://creativecommons.org/licenses/by-sa/3.0)], via Wikimedia Commons

provinces, Anatolia remained as the heartland of the Turkish-speaking people. It was the critical region for their prospective self-determination, and thus the emergence of the Armenian problem as a potential threat to the Turkish homeland.

Haik Nahapet
The Legendary Patriarch of the Armenian Nation

By Mkrtum Hovnatanian (1779–1846) (http://www.gallery.am/hy/database/item/937/) [Public domain], via Wikimedia Commons

Anatolia, especially in the west, developed impressively like the rest of the Empire during the 19th century. Eastern Anatolia remained less developed and there was considerable social and political tension between the Armenians (Christians), and the Kurds (Sunni Muslims), in this part of Anatolia, where there was a particularly large Armenian population. During the 19th century, an Armenian national consciousness developed under the intensive influence of Western sources, especially through the American Protestant missionaries, who were active amongst the Armenians.

European powers tended to intervene on their behalf and cooperation with Russia, for example, also meant collaboration of the Armenians with the traditional enemy of the Ottomans. Tensions between the Turkish-speaking Muslims and the Armenians rose and there were massacres of Armenians perpetrated by units of the Ottoman army in the eastern part of Anatolia in the mid-1890s, motivated mainly by the suspicion towards the Armenians as a national movement that threatened what the Turks had left of their Empire.

Hamidian Massacres of 1894–1896

By Bain News Service, publisher [Public domain], via Wikimedia Commons

These events set the stage for the Armenian genocide that took place in the early years of the First World War. Some Armenians in eastern Anatolia had fought with the Russians against the Ottomans. Others had engaged in guerrilla operations, and some Armenian populations rose against the Ottomans during the war, in response to Ottoman suppression. In the spring of 1915, with the British attacking at the Dardanelles, the Russians attacking in the east and the British apparently advancing on Baghdad, the Ottomans decided on the deportation of the Armenians in eastern Anatolia.

Ottoman Empire, 1915

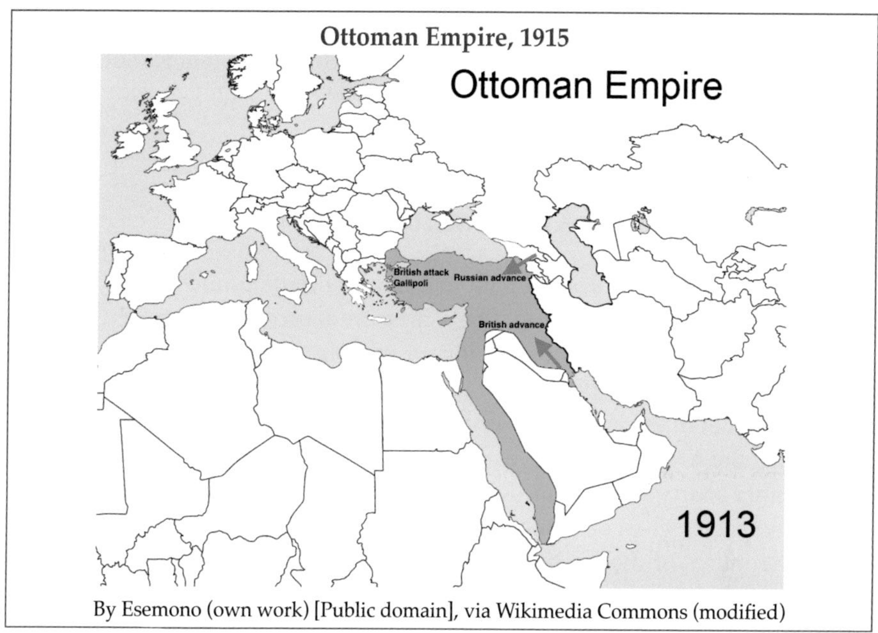

By Esemono (own work) [Public domain], via Wikimedia Commons (modified)

In this process of deportation, one million to one-and-a-half million Armenians, perished in the harsh conditions, dying of hunger, disease and exposure. Many thousands were also systematically murdered by the Ottoman authorities and by local Kurdish villagers and tribesmen.

What turned into the Armenian genocide was part of the larger transition from communal identity to territorial self-determination. This had some very unfortunate consequences on the ground. The transition from communal co-existence, whereby religious communities lived side by side, Ottoman style, to territorial nationalism, European style, required some degree of territorial contiguity.

The Armenian Genocide

By Henry Morgenthau [Public domain], via Wikimedia Commons

The need for communities now to acquire territorial contiguity in the name of self-determination, rather than communities living side by side, created unavoidable clashes between the mosaic of minorities within the Ottoman Empire, accompanied by horrific bloodshed. The Balkans of those days (and latter-day Yugoslavia of the 1990s) were one example. The Armenians in Anatolia were another. Not all products of modernity and change had positive results. Some were quite catastrophic. Indeed, the Armenian genocide was the worst example of this unfortunate reality.

Arab Nationalism

The intellectual origins of Arab nationalism were to be found in two sources: one Christian and one Muslim. The Christian source was that of Christian scholars and writers in the new missionary schools, producing new scholarship on Arabic language and culture. It was this new scholarship on Arabic language and culture that made a major contribution to the evolution of the idea that the speakers of the Arabic language were a nation.

The other source was Islamic Reform. As mentioned in Chapter Two, Islamic reformers spoke a great deal about the revival of the original Islam of the Arabs and of the return of the Arabs to a predominant role in the world of Islam, to recapture the primacy of the Arabs in Islamic civilization. Such sentiments naturally contributed to the sense of a particular Arab nationalist identity. But for years after the emergence of Arab nationalism, Arab nationalists did not demand secession from the Empire. Even as Arab nationalists, they continued to recognize the Islamic legitimacy of the Ottoman Empire and their demands focused on decentralization, not secession.

Returning to the Christian intellectual roots of Arab nationalism, one must recognize that during the 19th century, and in particular the second half of it during the *Tanzimat*, Syria evolved into a far more orderly region with a much better and more intensive connection with Europe. One of the results of these changes was a very significant expansion of the Christian school system, especially of church and missionary schools. By 1914 there were some 500 French schools in Syria and Lebanon. There were American Protestant schools too, one of which became the American University of Beirut, established in 1866, and still in existence today. American and French missionary schools in Syria and Lebanon brought many Arabs, mainly Christians, into close contact with the West and Western ideas.

Ottoman government schools did the same. But the Arab literary revival through the printing press, journalism, periodicals, dictionaries, grammar books and new literature was very much a cultural revival in which Christians were predominant. The dissemination of new ideas in this cultural revival focused on the idea of nationalism, and especially on Arab nationalism. Just to name a few of the Christians who were involved in this cultural revival: Nasif al-Yaziji, Butrus al-Bustani, Faris Shidyaq (who converted to Islam), Ya'aqub Sarruf, Faris

Nimr and Jurji Zaydan. It is important to mention that Faris Shidyaq was not the only Christian ideologue of Arab nationalism to convert. This was maybe a function of the recognition by Christians of the intimate association, at the end of the day, between Arab nationalism and Islam.

Mount Lebanon

By George Saliba (own work) [Public domain], via Wikimedia Commons

But many of the Christians in Lebanon and Syria were different from other Christians in the Empire in that they spoke the same language (Arabic) as their Muslim neighbors, as opposed to the Christians of the Balkans, or the Armenians of Anatolia, for example. They were Orthodox Christians and were not a compact minority, unlike the Maronite Catholics, who were very heavily concentrated in one area in Mount Lebanon. The Orthodox Christians were spread out through the Ottoman Empire and they had an interest in a common ground for political organization with their Arab Muslim neighbors. Spread out as they were, secession was not an option.

The importance of Arabic language in defining the land of Syria as a political entity

See page for author [Public domain], via Wikimedia Commons

There was tension in the hierarchy of the Orthodox Church between the Greek clergy, in the senior ranks of the church, and the Arabic-speaking clergy, in the lower ranks. This tension within the church between Greeks and Arabs also contributed to this sense of Arab distinction and Arab particular nationalist identity. There was a trend amongst the Christians to see the land of Syria as an Arabic-speaking geographic and political entity. Some went beyond Syria and spoke in terms of a larger state of Arabs, which would include Iraq and Arabia. Najib Azuri was one such Christian, a Syrian Catholic operating out of Paris, who spoke of a much larger Arab state. But who did Azuri really speak for? Apparently, not too many. For some Christians, a more liberal empire would have been good enough. For others, Arab nationalism and its essential link with Islam might possibly prove to be dangerous for Christians, driving them into an inferior status.

As for the Muslim public, the great majority of them were not initially attracted by Arab nationalism, certainly not that espoused by Christians. The

Muslim Arabs in Syria adopted the battle cry "Arabic shall not be Christianized" as a way of rejecting this form of Arab nationalism disseminated by Christian intellectuals.[1]

Muslims were indeed affected far more by the arguments of Islamic reformers on the primacy of the Arabs in Islam and on the fault of the Turks for Muslim decline, than they were influenced by Christian intellectuals. For Islamic reformers like Rashid Rida the revival of Arabic studies was an essential forerunner of Islamic revival as Arabic was the language of Islam.

From here it was an easy transition to the glorification of the Arabs and the argument for the essentiality of Arab nationalism. But Arab nationalism only captured the popular imagination of the Muslim masses after the dissolution of the Ottoman Empire and only after the special emphasis on the role of Islam in Arabism and the intimate connection between Arabism and Islam were established. After all, Islam was at the very heart of the cultural heritage of the Arabs. In the eyes of the Arabs, their greatest contribution to human civilization was, unquestionably, the religion and culture of Islam.

Before the First World War, Arab nationalists, for the most part, did not go beyond calls for greater autonomy and the recognition of Arabic as an official language in the Empire. There were secret societies that promoted Arab nationalism, but they had very little weight before 1914. An Arab nationalist conference was held in Paris in 1913. The conferees demanded autonomy for the Arab provinces (not secession), the recognition of Arabic as a language of government, and the appointment of more Arab officials. Whether this was about Arab nationalism or just the self-interest of the Arab educated class looking for good jobs in the government, was hard to say.

The Maronites

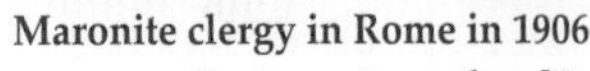

Maronite clergy in Rome in 1906

Maronite villagers building a church – 1920s

See page for author [Public domain], via Wikimedia Commons

1. C. E. Dawn, "From Ottomanism to Arabism: The Origins of an Ideology," in Albert Hourani, Philip Khoury and Mary Wilson (eds.), *The Modern Middle East: A Reader* (London: I.B. Tauris, 2011), p. 381.

It was only amongst the Maronite Catholics, that compact minority of Christians in Mount Lebanon, who had very clear ideas about a politically independent entity protected by France. However, that was not in the name of Arab nationalism, but in the name of a Christian dominated state of Lebanon.

In the provinces of Iraq, there was much less interest in Arab nationalism than in Syria, for example. There had been less substantial economic development and change in Iraq than there had been in Syria during the 19th century. There was a very large Shi'ite population in Iraq, and they saw Arabism as a form of Sunni Muslim revivalism, in which they obviously had no interest. The Christian catalyst that existed in Syria did not exist in Iraq. There were very few Christians in Iraq and they were not as intellectually prominent as the Christians in Syria. There was an important and sizeable Jewish minority in Iraq. But they were not very politicized and generally speaking were loyal Ottoman subjects. The Jews, after all, had no connections with Christian powers and could not possibly imagine secession.

After 1908 and the revival of the Ottoman parliament, there were much more intensive contacts between Arab representatives in the Empire. Parliament enabled them to come into contact with each other, and the interaction added to the awareness and appeal of Arab nationalism. But again, one must emphasize, the great majority of Muslims remained loyal subjects of the Ottoman Empire until the very end.

Egyptian Nationalism

Egypt differed from other Arabic-speaking lands. In Egypt of this period, the late 19th and early 20th century, one can speak of Egyptian nationalism, which one could not do in respect to countries like Syria or Iraq. Egypt differed from other Arabic-speaking lands in that it was a separate, clearly defined, independent entity. Egyptian nationalism emerged against the backdrop of British occupation, a very specific reality that existed

The Distinctiveness of Egypt and the Nile Valley

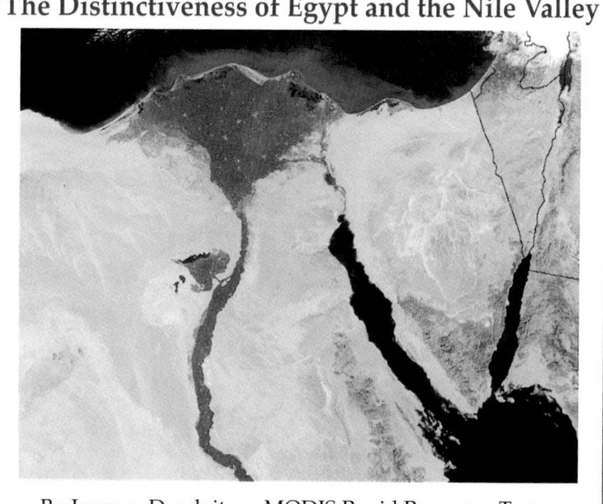

By Jacques Descloitres, MODIS Rapid Response Team, NASA/GSFC [Public domain], via Wikimedia Commons

only in Egypt and not in other Arab countries. There was, therefore, a specific Egyptian, rather than Arab, Muslim or Ottoman content to the nationalist movement that emerged in Egypt. It also had a specific geographical and political definition.

During the 19th century, as we have already seen, Egypt underwent a series of radical changes, as the foundations of the modern state of Egypt were built by Muhammad Ali. Egypt underwent an economic revolution of sorts, basing the economy on an export-oriented agriculture, particularly the growing of cotton for export and the sugar industry. As in other parts of the Ottoman Empire, there was considerable social change in Egypt of the 19th century with the development of the new school system, the printing press, journalism and legal reform, along with the introduction to the world of ideas and the lifestyle of Europe.

Egypt in the 1870s was in a situation of bankruptcy exposed to ever-increasing international intervention in Egypt's finances to ensure payment of the huge debt that the Egyptians had accumulated in the very rapid project of modernization instituted under the rule of Khedive Ismail. In 1879, Khedive Ismail was removed by the European powers in favor of his son Tawfiq. Egyptian Arabic-speaking officers of the Egyptian army began to express ever increasing disapproval of this international influence in Egypt's affairs.

Disapproval by the Arabic-speaking officers was also representative of more profound trends of social disaffection inside Egypt at that time. There was increasing tension between the Arabic-speaking Egyptians and the older upper class of Turco-Circassian officers and the landowning elite, also of Turco-Circassian background in many places, who had become predominant since Muhammad Ali's assumption of power. This Turco-Circassian elite was in part Turkish, that is, Turkish administrators and officers who had remained in Egypt and had become very prominent, or Circassians who had served with the

Archeological discoveries → Ancient past

https://commons.wikimedia.org/wiki/File: Jean_Pascal_Sebah,_Statue_de_Ramses_-_Memphis_-_18802.jpg

By National Media Museum [see page for license], via Wikimedia Commons

Mamluks, whose origins were in the Caucasus and who had become part of the new ruling elite in Egypt. They, together with Arab Egyptian landowners, were all equally interested in the restriction of foreign influence, which naturally eroded their stature too. These were the early stirrings of a clear cut, openly expressed Egyptian identity.

Educated Egyptians were also impressed by the new archeological discoveries of Egypt's glorious ancient past. There was an emerging sense of continuity between Egypt's great pre-Islamic past and its Islamic history. This had considerable impact on Egypt's collective identity. Valuing and glorifying Egypt's pre-Islamic past touches upon a core issue in the Islamic interpretation of history. In the Islamic interpretation of history the pre-Islamic past is known as the *Jahiliyya,* the period of ignorance and barbarism that was succeeded by the great, superior civilization of Islam. In that view of history there was nothing positive to say about Egypt's pre-Islamic past. But if, as a result of the great findings of Pharaonic Egypt, the pre-Islamic past of Egypt becomes a source of national pride, one is calling the Islamic interpretation of history into question, and thereby eroding the centrality of Islam in the Egyptian collective identity.

Rifa'a al-Tahtawi, who lived from 1801 to 1873 and, as already noted in Chapter Two, was one of the leading students in the Muhammad Ali era who studied in Paris from 1826 to 1831, was deeply influenced by European ideas. Tahtawi spoke of nations and countries and observed that a nation was bound to a specific territory. Egypt was one such country and the Egyptians were a nation, said Tahtawi, who should love their fatherland like the Europeans loved theirs. Tahtawi's writings about Egypt's uniqueness were published in 1869 in a book on the historical and geographical distinctiveness of Egypt.

Khedive Ismail built a national library and a museum and the introduction of pre-Islamic history into Egypt's schools was becoming an important facet of the evolution of a particular Egyptian identity. Writers like Ya'aqub Sanu' and Abdullah al-Nadim popularized the terms of Egypt, Egyptians and Egyptianness in the 1870s and the 1880s, and sounded the slogan of "Egypt for the Egyptians," which fueled the ever increasing opposition in Egypt to growing foreign influence.

Ya'aqub Sanu'

http://kjc-sv016.kjc.uni-heidelberg.de:8080/exist/apps/naddara/resources/images/images/1898_small.png

Opposition to increasing foreign influence was expressed in the early 1880s, in the Urabi Rebellion, led by an Arabic-speaking Egyptian officer by the name of Ahmad Urabi, who rose against the increasing foreign dominance in Egypt's internal affairs. There were various reasons for the disaffection of Urabi and his fellow Arabic-speaking Egyptian officers. Their promotion to the highest ranks in the military was blocked by the Turco-Circassian elite and many lost their jobs in the financial crisis of the 1870s. In 1881 and 1882, there were repeated uprisings of the officers under Urabi in protest against the economic situation, against Turco-Circassian domination and against increasing foreign intervention in Egypt's financial affairs. Urabi spoke, for the most part, in traditionally Islamic terms, but he also used the slogans of Abdullah al-Nadim on "Egypt for the Egyptians."

The Urabi Rebellion 1881–1882

By Anonymous [Public domain], via Wikimedia Commons

Alexandria after British bombardment, July 1882

By Argos'Dad at en.wikipedia [Public domain], via Wikimedia Commons

From May 1882, Egypt became increasingly rebellious and disorderly. Riots broke out in Alexandria in June and the European quarter of the city was sacked by the rioters. In July of 1882, the British navy shelled Alexandria. In September of that year, the British occupied Egypt. This was to be a temporary occupation, the British said. But in the end, it lasted for no less than 70 years. Urabi was exiled by the British to Ceylon, today's Sri Lanka.

Thus begins a new period in Egypt's history, the period of British occupation. The British occupation generated new forms of political expression and of particular Egyptian nationalism. Egypt had a peculiarly Egyptian status, formally still a part of the Ottoman Empire, but directly occupied by the British. Egyptian nationalism became ever more vociferous, especially in the decade preceding the First World War.

Further expansion of the school system under the British occupation also meant an extension of the relative freedom of speech that the British allowed in Egypt, more than there was in the Ottoman Empire. Expansion of education and freedom of expression contributed to the constant growth of Egyptian national sentiment and of a specifically Egyptian national consciousness, as did the continued competition between Arabic-speaking Egyptians and the Turco-Circassians over positions in the army and the bureaucracy.

Certain events, such as the infamous Dinshaway incident, also added to this sense of Egyptian patriotism. In 1906, British officers, hunting pigeons in the village of Dinshaway in the Nile Delta, got involved in a fracas with the local villagers, at the end of which a British officer died. The British response was vicious. Some of the people of Dinshaway, were tried and executed, many others were publicly flogged, leading to a widespread outcry in the name of the Egyptian people against the British occupation. In Egypt, as in other places in the region, the victory of Japan, the Asian power that had defeated the Russians of Europe in 1905, also encouraged the nationalist struggle of the Egyptians against European domination.

The year of 1907 was an important year for the establishment of modern-style political parties in Egypt. One of these was the nationalist party *al-Hizb al-Watani* led by Mustafa Kamil (1874 to 1908). The party that he established in the name of nationalism, *wataniyya* in Arabic, was an example of how the Arabic language was changing to incorporate new, modern meanings coming from Europe. Originally, the word *watan* simply meant one's place of birth. *Watan* had come to mean homeland in the French sense of *patrie*. Like European nationalism, *wataniyya* now included this novel sense of attachment and loyalty to the homeland, to the nation.

Ahmad Lutfi al-Sayyid (1872–1963)

By Zerida at en.wikipedia [Public domain], via Wikimedia Commons

Kamil was an exciting orator and a writer, but ideologically inconsistent. Above all else Kamil wanted the British out. He occasionally supported the Khedive, at times went along with the Ottomans, Islam, or secular Egyptian nationalism, anything that served his immediate political ends. He died in 1908 and was succeeded by his far less illustrious companion Muhammad Farid, who was more of an Islamist and usually pro-Ottoman.

Another political party established in 1907 was *Hizb al-Umma*. Founded by Ahmad Lutfi al-Sayyid (1872–1963), the name of the party also meant the nationalist party. *Umma* meant community, as in the community of believers. But in the modern era, *umma* had also come to mean the people, or the nation, in the modern nationalist sense.

Ahmad Lutfi al-Sayyid had been a disciple of Muhammad Abduh, who, as already noted in Chapter Two, was the greatest of the Islamic reformers. Abduh himself in his later years had become supportive of Egyptian nationalism. But Ahmad Lutfi took this a few steps further, shifting from Westernizing Islamic reform to uncompromising secularism. For Ahmad Lutfi, secular nationalism meant nationalism on a geographic, historic and linguistic foundation. Nationalism, as far as he was concerned, was not about religious identity and he rejected religion as the cohesive element of society.

Ahmad Lutfi was a classic European liberal, an intellectual giant known by his generation as *faylasuf al-jil*, the philosopher or the mentor of the generation. Countries ought to be guided by national interests, not religious belief and the Egyptian nation existed, he argued, independently of the Islamic community. Ahmad Lutfi believed in a territorially defined nation-state. But, as the British historian P.J. Vatikiotis has pointed out, he "underestimated the political power inherent in the instinctive adherence of Egyptians to their Islamic heritage."[2]

Ahmad Lutfi also differed with those who sought immediate British withdrawal. In his mind, the British presence was actually beneficial. It would enhance the modernization of the Muslims. He and Abduh believed that Egypt was not yet ready for their ideas, and the continuation of the British presence could actually further the promotion of modern secular, liberal ideas in Egyptian society. Only after that was achieved, they thought, the British should leave Egypt.

The Taba Issue of 1906

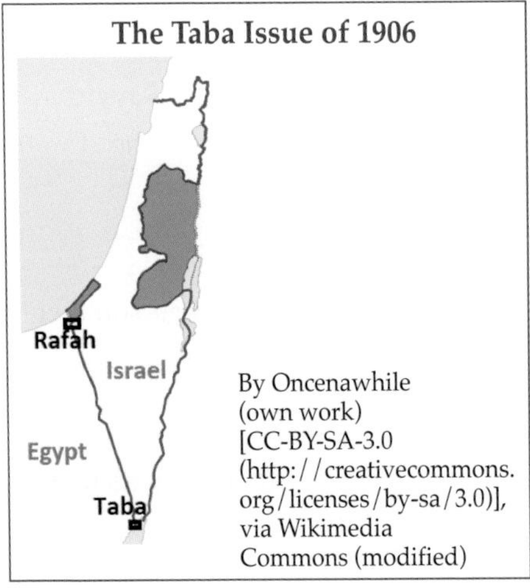

By Oncenawhile (own work) [CC-BY-SA-3.0 (http://creativecommons.org/licenses/by-sa/3.0)], via Wikimedia Commons (modified)

There were limits to nationalist appeal in this period before the First World War. Many people still had a strong Islamic-Ottoman allegiance. This was indicated in the rather strange incident related to the drawing of the border between Egypt and the Ottoman Empire, in a negotiation that was held between the Ottomans, on the one hand, and the British, as the *de facto* rulers of Egypt, on the other. In defining the boundary between Egypt and the Ottoman Empire, which is presently the border between Egypt

2. P. J. Vatikiotis, *The Modern History of Egypt*, pp. 230–234.

and Israel, the line runs from Rafah on the Mediterranean to Taba and Eilat on the Red Sea. In delineating the border in 1906, there was some disagreement between the British and the Ottomans. Yet, the Egyptian public actually supported the Ottomans against Egyptian territorial claims. These claims were being made by the British, while the people's loyalties were still to the Muslim Empire of the Ottomans.

Copts in Egypt

By American Colony (Jerusalem). Photo Dept. photographer [Public domain], via Wikimedia Commons

Religious fervor also contributed to continued sectarian tensions between Muslims and Coptic Christians in Egypt. The Coptic Christians were naturally very attracted to the idea of a secular Egyptian nationalism. Secular nationalism for the Christians, like in other parts of the region, was an ideology that would allow, at least in theory, for Christians and Muslims to share a collective identity as equals. However, if the community was to remain identified by Islam, it would make it much more difficult for the Christians or for other minorities to enjoy full equality with the Muslim majority.

Butrus Ghali
Prime minister of Egypt from 1908 to 1910

See page for author [Public domain], via Wikimedia Commons

Such tensions between the Copts and the Muslims in Egypt were expressed, for example, in the assassination in 1910 of the Coptic prime minister of Egypt, Butrus Ghali. He was assassinated by a Muslim who accused the Copts of being too supportive of the European powers. Copts, as a result, became somewhat disappointed in the nationalist movement in Egypt, and Coptic-Muslim suspicions and rivalries did not disappear. The Copts tended to stress Egyptianness, which was more convenient for them as Christians, while Muslims still attached much importance to Egypt's Islamic identity. There was an Arab dimension in Egyptian nationalism, but it was not very central. It was much more related to the hostility to the Turco-Circassian elite than to Arab nationalism. This hostility became increasingly irrelevant as the Turco-Circassians assimilated ever more into Egyptian society.

In conclusion to this discussion of nationalism it should be noted that nationalism remained the idea of a select, educated, urban elite. It was not the ideology of the masses, certainly not as long as the Ottoman Empire continued to exist. Most people were still profoundly influenced by Islamic tradition and by their religious identity. The old traditional education system had lost much of its power. It no longer supplied the bureaucrats and the judges who now graduated from the new schools. Not to mention the army officers who were at the vanguard of political and social change.

But in the villages of the rural Middle East, the old order was still very strong. The Sufi mystical religious orders had much sway over the people and the popular world view. Islam remained an important component of the nationalist movement, and one could not effectively mobilize the masses without it. Islam was still very much at the center of both Arabism and Ottomanism. Arabism and Ottomanism were forms of nationalist self-defense against the West and they both took pride in the past greatness of Islam. Moreover, in political terms, they both still sought the preservation of the Muslim empire, albeit in different ways.

The First World War and the Demise of Empire

The First World War spelt the end of the Ottoman Empire. At the end of the war the Ottoman Empire finally collapsed and ceased to be the governing body of the Arab lands that it had ruled for 400 years. From the ruins of Empire, the modern Middle Eastern state system was created.

Ottoman Empire's entry to WWI

By Unknown. Historical image, main source is the Turkish government. [Public domain], via Wikimedia Commons

As noted in the discussion of the "Eastern Question" in Chapters One and Two, the European powers sought to preserve the integrity of the Ottoman Empire for the sake of European peace. They feared that the possible collapse of the Ottoman Empire would result in a competition between the European powers to take over the remains of the Empire that might end in the eruption of a disastrous European war. But after the outbreak of the World War, the Europeans were already at war. The previous logic of maintaining the integrity of the Empire was no longer relevant. Moreover, the Ottoman decision to side with Germany and Austria in the war sealed the fate of their Empire.

The Western powers, Britain and France, and initially the Russians too, had every reason to seek the Empire's defeat and dismemberment. From an early phase in the war, there were secret talks between the powers about the eventual carving up of the Empire. The Russians wanted the Straits, the Bosphorus and the Dardanelles. The French wanted Syria, especially the coastal area, and Palestine too. The British wanted Iraq, because of the Persian Gulf and India, and the connection from there to the Mediterranean, which created an overlapping challenge to French interests in that area.

The Sykes-Picot Agreement

In early 1916, British and French officials, Mark Sykes on the British side and François Georges-Picot on the French side, signed the notorious Sykes-Picot Agreement that divided the central, mostly Arab, parts of the Middle East between Britain and France. France had a free hand in Cilicia (which is in southern Anatolia) and coastal Syria and Lebanon, and a sphere of influence stretching eastwards towards Mosul, which is in present-day Iraq.

The Sykes-Picot Agreement, 1916

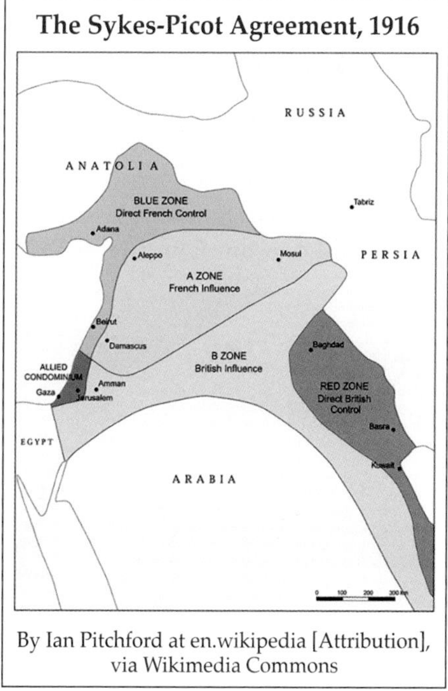

By Ian Pitchford at en.wikipedia [Attribution], via Wikimedia Commons

Britain got a free hand in Iraq including Basra and Baghdad, and a sphere of influence going west all the way to the Mediterranean. Britain also obtained the ports of Haifa and Acre in Palestine. Much of the rest of Palestine was put under an international administration together with France, with Russian agreement. The Russians were given control over some Armenian provinces. Russia, however, was overtaken by revolution in 1917 and opted out of the colonial spoils.

The McMahon-Hussein Correspondence

The Hashemites
Sharif Hussein Ibn Ali

See page for author [Public domain, Public domain, Public domain or Public domain], via Wikimedia Commons

Along with the Sykes-Picot Agreement, there was also an exchange of correspondence between the British High Commissioner in Egypt, Henry McMahon, and the leader of the Hashemite family in Mecca, Hussein Ibn Ali, about the future of the Arab provinces. The correspondence took place in 1915–16, and served an immediate British interest. Britain was deeply concerned by the Ottoman Sultan's appeal at the beginning of the war to Muslims everywhere to join in *jihad* against the enemies of the Ottoman Empire. The British were worried about the effect this appeal might have in India where there were millions of Muslim believers. The British were therefore in search of an Arab Muslim ally, with whom to fight against the Ottomans, and thus their interest in the connection with the Hashemites.

The Hashemites were a Muslim family of most prestigious lineage as descendants of the Prophet Muhammad. The Prophet himself was a member of the house of Hashim. The leader of the family, Hussein Ibn Ali, was the ruler, Emir, of the Muslim holy city of Mecca, as the representative of the Ottoman

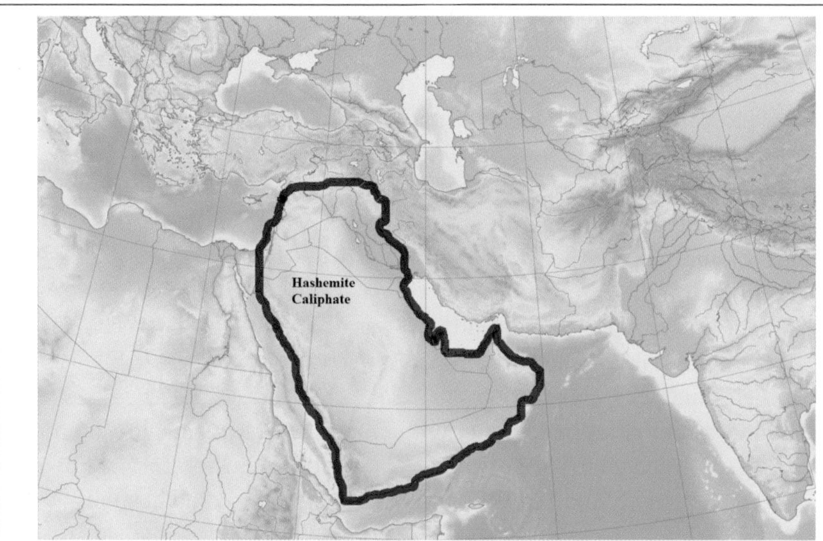

By Виктор В (https://commons.wikimedia.org/wiki/File:Relief_Map_of_Middle_East.jpg], via Wikimedia Commons

Empire. But even though they were the rulers of Mecca on behalf of the Ottomans, the Hashemites had grievances of their own with the Ottomans and had aspirations for Arab and Islamic leadership, independent of the Turks. In the summer of 1915, the Hashemites entered into negotiations with the British, demanding the formation of a Caliphate under Hashemite-Arab rule that would take over the Arab provinces of the Ottoman Empire.

The territory that the Hashemites demanded in their correspondence with the British, was the entire area stretching from the southern border of Turkey all the way to the Indian Ocean, and from the Mediterranean in the west, to the border with Iran in the east. The demands of the Hashemites from the British did not include Egypt or other parts of North Africa, which, at the time, were not seen as parts of the Arab world. Egypt was not demanded, also because the Hashemites were realistic enough not to ask the British for a territory that had been under British occupation for decades. Pretty much the same was true for the Arabic-speaking peoples of the Maghreb, who were under French colonial rule.

In this correspondence between the British and the Hashemites, McMahon agreed, with certain reservations, to the Arab demand. The British hoped and believed that the Arabs would contribute to the war effort by rising against the Turks, and that they would indeed rise against the Turks if they had a promise of territorial gain. The British also believed that siding with Arab nationalism would serve Britain's post-war interests in the Middle East in their competition with the French. With the Arabs on their side, it would be much easier for the British to exercise their own imperial control of the Arabic-speaking regions in the Middle East. These were important for the British because of imperial communications, especially the passage to India, as well as for oil for the great British fleet.

The Route to India

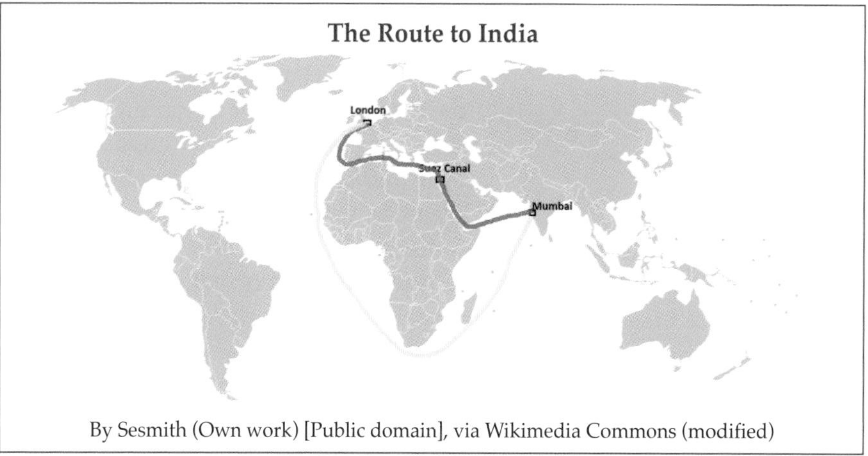

By Sesmith (Own work) [Public domain], via Wikimedia Commons (modified)

Some key reservations that the British made in the McMahon-Hussein correspondence related to certain areas that were excluded from the territory allocated to the Arab state, on the grounds that they were not purely Arab. This referred especially to the "portions of Syria lying to the west of the districts of Damascus, Homs, Hama and Aleppo." British promises also related only to those portions of the territory "wherein Great Britain is free to act without detriment to the interest of her ally, France."[3]

The reservations were cause for great controversy after the war, especially on the question of Palestine. But it was not that the British had promised the same territories twice to different players, as some often argue: "Palestine, the twice-promised land." In fact, there was no real, substantial discrepancy between the documents, the Sykes-Picot agreement, the Hussein-McMahon correspondence, and thereafter the Balfour Declaration. Generally, the British had been quite consistent.

The correspondence was indeed just that. It was a correspondence, not an agreement. There was no final agreement, but just the presentation of positions. The Zionists and the British tended to argue for a long time after the war that Palestine had been excluded from the Arab state on the basis of the sentence that speaks of the exclusion of the "portions of Syria lying to the west of the districts of Damascus, Homs, Hama and Aleppo." But to explain the exclusion of Palestine on those grounds was impossible. The argument that the Zionists and their supporters made could not be sustained by the text, nor by the reality on the ground.

By Patten, William and J.E. Homas (University of Alabama Map Library) [Public domain], via Wikimedia Commons

The Zionists and their supporters argued that by the word districts, the documents meant the equivalent of the Ottoman province, *vilayet*. Since the Vilayet of Damascus stretched all the way down south, including what became Trans-Jordan, then it stood to reason that "the portions of Syria" west of the Vilayet of Damascus, would exclude Palestine. But the word districts could not have meant *vilayet*s. Hama and Homs were not *vilayet*s, and to the west of the Vilayet of Aleppo was nothing

3. Laura Zittrain Eisenberg and Neil Caplan, *Negotiating Arab-Israeli Peace: Patterns, Problems, Possibilities* (Indiana University Press, 2010), Appendix B: Documents Online, Document 2, The McMahon-Husayn Correspondence, July 1915 to March 1916.

but the Mediterranean Sea. Districts meant environs and not *vilayets*. Palestine could not have been excluded on those grounds, as it was south of the areas in question. The exclusion of the portions of Syria lying to the west of the line, was a reference to Mount Lebanon and to its Maronite population, who did not see themselves as Arabs, and actively sought the protection of France.

But then there was the other reservation, that sentence which noted that the promises to the Arabs related only to "those portions of the territories wherein Great Britain is free to act without detriment to the interest of her ally, France." It is in accordance with that sentence that Britain could not have promised Palestine to the Arab state without consulting France. After all, as we have seen in the Sykes-Picot Agreement, Palestine was an area in which the French shared responsibility with the British.

So why did the British try to explain for years that the exclusion of Palestine was on the basis of this impossible *vilayet*s argument? They could simply have said that Palestine was excluded because of the previous secret understanding with France. In the aftermath of the First World War, to argue that the territories were excluded because they were not Arab was in accordance with the modern and politically acceptable principle of self-determination. Whereas to argue in the name of secret deals with the French or other colonial powers was no longer politically correct. With the rise of anti-colonial powers like the United States and the Soviet Union, it was no longer possible to argue in the name of old and discredited imperial rules and secret deals between great powers. Self-determination was the new name of the game, also according to the famous principles of US President Wilson. Therefore the argument about either the inclusion or exclusion of Palestine had to be made in the name of self-determination, even if in terms of the documentation, it could hardly make sense.

The Arab Revolt, 1916

See page for author [Public domain], via Wikimedia Commons

As for the Arab uprising that the British had hoped for, not much actually happened. Hussein declared his revolt against the Ottomans in June 1916, accusing them of religious deviation, that is, they were too secular, too reformist and not Islamic enough. The

Lawrence of Arabia (Thomas Edward Lawrence)

By Lowell Thomas (photographer) [Public domain], via Wikimedia Commons

revolt, therefore, was not really in the name of Arab nationalism. All the same, the great majority of Arabs did not rebel. They were unwilling to join in an uprising against the Ottoman Sultan, who they still regarded as their legitimate leader and thus remained loyal to the Empire. The Arab Revolt, in the end, did not really make much of a contribution to the war effort. In the words of T.E. Lawrence, the famous Lawrence of Arabia, the Arab Revolt was nothing but "a side show of a side show." The British in Cairo had been unrealistic in their views about the attraction of Arab nationalism. They had given Arab nationalism far more weight than the peoples of the Middle East had actually attached to it.

The Balfour Declaration

The war opened new opportunities for the Zionist movement. Palestine, as we have seen, had not been promised to the Arabs. But it was not promised to the Jews either. One ought to carefully examine the Balfour Declaration to see why it was issued and what it really said. The outbreak of the First World War and the fact that it meant the impending dissolution of the Ottoman Empire gave the

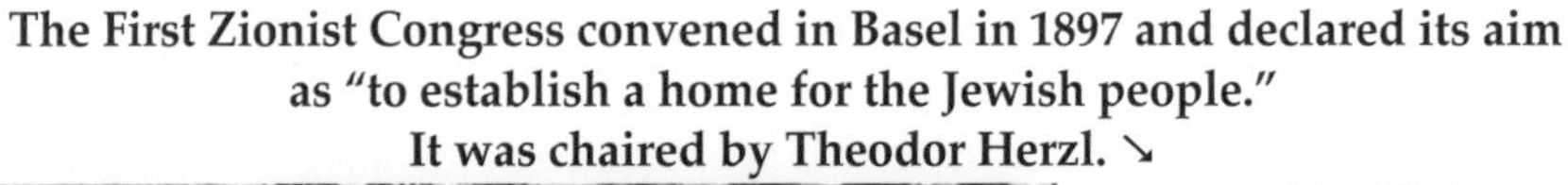

The First Zionist Congress convened in Basel in 1897 and declared its aim as "to establish a home for the Jewish people." It was chaired by Theodor Herzl. ↘

By Epson291 at en.wikipedia [Public domain], via Wikimedia Commons

Carl Pietzner [Public domain], via Wikimedia Commons

Zionists an opportunity that they had been waiting for. If the Empire was going to be dismantled, maybe the Zionists could secure Palestine for themselves.

David Lloyd George
Prime Minister of Britain
(1916–1922)

By Harris & Ewing [Public domain], via Wikimedia Commons

The British had their own interests in Palestine. As part of the general Middle Eastern strategic zone, adjacent to the Suez Canal and the passage to India, Palestine was seen as important by the British for their imperial security. Prime Minister Lloyd George was one of those who was quick to recognize the imperial interest that Britain had in Palestine. Lloyd George was also a man with a certain religious upbringing and knowledge of the Bible. The idea of a British-protected Jewish colony also appealed to him as a person who associated the Jews with the Holy Land.

In November 1917, when the Balfour Declaration was issued, the position of the Allies in the war was in a rather sorry state. The war was slow and extremely costly in human life to the participants on both sides. There was great hope amongst the British that the United States would become more involved in the war and that Russia would not withdraw, because of its internal difficulties, and would remain fully engaged. The British thought that if they expressed support for Zionist

Lord Balfour and the Balfour Declaration

Foreign Office,
November 2nd, 1917.

Dear Lord Rothschild,

I have much pleasure in conveying to you, on behalf of His Majesty's Government, the following declaration of sympathy with Jewish Zionist aspirations which has been submitted to, and approved by, the Cabinet

"His Majesty's Government view with favour the establishment in Palestine of a national home for the Jewish people, and will use their best endeavours to facilitate the achievement of this object, it being clearly understood that nothing shall be done which may prejudice the civil and religious rights of existing non-Jewish communities in Palestine, or the rights and political status enjoyed by Jews in any other country"

I should be grateful if you would bring this declaration to the knowledge of the Zionist Federation.

See original image descriptions [Public domain or Public domain], via Wikimedia Commons

aspirations, this would help propaganda in the US and in Russia to secure greater support in both of these countries for the war effort. So they believed, thanks to the vast Jewish influence that they thought existed in both of these countries. This British belief that support for Zionist aspirations would significantly help propaganda in the US and Russia for the war effort, was a huge exaggeration of actual Jewish influence in these countries. But it was, nevertheless, exaggerated or not, a major reason for the British to issue the Balfour Declaration.

The Declaration itself was in the form of a letter from the British Foreign Secretary to the leader of the Jewish community in Britain, Lord Rothschild, in which the British government expressed their sympathy for Jewish Zionist aspirations. Sympathy, not support, wording no doubt chosen with great care. "His Majesty's Government," as we see in the Declaration, "view with favor the establishment in Palestine of a national home for the Jewish people." Sympathy and "view with favor," both suggested less than outright support. The British were being extremely limited and cautious in their commitment to the Zionist enterprise.

Moreover, "the establishment in Palestine of a national home for the Jewish people," did not mean the conversion of Palestine into a Jewish national home, which could be restricted to any part of the territory of Palestine. The Declaration does not speak of a state, only of a "national home" and it is not at all clear what that really means. On the other hand, on the positive side, "a national home for the Jewish people" means recognition of the Jewish people as a nation with a right to self-determination. The British government will use their best endeavors, the document says, "to facilitate the achievement of this object, it being clearly understood that nothing shall be done that may prejudice the civil and religious rights of existing non-Jewish communities in Palestine."

Whatever rights may be recognized for the Jews, the British were also saying that "nothing shall be done which may prejudice the civil and religious rights" of other communities in Palestine. But for the other communities in Palestine, two points should be mentioned. 1) They, the other communities, only had civil and religious rights. National rights were recognized only for the Jews and not for the other communities in Palestine. 2) They are defined as the "non-Jewish communities" as if they were the minority in a Palestine where the Jews were the majority. In 1917 the reverse was true.

But these "non-Jewish communities" were Arabs (Muslims, Christians) who all had an identity of their own which could not reasonably be defined solely as being "non-Jewish." There is no recognition of their separate identity nor of any national rights associated with that separate identity. But, if "nothing shall be done which may prejudice" their civil and religious rights, there was an obvious restriction on what the Jews could actually do, once they did establish some kind of political entity in Palestine.

The Zionists understood the Declaration to mean support for a Jewish state in Palestine, although that was not what the Declaration actually said. As the British historian Malcolm Yapp correctly concluded, the Declaration was "virtually meaningless and committed Britain to nothing."[4] However, after the war, when Britain became the mandatory power in Palestine, it was committed to the League of Nations to implement the Balfour Declaration. Britain's commitment to the Jews began to mean a lot more than just the Declaration, or letter to Lord Rothschild.

The Middle East at War's End

At the end of the war it was the British who held the lion's share of the Arab provinces of the Empire. The British historian and journalist Elizabeth Monroe defined this post-war period as Britain's moment in the Middle East, and indeed, Britain was, after the First World War, by far the superior power in the Middle East. The Ottoman Empire had come to an end. The French, who were completely preoccupied at the front in France, could spare only token forces for the Middle East. Russia was overtaken by revolution and British forces occupied most of the Arab areas of the Empire. They were in Syria, Iraq and in Palestine, and there was just a small French force in Lebanon.

Faisal, the son of Hussein Ibn Ali who had led the Arab rebellion against the Ottomans, was, at the end of the war, in control of an Arab state, the capital of which was Damascus in Syria, which had been taken by British forces with the assistance of the men of the Arab Revolt. Faisal remained in this Syrian-Arab state under his control until 1920, when he was finally evicted by the French, with actual British agreement. As for the rest, Britain was in control of Egypt and the Sudan as well as much of Arabia under various degrees and guises of British influence.

King Faisal
In control of Syria from the end of WWI to July 1920

See page for author [Public domain], via Wikimedia Commons

The French were in control of North Africa, Morocco, Algeria and Tunisia, all taken well before the war: Algeria in 1830, Tunisia in 1881 and Morocco in 1912. Libya had been under the Italians since 1911. The great powers, especially Britain, could shape the region now more or less as they wished. The borders of Middle Eastern states were drawn by British and French officials in accordance with various imperial interests and trade-offs. It was these imperial interests that shaped the borders of the Middle East, very

4. Malcom Yapp, *The Making of the Modern Near East*, p. 290.

often by imperial officials with rulers in their hands, rather than the interests and identities of the peoples in question.

Very important French concessions were made to the British in Palestine and in Iraq. According to Sykes-Picot, Palestine was to be shared between the British and the French. But after the war, the British wanted Palestine for themselves and had no interest in sharing it with the French. The British also wanted Mosul, which was supposed to be part of French-influenced Syria, to become part of British-influenced Iraq. The French conceded in Palestine and in Mosul and, in exchange, the British allowed the French to take over Syria that was in the hands of their erstwhile allies, Faisal and the men of the Arab rebellion. Thus the French went ahead and expelled Faisal from Syria in July 1920.

To understand British actions in favor of France and against their own Arab allies one has to appreciate the very complicated balance between European and Middle Eastern interests in British foreign policy. British foreign policy was made in various places. Obviously in London, but in Cairo too. British officials in Cairo were firm supporters of an Arab solution, that is, to create a series of Arab states in alliance with Britain without necessarily leaving much for the French. In London, however, the perspective was very different. In the Foreign Office it was deemed to be very important to allow the French what they deserved according to their wartime agreements, even though the French had very little power in the Middle East. For British foreign policy makers in London, France's importance was mainly as a European ally against Germany. In terms of British national security, as an ally against Germany, the importance of France outweighed the value of any territory in Beirut, Damascus or anywhere else in the Middle East, by far.

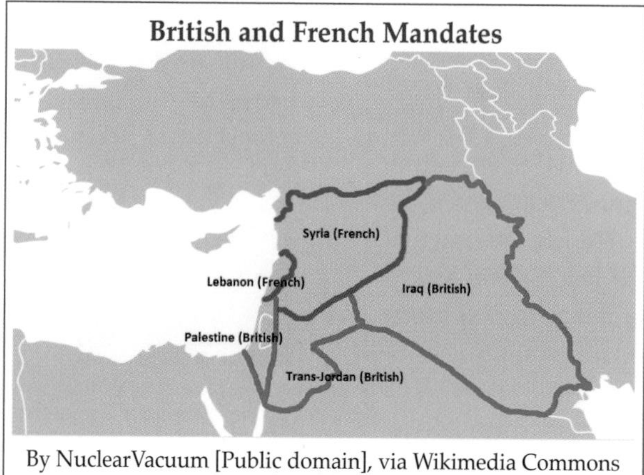

By NuclearVacuum [Public domain], via Wikimedia Commons (modified)

In the aftermath of the war, important Arab provinces of the Ottoman Empire were divided into territories that were called mandates, given to the British and to the French, in accordance with the decisions made at the conference of the victorious European powers in San Remo in April 1920. The mandates were divided as follows: The French obtained the mandates for Lebanon and Syria; the British were given the mandates for Palestine (which included Trans-Jordan) and Iraq.

The question arises as to the origins of this political concept known as a "mandate." The mandate was an essential colonial compromise with the principle of self-determination. In the aftermath of the First World War, with the emergence of the United States as a great power, and the principles put forth by President Wilson, including the principle of self-determination, the colonial powers could not simply ignore self-determination and impose endless colonial rule on foreign territory. The mandate was a colonial compromise whereby the mandate power committed itself to guide the mandated territory towards self-determination and independence. Thus it was the commitment of the French to guide Lebanon and Syria towards independence, as it was the commitment of the British to do the same for Palestine (including Trans-Jordan) and Iraq.

As for Turkey and what remained of the Ottoman Empire, the Turks were coerced into signing on to their defeat in the Treaty of Sèvres with the European powers in August 1920. The Treaty of Sèvres was a reflection of the European desire to enhance the prestige of the European powers and to punish the Turks as an Asian power that had urged Muslims everywhere to rise against their European rulers. They had to pay.

The Treaty of Sèvres, August 1920

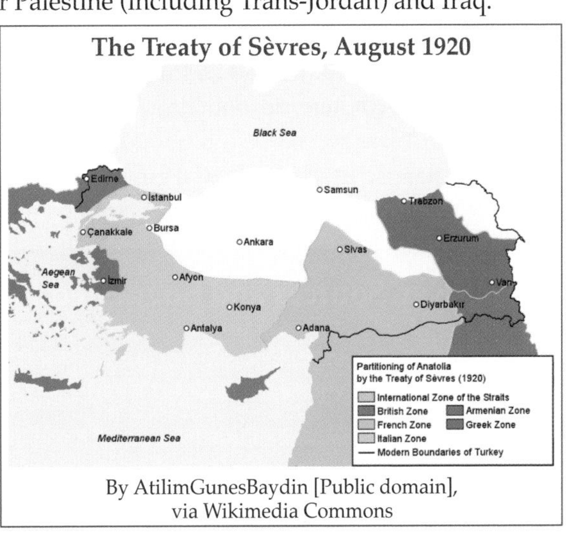

By AtilimGunesBaydin [Public domain], via Wikimedia Commons

The Greeks had already landed in Izmir (Smyrna) in May 1919. This was an extreme humiliation for the Turkish people. The Greeks were not just a

Greeks landing in Izmir, May 1919

See page for author [Public domain or Public domain], via Wikimedia Commons

By own work (Image:Turkey location map.svg) [CC-BY-SA-3.0 (http://creativecommons.org/license s/by-sa/3.0)], via Wikimedia Commons

foreign power, but a foreign power who, for centuries, had been under Turkish domination. There were demands of the Armenians in eastern Anatolia for an independent state of their own. The Turkish nationalist movement, for its part, demanded Turkish control of all the areas within the national boundaries that were inhabited by a Muslim majority at the time of the armistice that ended the war.

The Treaty of Sèvres as imposed on the Turks in August 1920 created an extremely humiliating situation. There was to be an international regime for the Straits; an Armenian state in the east and the possibility of a Kurdish state in the east, as well. There were Italian and French spheres of influence in southern Anatolia, Greek control of eastern Thrace and Izmir (Smyrna), and on top of all that, international financial controls over the Turkish economy.

This was not only the end of Empire, but the conversion of Turkey into a European semi-colonial dependency. The Turks rose in rebellion and waged what for the Turks would be a glorious war of liberation. That Turkish war of liberation changed the reality on the ground to such an extent that Sèvres became a dead letter and was subsequently replaced by another treaty altogether.

Key Sources and Suggested Further Reading

- Ayalon, Ami, *Language and Change in the Arab Middle East: The Evolution of Modern Arabic Political Discourse* (New York: Oxford University Press, 1987).
- Esposito, John, *Islam and Politics* (Syracuse University Press, 1991).
- Hourani, Albert, *A History of the Arab Peoples* (New York: Warner Books, 1991).
- Lewis, Bernard, *The Middle East: 2000 Years of History From the Rise of Christianity to the Present Day* (London: Weidenfeld and Nicolson, 1995).
- Dawn, C. Ernest, "From Ottomanism to Arabism: The Origin of an Ideology," in Hourani, Albert, Khoury, Philip and Wilson, Mary (Eds.), *The Modern Middle East: A Reader* (London: I.B. Tauris, 2011).
- Dawn, C. Ernest, "Hashemite Aims and Policy in the Light of Recent Scholarship on Anglo-Arab Relations during World War I," in C. Ernest Dawn, *From Ottomanism to Arabism: Essays on the Origins of Arab Nationalism* (Urbana: University of Illinois Press, 1973).
- Vatikiotis, P.J., *The Modern History of Egypt* (London: Weidenfeld and Nicolson, 1969).
- Yapp, Malcolm, *The Making of the Modern Near East, 1792-1923* (London: Longman, 1987).
- Zürcher, Erik, *Turkey: A Modern History* (London: I.B. Tauris, 2004).

Chapter Four

The Creation of the Middle East State System

The Ascendance of the Western Powers

The Middle East state system was created in the aftermath of the First World War, following the dissolution of the Ottoman Empire. This was the period of ascendance of the Western powers, Britain and France, in the Middle East and it was they who created much of this new state system.

The British and the French did not have similar perceptions of the Middle East. In the eyes of the French, the Middle East was a heterogeneous mosaic of religious sects and minorities, which clashed with the British view that tended to see the Middle East as a more homogeneous Arab world, populated by the Arab nation. Looking at the Middle East in retrospect, it would appear that the French were more on the mark than their British counterparts.

But at the time, in the aftermath of the First World War, in making their decisions the British had to take into consideration a variety of different points of view on policy in the Middle East. On the one hand, there was the view from London which sought compromise with France because of France's importance in the European context. France was a critical ally of the British against Germany, and even though the war was over, the British were still very concerned with the balance of power in Europe, and in that respect, France was a necessary partner.

The British view from Cairo, however, was very different. For the British in Cairo, the French in the Middle East were a disruptive irritant. The British experts in Cairo believed in the emergence of Arab nationalism and that Britain ought to side with Arab nationalism and unite the Arab Middle East under British influence in cooperation with the Arab nationalists, without any necessary deference to France. But it was the view from London that prevailed, which meant consideration for France's interests, while simultaneously taking Arab nationalism into account. Arab nationalism after the First World War had made its mark in the international community, and the great powers could not ignore this reality and establish in the Middle East some form of colonial order, as if nothing had happened during the war. Thus came the invention of the mandate compromise between colonial interests and the need to acquiesce in the self-determination of peoples. The great powers could exercise their influence in the region, but they also had to commit themselves to lead the peoples of the region to independence.

Britain's interests had to be balanced against those of France, and their divergent perceptions tended to clash once again. The British saw the region as one strategic theater on the way to their important imperial possession of India. In the French view, however, the region was not a single strategic theater. In their minds, the areas of Syria and Lebanon in the Levant, should be seen as separate from France's possessions in North Africa. In fact, France wanted as little influence as possible of Arab nationalism in Syria and Lebanon, to affect its position in North Africa in general, and in Algeria, their most important colonial possession, in particular. The French were very suspicious of Arab nationalism, and very suspicious of the British association with the Arab nationalist movement, which they constantly suspected was just an instrument to undermine their colonial interests in the Middle East.

The Arab nationalist movement, thanks to the Arab Revolt against the Turks during the First World War, had achieved a measure of international recognition. The international community did recognize that there was an Arab nationalist movement and that there were Arab national rights that had to be addressed. It was a combination of all these complex factors related to Arab national rights, on the one hand, and colonial interests, on the other, that eventually determined the state structure of the Middle East. A number of Arab states established on the ruins of the Ottoman Empire were new inventions that had never existed as defined political entities before 1920.

Egypt

The most notable exception to this rule was Egypt. Egypt was a country which had been in existence as a separate entity for centuries. When the war began, the British transformed Egypt into a protectorate governed by a British High Commissioner and thereby finally and formally detached Egypt from the Ottoman Empire, with whom the British were now at war. At the end of the war in November 1918, a delegation of Egyptians led by Sa'ad Zaghlul, who was to become one of Egypt's most prominent politicians until his death in 1927, was formed to negotiate with the British about independence. The delegation, known as the *Wafd* (delegation in Arabic), was to become

Hizb al-Wafd: The Wafd Party

Wafd Members in 1922

one of the most important political parties in Egypt of the first half of the 20th century. Sa'ad Zaghlul, the leader of the *Wafd*, was a typical product of the era of reform and one of the disciples of Afghani and Abduh. He became a lawyer and a judge and was active in the modernization of Egypt's legal system. Zaghlul and the *Wafd* sought permission from the British High Commissioner to visit London to present Egypt's nationalist demands for independence. But he was turned down. In March 1919 he was arrested by the British and deported.

Sa'ad Zaghlul
1859–1927

W. Hanselman [Public domain], via Wikimedia Commons

The result of this British action were riots and protests that broke out throughout Egypt. This was the great uprising or revolution, *thawra* as it was called in Arabic, of 1919. The uprising encompassed virtually the entire population, in the cities and in the rural districts of Egypt. In the cities, students were often the leading force of the demonstrations, joined by civil servants and skilled workers. Subsequently, organized workers, like the railway workers, for example, joined in the struggle. The peasants often had a different agenda. They rebelled against government as such, but also against their landlords, voicing complaints about their dire poverty. The British eventually agreed to negotiate with Zaghlul and the nationalists, and talks went on from June 1920 until February 1922. But agreement was not reached and a compromise formula on Egyptian self-government (while protecting British strategic interests) was not found.

The 1919 Revolution *(Thawra)*

See page for author [Public domain], via Wikimedia Commons

So on the 28th of February 1922 for lack of any better choice, the British unilaterally declared Egypt's independence with four reserved points that remained in British control:

1. Defense and foreign affairs
2. The security of the Suez Canal

3. Capitulations: The capitulations were rights that were given to foreigners in the Ottoman Empire which allowed them not to be judged in criminal cases by local law but by the laws of their own countries through their diplomatic representation. The capitulations remained in place under British supervision.
4. The Sudan would remain separate of Egypt as opposed to the demands of the Egyptian nationalists to unite the Sudan with Egypt.

Constitutional Monarchy under King Fuad I

By Brain News Service (publisher) [Public domain], via Wikimedia Commons

After the unilateral declaration of independence, a constitutional monarchy was established under King Fuad I, who was a continuation of the Muhammad Ali dynasty, which had ruled Egypt since the beginning of the 19th century. The British, the King and the political parties that were dominated by the Egyptian landowning elite, were engaged in never ending devious power struggles. The end result was the complete corruption of the parliamentary system. Parliamentary government and its institutions were quickly discredited in Egypt and never really took hold in the country.

This new phase of Egyptian statehood gave rise to a fascinating domestic debate on religion and identity in yet another round in the ongoing contest between the forces of modernity and tradition. The 1920s were the golden age of Egyptian-ness and secular liberal politics. Egyptian-ness meant a collective identity according to which people were

Egypt's Illustrious Past

By unknown Egyptian artisan (Jon Bodsworth (photographer)) [Public domain], via Wikimedia Commons

By Jerzy Strzelecki (Own work) [GFDL (http://www.gnu.org/copyleft/fdl.html) or CC-BY-SA-3.0 (http://creativecommons.org/licenses/by-sa/3.0)], via Wikimedia Commons

defined by their attachment to the land of Egypt, by the fact that they were born and bred in the country of Egypt, and not by their religion. Egyptian-ness, therefore, was a secular concept of identity and Egyptian secular nationalism went hand in hand with secular liberal politics.

In the early 1920s in this age of political liberalism in Egypt, Egyptian intellectuals spoke of the "Egyptian character", the "Egyptian mentality" and the "Egyptian spirit".[1] Islam in this form of identity was only one phase in Egypt's long history which went back thousands of years to Pharaonic times. The Egyptians, in this worldview, were not defined solely by Islam. Identifying a peculiarly Egyptian culture and identity was an indirect assault on the centrality of Islam and its values. Thus in the 1920s Egypt experienced what the British historian P. J. Vatikiotis has called the "attack upon tradition."[2]

The legal system in Egypt under the British occupation had been Westernized to a large degree and secularized even more than in the Ottoman Empire. The role of the Shari'a was steadily reduced to issues of personal status, inheritance and the management of *awqaf*, the religious endowments. The establishment of a constitutional monarchy in the early 1920s with a parliament and the holding of general elections formalized and institutionalized the practice of man-made legislation.

The established practice of man-made legislation automatically gave rise to the question of the residual role of religion in society and politics. There were some in Egypt in the 1920s who argued that there was no role for religion in the political order. Ali Abd al-Raziq, though a Shari'a judge, published a book on *Islam and the Principles of Government* in 1925. Abd al-Raziq argued that there was no need for a Caliphate in Islam, and that the Shari'a was a spiritual and moral law that was unrelated to the earthly governing of men. Abd al-Raziq was summarily expelled from the ranks of the *ulama*, the men of religion.

Taha Hussein (1889–1973)

By Van Leo (Leon Boyadijan) ([1]) [Public domain], via Wikimedia Commons

But, he was not the only person, who engaged in this attack on tradition. Taha Hussein, one of the most famous of Egypt's intellectuals and writers of the 20th century, published a book in

1. Israel Gershoni, *The Emergence of Pan-Arabism in Egypt* (Tel Aviv University, Shiloah Center, 1981), p. 31.
2. P. J. Vatikiotis, *The Modern History of Egypt*, Chapter 13.

1926 on pre-Islamic poetry. He argued that the *ulama*'s traditional, religious interpretation of the Qur'an and the Sunna (traditions of the Prophet) ought to be corrected. A much more rational method of literary criticism should be introduced into the interpretation of the religious sources. Rashid Rida, one of the initial group of Islamic reformers, as we have seen in Chapters Two and Three, and who also became one of the mentors of the Muslim Brethren, branded Taha Hussein as an apostate and demanded his removal from the university, which did eventually happen a few years later.

There were others in Egypt who wrote, for example, in favor of Darwinism and the ideas of evolution and in support of Western civilization as the highest stage of man's spiritual and material development. They attacked Islamic culture and civilization as dead and useless, and advocated the adoption of Western civilization as the only way towards progress. The secularizing reforms in Turkey in the 1920s (discussed below) strengthened the hand of those who sought the further weakening of the religious establishment.

Hasan al-Banna (1906–1949) founded the Muslim Brethren in 1928

See page for author [Public domain], via Wikimedia Commons

But to this assault on tradition, there was bound to be a response, and the reaction came in the late 1920s and during the 1930s. The Muslim Brethren were established in 1928 by Hasan al-Banna from the town of Ismailia, which is along the Suez Canal. Perhaps it is not accidental that the Muslim Brethren were formed initially in a town along the Suez Canal, that monument to external Western intervention in Egypt's affairs. The Muslim Brethren argued for the development of a modern society that was to be governed by the Shari'a, that is, modernity within the framework of the Shari'a, and not without it.

Leading modernists in the 1930s like Taha Hussein and others retreated hastily from their previous positions that had attacked tradition. In the 1930s they produced works on the ethical quality of early Islam and the genius of the Prophet, effectively abandoning their previous positions in unqualified favor of Western civilization. These new works of theirs in favor of a more traditional view were very popular.

They reinforced the conservative forces of the time, such as the Muslim Brethren, and during the 1930s, there was a steady shift towards Islam and Arab nationalism and away from narrow Egyptian-ness. Arab nationalism became very attractive to the masses of people in Egypt and elsewhere. This initial success of Arab nationalism could be ascribed to its "neo-traditionalist" formula. Arab nationalism had strong Islamic undertones and Islamic reformers had focused on the essential centrality of the Arabs to the reformation of Islam. Arab nationalism, with its religious link, was much easier for the masses in Egypt and elsewhere to accept than the more radically secular form of Egyptian nationalism, or other forms of territorial nationalism, that had no religious content.[3] The liberalizing phase of the 1920s, the attack on tradition and the effort to push Islam onto the margins of Egyptian politics and society, had ended in failure.

The Fertile Crescent

The Fertile Crescent is the region that stretches from the Mediterranean in the west to the Persian Gulf in the east, including the countries of Lebanon, Syria, Iraq, Trans-Jordan, Palestine and Israel. Comparison, they say, is the mother of all analysis. Looking at the Fertile Crescent, one should first compare with Egypt, in terms of topography and demography.

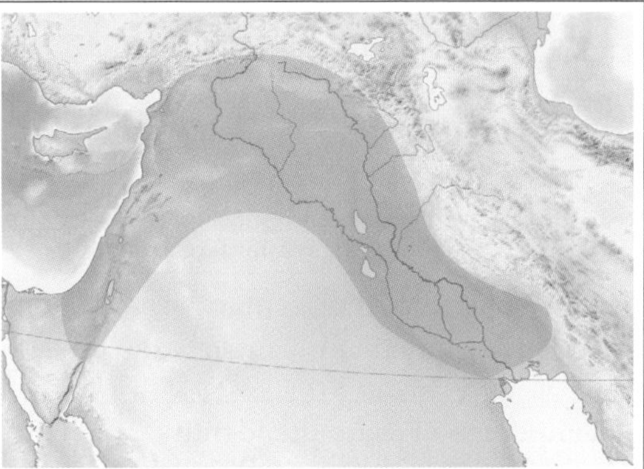

By Sémhur derivative work: Rafy (Middle East topographic map-blank.svg) [CC-BY-SA-2.5-2.0-1.0 (http://creativecommons.org/licenses/by-sa/2.5-2.0-1.0), CC-BY-SA-3.0 (http://creativecommons.org/licenses/by-sa/3.0/) or GFDL (http://www.gnu.org/copyleft/fdl.html)], via Wikimedia Commons

As opposed to Egypt, which has a very homogeneous population, the populations of the Fertile Crescent, in countries like Lebanon, Syria and Iraq, are very heterogeneous. These are countries that have populations composed of various different sects and minorities, which make the formation of cohesive states much more difficult than in the Egyptian case.

The French Mandates

The Establishment of Greater Lebanon

Greater Lebanon is the Lebanon that we know today. Its origins are to be found in the mid-19th century.

3. Israel Gershoni, "The Evolution of National Culture in Modern Egypt: Intellectual Formation and Social Diffusion, 1892-1945," *Poetics Today*, Vol. 13, No. 2 (Summer 1992), pp. 325–350.

Syria: Heterogeneous Populations

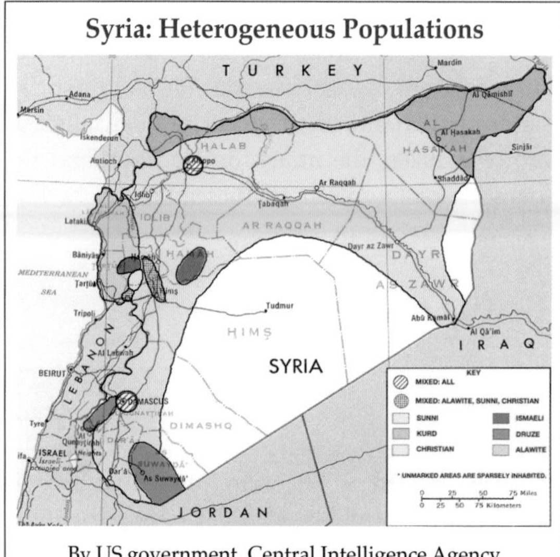

By US government, Central Intelligence Agency [Public domain], via Wikimedia Commons

As Christians and Catholics, the Maronites in Lebanon had a very distinct sense of identity in reference to all other communities in the Fertile Crescent who were either Muslim or Eastern Christian. In that respect, the Maronites were unique. They were also a compact minority, that is, a community situated in the particularly well-defined territory of Mount Lebanon. They had a historical affinity with France and a formal link with the Catholic Church since the 18th century. The Maronites had enjoyed long periods of relative autonomy, under the protection of local Druze and Maronite potentates in Mount Lebanon. In the 1840s, tensions mounted between the two main communities of Mount

The Area of Mount Lebanon

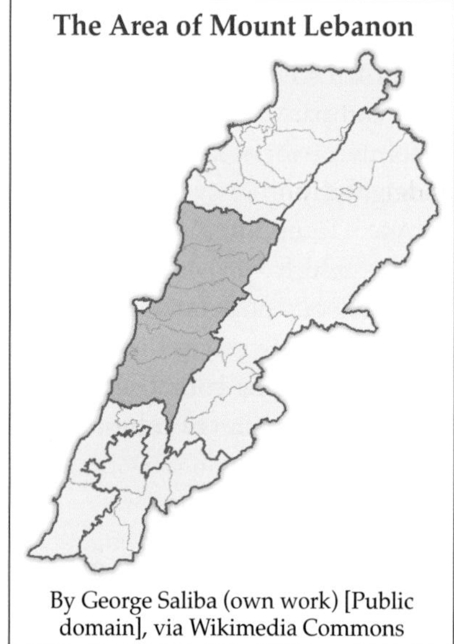

By George Saliba (own work) [Public domain], via Wikimedia Commons

Uniquiness of Maronite Identity

St. Maron: The spiritual leader of Maronite Christians, who lived in the 5th century AD

By unknown [Public domain], via Wikimedia Commons

Lebanon, the Druze and the Maronites. This eventually deteriorated into a major civil war, in which the Druze trounced the Maronites. In June 1860, thousands of Maronites were killed and about 100,000 became refugees.

Almost simultaneous was the massacre of Christians in Damascus, in July 1860, related (as noted in Chapter Two) to the opposition to the *Tanzimat*. It was these events involving the Christian minorities that led to the military intervention of France on their behalf in the summer of 1860.

The French Expedition in Syria 1860

Jean-Adolphe Beaucé [Public domain], via Wikimedia Commons

As a result of the French military intervention, an international accord was reached between the Ottomans, France, Britain, Austria, Russia and Prussia to form the autonomous province of Mount Lebanon. In 1861, this Mount Lebanon autonomous district was established by international agreement. This autonomous district would be run by a Christian governor from outside the mountain area, but appointed by Istanbul and therefore under the authority of the Ottoman Empire. This Christian governor was to be assisted by councils that would be based on sectarian representation. It was this basis of sectarian representation that created the pattern of government according to which Lebanon was established subsequently as an independent state.

Mount Lebanon Autonomous District, 1861

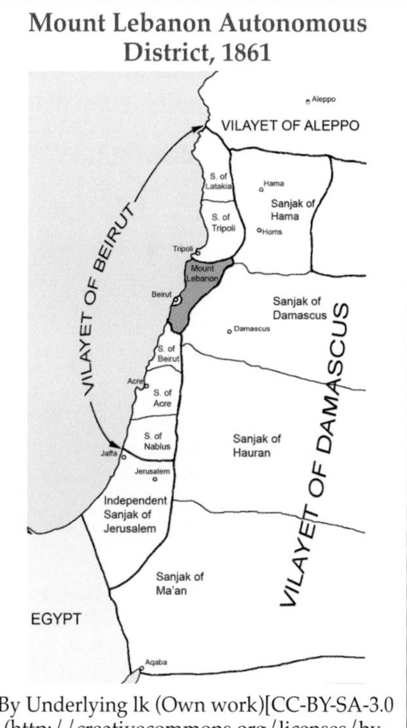

By Underlying lk (Own work)[CC-BY-SA-3.0 (http://creativecommons.org/licenses/by-sa/3.0)], via Wikimedia Commons

In 1920 Greater Lebanon was established in a territory much larger and more diverse than the cohesive Maronite area of Mount Lebanon. There are a number of reasons for the expansion. First of all, the Maronites themselves wanted more territory. The Maronites lobbied very intensively at the Paris Peace Conference after the war for the inclusion of more territory in the future state of Lebanon. The Maronites had historical aspirations that went way beyond the Mountain. Moreover, during the First World War, the Maronites had suffered awful losses from the ravages of war and starvation, as a result of which they desired to control the Biqa' Valley to the east and the mountainous area to the south. These were agricultural areas that the Maronites wanted to bring under their own authority. The affinity and protective connection with France also required the Maronites to control the coastal cities which were not included in the original autonomous area, Beirut, Tripoli, Sidon and Tyre, and all of these became part of Greater Lebanon.

The creation of Greater Lebanon changed the population ratios very dramatically. In autonomous Mount Lebanon, there had been 400,000 people of whom 80 percent were Christians and about 60 percent were Maronites. In the new Greater Lebanon, Christians were barely the majority, hardly more than 50 percent and Maronites were only one third of the population. This of course was to influence Lebanese politics very profoundly in the years ahead. Lebanon was now a confederation of Maronites, Sunnis, Shi'is and Druze, and with time, demographic trends shifted further against the Christians. Birthrates amongst the Christians were lower and emigration amongst Christians was higher. As a result, the population grew in favor of the Muslims, especially the Shi'is. As time passed it was the Shi'is who became the largest community in Lebanon, displacing the Maronites from that position.

Current sectarian distribution in Lebanon

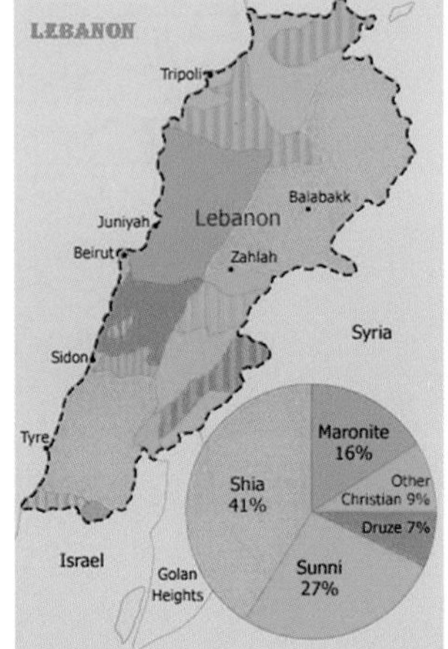

Ahmadhibrahim at en.wikipedia [CC-BY-SA-3.0 (http://creativecommons.org/licenses/by-sa/3.0) or GFDL (http://www.gnu.org/copyleft/fdl.html)], via Wikimedia Commons

The Sunnis in this new Greater Lebanon, who had previously been part of the majority in the Ottoman Empire, at least initially, deeply resented their separation from Syria and their subordination to the Maronite Christians in this new state of Lebanon. These tensions gave rise to a debate on the true face of Lebanon. Was Lebanon a Western-Christian dominated state? Or alternatively, was Lebanon an Arab state? In later years, the discussion would focus on whether Lebanon was part the Shi'ite Iranian sphere of influence or part of the

Sunni Arab camp. These questions were given answers that led eventually to breakdown and civil war on more than one occasion.

The Establishment of Syria

Like Lebanon, Syria was a mosaic of minorities too, but without a distinct territorial core like the Maronites of Mount Lebanon. The sectarian composition of the population of just over 2 million in the 1920s was as follows: Sunni Muslims in Syria were about 70 percent of the population; of that 70 percent 60 percent were Sunni Arabs and about 8 to 10 percent were Kurds, that is, people who speak Kurdish and not Arabic, Sunni Muslims by their religion, but Kurds in their ethnic identity. There were various other minorities, including the Alawis, one of the breakaway sects from Shi'a, who were 11 to 12 percent of the population, and other smaller minorities like the Druze and the Shi'is. There were some 12 percent of Christians of various denominations: Greek Orthodox, Greek Catholics and Armenians.

The Ottoman legacy and French political conduct in Syria tended to maintain and even to exacerbate sectarian differences. Historically Syria was not a

The Overlap between Sect and Social Class

Sunni landowners in the Alawite regions

By Whiting, John D. (John David), 1882–1951, and Matson, G. Eric (Gästgifvar Eric), 1888–1977 [Public domain], via Wikimedia Commons

Alawite peasant women

See page for author [Public domain], via Wikimedia Commons

consolidated unit. Rivalries that abounded between city and village, between the Sunni urban elite and the rural Sunni population and rural minorities were part and parcel of the Syrian political heritage. There was also a certain overlap between sect and social class, like Sunni landowners in the Alawi regions, who were the upper class, and the Alawis who were not only a religious minority, but also a downtrodden underclass.

Thus urban Sunnis were the only group which fully identified with Ottomanism and with the Ottoman Empire. But even amongst them, there were opponents of the *Tanzimat*, and it was they who waged the attacks on the Christian populations of Aleppo in 1850, and of Damascus in 1860. Muslims and Christians were educated in separate schools and social interaction between them was limited. Muslim hostility towards Christians was due to their relative affluence and the suspicion towards Christians as a potential pro-European fifth column. Christian Arab nationalists could not really enjoy the support of the Sunni elite and Sunni Arab nationalism was shaped, as we have already seen, more by their disappointment with the Ottomans and by Islamic reformism rather than by Christian ideologues.

French Division of Syria

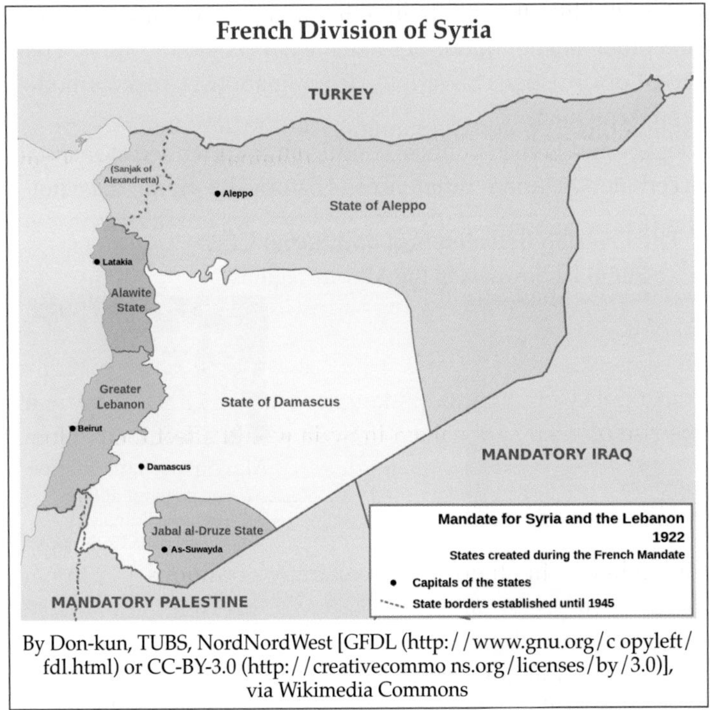

By Don-kun, TUBS, NordNordWest [GFDL (http://www.gnu.org/c opyleft/fdl.html) or CC-BY-3.0 (http://creativecommo ns.org/licenses/by/3.0)], via Wikimedia Commons

At the time of the establishment of the Syrian state, there was no sense of political community, centralized authority, or any widely accepted ideology. At first, the French even divided Damascus and Aleppo into two different states until 1924, when they succumbed to nationalist pressure and united the two in one state. But the French accorded autonomy to both the Druze and to the Alawi areas. These were eventually fully incorporated into Syria in 1936. As opposed to the British in Iraq, who united the entire country in the name of Arabism, Syria was ruled by the French with an emphasis on minority distinctiveness and autonomy.

Syria was overtaken by local rebellion against the French between 1925 and 1927. But this was more of a tribal than a nationalist affair. It began amongst the Druze minority in southern Syria in the summer of 1925. They demanded greater autonomy and less French interference in their affairs. They were joined by Arab nationalists, who were similarly disaffected by French rule and who demanded independence.

French Suppressed the Rebellion in 1927

By Markaz al-Wathâiq al-Târîkhiyya, Damascus [Public domain], via Wikimedia Commons

The French resorted to force, reconquered the Druze mountain area (Jabal Druze) in April 1926 and by early 1927, the rebellion had been suppressed. Though the rebellion was often presented as a nationalist uprising, it was not really. There was not much general participation in the rebellion, which was dominated by the Druze and by Bedouin tribesmen. It was more of a traditional affair, fueled by religion and sectarian rivalries. Some Muslim merchants were involved because of their concerns about Christian competition, while the Christians, for the most part, opposed the rebellion and tended to stay out of it.

As for the French, general hostility and suspicion towards Arab nationalism determined a distinct policy of minority preference. The French were extremely concerned that the rise of Arab nationalism in Syria would affect their colonial possessions in North Africa. The spread of Arab nationalism through North Africa, to Algeria and to Morocco and Tunisia, would make the French presence there much harder to maintain. The French therefore had their minority preference, that is, to have Christians in administrative positions and to have various minorities serve in the local army. Whatever the French could do to subdue Arab nationalism, they did. After the rebellion of 1925–1927, the French tried to be more accommodating towards the nationalists. But unlike the British, who had greater success in their dealings with Arab nationalism, the French never managed to achieve an agreement with the nationalists.

As opposed to Egypt, there was great difficulty in consolidating the Syrian state and in maintaining stability during the first decades of Syrian independence largely due to the persistently divisive sectarian identities, which had been encouraged by the French, and by the Ottomans before them. Syria became the most unstable of Arab states. There were more coups in Syria than in any other Arab state, and the country was only stabilized finally by the ascent to power of the Ba'th Party in the mid-1960s.

The British Mandates

As for the British Mandates of Palestine, Trans-Jordan and Iraq, one has to first clarify that Palestine and Trans-Jordan were both formally part of the mandate for Palestine, while Iraq was a separate mandate unto itself. But the question arises, if Palestine, Trans-Jordan and Iraq were all under British mandate, why did the British divide these into three different states? After all, they could have formed just one united Arab state linking the Mediterranean with the Persian Gulf, including Palestine, Trans-Jordan and Iraq.

The Palestine Question

The answer to that question is to be found in Palestine. It is because of the Palestine question, the Balfour Declaration and the idea of establishing a Jewish national home in Palestine that Palestine had to be clearly defined as a separate territory. Trans-Jordan was not included in Palestine and it became part of what one could call the Hashemite arrangement. The British, who had cooperated with the Hashemites in fomenting the Arab rebellion in the First World War, felt that they owed the Hashemites political compensation. Thus the Emirate of Trans-Jordan and later, also the Kingdom of Iraq, were created as Hashemite controlled states.

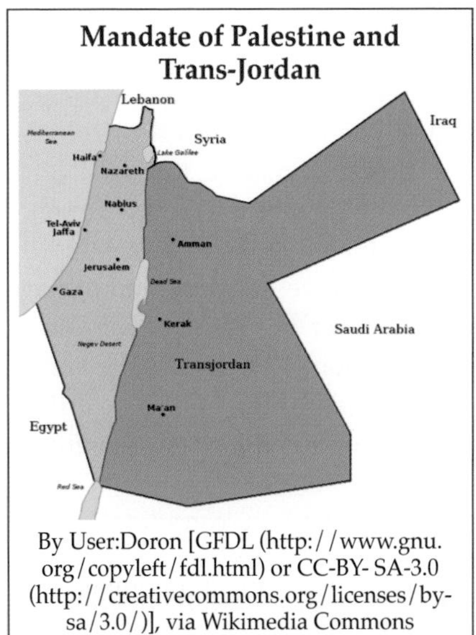

By User:Doron [GFDL (http://www.gnu.org/copyleft/fdl.html) or CC-BY- SA-3.0 (http://creativecommons.org/licenses/by-sa/3.0/)], via Wikimedia Commons

The formation of Palestine as a British mandate required an agreement with France. According to the Sykes-Picot agreement, the French were to share influence in Palestine with the British. However, following upon the British agreement to allow the French to take Lebanon and Syria, and even expel their allies, the Hashemites, from Syria, the French had to compensate the British. This came, in part, from Palestine, where the French conceded their former claims.

As for the Arabs of Palestine, one cannot really speak of a people with a clearly defined Palestinian identity when Palestine was established in 1920. In Palestine of 1920, the Arabs either identified as Muslims or Christians, perhaps gravitating in some measure towards Arab nationalism. Palestinian-ness and Palestinian nationalism evolved much later, as a result of the conflict with the Jews in Palestine, which developed into the crucible of a unique Palestinian national consciousness.

The Emirate of Trans-Jordan

Trans-Jordan was established as a separate entity, primarily to avoid the inclusion of the country in the Zionist project. It was clear to the British from the very early stages of their occupation in Palestine that Arab opposition would make the implementation of the Zionist program difficult, to put it mildly. Therefore, the decision was made not to include Trans-Jordan in the Zionist project and to have it develop from the start as an Arab state. At the end of 1920, the Emir Abdullah, one of the sons of Hussein Ibn Ali, who had led the Arab rebellion against the Ottomans in cooperation with the British, arrived in Trans-Jordan from the Hijaz, after having been ignominiously defeated by the Saudis (see below). Abdullah came to Trans-Jordan, ostensibly to take revenge against the French, who, as we have seen, had expelled his brother Faisal from Syria in July of that year.

The Agreement with the British in 1921

By American Colony (Jerusalem). Photo Department photographer. [Public domain], via Wikimedia Commons

The British at the same time were not quite sure what it was that they wanted to do with Trans-Jordan and they had no firm political arrangement for the territory. In March 1921, Abdullah and the British came to an agreement, whereby he would become the Emir (Prince) of Trans-Jordan. He would rule Trans-Jordan, at least temporarily, and if things went well, he would continue under a commitment not to attack the French in Syria. The British needed an arrangement, according to which Abdullah would keep the peace in Trans-

The Arrival of Abdullah in Amman

By American Colony (Jerusalem), Photo Department photographer. [Public domain], via Wikimedia Commons

Jordan, and would not disturb their French allies in Syria. It was within these constraints that Abdullah agreed to take over Trans-Jordan.

Trans-Jordan had very strange borders, perhaps the most unusual of all the borders of the new Arab countries, with the so-called "duck's bill" protruding eastwards towards Iraq. There are various explanations for this oddity. One explanation was the importance of a controllable land connection between Trans-Jordan and Iraq, and at the same time, to separate Arabia, which was already very much under the aegis of the Saudis and their very radical Wahhabi Islamic ideology, from the French allies of the British in Syria. Another theory was related to the importance for the British to have this territory in order to establish air fields that would enable steady and uninterrupted air traffic from the Mediterranean to the British possessions in the Gulf. No explanations, needless to say, had anything to do with the needs or desires of the people on the ground.

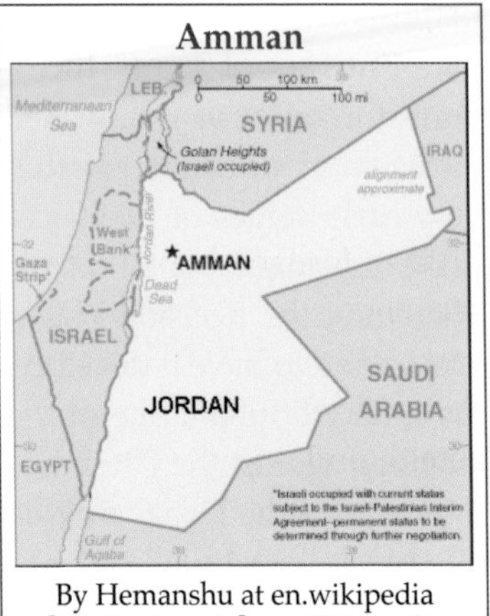

By Hemanshu at en.wikipedia [Public domain], via Wikimedia Commons

Trans-Jordan was often seen as the most artificial of the Arab states that were created in the 1920s. It was, indeed, artificial in the sense that Jordan, when established, had no urban centers. Amman, which is today a bustling metropolis of some two million, was then a very small village of just 2,000 people. There were no cities in Trans-Jordan, no Damascus, no Baghdad and no Beirut, only a number of small towns of which there were not too many either. The overall population was barely a quarter of a million. In these respects Jordan really was artificial.

But if one compares Jordan to the other countries of the Fertile Crescent, Jordan was not a collage of minorities. Jordan was a homogeneous country of Sunni Muslim speakers of the Arabic language, who were the great majority, more than 90 percent of the population. The problems of ethnicity and minorities, so difficult in countries like Lebanon, Syria and Iraq, were not present in Jordan. As a result, whatever people may say about Jordan's initial artificiality, in the long run, Jordan has proved to be the most stable of these new states that came into being in the early 1920s.

Jordan from the outset, though not included in Palestine, had a very strong historical affinity with Palestine. Jordan was part of the Palestine mandate, (although excluded from Zionist settlement) and Jordan had always been close to Palestine territorially, and intimately associated with the people of

Palestine because of the topographical structure of Jordan. In Jordan, there are a number of rivers, the Yarmuk in the north, the Zarqa in the center, and the Mujib in the south, that divide Jordan into three sections in their flow from east to west. Historically there was much easier access and movement on the east-west axis than on the north-south axis. Consequently, towns on the East Bank of the Jordan had very close relations with towns on the West Bank of the Jordan, and the peoples of Jordan and Palestine have historically been closely related.

Topography of Jordan

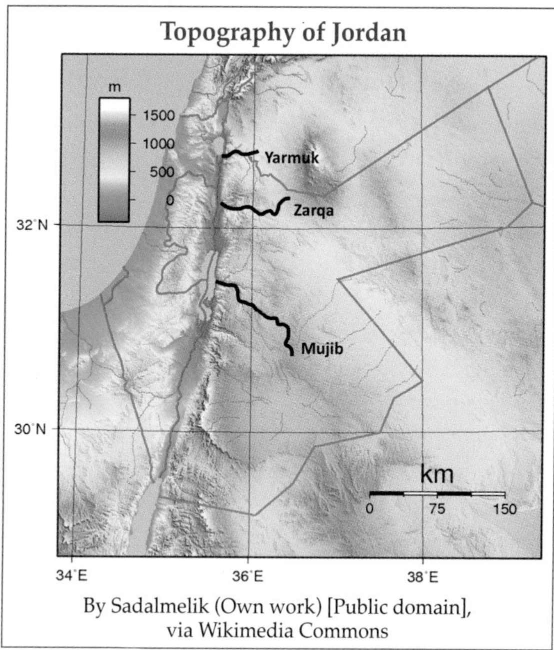

By Sadalmelik (Own work) [Public domain], via Wikimedia Commons

Abdullah was dissatisfied with the small desert principality which he had obtained, with just a few hundred thousand people and no urban centers to speak of. Abdullah had an ambition for expansion and his dream was to reign and rule in Damascus. Abdullah was obsessed with the idea of Greater Syria, rather than his dusty principality of Trans-Jordan. But that was an obsession that he could never realize. He was more successful in expanding in the direction of Palestine and in the War of 1948 the Jordanians obtained more territory for their kingdom from the land of Palestine.

Looking at Jordan through the test of survivability the kingdom established an effective ruling elite composed of the Hashemite family, the important families and the tribes of Jordan. They succeeded in promoting a sense of Jordanian-ness and in creating a loyal security and military establishment. Thanks to Jordan's geopolitical centrality, at the core of the Fertile Crescent, there are many external players that actively seek to maintain Jordanian stability, as a key component of regional security. Therefore, the Jordanian state has actually survived for longer than most would have imagined, as a good example of a state-nation rather than a nation-state, that is, as a state that was formed first and the nation evolving thereafter, rather than the other way round.

The Kingdom of Iraq

Mesopotamia: Land between Rivers

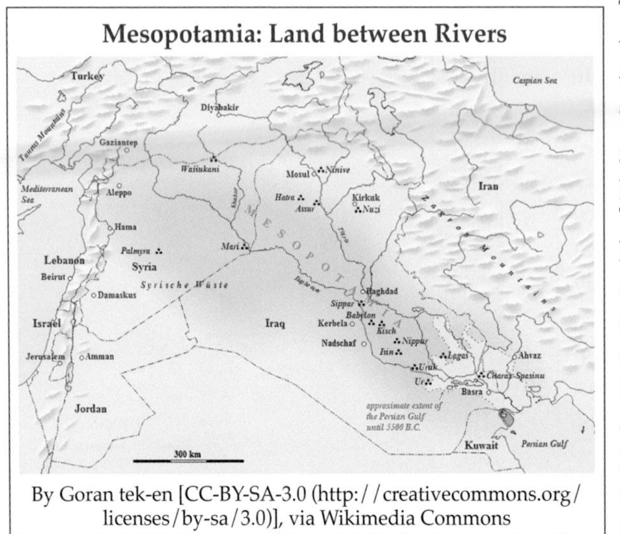

The Kingdom of Iraq was established in historical Mesopotamia, that area of the two great rivers of the Euphrates and the Tigris. These great rivers, however, did not serve as the Nile did in Egypt as an artery of effective central government. In Egypt, virtually everyone lived along the Nile. That was not true of the Euphrates and the Tigris in Iraq. There are mountainous areas in the north populated mainly by the Kurds and an extensive swampy region in the south populated predominantly by Shi'is. Iraq was always a country which was much more difficult to rule in a unified form than Egypt ever was.

The Shi'is in Iraq under the Ottomans were suspected of loyalty to Shi'ite Persia (Iran). They were never really regarded as loyal Ottoman subjects and were never integrated into the state. Moreover, the Shi'is themselves wanted no part of the Ottoman system. They did not send their children to Ottoman schools, nor did they serve in the military or in the bureaucracy. The Shi'is lagged behind the Sunnis to the north, who were more exposed and more involved in the 19th century reforms and modernization. The Shi'is were discriminated against and underprivileged, an underclass that remained un-

Shi'ite Persia

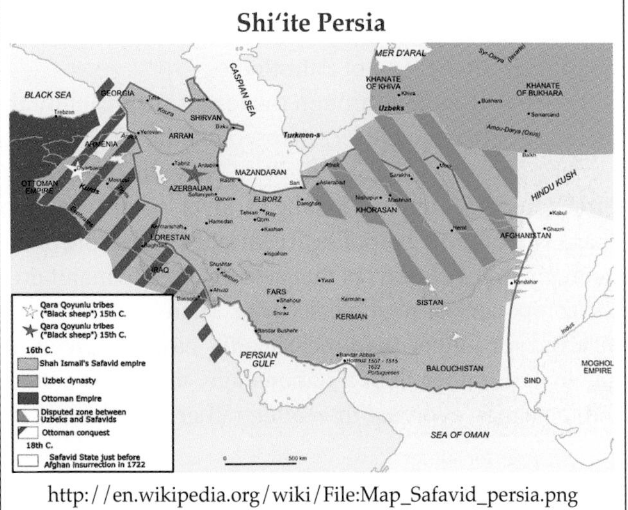

http://en.wikipedia.org/wiki/File:Map_Safavid_persia.png

educated, less economically developed and living in the underdeveloped south, the distant perimeter of the Ottoman Empire.

Shi'i consciousness, however, was particularly powerful in Iraq, the birthplace of Shi'a. The most holy places of Shi'a are situated in Iraq, in Najaf, Karbala and Kadhimayn, which is part of Baghdad. Moreover, the influence of the men of religion over their flock has historically been especially powerful in the Shi'i tradition, more so than in Sunni Islam.

Najaf

By U.S. Navy photo by Photographer's Mate 1st Class Arlo K. Abrahamson. [Public domain], via Wikimedia Commons

Karbala

By Toushiro (Own work) [Public domain], via Wikimedia Commons

The Hashemite arrangement in Iraq, seemingly the most promising when it began, failed, as opposed to the Hashemite arrangement in Jordan, which succeeded, even though the Hashemite arrangement in Trans-Jordan initially looked far more fragile and difficult to implement. Abdullah and the British created Jordan from scratch. It was, therefore, much easier for them to create Jordan in the image that they desired than was possible in Iraq, with all the problems that Iraq had inherited from the moment of its creation.

Kadhimayn

By Toushiro (Own work) [Public domain], via Wikimedia Commons

1958 Revolution: The Overthrow of the Hashemite Monarchy

See page for author [Public domain], via Wikimedia Commons

The Three Vilayets of Iraq

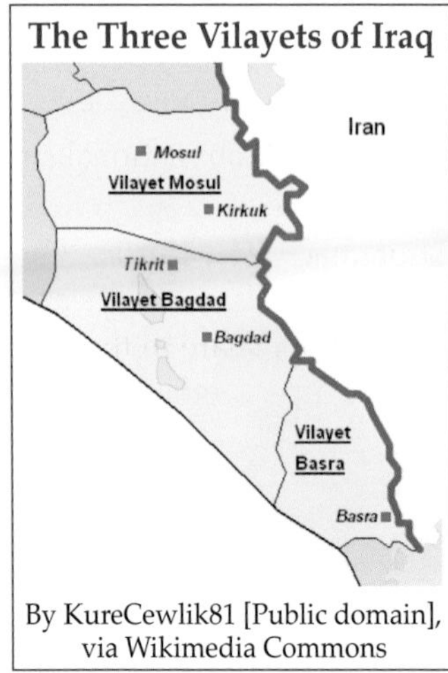

By KureCewlik81 [Public domain], via Wikimedia Commons

In Iraq, as opposed to the case of Trans-Jordan, from the very beginning, the Hashemites had to deal with a most unwieldy situation, and the existing reality in the kingdom eventually destroyed the Hashemites, who were overthrown in 1958. Iraq was made up of three Ottoman vilayets, the provinces of Basra, Baghdad and Mosul, that were lumped together to form the Kingdom of Iraq. Mosul originally was supposed to be part of the French mandate in Syria. But, in order to obtain British agreement for the French occupation of Lebanon and Syria, the French, as we have seen, compromised in Palestine and they compromised in Iraq too, by agreeing that Mosul become part of British Iraq instead of French Syria.

Of the population of Iraq, approximately 3 million in the early 1920s, 90 percent were Muslims, the rest were composed of small minorities of mainly Jews and Christians. On the face of it, that looked rather promising, but it was not really. The Muslims were made up of Sunnis and Shi'is, and it was the Shi'is who were actually the majority with a ratio of some seven to five, more or less. And of the Sunnis, half were Kurds and not Arabs. In Iraq, therefore, there was a Shi'ite majority with a Sunni minority, and the Sunni minority was divided into two, partly Arab and partly Kurdish.

Baghdad in 1930

See page for author [Public domain], via Wikimedia Commons

Baghdad was the main city and the capital with a population of 200,000, with a very large Jewish minority. In fact, the Jews in Baghdad, 80,000 in number, were the largest ethnic group in Baghdad. The other 120,000, who were the Muslim majority, were divided between Sunnis and Shi'is.

People in Iraq in the early 1920s did not generally define themselves nor identify as Iraqis. Most people identified themselves by their sect, their ethnicity or their tribe. The British created Arab Iraq in the name of Arabism which was not a shared value for very many of the people who became part of this Arab state. The Sunni Arabs, who were only about a quarter of the population, did

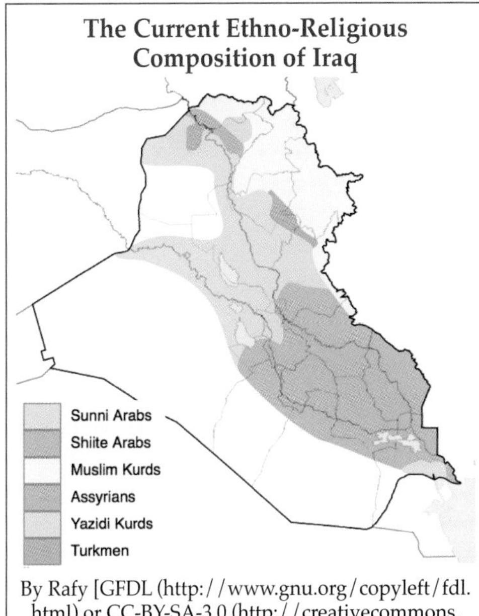

By Rafy [GFDL (http://www.gnu.org/copyleft/fdl.html) or CC-BY-SA-3.0 (http://creativecommons.org/licenses/by-sa/3.0)], via Wikimedia Commons

identify quite strongly with Arab nationalism. But the Shi'ite Arabs did not. The Shi'ite Arabs generally saw Arab nationalism as a Sunni device to engineer their own supremacy. The Kurds, who were Sunnis, were not Arabs and certainly did not share in the idea of an Arab state.

From July to October 1920 Iraq was overtaken by an anti-British rebellion. There are those who tried to explain the revolt in terms of notions borrowed from Arab nationalism and to argue that this was an Arab nationalist revolt. But in fact, it was in the main a reaction of the Shi'i tribes to the new reality in Iraq. The Shi'i tribes rose in revolt, because of their hostility to the British, deeply encouraged by the men of religion, many of whom were actually Persian in origin with no loyalty either to the state of Iraq, nor to Arab nationalism. As Elie Kedourie, the British Iraqi historian has put it, "in fomenting an anti-British rising in 1920, the Shi'ite divines no doubt hoped to gain and establish ascendancy for their community in a country where the Shi'ites were the majority, albeit hitherto a powerless one. It is difficult to say whether the failure of the uprising or the importation of Faisal and his men which followed was more galling" to them. The Hashemites in Baghdad "at all events, spelt renewed Sunni dominance." For the Shi'is, the government in Baghdad that was now being imposed upon them "was a creature of the British and an instrument of Sunni persecution, different from its Ottoman predecessor only in that is was without benefit of longtime legitimate possession, and that its rule did not derive from conquest, but was bestowed upon it by the British."[4]

But, that was not all. Aside from Shi'i disapproval of the new order in Iraq, there was the Kurdish problem. The Kurds were now in the uneasy situation of becoming a minority in an Arab Iraq, whereas under the Ottomans, they had been part of the ruling majority which was Sunni Muslim, just as they were. The Kurds were these new unhappy members of this Iraqi state in which they

4. Elie Kedourie, *The Chatham House Version and other Middle Eastern Studies* (Hanover, NH: University Press of New England, 1984), pp. 250–251.

sought at least autonomy, if not outright secession. The Shi'is, on the other hand, did not wish to secede. On the contrary, being the majority the Shi'is wanted to dominate Iraq.

The Kurdish Inhabited Area

By English: Source stated "The following maps were produced by the U.S. Central Intelligence Agency, unless otherwise indicated."
[Public domain], via Wikimedia Commons

Despite the Kurdish problem, and despite the Shi'i majority, Iraq was ruled by minority Sunni Arab predominance for decades. Faisal, the Hashemite prince, was installed as the King of Iraq in 1921, with a referendum that was carefully stage-managed by the British to produce the desired result of popular Iraqi approval. The ruling political elite of Hashemite Iraq was decidedly Sunni. Between 1921 and 1936, 71 percent of the ministerial posts were held by Sunnis and only 24 percent, and mostly minor posts at that, were held by Shi'is. In 1928, among the 88 deputies elected to the Parliament in Iraq, only 26 were Shi'is. In 1946, only three of 80 senior officers of the Iraqi military were Shi'is, and all the rest were Sunnis.

The Coronation of King Faisal I, 1921

See page for author [Public domain], via Wikimedia Commons

The British, however, were relatively liberal when it came to the question of independence. The British understood the Revolt of 1920 to be an Arab nationalist revolt, meaning that they must move quickly in according the Iraqis political independence. Indeed, in a treaty already signed in 1922, Britain devolved more responsibilities onto the Iraqi government. In a new treaty that was signed in 1930, which further restricted British powers, Iraq became independent. Iraq was admitted into the League of Nations in 1932 and was the first Arab state to become a member.

Before his death, in 1933, Iraq's King Faisal, noted that: "In Iraq there is still [...] no Iraqi people, but unimaginable masses of human beings, devoid of any patriotic ideal, imbued with religious traditions and absurdities, connected by no common tie, giving ear to evil, prone to anarchy, and perpetually ready to rise against any government whatsoever."[5] So said the first King of Iraq about his country.

Elie Kedourie, summarized the history of Iraq as follows: "From the very foundation of the Iraqi kingdom, there was this nagging feeling that it was a make-believe kingdom, built on false pretenses and kept going by a British design and for a British purpose."[6]

The new Arab states that were created in this fashion had, of course, questionable legitimacy. As a result, independence movements in countries like Syria, Iraq and Trans-Jordan were fighting for the independence of states, whose right to actually exist as independent entities was hardly accepted and was still questioned by these very same movements themselves. There was, therefore, great appeal for the idea of Arab unity. There were various unity schemes, such as those of the Iraqi Hashemites, to unite the Fertile Crescent, which was to unite Iraq with Syria, Lebanon, Jordan and Palestine in one Arab country, where, at long last, the Sunnis would be the majority, allowing them to overcome their Shi'ite majority problem in Iraq. Abdullah had his own ideas of Greater Syria which meant a union between Syria and Lebanon, Trans-Jordan and Palestine, which would of course have him as the King of Greater Syria sitting on his throne in Damascus. Then there were in later years the Ba'th party in Syria and in Iraq and Abd al-Nasser, as the President of Egypt, who were all fervent advocates of pan-Arab unity, in the 1950s and the 1960s.

The Saudis and the Hashemites in the Arabian Peninsula

For centuries in Arabia there was a powerful alliance between the Wahhabiyya, a radical school of Islamic puritanical fundamentalism, and the Saudi family. It was this Saudi-Wahhabi alliance which became the backbone of the Saudi Arabian kingdom.

King Faisal I and King Abd al-Aziz

See page for author [Public domain], via Wikimedia Commons

The Wahhabis were a radical, puritanical movement that appeared in the 18th century, and opposed any form of modernization or change in Islam. They, together with the family of Saud, controlled much of the Arabian Penin-

5. Hanna Batatu, *Old Social Classes and the Revolutionary Movements of Iraq* (Princeton University Press, 1978), pp. 25–26.
6. Elie Kedourie, *The Chatham House Version*, p. 278.

sula. In the early 19th century, the Ottomans, as we have already seen, used Muhammed Ali from Egypt every now and then to try and put them down, but with no lasting success. In the early 20th century the Wahhabi-Saudi alliance was the master of most of Arabia, while the Hashemites controlled the Hijaz, the coastal area of western Arabia, which included the holy cities of Mecca and Medina. The competitive relationship that evolved between the Saudis and the Hashemites in the Arabian Peninsula, led eventually to the creation of the independent Kingdom of Saudi Arabia in the borders as we know them today.

The Hijaz Railway

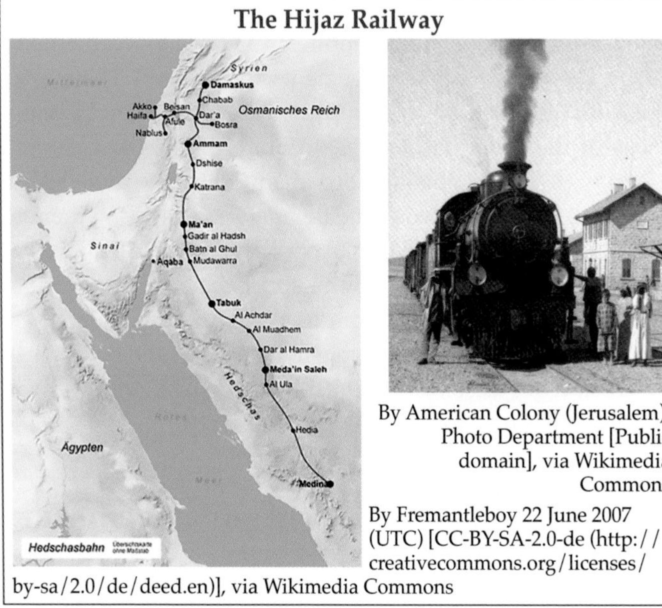

By American Colony (Jerusalem). Photo Department [Public domain], via Wikimedia Commons

By Fremantleboy 22 June 2007 (UTC) [CC-BY-SA-2.0-de (http://creativecommons.org/licenses/by-sa/2.0/de/deed.en)], via Wikimedia Commons

Not much is known about the Arabian Peninsula at the beginning of the 20th century. The population was perhaps somewhere around seven million, maybe even a lot less than that. There is no knowing what the largest city of the region was, whether it was Mecca, Jeddah, Aden or Sana'a. None had a population of more than a 100,000 inhabitants and the area was hardly affected by the reforms of the 19th century, which had such a far-reaching impact in other parts of the region. Though the Ottomans, towards the very end of their rule, did manage to extend a more effective presence, at least to the Hijaz, thanks to the building of the railway that reached as far south as Medina by 1908.

Following the Ottoman collapse in the First World War, Britain had the upper hand in the region, in which it had already formed alliances with local tribal centers of power long before. One of these was the House of Saud, which was the strongest in the Arabian Peninsula in the aftermath of the war. The Saudis, however, were the rivals of Britain's other tribal allies, the Hashemites, who as we have seen, cooperated with the British in the Arab Revolt against the Ottomans during the war. The Hashemites, under Hussein Ibn Ali, had great ambitions, more than their real power could sustain. Their ambitions set

The House of Saud

King Abd al-Aziz Ibn Saud with members of his family
By zamanalsamt (Saud family) http://www.flickr.com/photos/92278137@N04/9639340291/sizes

the Hashemites on a collision course with the Saudis, who proved to be a lot stronger.

In 1917, Hussein Ibn Ali proclaimed himself "King of the Arabs." He was recognized as such by no one, including the British, who would only accept him as the King of the Hijaz. With their Wahhabi forces, the Saudis defeated the Hashemites in a series of clashes in the first years after the war. Though in a precarious position, Hussein refused to accept Britain's precondition for cooperation, which was to acquiesce in the terms of the post-war mandate order, especially in Palestine. The British eventually lost their patience with Hussein, abandoned him to his fate and left him to be routed by the Saudis.

The Hashemites

Hussein Ibn Ali and his sons Abdullah and Faisal
Not available (The Online Museum of Syrian History) [Public domain or Public domain], via Wikimedia Commons

Hussein made the ultimate provocation by declaring himself Caliph in 1924, immediately after the Turks had abolished the Caliphate. The Saudis made their final offensive and defeated the Hashemites yet again. They annexed the Hijaz in 1925, and sent the Hashemites packing into exile.

Present-Day Persian Gulf Countries

http://en.wikipedia.org/wiki/File:Persian_Gulf_Arab_States_english.PNG

A few years later, the Kingdom of Saudi Arabia in its present borders was established under the leadership of King Abd al-Aziz Ibn Saud, and it became an independent state in 1932. As for the Persian Gulf principalities, they had been under British influence through long standing alliances with local sheikhs that were formed in the late 19th century in places like Kuwait, Qatar, Trucial Oman, which is now the United Arab Emirates, and the island of Bahrain.

The Non-Arab States

The Republic of Turkey

The Allied powers after the First World War wanted to teach the Ottomans a lesson for having attempted to rally the Arabs and other Muslims against the European powers under the banner of pan-Islamism. Since resuscitating the Empire was not an option, the powers wanted to dismantle it, weaken the Turks and even create a system of control and oversight over Turkey.

Turkish Liberation of Izmir

Başkanlığını Aydın Erkmen, "The Turkish Army's entry into Izmir" (https://commons.wikimedia.org/wiki/File:KiMOiG.jpg)

The Arab regions had been successfully separated from the Empire by the Treaty of Sèvres that was signed in August 1920. This was not the case however with Anatolia and eastern Thrace. Turkish nationalists refused to accept the partition plans that had been devised for these areas and they rose in rebellion against the Treaty of Sèvres. The Turks emerged victorious and the Treaty of Sèvres was replaced by the Treaty of Lausanne in July 1923. The Treaty of Lausanne created an entirely different reality. Thanks to the War of Independence that the Turks fought successfully, the oppressive Treaty of Sèvres was scrapped and replaced by a new arrangement which guaranteed the establishment of the independent Turkish Republic.

Immediately after the First World War the Greeks made claims over western Anatolia. They landed forces in Izmir (Smyrna for the Greeks) in May 1919. For the Turks, this was an insufferable provocation. The Greek conquerors were the former subjects of the Ottoman Empire, part of the Greek minority that had traditionally been governed by the Turks. Moreover, the Greeks had committed various atrocities against the Turks during their occupation of Izmir.

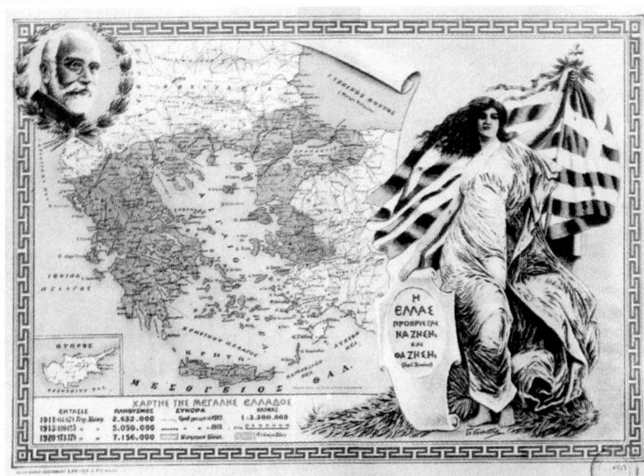

Megali Idea (Big Idea): An irredentist Greek concept the aim of which was to unite all Greek-inhabited territories under a large Greek state

See page for author [Public domain], via Wikimedia Commons

Turkish nationalists rose up in revolt under the leadership of a successful military officer and war hero of the First World War, Mustafa Kemal, who was later to assume the name Atatürk, as the first president of the new and independent Turkish Republic. Turkish resistance was especially forceful against Greek and Armenian claims in Anatolia, which provoked a powerful spirit of resentment amongst the Muslim public. In the War of Independence, the revolutionaries recaptured Izmir, ending Greek control in September 1922, and shortly thereafter, the Greeks evacuated eastern Thrace as well.

Kuva-i Milliye (National Forces): Irregular Turkish forces who fought in the War of Liberation

Original photographer is unknown [Public domain], via Wikimedia Commons

Turkish Delegation at Lausanne

By Frank and Frances Carpenter Collection. [Public domain], via Wikimedia Commons

The Ottoman Sultanate was abolished in November 1922, thus creating one central nationalist government of the revolutionaries in Ankara, which now entered into new negotiations with the European allied powers. These produced the Treaty of Lausanne in July 1923. The Arab lands were given up completely, but Anatolia was jealously protected and

Treaty of Lausanne, 1923

https://commons.wikimedia.org/wiki/File:Turkey-Greece-Bulgaria_on_Treaty_of_Lausanne.png

preserved. Kurdish and Armenian claims now disappeared as if they had never existed. Neither were there any French or Italian protectorate zones in Anatolia. Turkey also controlled the Straits, and had therefore successfully restored complete and total Turkish independence.

As for the role of modern nationalism in this revolutionary retrieval of Turkish independence, it appears that Turkish nationalism really took root during the war with the Greeks, but with very strong Islamic undertones. Turkish nationalism was an effective mobilizing force, together with Islam, in the war against the Greek infidels. Mustafa Kemal bore the title "Gazi," which had a distinctly Islamic significance, going back to the early days of Muslim conquest, as the title of a conqueror in the name of Islam.

Gazi Mustafa Kemal

Mustafa Kemal was given the title "Gazi" in 1921 by the Turkish Grand National Assembly.

Gazi: the title given to Muslim warriors

http://commons.wikimedia.org/wiki/File:Mustafakemal16.jpg

Only Muslims were considered real Turks in the full sense of the term. In the negotiations for the Lausanne Treaty of July 1923, an agreement was also achieved between Turkey and Greece on a population exchange. About one million Greeks were "repatriated" from Turkey to Greece, and a lesser number of Turks were "repatriated" from Greece to Turkey. It is particularly interesting to note that in this question it was religion that defined nationality and not language. Therefore, Christians, even if they spoke Turkish, were defined as Greeks and were sent accordingly to Greece, and Muslims who spoke Greek were defined as Turks and sent to Turkey. By this exchange of population, both Turkey and Greece became more homogeneous nation-states.

1923 Population Exchange between Turkey and Greece

Greeks from Turkey

Turks from Greece

By Frank America [Public domain], via Wikimedia Commons

The population of Turkey had declined as a result of the ravages of war and the population exchange. A census in 1927 showed that the population of Turkey was only 13.6 million. Of these, however, 98 percent were Muslim. Of the Muslim population, some 10 percent were Kurdish. The Greek and Armenian populations had sharply declined after the war, the Armenian genocide, and the population exchange.

The main ideologue of Turkish nationalism, as we have already seen in Chapter Three, was Ziya Gökalp. Now that the Empire no longer existed Gökalp's ideas of a more narrowly based Turkishness were more readily accepted. There were no significant non-Turkish populations left in the new Turkey, as there had been in the Ottoman Empire. Gökalp had been deeply influenced by the French philosopher and sociologist Émile Durkheim, who regarded nationalism as a form of civil religion. Accordingly, in Gökalp's version of nationalism, Islam remained an inseparable part of the Turkish cultural heritage. But it was not the sole cohesive element of society, only one of a number that included language, history and culture. Religion, moreover, was separated from the state, reduced to a matter of personal belief, and replaced, at least in theory, by secular nationalism.

David Émile Durkheim (1858–1917)

See page for author [Public domain], via Wikimedia Commons

The collapse of the Empire and Atatürk's decision not to expand the borders paved the way for a process of radically secularizing reforms that went hand in hand with the founding of the new Turkish Republic. The Sultan's deep hostility towards the nationalist movement only served to accelerate the process of radical reform. At the end of 1922 Ankara was determined as the new capital of Turkey, shifting the center of gravity of Turkish politics from the Imperial Ottoman capital of Istanbul to the Turkish heartland of Anatolia. At the same time the Sultanate was abolished and Sultan Mehmet VI fled into exile to be replaced by Abdülmecid II, who was appointed Caliph, a purely ceremonial position with no political power. In October 1923, Turkey formally became a Republic and in March 1924, the Caliphate was finally abolished.

Ankara as the New Capital, 1922

Opening of the 1st Turkish Grand National Assembly in Ankara (1920)
NordNordWest [GFDL (http://www.gnu.org/copyleft/fdl.html) or CC-BY-SA-3.0 (http://creativecommons.org/licenses/by-sa/3.0)], via Wikimedia Commons

The Abolition of the Sultanate, 1922

The last Ottoman sultan, Mehmet VI, leaves Istanbul
See page for author [Public domain], via Wikimedia Commons

The role of Islam in law and education was terminated. The Shari'a courts were abolished. Shari'a personal status law was replaced by a version of the Swiss civil code in 1926. The Sufi mystical orders were banned. In 1925, a special Hat Law was passed, requiring men to wear hats with brims. Though a seemingly innocuous introduction of a new law, it actually had great political

The Closure of Sufi Orders, 1925

By Uncredited photographer [Public domain], via Wikimedia Commons

and cultural importance. The hats with brims were designed to obstruct the regular performance of prayer. This was a way of imposing secularizing and secular reform.

Between 1928 and 1937 secularism was established as a principle of governance in the Turkish constitution. Turkey was the only country in the Middle East to include such a clause in its constitution. The Latin alphabet was introduced in 1928. This was an obvious attempt to erase the influence of Arabic and Persian in the Turkish language, and by changing the alphabet, to create a major disconnect between the present and the past. No other country in the Middle East ever went that far in the formal process of secularization. This was all part of a very deliberate effort by Atatürk to break with the past and to emphasize the uniqueness of the Turkish nation. There was opposition, though not very substantial, coming mainly from some religious or Kurdish sources in the east. The opposition was ruthlessly crushed by the republican regime, which was unquestionably autocratic.

The Hat Law of 1925

By NA (Türkiye Cumhuriyeti Cumhurbaşkanlığı) [Public domain], via Wikimedia Commons

The Adoption of the Latin Alphabet, 1928

By Presidency of the Republic of Turkey (http://www.tccb.gov.tr/sayfa/ata_ozel/fotograf/) [Public domain], via Wikimedia Commons

The Israeli Ottoman historian Uriel Heyd noted that Kemalism was the logical result of the very long process of Westernization, which had created a secular upper

Kurdish Rebellions

One of the most important Kurdish uprisings was the Sheikh Said Rebellion of 1925

See page for author [Public domain], via Wikimedia Commons

class in Turkey. The reform was also facilitated by the remarkable prestige and legitimacy of Atatürk, the great leader of the courageous War of Liberation that the Turks had fought for their independence. The collapse of Empire had also dealt a blow to the status and prestige of the Ottoman legacy which was seemingly overridden with ease. In later years however, this would all change again.

The Legitimacy of Atatürk

http://commons.wikimedia.org/wiki/File:Ataturk13.JPG

By Original photographer unknown. [Public domain], via Wikimedia Commons

Iran

Like Turkey, Iran was not a new state created by the great powers, but a country with a long historical and cultural tradition that went back thousands of years. In 1900 Iran had a population of about 10 million.

As of 1501, the Safavids had been established as the ruling dynasty of Iran. Since the rule of the Safavids, Iran had become a Shi'ite controlled state. As a state governed by Shi'ite Islam, Iran was a natural competitor with its Sunni Muslim Ottoman neighbors. The Safavids ruled until the early 18th century, followed by a prolonged period of political instability. At the end of the 18th century the Qajar dynasty came to power and lasted until 1925.

The Safavid Empire

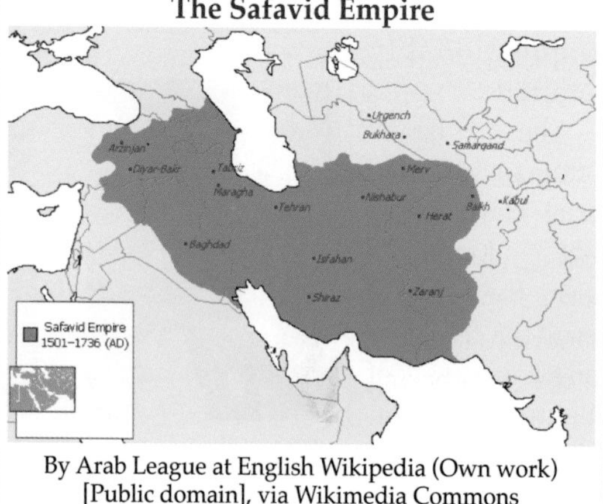

By Arab League at English Wikipedia (Own work) [Public domain], via Wikimedia Commons

Iran was characterized by a long tradition of weak central government. This had very much to do with the lay of the land, either very high mountain ranges in the north and the west, or huge deserts in the center that covered almost all of Iran's land space. So until the advent of modern means of transport and communications it was very difficult to maintain effective central government or economic modernization, for that matter. Iran had no real army to speak of like the Ottomans or Muhammad Ali in Egypt, except for usually not very effective forces raised by provincial governors.

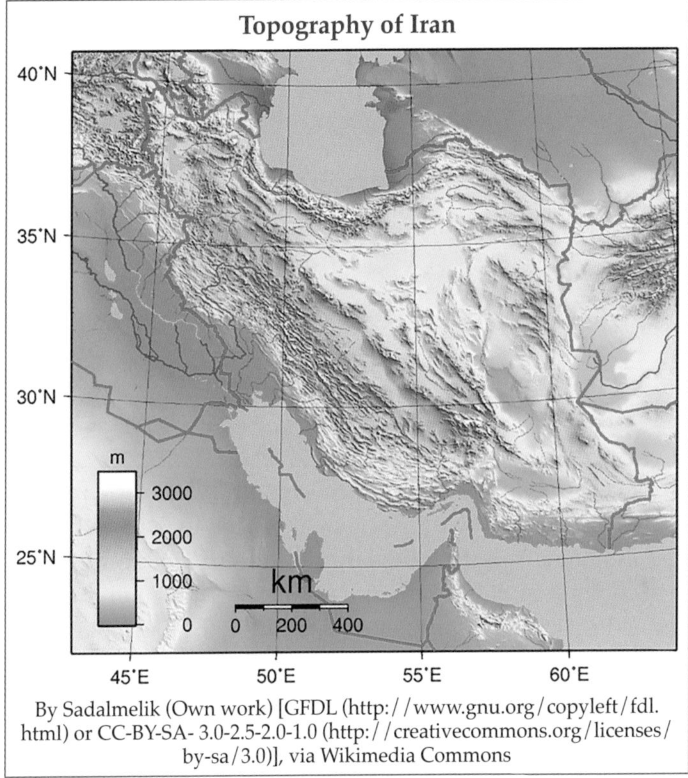

By Sadalmelik (Own work) [GFDL (http://www.gnu.org/copyleft/fdl.html) or CC-BY-SA- 3.0-2.5-2.0-1.0 (http://creativecommons.org/licenses/by-sa/3.0)], via Wikimedia Commons

Iran was territorially isolated and very far from Europe. In the 19th century, Iran managed only a very slow pace of reform. There were some changes in education but always about half a century later and less extensive than was the case with the Ottomans or Egypt. There was, however, growing economic influence of outside forces and ensuing economic difficulties.

Iran was a country historically troubled by the threat of external influence and penetration. The borders of Iran were particularly problematic. Iran was populated by a series of minorities that lived along the borders, and these ethnic minorities straddled the frontiers with part of their population in Iran and part in the neighboring countries. The Azeris, had part of their population in Iran and part in Azerbaijan, the Kurds were in Iran and in Iraq and Turkey, the Arabs in Iran and in Iraq, or the Baluchis in the east, who had part of their population in Iran, and part in Pakistan.

http://commons.wikimedia.org/wiki/File:Iran_ethnoreligious_distribution_2004.jpg

In Iran, a country with a long tradition of weak central government, the men of religion wielded extraordinary power. In the Shi'i branch of Islam the *ulama* tended to be considerably more influential than their Sunni rivals in other countries. In Sunni Islam, as we have already noted, the gates of *ijtihad* (independent interpretation), were closed in the 10th century. But the gates of *ijtihad* were never closed in Shi'a and there was always the opportunity which continues until the present day for the men of religion in Shi'a to engage in independent interpretation, *ijtihad*. In the late 18th century, there were two competing schools of thought in Shi'i Islam in Iran, the Akhbaris and the Usulis. The Akhbaris argued that all answers could be found in the Qur'an and the Sunna (the traditions of the Prophet), while the Usulis contended that answers should be given by a living interpreter, the *mujtahid*, he who conducts *ijtihad*, and it was they who emerged victorious.

Further, according to the principle of imitation the living *mujtahid* (the interpreter) was expected to be imitated by his flock, the believers. The Ayatollahs were the interpreters, the "imitated," and the rank and file were the "imitators" of the "imitated." The men of religion were financially independent of the regime, because they were maintained by their flock. As such, they had a strong economic and political tie to the masses, which provided them with a great deal of political influence, and at the same time considerable independence of the regime. Conversely, the Sunni *ulama* were usually bureaucrats of the government, as it was in the Ottoman Empire or in Egypt under Muhammad Ali.

There was a constitutional revolution in Iran in 1906. This constitution remained in force for five years until 1911. It was the result of a relatively small movement, but the *ulama* were a central driving force in the group that forced a constitution on the Shah of Iran. Taking advantage of the relative weakness of the Qajar regime and the central government, they sought to enhance their own influence by imposing a constitution on the Shah. But this constitutional revolution, though likened to the Young Turk Revolution of 1908, was not really similar. The Young Turk Revolution came in the wake of a prolonged process of reform in Ottoman government and society which was part of a longstanding modernization process.

The Constitutional Revolution of 1906

See page for author [Public domain], via Wikimedia Commons

In the case of the Iranian constitutional revolution, the modernization process had not yet begun in any serious fashion. In Turkey, it was the forces of modernity that were central to the promotion of the Revolution of the Young Turks. But in Iran, it was actually a coalition of various forces of tradition and opponents of modernization and foreign influence that had imposed the constitution on the regime.

The weakness of the Qajars attracted growing foreign interference. In the years preceding the First World War large areas of Iran were under direct foreign influence and occupation: Britain coming from India in the south and Russia from the north. After the war, the Russians were consumed by their own revolution and Britain had no real rivals to challenge her influence in Iran. But Britain also had other issues to deal with in the Middle East and in India, and in Iran itself, her power was in decline.

The 1921 Coup d'état Riza Khan

Antoin Sevruguin (1830s-1933) [Public domain], via Wikimedia Commons

Iran was the country least experienced in modernization in the region. In 1921 a coup d'état was staged by Riza Khan, an Iranian military officer, who filled the power vacuum. He did not apparently obtain direct assistance from the British, but his rise to power was certainly not against Britain's will. In 1925, he managed to pressure the *majlis*, the parliament, to abolish Qajar rule. Riza crowned himself as the Shah of Iran in April 1926 and established the Pahlavi Dynasty, taking its name from pre-Islamic Iran. The Pahlavis had an image problem from the very beginning. Theirs was an image of a regime that rested on foreign influence and intervention and the Pahlavis to their misfortune never managed to rid themselves of it until they were finally overthrown by the Islamic Revolution of 1979.

The Coronation of Riza Shah Pahlavi (1926)

See page for author [Public domain], via Wikimedia Commons

Riza was deeply influenced and inspired by Atatürk. He saw himself as some kind of Iranian example of the Turkish model. But any comparison between Turkey and Iran would reveal numerous differences. First of all, the Ottomans were exposed to Western-style modernization as of the end of the 18th century, long before Iran. Turkey, though known as the "sick man of Europe" was still seen by itself and by its rivals as part of Europe.

Iran, on the other hand, was largely a country closed to European influences. The distance from Europe, the isolating topographic structure of the mountains and deserts, and the weakness of central government, were not conducive to the introduction of European influence or the creation of a more effective central government as existed in Turkey. There was much less of a Westernizing elite in Iran to serve as the standard bearers of modernization as there was in Turkey from the *Tanzimat* onwards. It was they who served as the backbone of a modernization process that was easily accelerated when Atatürk came to power. All of this was not in place for Riza when he assumed power in Iran of the 1920s.

In Iran, the religious institution, as we have seen in the comparison between Sunni and Shi'ite *ulama*, had far greater relative strength and influence. In Turkey, Atatürk had the prestige and the legitimacy of the "Gazi," the great conqueror in the name of Islam as compared to the Pahlavis in Iran, who had their problematic image of rulers propped up by foreign influence.

The demographic composition of Iran was also very different to that of Turkey. As we have already seen, Iran had various minorities straddling the borders with other countries, creating a constant fear in Iran of foreign interference. Ethnically Iran was far less uniform than Turkey. It had minorities that were Turkish, Kurdish, Arabic and Baluch speaking. In Iran people also spoke in various Persian dialects. Though the political elite was overwhelmingly Persian in culture, true speakers of Persian were just half of the population.

Concluding Remarks

In describing the creation of the new states it was common to speak of the nationalist movements in Egypt, Iraq and Turkey which had forced the great powers to change their policies. But was it nationalism or the more traditional identities of ethnicity, sect and tribe that drove the political movements in these countries? There were nationalist leaderships in Egypt and in Turkey, as well as in countries like Syria and Iraq. In Turkey, the Arab states, and in Iran too, it was the modernizers who were in power.

But those involved in the revolutionary movements often fought for traditional religious or tribal values rather than secular nationalism. So why did nationalism win? The British historian Malcolm Yapp suggests the following on the great powers and their understanding of the region: "The Europeans made errors in their identification of the opposition and greatly overestimated the role of nationalism in it. To some extent, they were the victims of their own propaganda of the last years of the war which had depicted an enemy world full of nations [...] ready to emerge [...] under the banner of self-determination. But perhaps more importantly, the Europeans wanted nationalism to be the most prominent element; nationalism they understood — it was a modern European doctrine and those who professed it talked the language of debating chambers. Islam and tribalism, on the other hand, seemed dark and dangerous factors, elemental passions rather than doctrines; and their leaders, if they could be discovered, were hard, uncompromising men uncorrupted by reason."[7]

7. Malcolm Yapp, *The Making of the Modern Near East*, pp. 350–351.

Key Sources and Suggested Further Reading

- Batatu, Hanna, *Old Social Classes and the Revolutionary Movements of Iraq* (Princeton University Press, 1978).
- Gershoni, Israel, and Jankowski, James, *Egypt, Islam, and the Arabs: The Search for Egyptian Nationhood, 1900-1930* (New York: Oxford University Press, 1986).
- Hourani, Albert, *A History of the Arab Peoples* (New York: Warner Books, 1991).
- Keddie, Nikki, *Modern Iran; Roots and Results of Revolution* (New Haven: Yale University Press, 2006).
- Kedourie, Elie, *The Chatham House Version and other Middle Eastern Studies* (Hanover, NH: University Press of New England, 1984).
- Lewis, Bernard, *The Emergence of Modern Turkey* (New York: Oxford University Press, 2002).
- Harris, William, *Lebanon: A History, 600-2011* (New York: Oxford University Press, 2012).
- Khoury, Philip, *Syria and the French Mandate: The Politics of Arab Nationalism, 1920-1945* (Princeton University Press, 1987).
- Nakash, Yitzhak, *The Shi'is of Iraq* (Princeton University Press, 2003).
- Tripp, Charles, *A History of Iraq* (Cambridge University Press, 2007).
- Vatikiotis, P.J., *The Modern History of Egypt* (London: Weidenfeld and Nicolson, 1969).
- Wilson, Mary, *King Abdullah, Britain and the Making of Jordan* (Cambridge University Press, 1987).
- Yapp, Malcolm, *The Making of the Modern Near East, 1792-1923* (London: Longman, 1987).
- Zürcher, Erik, *Turkey: A Modern History* (London: I.B. Tauris, 2004).

Chapter Five

Arab Independence and Revolution

In various key Arab states, political independence was rapidly followed by periods of revolutionary politics. In the 1950s and the 1960s, a number of Arab states, particularly those that were relatively poor, went through a phase of revolutionary politics in response to a widely felt sense of failure in the process of modernization. These were countries that suffered significant social and economic crisis. The landowning elites that were in power in countries like Egypt, Syria or Iraq, did not have much of a social agenda and they did not foster policies that were beneficial to the great masses of the people. The parliamentary political systems that had been created under the British were totally corrupted by the monarchies, the British, and the political parties in Egypt and Iraq. Under the French in Syria parliamentary performance was no better. Then came the ignominious defeat in the war with Israel in 1948, the first real test that these newly independent Arab states had to face. For the most part they failed miserably.

Egypt: Social Crisis and Revolution

In 1936, Egypt and Great Britain, after long years of failed negotiations, signed a treaty of alliance. Egypt was now formally an independent state, though with a special association with Britain, which allowed for the British to maintain a military presence in the Suez Canal Zone for 20 years. In the event of a war, Egypt's facilities were to be made available to the British.

Now that relations with the British were on the back burner, Egypt could turn inwards and begin to look at its domestic politics. In 1938, two very important books were published in Egypt, one by Mirrit Butrus Ghali, *Siyasat al-Ghad* (*The Politics of Tomorrow*) and the other by Hafiz Afifi, *Ala Hamish al-Siyasa (On the Margins of Politics)*. Both dealt with Egypt's socio-economic ills.[1]

They included a pessimistic forecast on population growth and the dire consequences in the event of insufficient economic development. Egypt's

1. P.J. Vatikiotis, *The Modern History of Egypt*, pp. 309–311.

population in 1900 was 10 million. In 1937, it had reached 16 million and some 20 million were forecast for 1957. But in fact, Egypt reached that number already in 1949. In the second decade of the 21st century, the population of Egypt had reached 85 million and was growing by about a million a year.

Egypt suffered from a growing gap between resources and population. These experts in the late 1930s called for essential and rapid economic development, to keep up with population growth. But in practice, nothing much was really done. The Egyptian economy remained stagnant and hardly kept up with the growth of population.

Faltering modernization led in the 1930s to an era of Islamic revival. In Egypt of the 1920s there had been an attack on tradition, but in the 1930s, there was a noticeable retreat even by some of the very same intellectuals who had waged this attack on tradition. The Muslim Brotherhood's core agenda, calling for the modernization of Egypt in accordance with the Shari'a, became a very dominant facet of Egyptian politics. The Muslim Brotherhood was not opposed to modernization, but it advocated modernization that would be in accordance with Islamic tradition, rather than abandoning the one for the other.

The Brotherhood's appeal was very popular. It effectively organized in a countrywide network of branches and paramilitary groups. It developed its own economic ventures and networks of social services. The Muslim Brotherhood in Egypt had a membership in the 1940s of hundreds of thousands and a following of millions. There was no grassroots mass movement like the Muslim Brotherhood anywhere in the region.

Hasan al-Banna (1906–1949) founded the Muslim Brethren in 1928

See page for author [Public domain], via Wikimedia Commons

As of the 1920s, Egypt suffered from political violence, which became quite common. Political parties tended to have paramilitary organizations. The Muslim Brotherhood had a paramilitary organization and other political parties tended to have the same. After 1945, political violence became endemic in Egypt as the Muslim Brotherhood played a leading role in the political assassination of its Egyptian rivals and in military operations against the British presence in Egypt.

In December 1948, no doubt influenced by the war in Palestine, after a spate of violence against foreign, Jewish and government targets, the prime minister of Egypt, Mahmud al-Nuqrashi ordered the dissolution of the Muslim Brotherhood. Nuqrashi was assassinated later in December by the Brotherhood, followed by the assassination of the leader of the Brotherhood, Hasan al-Banna, in

February 1949, no doubt inspired or ordered by the government. The chaos continued into the early 1950s with Egyptian governments finding it increasingly difficult to assert control.

Mahmud al-Nuqrashi (1888–1948)

http://arz.wikipedia.org/wiki/ملف:محمود_فهمى_النقراشى.jpg

When, in 1952, the government called in the army to restore order, the stage was set for the coup d'état of the 23 July 1952, which brought the army to power in Egypt. This was the beginning of a new revolutionary era not only in Egypt, but in the region as a whole. Revolution spelt the end of the monarchy in Egypt. King Faruq, who had succeeded King Fuad in 1936, abdicated a few days after the coup. The monarchy was finally abolished a year later and Egypt became a republic. In 1954, the new regime signed the final agreement with Britain on withdrawal. The British were out of Egypt by 1955 making Egypt, at long last, a truly independent country.

Cairo Fire

A series of riots against the British presence took place in downtown Cairo in January 1952.
Not available (Al-Ahram Weekly Online) [Public domain], via Wikimedia Commons

The officers who engineered the coup of 1952 were members of what was to become the new ruling class. This was a dramatic change in the power structure in Egypt. A new ruling elite emerged, composed mainly of a new generation of officers, who came from lower middle class origins and often from rural backgrounds, as opposed to their predecessors who were usually the sons of wealthy notables.

They were graduates of the military academy of the late 1930s and were unhappy with the general state of affairs in Egypt, aggravated by the performance of the army in the war with Israel in 1948. Some of these officers formed what was called the "Free Officers Movement" in 1949. From then on, it was they who were readying themselves to take over.

The 1952 Coup d'état

Not credited ([1] at Bibliotheca Alexandrina) [Public domain], via Wikimedia Commons

The leading figure of the Free Officers was a young lieutenant colonel by the name of Gamal Abd al-Nasser. In his early thirties at the time, he was the son of a postal clerk, just like others, of a modest background. They immediately set about removing the landowning elite, which had ruled since the 19th century. The constitution of Egypt was abolished in December 1952 and the political bases of the ruling elite, such as the political parties, were all dissolved and banned in January 1953.

Gamal Abd al-Nasser

Not credited [Public domain], via Wikimedia Commons

Furthermore, the source of the old elite's economic power was expropriated by an agrarian reform. Agrarian reform redistributed land in Egypt and thereby denied the landowning elite much of its wealth. Before the agrarian reform, 70 percent of the arable land in Egypt was in the control of only 1 percent of the population. The redistribution of land on a much fairer basis was thus a most devastating tool for the elimination of the political power of the old landowning elite. By early 1954, Abd al-Nasser was in complete control and the only competition left was from the Muslim Brotherhood. As of late 1954, a systematic crackdown on the Muslim Brotherhood forced them underground. For very many years, they were unable to play a serious role in Egyptian politics.

The structure of the regime was based on a very powerful presidency, a quiescent and essentially powerless parliament, and a mass state-controlled ruling party. The party had branches throughout the country and was a means of state control rather than a vehicle of popular representation. The party through the years went under various different names. The Liberation Rally founded in 1953 was then changed to the National Union in 1956, and then changed again to the Arab Socialist Union in 1962. But it was essentially the same all along, a tool for very effective centralized government.

The new regime had not only a highly centralized government but also a centralized economy, not driven so much by ideology, but by political pragmatism. The impact of agrarian reform by destroying the old elite was far more political than it was economic. Population growth soon devoured any of the economic gains that had been made by the agricultural reforms.

The Aswan Dam that was completed in 1970 did not meet expectations either. Initially the dam was presented as a panacea for all the ills of the Egyptian economy, and as the great symbol of Egypt's modernization. It would expand arable land, create hydroelectric power and catapult Egypt into the modern era. But in the end, the Aswan Dam changed very little. Again, because of the rapid growth of population, development could not keep up with the steady increase in the number of mouths that Egypt had to feed. The dam also caused a variety of ecological problems that have been detrimental to Egypt's economy ever since its completion.

The centralization of the economy from the mid-1950s onwards was part and parcel of Egypt's growing political independence, as it rid itself of all remaining vestiges of foreign influence, while creating a very domineering, centralizing, powerful government. As part of Egypt's confrontation with the Western powers, the Suez Canal was nationalized in 1956. British and French banks were also nationalized at the end of the same year, all part of the process designed to speed up the industrialization of Egypt.

The Aswan Dam

Nasser observing the construction of the Aswan Dam

Not credited ([1] at Bibliotheca Alexandrina) [Public domain], via Wikimedia Commons

Nationalization of the Suez Canal, 1956

Nasser is received by a jubilant crowd following the announcement of the nationalization of the Suez Canal on July 26th, 1956

See page for author [Public domain], via Wikimedia Commons

But, in fact, politics came first, and the main motivation was to create a centralized regime without any serious competition. The ideological explanation, which had a lot to say about Arab socialism, was an afterthought and a legitimizer, but not the real cause for these political and economic changes.

The achievements, as we have already noted, were limited in the face of a growing population. Egypt's population in 1950 was about 20 million, in 1966 it was already 30 million and 36 million by 1976. In 1986 it had reached 50 million, approaching 90 million in the second decade of the 21st century and steadily increasing. Massive population growth also led to massive urbanization. Rural Egypt could no longer sustain the huge population that was being born there and people migrated to the cities in their millions.

Education was a very high priority for the new regime in Egypt, but the achievements were modest, if not poor. The illiteracy rate in Egypt dropped to 53 percent in 1982 from the very high percentage of 75 that it had been in 1950. By the second decade of the 21st century the illiteracy rate in Egypt was down to approximately 28 percent, which was a great improvement in comparison to the past, but still left Egypt very low in the international rankings, at 160th in the world.

The Secular Nature of the Regime

Nasser at al-Azhar
Not credited ([1] at Bibliotheca Alexandrina) [Public domain], via Wikimedia Commons

The revolutionary regime allowed for a huge expansion of the universities. But this came at the expense of standards in these Egyptian schools of higher learning. The universities became the base for the building of a massive bureaucracy as a means of maintaining power and as a source of employment. From 1962 onwards, every university graduate was promised a job in the government. But this had more to do with the insurance of political stability than with economic development or bureaucratic efficiency.

The Islamist revival of the 1930s and the 1940s was checked by the officer regime. Had it not been for the officer regime, the Brotherhood may have risen to power in Egypt in the early 1950s. It was the officers who kept them out of power. The officers also implemented an essentially secular policy. The Shari'a courts were shut down altogether in Egypt in 1956, the Sufi mystical orders were formally abolished in 1961 (though they continued to flourish in practice) and the renowned religious University of al-Azhar in Cairo was brought under strict government control.

Then came the defeat to Israel in the 1967 Six Day War. The great hopes of the Nasserist era were now in tatters. This was the beginning of a political, economic and global reorientation for Egypt, and the gradual abandonment of the key policies of the Nasserist era. After the war there was a steady shift away from the Soviet Union into the American camp, the creation of a more liberalized economy, and in the end, even peace with Israel.

Iraq: From the Overthrow of the Hashemites to Saddam Hussein

In 1930, Iraq was the first of the British mandated countries to achieve independence, and in 1932, Iraq was the first Arab state to join the League of Nations, the predecessor to today's UN. But the Iraqi monarchy was not able to consolidate a cohesive Iraqi state. Fortunately for the regime, the opposition was not coherent either. The Kurds and the Shi'is were relatively weak, located in the northern and southern periphery respectively and could not effectively cooperate against the Sunni dominated regime.

Iraqi Independence, 1930

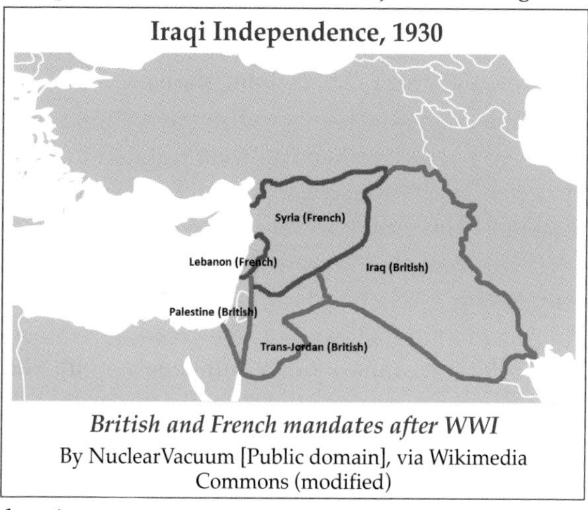

British and French mandates after WWI
By NuclearVacuum [Public domain], via Wikimedia Commons (modified)

From the outset, the regime was dominated by the Sunni-Arab minority led by the Hashemite monarchy. Like in Egypt, the parliamentary system was corrupted by the main powers of Iraqi politics: the British, the monarchy, the urban notables and the tribal sheikhs. The elections were always stage managed in one way or another by the government.

Interference of the army in politics began early in Iraq. The building of a national army based on conscription began in 1934. Pressure from the army in regard to government formation was already apparent

http://commons.wikimedia.org/wiki/File:Iraq_2004_CIA_map.jpg

The Ottoman Vilayet of Mosul

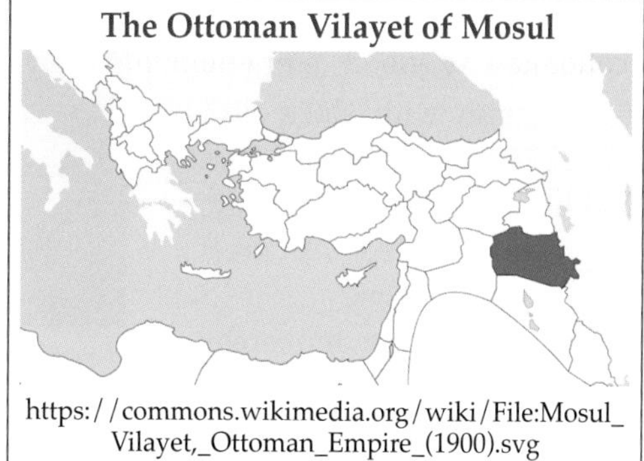

https://commons.wikimedia.org/wiki/File:Mosul_Vilayet,_Ottoman_Empire_(1900).svg

in the mid-1930s. The army was successful in suppressing the Shi'ite tribes in the south, but much less successful in reference to the Kurdish minority in the area of Mosul in the north. The Kurds were the majority in the former Vilayet of Mosul, and were never entirely subdued by the state.

After the fall of France in June 1940, a pro-German government headed by Rashid Ali al-Kaylani, supported by military officers, came to power in the spring of 1941. The Hashemites were forced to leave the country. Thanks to the intervention of the British army, the Hashemites were restored to power. But from mid-1941 onwards, the Hashemites were essentially living on borrowed time.

Rashid Ali al-Kaylani (1892–1965)

See page for author [FAL], via Wikimedia Commons

There were significant social changes in post war Iraq. Rising levels of education led to the increased politicization of Iraqi society. The growing number of high school graduates had insufficient opportunities for suitable employment. They were attracted to radical parties and with the rapid process of urbanization frequent street protests became a very common feature of Iraqi politics of the late 1940s. The poor urban masses were exposed to the influence of radical parties, particularly the Ba'th Party, on the one hand, and the Communists, on the other. The defeat in Palestine in 1948 naturally had its damaging influence on the stature of the government in the eyes of the people. A "Free Officers Movement" began to form in the Iraqi army, under the impact of the military coup of 1952 in Egypt, which served as a model for Iraqi officers too.

The early 1950s were actually good years for the regime. Iraq was beginning to enjoy its oil wealth. But all of that rested on very shaky foundations, and in July 1958, a military coup overthrew the regime with incredible ease. The general public was delighted with the coup, which was received with great popular enthusiasm.

The Hashemite monarchy in Iraq was, after all, a small elite group without any really large social basis. As a pro-

1958 Revolution: The Overthrow of the Hashemite Monarchy

The revolution was led by Abd al-Karim Qasim (standing in the middle) who ruled Iraq until 1963.
https://commons.wikimedia.org/wiki/File:Leaders_of_July_14_1958_Revolution.jpg

Western monarchy, it was not popular. The leader of the coup was Brigadier Abd al-Karim Qasim, who brought about the abolition of the monarchy by the execution of its leading figures.

Like in Egypt, this was followed by the demise of the landowning elite. Here too, land reform was designed to destroy the big landlords. The old elite was replaced by the rule of a civil and military bureaucracy. At the top were Sunni officers mainly from the middle and lower classes, and a very small minority of Shi'is. The coup did not build strong institutions, and everything revolved around the personality of Qasim himself. He and his number two, Abd al-Salam Arif, soon split in disagreement on the pace of unity with the United Arab Republic that had been formed by the union between Egypt and Syria in early 1958. Other enemies were eliminated through the regular use of the revolutionary court, which dispensed with most of Qasim's challengers.

Popular support was built up by extensive social welfare programs that were managed in the towns in particular. This was an urban revolution, and Qasim invested in the well-being of the urban population at the expense of the villagers in order to create a loyal constituency for his regime. Agrarian reform did not change a great deal in the rural areas and the pattern of massive migration to the cities continued unabated. Population growth continued to bring pressure to bear on the standard of living. In the 20 years between 1957 and 1977, the population of Iraq doubled from about 6 million to 12 million. In the next 20 years, it almost doubled again to 22 million in 1997 and by the second decade of the 21st century it had passed 30 million.

Fortunately for Iraq, oil wealth was available to improve the economy. But the regime was deeply divided within itself. Qasim did not have the charisma of Abd al-Nasser and he never captured the imagination of the masses like the Egyptian president. Competing factions of officers within the military joined with civilians in the Ba'th Party to set the stage for yet another coup. The Ba'th party that was actually established in Syria in the early 1940s, was a secular Arab nationalist party that believed in Arab unity and socialism as the avenue to Arab revival (*Ba'th* in Arabic).

Qasim Overthrown and Executed in February 1963

Credits for w:ar:مستخدم:Jalal Naimi – Iraqi governers Book [Public domain], via Wikimedia Commons

Qasim was overthrown in February 1963 and executed by the new rulers, many of whom came from the Ba'th. The new rulers, however, were not united amongst themselves and internal power struggles gave birth to another coup in November 1963 led by Abd al-Salam Arif, and the Ba'th supporters were ejected from the new ruling group. The Arif regime, like its predecessor, was made up of a few personalities, loose army factions and cronies, but no serious building of supportive institutions. The regime lasted for five more years until the rise to power of the Ba'th in July 1968.

Saddam Hussein Became President in 1979

By INA (Iraqi News Agency) (Dar al-Ma'mun) [Public domain or Public domain], via Wikimedia Commons

Now the Ba'th was much better organized and the party dominated the new regime entirely. For the first time since the monarchy, a regime of institutions was actually created. Ba'th party branches were established all over Iraq, which led to an effective and centralized government. The party imposed its authority over all organizations such as professional and trade unions, and, most importantly, it was the party that ruled over the army and not vice versa.

The two key figures in the regime were Ahmad Hasan al-Bakr and Saddam Hussein, both Sunnis of provincial background from the town of Tikrit, north of Baghdad, and of modest lower middle class backgrounds. Saddam Hussein was the real strong man of the regime and he became president in 1979. The Saddam Hussein regime was dominated not just by Sunni members of the Ba'th Party, but by Sunnis from one particular town in Iraq. In 1987, for example, one third of the senior Ba'th party leadership, was composed of people from Tikrit.

Saddam Hussein and Ahmad Hasan al-Bakr

http://www.flickr.com/photos/ethiosudanese/4149880302/

By NordNordWest, via Wikimedia Commons (modified)

The regime was socialist and secular and the economy was state controlled. Oil was nationalized in the early 1970s, and the state bureaucracy was a major employer giving many a vested interest in the political status quo. There was a common sectarian interest in being Sunni as well as a member of the Ba'th. Secular politics, forcing religion to the margins of society, served the interests of the Sunni minority. After all, if politics in a country like Iraq were to be religious, the Shi'i majority would most probably be the major beneficiary. The Sunni Arab minority in power, therefore, had no particular interest in promoting religious politics and secularism, therefore, served the particular sectarian interest of the minority.

The Ba'th encountered increasing religious opposition, especially from the Shi'is, to the secularizing tendencies of the regime from the late 1960s onwards. The regime, consequently assumed a more religious character of its own to defend itself against this kind of criticism. It enforced religious observance on Ramadan, for example. Even Saddam exhibited a more observant posture.

The Islamic Revolution in Iran in 1979 added to the regime's anxiety about the possible effects of Khomeini's revolution on the Shi'i population of Iraq. The fear of the revolutionary fervor of Shi'ite Iran drove Saddam Hussein to launch a war against Iran, which lasted for eight destructive years from 1980 to 1988. Saddam launched his war against Iran in the expectation of rapid victory over a country in post-revolutionary disarray. But the war dragged on at huge cost, with hundreds of thousands of causalities on both sides.

Iraq's ethno-religious composition

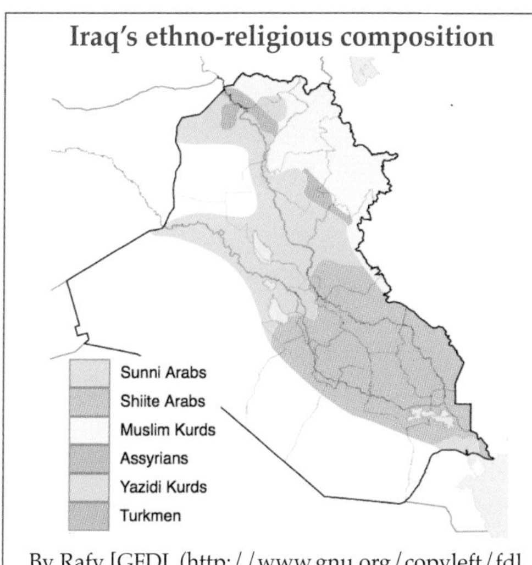

By Rafy [GFDL (http://www.gnu.org/copyleft/fdl.html) or CC-BY-SA-3.0 (http://creativecommons.org/licenses/by-sa/3.0)], via Wikimedia Commons

Ayatollah Khomeini's Islamic Revolution in Iran, 1979

By نامعلوم (پایگاه اطلاع‌رسانی امام خمینی) [Public domain], via Wikimedia Commons

Another issue that Iraq never really resolved, aside from the problem of its Shi'i majority, was the question of the Kurdish minority and its longstanding opposition to the central government in Iraq. Between 1961 and 1975, the Kurds fought the regime for greater autonomy, only to be constantly repressed by all the various governments in power. In 1975, following an agreement between Iran and Iraq, the Iranians ceased their support for the Iraqi Kurds, and the Kurdish struggle collapsed.

Kurdish Leader Mustafa Barzani (1903–1979)

By Jan Sefti, https://flic.kr/p/66VuXM

The Kurdish struggle was resumed during the Iran-Iraq War, with renewed Iranian support. In the closing phases of the war, mainly during the year of 1988, the Kurds were ruthlessly crushed by the Iraqi regime. The Anfal Campaigns, as they were called, included the killing of tens of thousands, the mass deportation of Kurds from thousands of villages that were destroyed, and other unspeakable atrocities like the gassing of the people of Halabja in March 1988, in which some 5000 people perished.

The Anfal Campaigns, 1988

By Sa.vakilian at en.wikipedia Later versions were uploaded by Abu badali at en.wikipedia. [GFDL (http://www.gnu.org/copyleft/fdl.html) or CC-BY-SA-3.0 (http://creativecommons.org/licenses/by-sa/3.0/)], from Wikimedia Commons

Iraq's basic problem of collective identity was never really resolved. Shi'is, Sunnis, and Kurds never fully shared the Arab identity of the Iraqi state. Shi'is, after all, saw Arabism as just another means of Sunni domination. The Kurds were not Arabs at all and Arab nationalism hardly appealed to them. The attempt to promote a particular Iraqi identity resting on the glorious past of ancient Babylon, was artificial and neither Sunni Arabs, nor Shi'is or Kurds, were

Saddam Hussein, 1982

File: Saddam Hussein 1982.jpg [Public domain], via Wikimedia Commons

particularly impressed. Therefore, whether it was Arabism, Iraqiness or Islam, which could not possibly unite both Sunnis and Shi'is, all were problematic in one way or another. Saddam, therefore, ruled by the ruthless suppression of the secret police in the creation of a state described by an Iraqi author, Kanan Makiya, as the "Republic of Fear." The state ruled with an iron fist of gruesome repression. This only came to an end by the external intervention of the United States in 2003.

The US Invasion of Iraq and the Fall of Saddam Hussein 2003

By Unknown U.S. military or Department of Defense employee [Public domain], via Wikimedia Commons

Syria's Prolonged Instability

Syria, like other Arab countries, also went through a prolonged period of instability. As opposed to the British in Iraq, the French and the Syrians failed in their efforts to arrive at an agreement on a treaty of alliance that would pave the way to complete independence. Syrian politics, republican in form according to the French model, were dominated by the Sunni urban notables who had become fervent Arab nationalists for the most part and were not inclined to compromise with the French.

Things seemed to change in the mid-1930s. In Syria there were new more radical political forces that were emerging, giving the urban notables something to worry about. Egypt and Iraq had established treaties with the British, encouraging the Syrians to do the same. In France a left wing government came to power in 1936 and with the rise of the fascist powers of Italy and Germany, the French were also more inclined to compromise with Syria.

The National Bloc, the leading Syrian party, and Léon Blum's Popular Front left-wing government in France, signed a treaty in September 1936 promising Syria independence in exchange for a 25 year alliance with France, similar to the agreements that the British had signed with Iraq and Egypt. But the treaty between Syria and France was never ratified. The Blum government fell as the political right was on the rise in France, and in November 1938 France refused to ratify the treaty. Syria, therefore, did not gain its independence in the 1930s like Iraq and Egypt.

The Second World War, however, changed everything. France fell to Germany in June 1940 and the French mandated territories of Syria and Lebanon came under the control of the Vichy French, who collaborated with the Nazis. The fear of the British was that Syria and Lebanon under the Vichy French would soon become bases for the German air force and other axis forces. The British preempted by occupying Syria and Lebanon in June 1941.

Thus an extraordinary situation transpired. Syria and Lebanon, remained under French mandate, now administered by the Free French, under General de Gaulle, but under British occupation. Though the French were still in power, their real control of events was sharply reduced. The British, who became the real movers and shakers in Syria and Lebanon, constantly pressured the French to move towards independence for these two countries. In the elections held in Syria in the summer of 1943, the nationalists won easily, mainly because the French could not rig the elections under the watchful eye of the British occupation. The French position became increasingly untenable, and in 1946 they and the British forces withdrew.

Syria had finally become a fully independent country now under the leadership of the most prominent of Syria's nationalists of the mandate period, President Shukri al-Quwatli. Independence was the victory of the Sunni urban notables who had led the struggle against France. But they did not last in power for very long before being overtaken by chronic Syrian domestic instability. Ironically, the continuation of the French mandate had allowed for their political supremacy. Independence meant the intervention of the military in politics, and against the officers, the notables never had a chance.

Syria Gains Independence, 1946
First President: Shukri al-Quwatli (1891–1967)

See page for author [Public domain], via Wikimedia Commons

The urban notables were always deeply factionalized. Split along family and regional lines, such as between Damascus and Aleppo. In government they proved to be inept too. They had no solutions for the usual problems of increasing population, urbanization, housing and unemployment. The education system continued to produce graduates for whom jobs did not exist. The Sunni notables feared the potential power of the military which was heavily reliant on minorities, such as the Alawis, the Kurds and the Druze, as a result of the former French minority policy and the customary reluctance of Sunni notable families to send their own sons to serve in the military. The Syrian government, therefore, decided to reduce the size of the military from some 7,000 to no more than 2,500, a decision made just before the war in Palestine in 1948.[2]

The defeat against Israel generated much acrimony between the military and the politicians, culminating in 1949 in a series of three coups within less than a year. In March 1949, Colonel Husni Za'im came to power. He was overthrown in August by another colonel, Sami al-Hinnawi, who was ejected by yet another senior officer of the Syrian army, Adib Shishakli, in December 1949. Shishakli remained in power for nearly five years until February 1954. Za'im immediately increased the size of the army to 27,000 and the Syrian army from then onwards increased in size consistently, reaching as many as half a million men in the 1980s. Henceforth, there could be no Syrian politics without the army playing a central role.

Three Coups in 1949

Husni Za'im *Sami Hinnawi* *Adib Shishakli*

See page for author [Public domain], via Wikimedia Commons

After Shishakli's overthrow in early 1954, the urban notables returned momentarily to the leadership of the country. But they were never secure in their seats and were soon challenged by the new ideological parties, especially the Ba'th and the Communists, while the army lurked in the background, always potentially influential in Syrian politics. Political disarray was most acute between the various regions and factions and between the Sunnis and the minorities. The Ba'th, fearing a takeover from the far left, that is, the Communists and some in the army, appealed to Abd al-Nasser to form a union with Syria. In February 1958, Syria joined what was called the United Arab Republic, the

2. Hanna Batatu, "Some Observations on the Social Roots of Syria's Ruling, Military Group and the Causes for its Dominance," *Middle East Journal*, Vol. 35, No. 3 (Summer 1981), p. 341.

union with Egypt, because of fears of a Communist takeover or, alternatively, possible Turkish or Iraqi intervention. Both countries, then allied with the West, might have intervened in Syria had there been a Communist takeover. Syria, as an independent state, ceased to exist.

But the union between Egypt and Syria did not work well, mainly because of Egypt's domineering policies. This eventually led to the dissolution of the United Arab Republic, which was ended by a military coup in Syria in September 1961.

The United Arab Republic (1958–1961)

Egypt's Abd al-Nasser and Syria's Shukri al-Quwatli signing the pact which created the UAR in 1958

https://southcarolina1670.wordpress.com/2011/11/15/recalling-the-union-of-egypt-and-syria/

For a while it was back to the politics of the urban notables, but that did not last for very long either. In March 1963, the Ba'th ascended to power, perhaps inspired by their Ba'thi colleagues who had just engineered the coup that had overthrown Qasim in neighboring Iraq. As in the Egyptian and Iraqi cases, the army was the driving force of the revolution. But in Syria the coup had revolutionary social and political implications that were more far reaching than in Iraq and in Egypt. Like in Nasser's Egypt and Ba'thi Iraq, there was a new elite group from the rural periphery that displaced the ruling land owning classes. In Syria, however, the revolution was also linked to the overlap of sect and social class with the rise to power of the Alawis, a small minority of just 12 percent of the population, who were also a social underclass.

It was the Ba'this, and the Alawis amongst the Ba'this, who dominated the new regime, especially after the more radical neo-Ba'th, came to power in 1966. From then onwards, it was the Alawis who were very much in the driving seat of Syrian politics. The Sunni military leadership had already been exhausted by previous struggles. This paved the way for the Alawis and the Ba'th to rise to power. For the Alawis and the Ba'th, secularism and secular politics were important means for overcoming the disadvantage of their religious minority status in a Sunni majority country like Syria. For the Alawis and the Ba'th, the army was their vehicle for social mobility and their rise to power. The regime relied very heavily on the military and the security apparatus, in which there were dominant groups of Alawis and of Sunnis, but these Sunnis were from the Syrian periphery, who together with the Alawis had finally ousted the urban Sunnis from their historically superior status. This was a radical change in the balance of power. The Alawis, after all, were a historically downtrodden underclass at the very bottom of the Syrian social ladder, and it was they who had turned the tables and come to power.

Hafiz al-Asad, president as of November 1970 was the unquestioned strong man of the Syrian state, who reinforced the regime through the vehicle of a very powerful presidency. According to the 1973 constitution, all power was invested in the president. There was no real separation of powers. The Syrian model had a strong presidency, a ruling party affiliated with the regime, the Ba'th, and a policy, at least in terms of its formal ideology, of Arab socialism. But rather than ideology, these were all tools for regime control, very similar to the Soviet model. The Ba'th Party was an instrument for mass mobilization and government control. It was not about popular representation.

Hafiz al-Asad (1930–2000)

By Syrian government [Public domain], via Wikimedia Commons

There was a special meaning to the rule of the Alawis. In the eyes of the Sunni urban class, the Alawis were coarse mountaineers who were hardly expected ever to become the rulers of Syria.[3] What made matters worse was the fact that the Alawis, a breakaway sect from Shi'a, were not really Muslims. Amongst Sunnis there was a natural opposition to the secularism and sectarian character of the Ba'th. The opposition was most forcefully expressed by the Muslim Brotherhood, which was banned in 1963, after the ascent of the Ba'th to power. An uprising in Hama led by the Brotherhood in 1964 was suppressed, but armed resistance and suppression continued.

In 1969, the regime removed from the constitution the clause which required the president of the state be a Muslim. The move was intended to pave the way for the Alawis to assume the presidency, which they had refrained from doing until then. The controversial clause was, however, reinstated in the 1973 constitution, by Hafiz al-Asad after he became president. The reinstatement was preceded by a political arrangement with the leader of the Shi'ite community in Lebanon, Musa al-Sadr, who accepted the Alawis as Shi'is and, therefore, as Muslims. The Alawis were now ostensibly eligible for the presidency.

These patently obvious political maneuvers did not satisfy the Muslim Brotherhood, and they rose in rebellion of holy war, *jihad*, against the Ba'thi

3. Hanna Batatu, "Some Observations," pp. 331–344.

regime, waged from 1976 onwards. The Brotherhood engaged in the killing of regime officials and supporters and led riots in the cities of Aleppo, Hama and Homs. They were finally crushed by the regime in February 1982. The last redoubt of the Brotherhood, in Hama, was reduced to rubble by an artillery bombardment which reportedly killed thousands, maybe even tens of thousands.

The Hama Massacre of 1982

See page for author [Public domain], via Wikimedia Commons

The ruthless repression of the Ba'thi dictatorship established stable government in Syria for the first time since independence. Until his death in 2000, Hafiz al-Asad ruled with a high hand and was successfully succeeded by his son, Bashar. From a most unstable state, one for which external players competed, Syria under Hafiz al-Asad was transformed into a regional power with a dominant position in neighboring Lebanon and a leading role in the ongoing conflict with Israel.

As for the Syrian economy, since the rise of the Ba'th, economic change was accelerated far more by the demands of population growth than by the socialist ideology of the revolution. The population increased from 3 million during the 1940s to 9 million in the 1980s, to 14 million in the 1990s and to 23 million in 2013. Agricultural reform and nationalization had been effectively employed to destroy the old elites. Thereafter, Syria was in urgent need of greater industrialization. Rapid urbanization and industrialization led to agriculture losing much of its importance in the Syrian economy and by 1971, industry had surpassed agriculture in its contribution to the Syrian GDP. But Syria's economy could not meet the economic and demographic challenge effectively. There can be no doubt that the outbreak of the "Arab Spring" in 2011 in Syria, just like in other countries, had powerful economic causes.

Hafiz al-Asad	**Bashar al-Asad**

By Government Photographer ([1]) [Public domain or Public domain], via Wikimedia Commons	By Fabio Rodrigues Pozzebom/ABr derivative work: César (Bashar_al-Assad.jpg) [CC- BY-3.0-br (http://creativecommons.org/licenses/by/3.0/br/deed.en)], via Wikimedia Commons

Lebanon's Civil Wars

Lebanon was also beset by frequent instability which degenerated on two occasions into outright civil war.

The 1926 constitution, on the basis of which the Lebanese Republic was formed, was founded on the confessional system, whereby power was divided between the religious communities according to their relative size. It rapidly transpired that the creation of Greater Lebanon was a fateful error on the part of the Christians. Higher natural increase and lower rates of emigration consistently shifted the demographic balance in favor of the Muslims, particularly of the Shi'ite Muslim community.

According to the census of 1932, only 51 percent of the Lebanese were Christians. No more official counts were taken in Lebanon, as the Christians clearly did not want the obvious truth to become known, that they had lost the majority in the meantime. There was an internal Maronite debate on how to handle the problem of safeguarding the status of the Maronites in a country in which their relative numbers were steadily decreasing.

There were two schools of thought in the Maronite community, one led by Émile Eddé and the other by Bishara al-Khuri. Eddé believed in a smaller Lebanon in which those parts that were added on to Mount Lebanon to create Greater Lebanon, which included large non-Christian populations, ought to be ceded and to have this smaller Lebanon protected by France. Bishara al-Khuri, on the other hand, believed that the Lebanese Maronites would only be secure if they established an agreement with the Sunni Muslims of Lebanon and the surrounding Arab states. The Maronites, in Khuri's mind, would not be able to secure their future in the long term through a foreign power. Christian Lebanon could only be preserved by agreement with the Arab world, rather than French protection.

In the new conditions created by the Second World War, the Eddé school which rested on French protection, was completely defeated. If France fell to the Nazis and the French could not protect France, how could they ever protect the Christians of Lebanon? Lebanon, like Syria, came under British occupation as of the summer of 1941. Under British occupation, Lebanon was more inclined towards an arrangement with the Arab world which also coincided with Britain's more intimate association with the Arabs than the French Arab connection.

Thus came into being the National Pact of 1943. This was an unwritten agreement between the Maronites and the Sunni Muslims of Lebanon, the two leading communities, led by Bishara al-Khuri for the Maronites and by Riyad al-Sulh for the Sunnis. The National Pact acquiesced in Maronite political supremacy, by according them the powerful presidency, the chief executive office. The Sunnis were given the second spot, which was the premiership, and the Shi'is, the weakest of the three large communities (who were not even at the table), got the crumbs, the speakership of parliament and no more. In parliament, a 6:5 ratio in favor of the Christians was set for the parliamentary representation of the people of Lebanon. Lebanon, according to the National Pact, would not be a bridgehead of foreign influence either, which meant the severance of the Maronites' political umbilical cord to France and reliance on the Arab states to maintain the political status quo in the country.

The problem with the National Pact was how to accommodate change without collapsing the system. After Lebanon's final independence in 1946, the first serious crisis came in 1958, which quickly degenerated into civil war. The challenge of pan-Arabism, when Nasserism was at its all-time high, and at the peak of its attraction to the Sunni Muslim population, upset the fragile domestic political balance in Lebanon. Pan-Arabism under the charismatic leadership of Abd al-Nasser was much more attractive to the Sunni Muslim population than it was to the Maronites. The Maronite Christians never really regarded themselves as an integral part of the Arab world and had a much more pro-Western orientation, at least in their own self-perception.

There were also serious complaints about the demographic shifts that had not been given due political representation. After all, the Maronites were becoming an ever smaller percentage of the population, and nevertheless, they continued to preserve their position of supremacy through the presidency. The union that came into effect between Egypt and Syria in February 1958 fanned the flames and soon led to an outbreak of civil war between Muslims and Christians, where the Muslims, the Sunnis in particular, were far more enthusiastic about joining the United Arab Republic than the Christians were, needless to say.

The Maronite President Camille Chamoun appealed to the United States for assistance. The landing of US Marines in Beirut in July 1958 restored calm, and the political status quo was maintained. The US military intervention came on the heels of the establishment of the United Arab Republic and the overthrow of the pro-Western Hashemite regime in Iraq in 1958, just shortly before. The US was therefore taking a stand for pro-Western regimes in the region at the height of the Cold War.

US Military Intervention in Lebanon, July 1958

By Thomas J. O'Halloran, U.S. News & World Report Magazine [Public domain], via Wikimedia Commons

By USAF [Public domain], via Wikimedia Commons

But stability in Lebanon depended, in the main, on the continued acceptance of the power sharing agreement between the various religious communities. This agreement, however, was steadily undermined until the outbreak of the second civil war, which tore the country apart from 1975 to 1989. Demographic changes continued to erode the Christian communities while the system, preferring the now non-existent Christian majority, remained unchanged much to the disaffection of the Muslim communities, both Sunni and Shi'ite.

A Palestinian Base: Lebanon

Fatah militants, known as fedayeen, at a parade in Beirut, 1979
https://en.wikipedia.org/wiki/Palestinian_insurgency_in_South_Lebanon#/media/File:FatehMilitia.jpg

The Palestinian refugee population, which had arrived in Lebanon in 1948, at that time some 150,000, steadily increased in number to over 300,000. They were kept in refugee camps and were not integrated into the Lebanese population, contributing further to the destabilization of the Lebanese system. In the late 1960s, Palestinian armed groups, concentrated in Lebanon's refugee camps and in numerous bases for operations against Israel in southern Lebanon, provoked regular Israeli retaliation strikes against targets in Lebanon.

After the civil war in Jordan in 1970–1971 (see below) and the consequent expulsion of Palestinian fighting forces, Lebanon became the sole semi-autonomous base of operations for the Palestinians against Israel, seriously exacerbating internal Lebanese tensions between the Sunnis and the Maronites.

The Sunnis, who preferred to see Lebanon as an Arab state deeply committed to the conflict with Israel, were generally more supportive of the Palestinian struggle waged from Lebanon. Conversely, the Maronites saw Lebanon as a Christian dominated pro-Western state that had no real interest in the fight with Israel.

Thus, a combination of domestic tensions and external factors contributed to the eventual outbreak of civil war yet again in Lebanon. In April 1975, clashes erupted between Palestinian forces and the Maronite Phalange militia, which rapidly degenerated into a more general conflict between Christians and Muslims. The Lebanese army could not be counted on to restore order. The army collapsed into its sectarian components as many of its men joined the rival forces in the civil war, in accordance with their respective sectarian origins.

The Maronite Phalange Militia

By Jinanez at the English language Wikipedia. [https://upload.wikimedia.org/wikipedia/commons/3/3d/Bashir_Gemayel_and_William_Hawi_inspecting_the_Kataeb_troops.jpg]

Syria, however, was now strong and stable under Hafiz al-Asad, and it was Syrian intervention that brought the first phase of the war to its conclusion. Most surprisingly, Syria intervened in May 1976 on behalf of the Christians, who were facing defeat by the Palestinians and the radical Sunni Muslim alliance. Syria, as a radical state in the conflict with Israel, could be expected to side with the Palestinians against the Maronites. But in May 1976, the Syrians did precisely the opposite. Syria took advantage of the war to enhance its regional clout and prestige by assuming virtual control of Lebanon. Syria was presumably also concerned that a radical takeover of Lebanon would expose Syria to possible war with Israel at a time not of Syria's choosing. Syria could hardly allow the Palestinians in Lebanon the leeway to make decisions that could have far reaching effect on its national security.

As a result of the civil war, Lebanon was informally divided into its various sectarian strongholds. The Maronites, under the leadership of Bashir al-Jumayyil, sought to reassert Maronite supremacy in an alliance with Israel. Israel, like the Maronites, was opposed to the Palestinian military presence in Lebanon.

Bashir al-Jumayyil (1947–1982)

http://pam.wikipedia.org/wiki/Bashir_Gemayel

Israel and the Palestinians frequently traded blows, and in the summer of 1982 Israel invaded Lebanon with the objective of removing the Palestinian fighting forces from their Lebanese stronghold. Israel also sought to restore Maronite supremacy in Lebanon and seemed to be achieving its objectives when Bashir al-Jumayyil was elected president in August 1982 as Israeli forces occupied Beirut.

The bulk of the Palestinian fighting forces were compelled to withdraw from Lebanon in early September to be dispersed in various distant Arab states. Israel appeared to be having its way, but Syria would not let that be. Bashir was assassinated by operatives on Syria's behalf in mid-September resulting in the notorious Maronite massacre of revenge against Palestinians in the refugee camps of Sabra and Shatila in Beirut. Since the Israeli military was still present in the area, many accusations were leveled against Israel for not having done what it was believed that it should have or could have done to prevent the massacre.

Amin Pierre al-Jumayyil

By Michael Gross, State Department [Public domain], via Wikimedia Commons

Bashir al-Jumayyil was replaced by his brother Amin as president of Lebanon, but Amin and Bashir, though brothers, were similar in their divergent outlooks to Bishara al-Khuri and Émile Eddé of the 1930s and the 1940s. Amin al-Jumayyil, like Bishara al-Khuri before him, believed in securing the Maronites in an agreement with the Arab world which, in the new circumstances, meant subservience to Syria. Bashir had sought an alliance with Israel, which replaced France, as had been the case in Eddé's formula of old. But the assassination of Bashir and the massacre in Sabra and Shatila had emptied the Maronite-Israeli alliance of any practical content. Israel wanted no more to do with Lebanese domestic affairs and restricted its interest in Lebanon to the defense of its northern border. Israel therefore withdrew from Lebanon in 1985 except for a narrow security zone in the south and it finally withdrew from there too in 2000.

Israeli Withdrawal from Lebanon

http://commons.wikimedia.org/wiki/File:BlueLine.jpg

In the meantime, as the Maronites continued their political decline, the Shi'is shifted from the periphery to the center of Lebanese politics. Syria, allied with the Shi'is, was the hegemonic power in Lebanon until it finally withdrew its forces in 2005.

Socio-economic developments of the 1950s and the 1960s led many Shi'is to migrate from their traditional locations in the south and in the Biqa', that is eastern Lebanon, to the capital of Beirut. Their rate of natural increase outstripped that of other communities, and they displaced the Maronites as the most populous community in the country. By the mid-1970s all Christians, Maronites together with other Christian minorities, were hardly 40 percent of the total. Under the charismatic leadership in the 1960s and 1970s of the Shi'i cleric Imam Musa al-Sadr, the community became considerably more assertive in demanding their fair share of the Lebanese pie in accordance with their increasing demographic weight.

Musa al-Sadr (1928–1978) and the Rise of the Shi'a in Lebanon

https://commons.wikimedia.org/wiki/File:Musa_Al-Sadr_and_AbdulNaser.jpg

The civil war further enhanced Shi'i political assertiveness as they formed their own militias, first Amal and then Hizballah, which

Orthuberra at the English language Wikipedia [GFDL (www.gnu.org/copyleft/fdl.html) or CC-BY-SA-3.0 (http://creativecommons.org/licenses/by-sa/3.0/)], via Wikimedia Commons

became the major Shi'ite force politically and militarily in the 1980s. In April 1985, the Shi'is took over west Beirut, thus physically cementing their growing power at the very center of Lebanese politics. The civil war finally came to an end in 1989 with the signing of the Ta'if Accords. Ta'if, in Saudi Arabia, was where the Saudis and other Arab states gave their auspices to the new agreement for peace in Lebanon.

The Ta'if Accords formalized the ascendance of the Shi'is. In the 1943 National Pact, they were only third in line and received the crumbs left to them by the Maronites and the Sunnis. Now, they were formally on a par with the Maronites and the Sunnis, and that was only formally. In fact, they were the most powerful community in Lebanon, both demographically and politically, backed by the punch of their armed militia Hizballah, for which the Lebanese army was no match and for which no other community had any answer. To that one must add Syria's managing influence over Lebanese politics at the time, which further strengthened the hand of the Shi'is. Christian-dominated Lebanon under the hegemony of the Maronites, as established in Greater Lebanon of 1920, no longer exists. If the question once was whether Lebanon was an Arab state or a Christian-dominated pro-Western country, the question has now become whether Lebanon was still part of the Sunni Arab world or was it becoming a client and an outpost of non-Arab Shi'ite Iran, thanks to the preeminence of Hizballah and the Shi'is in Lebanese politics.

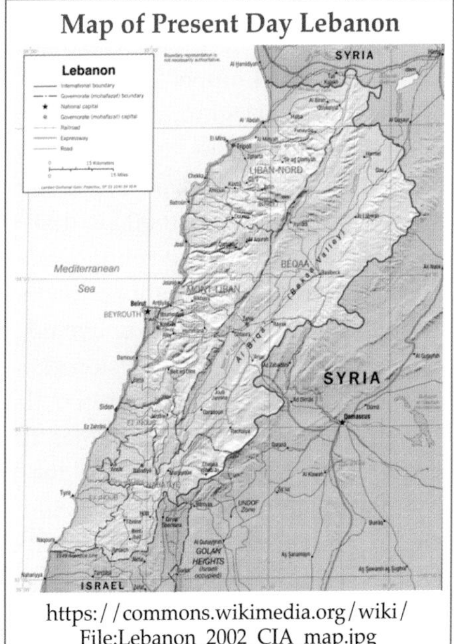

https://commons.wikimedia.org/wiki/File:Lebanon_2002_CIA_map.jpg

The Surprising Stability of the Arab Monarchies

Having discussed the destabilizing revolutionary experiences of the republics in the Middle East of the 1950s, 1960s and 1970s the stability of the Arab monarchies was especially surprising. It was the monarchies that were expected to be bowled over one after the other, but it was, for the most part, the monarchies that have been the most stable states in the region.

Some observers have argued that the strength of the monarchies lies in their wealth. While that was probably true for most of them, countries like Saudi Arabia or the Gulf states, it was obviously not true in a case like Jordan. Jordan was a poor country, relatively speaking, but a very stable one all the same. Others have noted that the authority of royal families, like in Jordan, Saudi Arabia or Morocco, stems from their integral role in the nation-building and state formation processes in their respective countries.

One of the most salient explanations for the stability of the monarchies, especially in countries that have very strong tribal traditions, like Jordan, Saudi Arabia and the Gulf States, was the deep-rootedness of the dynastic principle itself. Hereditary succession has been an accepted long-established practice for centuries in many parts of the Middle East, from the nomadic tribes to the Muslim Caliphates and the Ottoman Sultanate. As for the Hashemites who are still in power in Jordan, their dynastic legitimacy was reinforced by their descent from the Prophet Muhammad himself.

These were all legitimizing assets but, needless to say, they did not guarantee political immunity for these regimes. Monarchies were indeed overthrown in rapid succession as we have seen in the Middle East of the 1950s and the 1960s. But the military regimes that replaced the monarchies have generally been dismal failures. The ruling officers, lacking the ancestral authority of the monarchs, based their legitimacy on the promised attainment of power, prestige, and prosperity. They never delivered, and subsequently faced rebellion in the "Arab Spring" by their disillusioned peoples.

The monarchs never promised their peoples messianic deliverance on a Nasserist or a Ba'thi model. Rather, from Hussein in Jordan in his early years, to Abdullah II, king since 1999, the Hashemites have offered nothing more ambitious than securing a "better life" for all Jordanians. By comparison with other regimes in the neighborhood, they have actually delivered, as attested to most recently by the hundreds of thousands of Syrians who have been flocking to take refuge in the Jordanian haven from the disastrous bloodshed of the Syrian civil war of recent years.

Jordan

Jordan, as opposed to the other Arab states, came out relatively well from the war with Israel in 1948. Jordan was not defeated by the Israelis and they more or less obtained their key objective, which was to hang on to the bulk of Arab Palestine and to annex it to Jordan. This was the area that after the war became known as the West Bank, including the Arab part of Jerusalem that was annexed by the Jordanians.

Jordan's Achievements in 1948

By Chesdovi (File:Amman location.png) [Public domain], via Wikimedia Commons

Jordan sought to incorporate the Palestinians into the kingdom even though they outnumbered the original Jordanians by about two to one, some 900,000 Palestinians compared to 450,000 original Jordanians. Such an incorporation was a tall order. The Palestinians, for the most part, did not share the basic interests of the regime. While the regime sought to preserve the status quo with Israel, the Palestinians desperately wanted to turn the clock of history back and regain what they had lost in 1948.

King Abdullah I of Jordan, who had led Jordan into the war in 1948, was assassinated by Palestinians in 1951. He was succeeded by his son Talal, who was mentally ill, and was therefore replaced by his son, Hussein, who became the King of Jordan in 1953. Hussein's ascent to the throne coincided with the

King Abdullah I (1882–1951)

Cecil Beaton [Public domain], via Wikimedia Commons

King Hussein (1935–1999)

ErlingMandelmann.ch [CC-BY-SA-3.0 (http://creativecommons.org/licenses/by-sa/3.0)], via Wikimedia Commons

rise of the officer regime in Egypt, in 1952, which, as already noted, was a major turning point in the history of the Middle East.

The Palestinians were great believers in President Abd al-Nasser's revolutionary Egypt that would deliver Palestine. They became the natural allies of Abd al-Nasser in their common effort to transform Jordan from a pro-Western monarchy that believed in the status quo with Israel, into the main Arab staging ground and platform for the liberation of Palestine.

Nasser and the Palestinians

By Al Ameer son at en.wikipedia (Transferred from en.wikipedia) [Public domain], from Wikimedia Commons

The Palestinians in the West Bank did not seek to break away from Jordan and create a separate Palestinian state that would probably invite an Israeli attack. Their real ambition was to overthrow the Hashemite monarchy and to transform Jordan into a radical, pan-Arab state, in alliance with Egypt and the Soviet Union against Israel and the Western powers. The struggle was fought intensively in the mid-1950s, with the Palestinian people in Jordan serving as an available and willingly cooperative instrument in the hands of Abd al-Nasser to pressure the Jordanian regime into submission by political opposition, mass protest and subversion.

They almost succeeded, and to many observers in the mid-1950s it seemed as though the days of the Hashemite regime in Jordan were numbered. But the Hashemites survived and Jordan pulled through. There were three components of this durability of the Jordanian regime:

1) First, the loyalty of the Jordanian elite. Though Jordan was an artificial creation, with the passage of time, a Jordanian political elite was formed of those who firmly believed that Jordan was their political patrimony, for which they had no alternative. They were the loyal supporters of the Hashemite monarchy.

2) Alongside the elite, the loyalty of the defense establishment, that is the army and the security services, which rested very heavily on the Bedouin tribes of Jordan, who were the steady and stable supporters of the monarchy since the 1930s.

3) And thirdly, because of Jordan's geopolitical centrality — sandwiched between Israel-Palestine and Iraq, between Saudi Arabia and Syria — Jordan's geopolitical centrality gave it a special importance for the stability of the entire region. As a result, Jordan was consistently supported by powers from the region itself, and from the broader international community, in order to preserve Middle Eastern stability.

The regime, therefore, survived. But it failed to 'Jordanize' the Palestinians. If the regime had hoped for the incorporation of the Palestinians into the Jordanian state and for the Palestinians to become fully loyal Jordanians, by gradually shedding their Palestinian identity, this did not materialize.

The Geopolitical Centrality of Jordan

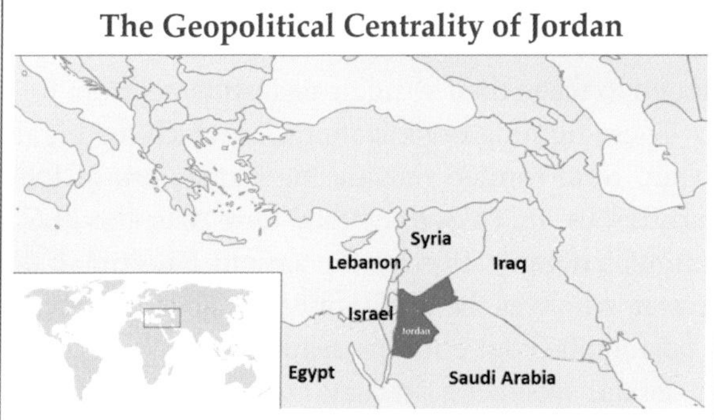

By Rei-artur pt en Rei-artur blog [GFDL (http://www.gnu.org/copyleft/fdl.html), CC-BY-SA-3.0 (http://creativecommons.org/licenses/by-sa/3.0/), via Wikimedia Commons (modified)

In the late 1950s, a movement for the revival of the Palestinian entity and identity developed in the Arab world through public initiatives by member states of the Arab League, on the one hand, and by clandestine independent Palestinian initiatives, on the other. This eventually led to the formation under the auspices of the Arab League of the Palestine Liberation Organization (PLO) in 1964. It also led at the same time, outside the framework of the PLO, to the establishment of other Palestinian organizations like Fatah and others, who launched their armed struggle against Israel.

The PLO and Jordan were soon at loggerheads in the struggle for control of the destiny of the Palestinian people. The PLO demanded freedom to operate politically and militarily in the West Bank, but Jordan, naturally, refused, since the West Bank was in their minds their own sovereign territory and they were not about to allow the PLO to operate freely against Jordan's own national interests. Without access to the West Bank, the PLO could not operate effectively as the official representative of the Palestinian people. After all, the West Bank was the most important part of Palestine that still remained under Arab control. But Jordan, seeing itself as the inheritor of Palestine, did not have the slightest intention of conceding its sovereign control of the West Bank to the PLO.

Under Israeli Control After 1967 War

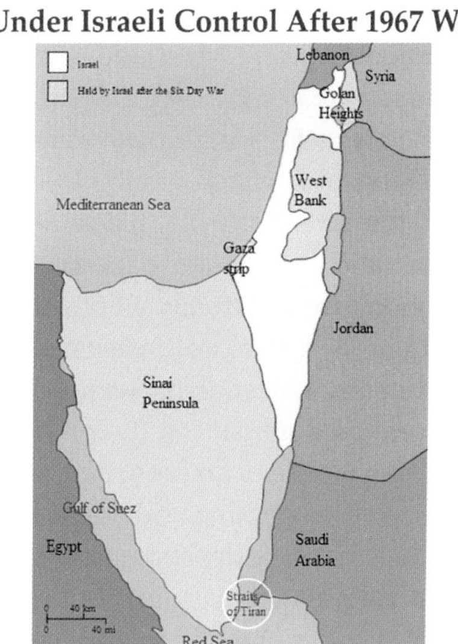

By Ling.Nut derivative work: Rafy (Six_Day_War_Terrritories.png) [CC-BY-SA-3.0 (http://creativecommons.org/licenses/by-sa/3.0)], via Wikimedia Commons

Jordan lost the West Bank to Israel in the 1967 War and thereby also lost its manipulative control of the Palestinian destiny. Moreover, in their hour of weakness after the war in 1967, the Jordanians were compelled to allow the deployment on their territory of the Palestinian fighting organizations that continued to wage their struggle against Israel from Jordan after the 1967 debacle.

These fighting organizations, of which the biggest and most important was Fatah, were formed outside the framework of the PLO in the late 1950s and early 1960s. In 1968–1969, they took over the PLO and transformed it into an umbrella organization for the various Palestinian fighting organizations. Yasser Arafat, who was the leader of Fatah, now also became the chairman of the PLO, a position he kept until his death in 2004.

The PLO and Yasser Arafat

http://america.aljazeera.com/articles/2013/11/6/who-was-yasser-arafat.html

Israel, needless to say, would not tolerate the operations of the Palestinian guerrilla groups against its territory and retaliated forcefully against them in Jordan, gradually forcing the guerrillas away from the border zone with Israel further into the interior of Jordan. The Palestinian organizations established a kind of "state within a state" in Jordan, particularly in the Palestinian refugee camps in Amman and other Jordanian cities, threatening the stability of the Jordanian monarchy.

This eventually led to a major clash between the Jordanian army and the PLO forces, in September of 1970, in what the Palestinians called "Black September," during which the Palestinian forces were routed by the Jordanians. By the summer of 1971, all Palestinian fighting forces were forced out of Jordan completely, from where they went to Lebanon, as already noted above in the discussion on Lebanon.

In the aftermath of "Black September," Jordan underwent a process of Jordanization, which now meant the exclusion of Palestinians, with very few exceptions, from virtually all positions of influence in the Kingdom.

Thus, a functional cleavage was created between Jordanians and Palestinians. Palestinians were almost entirely excluded from government, but were predominant in the private sector, with a controlling influence in the Jordanian economy and much of the professional class. Jordanians, on the other hand, were predominant in the bureaucracy and the security establishment, and generally far more dependent on government employment and social services.

Jordan's national priorities were shifting towards the East Bank, as the involvement in the West Bank and the Palestine cause was increasingly seen by members of the Jordanian elite as an unnecessary burden. After the Civil War of 1970, there were many in the Jordanian elite who were very suspicious and distrustful of the Palestinians, and who thought that Jordan would best be served by disengaging from the West Bank and from the Palestinian cause.

In the October 1973 War, in which Egypt and Syria launched a surprise attack on Israel (see below Chapter Eight), Jordan stayed out of the direct confrontation and refrained from opening a third front against Israel along the Jordanian border. Jordan participated only partially and indirectly by sending some of its forces to assist the Syrians in their battle with the Israelis on the Golan. Jordan's limited participation made it all the more difficult after the war for Jordan to maintain its recognized representative role in the Palestine question.

In October 1974, after an intensive inter-Arab diplomatic struggle, Jordan was compelled to concede the mantle of Palestinian representation to the PLO, which was recognized by the Arab League as the "sole legitimate representative of the Palestinian people." Jordan was thus disqualified as a contender for retrieving the West Bank from Israel.

King Hussein, as opposed to others in the elite, was extremely reluctant to finally concede on Palestine. Since the late 1950s, he had argued passionately that "Jordan is Palestine, and Palestine is Jordan" as a way of emphasizing Jordan's permanent role in Palestine. But as of the mid-1980s he began to change course, too. "Jordan is Jordan and Palestine is Palestine," he now proclaimed. He realized that the slogan of "Jordan is Palestine" could be working against Jordan, as some Israelis and Palestinians might use it to further their respective agendas against Jordan; that is, to transform Jordan, perhaps, into the state of the Palestinians.

King Hussein

"Jordan is Palestine"
https://www.britannica.com/biography/Hussein

In December 1987, the first Palestinian uprising against the Israeli occupation broke out in the West Bank and Gaza. In the West Bank, there were strident anti-Jordanian protests too. Hussein finally came to the conclusion that his Palestinian aspirations were beyond reach and he declared Jordan's official disengagement from the West Bank in July 1988.

The late 1980s were also bad times for Jordan's economy, and in 1989 Jordan faced serious domestic instability as a result of the economic crisis. The crisis was very much a consequence of the inability of Jordan's resource-strapped economy to make ends meet at a time of rapid population growth. Jordan had no choice but to follow the neo-liberal economic advice of the World Bank and the International Monetary Fund, and to drastically cut government spending and privatize public enterprises.

The cutback in government spending was especially damaging to the original Jordanians, the loyal backbone of the monarchy who were far more dependent than their Palestinian compatriots on government spending and on government jobs. Privatization also seemed to benefit the Palestinians in the private sector, at the expense of the original Jordanians. Whether this was really true or not, did not matter. It was the public perception that counted. The original Jordanians began to feel that their unwritten social contract with the Hashemite monarchy, which prescribed unfettered loyalty in exchange for employment and economic security, was being undermined by the monarchy.

Cracks did begin to appear in the edifice of unswerving loyalty of Jordanians to the regime. The problem was handled with much skill and forbearance by Hussein, buttressed by the groundswell of support and even admiration that the Jordanians as a whole had for the king, as elder statesman, in his last years in power.

The Israeli-Jordanian Peace Treaty, 1994

By White House [Public domain], via Wikimedia Commons

One of the king's motivations for making peace with Israel in 1994 was the belief that it would not only serve Jordan's interests in regional stability and security, but that the peace dividend would also greatly benefit Jordan's economy. This unfortunately proved to be an unrealistic assumption.

Hussein died after 46 years at the helm in February 1999. He was succeeded by his eldest son, Abdullah, who had much more

King Hussein (1935–1999)

By Helene C. Stikkel [Public domain], via Wikimedia Commons

King Abdullah II (1962–)

By World Economic Forum [CC-BY-SA-2.0 (http://creativecommons.org/licenses/by-sa/2.0)], via Wikimedia Commons

difficulty in securing the popularity of the monarchy. Condemnation of King Abdullah II has regularly surfaced from within the inner sanctums of the East Banker Jordanian elite.

The outbreak of the "Arab Spring" in neighboring countries in late 2010 and early 2011 provided a convenient background for some of the more embittered Jordanians to vent their disapproval of the king. Abdullah II did not have quite the charisma or monarchical presence of his father. Nor did he have the kind of intimacy his father had cultivated with the Bedouin tribes. Abdullah, born to a British mother, and having grown up and been educated mostly abroad in England and the US, was seen as something of an outsider.

While both non-Islamist East Bankers and mainly Palestinian Islamists called for greater democratization, the East Bankers actually faced a serious dilemma. They sought more influence in determining how wealth and power were distributed in the kingdom, but they were hardly interested in a democratization process that would almost certainly empower the Islamists and the Palestinians at their expense. Therefore, notwithstanding the cracks in the edifice of the East Banker elite, the fractious opposition had yet to come up with a viable alternative to the status quo.

Thanks to the three historic stabilizing factors — the still predominately loyal elite, the unshaken reliability of the security establishment, and the external support of regional players like Saudi Arabia and international powers like the US — the Jordanians have, thus far, successfully weathered the various storms of Middle Eastern politics.

Saudi Arabia

In Saudi Arabia, the same regime of the Saudi family has been in power since the establishment of the state in 1932. In the words of Joseph Kostiner and Joshua Teitelbaum, "The institution of the monarchy in the Kingdom of Saudi Arabia has traditionally been regarded as fundamentally congruent with the Kingdom's basic sociocultural characteristics, a factor that has accounted for the institution's durability and popular support. The Saudi royal family, which heads the monarchy, is integrally linked with it and structured to befit the tribal formations that underpin Saudi society."[4]

The royal family has married into the main tribal groups, urban centers, the business community and the religious establishment. To that, one ought

---

4. Joseph Kostiner and Joshua Teitelbaum, "State Formation and the Saudi Monarchy," in Joseph Kostiner (Ed.), *Middle East Monarchies: The Challenge of Modernity* (Boulder, CO: Lynne Rienner, 2000), p. 131.

to add the Wahhabi factor, the fact that the Saudi monarchy also evolved in congruence with the extremely puritanical Wahhabi religious tenets of most of Saudi society. The Saudi family has been in alliance with the Wahhabi Islamists for more than two centuries. The Saudi king, therefore, is also the leader or the imam of the Saudi Wahhabi community of believers and is subordinate only to the Shari'a.

Saudi Oil Wealth

https://www.venturesonsite.com/news/wp-content/uploads/2016/09/pet-3-web.jpg

A combination of lasting and effective tribal religious alliances and great wealth have provided for prolonged stability, though not without problems, and sometimes serious ones, too.

The leaders of major tribes are conciliated with pensions, jobs for their followers and privileged treatment in legal matters. The *ulama*, the men of religion, were frequently recruited to support government policy and were given in exchange full and unfettered control of the legal system, which remained based entirely on the Shari'a, according to the more radical Hanbali school of Islamic jurisprudence.

Saudi Arabia is a classic rentier state, that is, a state whose revenues come almost entirely from the sale of natural resources — oil in this case — and not from taxation.

The state, as embodied by the Saudi royal family, acts as a distributor of resources, and the citizens of the state as beneficiaries, in accordance with an unwritten social contract, whereby the royal family runs a cradle-to-the-grave social welfare system and guarantees employment in the public sector in exchange for the people's loyalty. The state has assumed the role of provider, a function that fitted well with earlier tribal practices, patterns and values. In Saudi Arabia, it is, therefore, no taxation and no representation.

A large proportion of public spending has gone to public health, hospitals, housing and education. So Saudi Arabia has developed into a modern and far more centralized state. It has a huge bureaucracy and the government is the largest employer in the country. Saudis are therefore healthier, better educated but also far more numerous.

Population growth has been more than threefold since the mid-1970s, from some 7 million to around 26.5 million, of whom 21 million are Saudi nationals and others are foreigners from various countries. Income per capita has actually declined in Saudi Arabia in recent decades.

In the economic downturn of the 1990s, there was increasing criticism coming from the so-called new middle class of academics and professionals and educated technocrats. They were negatively affected by the declining oil prices and a consequent limitation on the state's ability to absorb the effects of rapid population growth.

There were domestic critics of various kinds in Saudi Arabia. There were the more extreme puritans for whom the regime was not religious enough. It was people like these who seized the Grand Mosque in Mecca in November 1979. They were radical tribesmen and Islamic fundamentalists, who accused the monarchy of corruption and religious deviation and called for rolling back modernization by banning television and professional soccer, as well as the employment of women in public places. These rebels were eventually subdued by force and many were executed, beheaded in public to teach everyone a lesson.

The Grand Mosque in Mecca

By Al Jazeera English (A packed house) [CC-BY-SA-2.0 (http://creativecommons.org/licenses/by-sa/2.0)], via Wikimedia Commons

In the 1990s, after the Iraqi invasion of Kuwait and the deployment of hundreds of thousands of US troops in the country, a group of younger clerics repeatedly challenged the regime on the grounds that it was humiliating the country by seeking the protection of Christian powers and was not generally upholding Islamic values as it should.

Insurgents in Custody

By واس (وكالات الانباء السعودية) - spa [Public domain], via Wikimedia Commons

While senior *ulama* continued to defend the royal family, a culture of opposition was said to have developed amongst younger *ulama*, raising serious questions about the Islamic legitimacy of the Saudi monarchy.

There were Muslim militants in Saudi Arabia influenced by the likes of Usama bin Ladin, who have carried out isolated attacks as they deny the right of the Saudi family to rule.

The Shi'ite Minority in Saudi Arabia: Located in the oil-rich Eastern Province

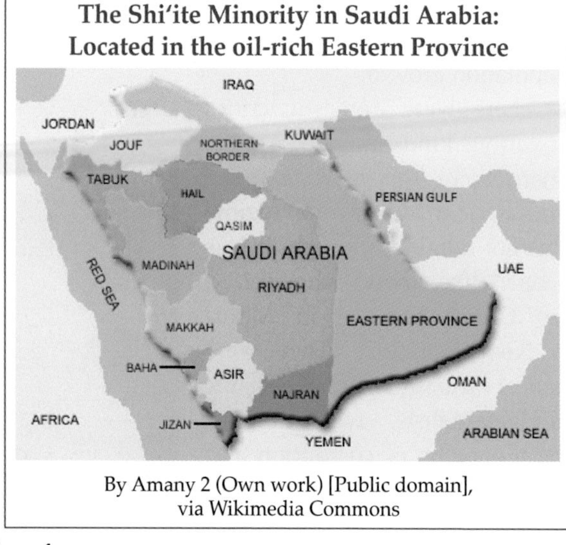

By Amany 2 (Own work) [Public domain], via Wikimedia Commons

Other critics come from the Shi'ite minority in Saudi Arabia, some 12 percent of the total population. This minority is located in the oil-rich Eastern Province and they have generally been severely suppressed by the Wahhabis who regard them as polytheists. They are opponents of the Saudi order, but have expressed this opposition only occasionally, and have not been a serious threat to internal stability thus far.

Another group of opponents was to be found in the young generation of Saudis, who were more questioning and also often unemployed. They could become harder to deal with if oil income declined and people might feel that the social contract was being violated. Therefore, the upswing in oil prices in the early 2000s made life a lot easier for the Saudis, and the transition from King Fahd to King Abdallah in 2005 was very smooth and untroubled.

Worried by the outbreak of the "Arab Spring," the Saudis quickly distributed no less than $130 billion in social spending to keep domestic peace and have thus far been successful.

King Fahd Ibn Abd al-Aziz al-Saud (r. 1982–2005)

By Helene C. Stikkel [Public domain], via Wikimedia Commons

King Abdullah Ibn Abd al-Aziz al-Saud (r. 2005–2015)

By Tina Hager [Public domain], via Wikimedia Commons

The state-tribal-family system was working well, and as long as oil prices remained high enough for the regime to dispense its largesse to the citizenry, there was more than a fair chance that stability in Saudi Arabia would be maintained.

The Arab Cold War

The 1950s and the 1960s in the Arab world were defined by the American historian Malcolm Kerr as the "Arab Cold War."[5] These were the years in which the great struggle between the so-called "progressive" states, the republican officer regimes, who were aligned with the Soviet Union, were arrayed in political battle with the so-called "reactionaries," the monarchies who remained in the camp of the pro-Western states.

The struggle was on the avenue to modernity. The "progressives" argued that they had the perfect formula. The alliance with the Soviet Union, Arab socialism and Arab unity under the charismatic appeal of Abd al-Nasser was the avenue to Arab victory.

But the humiliating defeat of the Arabs by Israel in 1967 exposed the "progressives" as empty vessels. The 1967 war was, therefore, the end of the Arab Cold War and the end of an era. The so-called "progressives" and the so-called "reactionaries" were all in the same boat, having been defeated equally by Israel. The previous ideological divisions became irrelevant. Pan-Arabism, so popular before 1967, was now a defeated force. The vacuum left by pan-Arabism was filled by the new forces of Islamic radicalism, which in different ways challenged them all, "progressives" and "reactionaries" alike. It was these challenges of Islamist politics which came to the fore in the latter part of the 20th century and with even greater effect in the so-called "Arab Spring."

---

5. Malcolm Kerr, *The Arab Cold War: Gamal 'Abd al-Nasir and His Rivals, 1958-1970* (Oxford University Press, 1971).

Key Sources and Suggested Further Reading

- Ajami, Fouad, *The Vanished Imam: Musa Sadr and the Shia of Lebanon* (Ithaca, NY: Cornell University Press, 1986).
- Batatu, Hanna, "Some Observations on the Social Roots of Syria's Ruling, Military Group and the Causes for Its Dominance," *Middle East Journal*, Vol. 35, No. 3 (Summer 1981), pp. 331-344.
- Goldschmidt, Arthur, *Modern Egypt: The Formation of a Nation-State* (Boulder, CO: Westview Press, 2004).
- Hourani, Albert, *A History of the Arab Peoples* (New York: Warner Books, 1991).
- Kerr, Malcolm, *The Arab Cold War: Gamal 'Abd al-Nasir and His Rivals, 1958-1970* (Oxford University Press, 1971).
- Khoury, Philip, *Syria and the French Mandate: The Politics of Arab Nationalism, 1920-1945* (Princeton University Press, 1987).
- Kostiner, Joseph (Ed.), *Middle East Monarchies: The Challenge of Modernity* (Boulder, CO: Lynne Rienner, 2000).
- Makiya, Kanan, *Republic of Fear: The Politics of Modern Iraq* (Berkeley: University of California Press, 1998).
- Rabinovich, Itamar, *The War for Lebanon: 1970-1985* (Ithaca, NY: Cornell University Press, 1985).
- Al-Rasheed, Madawi, *A History of Saudi Arabia* (Cambridge University Press, 2010).
- Robins, Philip, *A History of Jordan* (Cambridge University Press, 2004).
- Salibi, Kamal, *A House of Many Mansions: The History of Lebanon Reconsidered* (Berkeley: University of California Press, 1990).
- Sayigh, Yezid, *Armed Struggle and the Search for State: The Palestinian National Movement, 1949-1993* (Oxford: Clarendon Press, 1997).
- Seale, Patrick, *Asad of Syria: The Struggle for the Middle East* (London: I.B. Tauris, 1988).
- Susser, Asher (Ed.), *Challenges to the Cohesion of the Arab State* (Moshe Dayan Center, Tel Aviv University, 2008).
- Tripp, Charles, *A History of Iraq* (Cambridge University Press, 2007).
- Van Dam, Nikolaos, *The Struggle for Power in Syria: Politics and Society under Asad and the Ba'th Party* (London: I.B. Tauris, 2011).
- Vatikiotis, P.J., *The Modern History of Egypt* (London: Weidenfeld and Nicolson, 1969).
- Yapp, Malcolm, *The Near East since the First World War* (London: Longman, 1991).

Chapter Six

The Beginnings of the Arab-Israeli Conflict

On Contexts and Discourse

The contexts through which one tends to see the Arab-Israeli conflict influence one's understanding of the respective players. There are various contexts through which one might observe the developments that have taken place in the last century.

The first is the European context. The European origins of the conflict emanated from the European Jewish predicament that gave rise to the idea of the creation of a home for the Jewish people in Palestine, which, for the Jews, was their historic homeland. Then there is, of course, the Middle Eastern context, that is, the relationship between the Jews and the Arabs in the Middle East generally speaking, as the key to the understanding of the conflict. Is the conflict an Arab-Israeli conflict? Or is it a Palestinian-Israeli conflict? The definition of the conflict naturally influences the images observers have of it. If it is an overall Arab-Israeli conflict, the Arabs would appear to be the stronger party and the Israelis the weaker side. But if the conflict is defined as Palestinian-Israeli, it is the Israelis who would seem to have the upper hand over a considerably weaker Palestinian side.

The European Context

http://commons.wikimedia.org/wiki/File%3A1904_Russian_Tsar-Stop_your_cruel_oppression_of_the_Jews-LOC_hh0145s.jpg

Looking first at the European context, Zionism, the national movement of the Jewish people, was born out of a profound Jewish sense of disappointment with the results of modernity in Europe. Instead of emancipation, modernity gave rise to modern anti-Semitism, exposing the Jews to endless humiliations of everyday life, to the shame and anguish simply of being Jewish. It was against this background that Theodor Herzl promoted the idea of the creation of a Jewish state, a "state for Jews" as he called it.

Theodor Herzl (1860 to 1904) was a Hungarian-born Jewish journalist, who worked in Vienna for an Austrian newspaper. Herzl was obsessed with what

Theodor Herzl (1860–1904)

http://commons.wikimedia.org/wiki/File%3AHerzl-balcony.jpg

was known in German as *der Judenfrage*, the Jewish question that concerned the fate of the Jews in Europe, the question of Jewish self-respect and Jewish dignity and the problem of the non-acceptance of the Jews in an emancipated Europe. This sense of indignity, shame and suppression of the Jews was a powerful propelling force in the creation of the new national movement of the Jewish people. It was this misery of the Jews that served as the creative force that drove the Jews to seek a national solution to their problem.[1]

Dreyfus Affair (1894–1906)

http://commons.wikimedia.org/wiki/File%3ADegradation_alfred_dreyfus.jpg

Herzl covered the Dreyfus case as a journalist in 1895 in Paris. This was the notorious case of a Jewish officer in the French army who was unjustly accused of espionage only because of his Jewish background. The case exposed the force of European anti-Semitism, and in France of all places. The Dreyfus affair was especially shocking in that anti-Semitism could be so powerful in what had become the model for the most liberal and democratic of European states.

The State of the Jews (1896)

DER

JUDENSTAAT.

VERSUCH

MODERNEN LÖSUNG DER JUDENFRAGE

THEODOR HERZL

LEIPZIG und WIEN 1896.

http://commons.wikimedia.org/wiki/File%3ADE_Herzl_Judenstaat_01.jpg

Thus matured the idea in favor of the creation of a state for the Jewish people. In early 1896, Herzl published a pamphlet called *Der Judenstaat*, the state of the Jews, often mistranslated as "The Jewish State". What Herzl really meant was a secular state for the Jewish people and not a "Jewish" state which could be misconstrued to mean some form of theocracy. Classical Herzlian Zionism was about secular Jewish nationalism.

As a journalist, Herzl was acutely aware of the great power of the modern media. He, therefore,

1. David Vital, *The Origins of Zionism* (Oxford University Press, 1990), p. 261.

sought to make the Zionist cause a public issue and to bring the idea of Jewish statehood into the discourse of the European public domain.

Herzl sought to obtain Palestine for the Jews by diplomacy and in accordance with international law, that is, by an international charter that would award Palestine to the Jews. This was a rather unrealistic idea and not his only one. Herzl also suggested the possibility that the Jews purchase Palestine from the Ottomans. Herzl was naive and had no idea of the workings of the Ottoman Empire or about the place of the Jews in the Muslim political order, that is, of a minority with some form of autonomous religious rights, but hardly a sovereign state.

Herzl did manage to meet with the Ottoman Sultan and to negotiate with him in 1901. Not unexpectedly, his demands were turned down, but just the fact that Herzl had negotiated with the Ottoman Sultan was an achievement in its own right. The idea that the Jewish problem should be solved by statehood was gaining international exposure and momentum. Some established Western Jews were apprehensive about the idea, fearing that the notion of creating a Jewish state in Palestine would provoke the anti-Semites to demand that the Jews leave Europe. But for the Jewish masses in Eastern Europe, suffering from persecution and dire poverty, Herzl's ideas were very appealing.

Meeting Sultan Abdülhamid II (1901)

http://historiasdelahistoria.com/wordpress-2.3.1-ES-0.1-FULL/wp-content/uploads/2012/12/Abdul-Hamid-II.jpg

European Jews, by the turn of the century, were already at a rather advanced stage of secularization and were receptive to non-traditional ideas, of which there were a few. One of them was simply to emigrate from Europe to the New World. Another was to engage in socialist revolution, and Jews were indeed very prominently involved in socialist politics. The third option was the Zionist idea of solving the Jewish problem in Europe by the creation of a state for the Jewish people in their historical homeland in Palestine, Eretz Israel, in the eyes of the Jews.

Early Zionism

At the end of the 19th and early 20th century secular Jewish nationalism was based on the cultural identity of the Jews that was fostered through the Jewish languages of the time, Yiddish and Hebrew, that were both used by the Jews of Europe. Hebrew was used more by the educated classes and Yiddish by the common folk, the masses of the Jewish population. It is interesting to note that Jewish nationalism was generally not fostered in Russian or Polish that the Jews also spoke, but in Jewish languages, emphasizing the connection between language and nationhood, as other nations did in Europe at the time.

Nationalism was, of course, a secular idea. Nationalism was about the salvation of men by men, salvation of the human condition by the acts of men themselves, thus distancing people from the idea of salvation by God and by religious belief.

Herzl and the Zionist movement expected the Europeans to support the Zionist idea, but not because of any intrinsic sympathy for the Jewish plight. They were firmly convinced that anti-Semitism was so deeply rooted in Europe, that the gentiles would support Zionism as a way of ridding themselves of the Jews. That would allow the Europeans to appear progressive by supporting the idea of Jewish self-determination without seeming to be racist and in conflict with their own humanist and progressive self-image.[2]

The First Zionist Congress (1897)

https://upload.wikimedia.org/wikipedia/commons/5/58/Delegates_at_First_Zionist_Congress.jpg

The first Zionist Congress was held in Basel, Switzerland, in August 1897. The Congress allowed for much publicity for the Zionist idea and for the political mobilization of the Jewish people. Herzl, as a journalist, was also a man of public relations and appearances. It was therefore very important, as the pictures of the conference show, that the delegates to the conference appeared in tuxedos and top hats to make it look very serious and distinguished. But Herzl was not just about appearances. His emphasis was on self-help. Enough of this protected Jewry, *schutz Judentum*, that is, Jews as protected by their gentile neighbors, which was not always a safe policy. Zionism, as the historian David Vital points out, "re-created the Jews as a political nation; and by so doing it revolutionized their collective and private lives."[3] The Jews were now not just a religious community. The Jews were a people with national rights, not just a community of believers, at a moment in time when many Jews were no longer that observant in their religious practice. These Zionist Jews sought to formulate a new secular form of modern national and cultural Jewish identity.

2. Anita Shapira, *Land and Power; The Zionist Resort to Force, 1881–1948* (Stanford University Press, 1992), pp. 14–15.
3. David Vital, *The Origins of Zionism*, p. 371.

Ahad Ha'am (1856–1927)

https://upload.wikimedia.org/wikipedia/commons/thumb/a/a5/Ahad_Haam.jpg/220px-Ahad_Haam.jpg

Zionism was a radical departure for those who found the Jewish condition intolerable. Not all Jews agreed to this approach. One, for example, was the Jewish publicist of the late 19th and the early 20th century, Ahad Ha'am (the Hebrew pen name of Asher Ginsberg), who believed very strongly not in the creation of a state for the Jewish people, but rather in spiritual Zionism. He argued that the issue was not the predicament of the Jews, but the predicament of Judaism. There was a need not to solve the problem of the Jews, but to reform Judaism in accordance with the demands of modern times. The problem of the Jews, according to Ahad Ha'am, could be solved by emigration to the United States. Palestine rather than becoming a state for the Jewish people should be a center for spiritual revival. The creation of a state might turn into "just another Serbia," he argued. No state could be established without the eventual resort to force, and that was not Jewish. Mainstream Zionists preferred for the Jews to be a normal people just like all others.

Events in Europe also had a profound impact on this discussion. In 1903, a horrific pogrom was perpetrated against the Jews in Kishinev, in present-day Moldova, then part of the Russian Empire, where scores of Jews were raped and massacred by their gentile neighbors. The pogrom of Kishinev came after a long period of twenty years of relative quiet. The awful nature and the terrible losses of the killings in Kishinev were a huge shock for an entire generation of Jews in Eastern Europe. Change was imperative. The Jewish predicament in Europe was intolerable and it was incumbent upon the Jews to make their choice between the three options of emigration, socialist politics or the Zionist solution.

The Pogrom of Kishinev (1903)

http://commons.wikimedia.org/wiki/File%3APogrom_de_Chisinau_-_1903_-_2.jpg

In the poetry of the time, Hebrew poets wrote about the utter helplessness, shame and disgrace of the Jewish predicament. There was a need for self-defense. Indeed, the whole Zionist idea from the Jewish point of view was a historical act of self-defense against the tragic fate of the Jews. As some put it "a land without a people, for a people without a land." But, in fact, the Zionists knew a lot better than that very often-quoted sentence.

The Zionists knew, as Ahad Ha'am had often said and others had observed, the land was not empty. There was another people in Palestine, and the Zionists were acutely aware of that from the very beginning. But the Zionists tried to convince themselves that the Arabs were not really hostile, and would eventually acquiesce, as they too would ultimately benefit from the advantages that the Zionist project would bring to Palestine. The Zionists would bring modernity and prosperity and the Arabs would enjoy the consequences just as the Jews would. There would be no need to resort to force, so the Jews hoped and believed. The Jews, in the beginning, had no force to resort to anyway.

Initial Arab Resistance

The Arab response, however, was very different. As already noted in other contexts relating to the Middle East of the 19th century, the European challenge had eroded the longstanding historic sense of Muslim superiority, by exposing the current weakness and inadequacy of Muslim societies. The Zionist project was seen as an extension of this expansionist, modernizing, industrialized West in the Muslim heartlands, challenging the Arabs at a time of Muslim decline. Zionist success, against the odds, as things turned out later on, was understood by the Arabs as a symptom and a consequence of their own underdevelopment and political failure. Thus Israel, widely regarded by the Arabs as a Western bridgehead, was to be seen from the Arab side as a much resented monument to Arab ineptitude. The Arabs, therefore, had genuine and meaningful reasons to oppose the Zionist project from the very beginning.

As for the Zionists, they understood the Balfour Declaration from the outset to mean support for a Jewish state in Palestine, which was not exactly what the Declaration had actually said, as noted above in Chapter Three. The Zionists had made various basic assumptions some of which proved to be incorrect. They believed, for example, that they would soon be able to establish a Jewish majority in Palestine by immigration. The Jews would easily outnumber the Arabs in Palestine, who in the early 20th century, were less than 700,000. Once they had established a Jewish majority in Palestine, they would be able to establish their Jewish state.

But these Zionist assumptions were flawed. The immigration that they had expected, of some 70–80,000 a year, did not materialize. The belief that they could create a majority in about a decade or slightly more did not turn out to be true. By 1930, there were only 170,000 Jews in Palestine, that is, between 15 and 20 percent of the total population of the country, nowhere near a majority. Indeed, even until 1948 when the State of Israel was finally established, the Jews had not established a majority in all of Palestine.

The Arabs did not acquiesce as the Jews might have expected. Indeed, with hindsight one may ask, how could it have been otherwise? The Arabs argued, quite naturally, that if the Jews had problems with the nations of Europe, the solution to the Jewish question ought to be found in Europe, and not at their expense. It was not they, after all, who were the cause of the Jewish predicament in Europe. Moreover, the realization that the Zionists intended to transform Palestine into their own state by turning the Arabs into a minority was obviously greeted with trepidation by the Arab population. Another Arab contention was that, in an era of international recognition of the rights of peoples to self-determination, the Arabs of Palestine were never asked about the Balfour Declaration and needless to say they never gave their consent to the Jews to establish a state in all or part of Palestine. The whole idea, the Arabs complained, was being imposed on them against their will.

There were some exceptions on the Arab side. In January 1919, Prince Faisal, of the Hashemite family, whom we have already encountered through the Arab Revolt against the Turks in the First World War, came to an agreement with the leader of the Zionist movement, Chaim Weizmann. The accord was essentially an Arab acceptance of the idea of a Jewish Palestine. But Faisal was not really representative of the Arabs, generally speaking, and not of the Palestinian Arabs in particular. Therefore the agreement between Faisal and Weizmann never held much water and did not have much historical significance.

***Dr. Chaim Weizmann** (left) and*
***Prince Faisal** (right)*
January 1919

http://commons.wikimedia.org/wiki/File%3AWeizmann_and_feisal_1918.jpg

In April 1920, the mandates were handed out to the European powers, Britain and France, at the San Remo conference. The Balfour Declaration, as given by the British to the leadership of the Zionist community in Britain in 1917, was now incorporated into the British mandate over Palestine. This was a great achievement for the Jews as it signified an upgrading of the British commitment to the Zionists, which was now more than just a letter by Lord Balfour to the leader of the British Zionists, but an international obligation that Great Britain had undertaken at the highest level.

Arab-Palestinian opposition to the Zionist idea was already apparent before the First World War, but after the war Arab opposition became much more organized. The first form of organized opposition after the war were the Muslim-Christian Associations that formed in Palestine to resist the Zionists. It is interesting to note that these associations were called Muslim-Christian associations, suggesting that people continued to identify themselves, as they had for centuries upon centuries in the Middle East, by their religious affiliation rather than by their national identity, which was still in its most embryonic phase.

In early 1919 there was the first of a series of Palestinian congresses that were held throughout the years, emphasizing Palestinian opposition to the Zionist idea. In the early years after the war, there was a significant trend amongst the Arabs in Palestine that argued that Palestine was actually part of Southern Syria. This was the period during which Faisal was the Hashemite King of Syria in the name of the Arab Revolt against the Turks and in cooperation with Britain. But, as already noted, the French expelled Faisal from Damascus in July 1920, transforming Syria into a French mandate and putting an end to the Arab state that had existed there between 1918 and 1920. Once the French had taken over Syria, the idea of Palestine being Southern Syria did not make political sense any more. The idea of Southern Syria disappeared into the oblivion and the focus henceforth was on the struggle for Palestine as Palestine.

Serious riots erupted in Jerusalem in April 1920, and even more violent riots broke out in Jaffa in May 1921. Arab opposition to Zionism was very clear. For some British officials who were sympathetic to the Arabs, the violence of the early 1920s, gave them added reason to believe that British policy in Palestine was being forced upon the majority, for whom this policy was most distasteful.

Riots in Jerusalem, April 1920

http://commons.wikimedia.org/wiki/File%3A1920_demontration_Palestine.jpg

David Ben-Gurion

By ELDAN DAVID ([1] [Public domain], via Wikimedia Commons

On the Zionist side, there was a tendency to deny the extent of Arab opposition, and a willingness to explain that the violence was actually a consequence of incitement of the masses by the Arab upper classes or by the British. This was a rather futile effort of the Zionists to convince themselves that the opposition expressed by the people to the Zionist project was not truly reflective of majority opinion amongst Palestinian Arabs.

But the Zionist leadership, people like David Ben-Gurion and Moshe Sharett, leaders of the Zionist community in Palestine, from the outset knew better. They understood perfectly well that the opposition was a nationalist opposition to the Zionist enterprise. But they usually kept such sober assessments within the confines of the internal discussions of the leadership, and did not make them in public to keep up hope and morale. It was clear from early on that there was not just some minor misunderstanding between the parties in Palestine, who actually had common interests, but quite the opposite. They had virtually nothing in common and an existential conflict was brewing.

Moshe Sharett

By צבי אורון.תמרה at he.wikipedia [Public domain], via Wikimedia Commons

The mass violence of 1921 left the Zionist leadership with the ineradicable impression that their enterprise in Palestine rested on very precarious foundations.[4] Though they maintained the fiction in public that the hostility was not really genuine, they were quite aware of the fact that there was an Arab national movement implacably opposed to the Zionist enterprise. It was not the effendis, that is the educated upper class, nor British anti-Semites who were fomenting the opposition. Zionism itself was the problem for the great majority of the Arabs of Palestine and most Arabs wanted the Jewish community in Palestine, the *Yishuv* as it was known in Hebrew, simply to disappear. The Jews, on the other hand, aspired to become the majority in Palestine and to be the future masters of the land, and they expected to be treated accordingly by the British authorities. In their mind, they had the right to change the face of the land peacefully for the benefit of all its inhabitants.

Creating Trans-Jordan

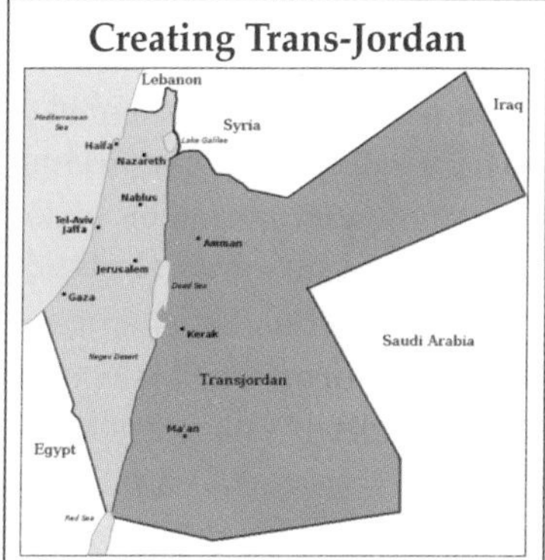

http://commons.wikimedia.org/wiki/File%3APalestineAndTransjordan.png

Understanding the emerging problems in Palestine, the British made a decision to exclude the Zionist project from the East Bank of the Jordan River. Trans-Jordan and Western Palestine were both part of the British mandate for Palestine. But as they saw the situation in Palestine evolving into a major conflict between the Jews and the Arabs, the British decided in 1921 to restrict the application of the Balfour Declaration to the western part of Palestine only. In other words,

4. Benny Morris, *Righteous Victims; A History of the Zionist Arab Conflict, 1881–1999* (New York: Knopf, 1999), p. 102.

that meant the non-inclusion of Trans-Jordan in the area of Palestine which would be open to Zionist settlement. Thus, the British made their decision, in March 1921, to establish the Hashemites as the founders of an Arab state in Trans-Jordan, possibly also as the beginning of a solution for Palestine. A Jewish state would be established in Western Palestine, but Trans-Jordan on the East Bank would be reserved for a strictly Arab state, where Jewish settlement would not be allowed.

The Jews and Arabs in Palestine were so politically far apart that, from the very beginning, they were unable to form joint political organizations. They tended to develop separately in all respects, politically, socially and economically. These were the first inklings of what was to come later — partition.[5]

Jews Mourn Losses in Hebron, 1929

http://commons.wikimedia.org/wiki/File%3AHebron_1929.jpg

In the meantime, hostility to the Zionist project only grew. It came to a head in a new height of violence against the Jewish community in Palestine in the riots of 1929. The riots of 1929, the worst the Jews had experienced in Palestine until then, had an especially powerful religious component.

The problem started at the Wailing (or Western) Wall in Jerusalem. The Jews wished to expand their rights of prayer at the Wall, giving rise to the fear amongst the Muslims that the Jews sought to undermine and perhaps even destroy the Muslim holy places on Temple Mount. The Palestinian leadership, from the early days of the British Mandate, was in the hands of a man of religion, Hajj Amin al-Husseini, who was a Mufti (one who issued religious interpretations of the Qur'an). The Mufti, as the leader of the Palestinian Arabs, led the opposition to the expansion of any Jewish rights at the Wailing Wall. It was against this background, that riots broke out in Jerusalem and other places in Palestine in 1929.

Hajj Amin al-Husseini (1897–1974)

http://commons.wikimedia.org/wiki/File%3AAl-Husayni1929head.jpg

The most serious of these expressions of hostility was the massacre that took place in the Jewish community of Hebron in August 1929, when scores of Jews were killed by their Muslim

5. Anita Shapira, *Land and Power*, p. 138.

neighbors. All in all, in the riots of 1929, over 100 people were killed on either side of the warring parties in Palestine.

The severity of the riots led to the establishment of a British commission of inquiry, which was appointed to study the causes of the violence in Palestine. The commission concluded that the root cause was the animosity of the Arab majority to the Zionists. The British consequently issued a White Paper, a statement of policy, in October 1930. In the White Paper, the Colonial Secretary, Lord Passfield, imposed restrictions on immigration and land purchases for the Zionist project. The Passfield White Paper also called for the establishment of a legislative council that would have an Arab majority. Essentially, the Passfield White Paper, if ever implemented, would have spelt the end of the Zionist project in Palestine.

The Passfield White Paper, 1930

PALESTINE

Statement of Policy
by His Majesty's Government
in the United Kingdom

Presented by the Secretary of State for the Colonies
to Parliament by Command of His Majesty,
October 1930

LONDON

1930

Cmd. 3692

http://commons.wikimedia.org/wiki/File%3AAl-Husayni1929head.jpg

The Zionists protested vehemently and the British eventually backed down. All the same, by the late 1920s and the early 1930s, the prospects of the Zionists in Palestine seemed dire. The project was in decline, reflected by the fact that more Jews were leaving Palestine than were coming to it. With Jews emigrating from Palestine to other places, the Zionist idea seemed to be courting failure.

The Passfield White Paper spoke of the Arab majority and the Jewish minority in Palestine, in recognition of the fact that by the early 1930s the Jews were not about to establish a majority in Palestine, as the Zionists had hoped. The Zionist response to that statement of fact was that the situation should not be judged according to the numbers as they were at present. The statistics in Palestine, the Zionists contended, should be judged with a view to the future, bearing in mind the universal aspiration of millions of Jews who would eventually immigrate to Palestine. In the long run, the Jews would become the majority and they should be treated as such. But in the meantime, the Muslims in Palestine were ratcheting up their opposition by mobilizing external support as well and in 1931 an international Islamic conference was convened in Jerusalem. Facing growing opposition in Palestine and declining immigration from abroad, it looked as if the Zionist project had very little chance of success.

Then, suddenly, things changed dramatically. The rise of fascism in Europe, Hitler in Germany and a radically anti-Semitic government in Poland, led to massive Jewish emigration from Europe to Palestine. The Jewish community in Palestine during the 1930s grew at an unprecedented pace. In the years between

1932 and 1935, the Jewish population in Palestine doubled from 185,000 to 375,000. By 1939, the Jewish population in Palestine was close to half a million. This was a sizable population that increased the confidence of the Jews in their power, simply by virtue of their numbers. On the Arab side, there was ever increasing fear of Jewish domination. If the Zionist enterprise at the end of the 1920s and the early 1930s looked like a temporary and fleeting feature, by the mid-1930s matters had changed very substantially. The Arabs could now imagine the very real possibility of the Jews taking over their country.

Arab Rebellion and Jewish Response

In 1936 an Arab Rebellion broke out against the Zionists and the British to bring an end to the idea of creating a Jewish state in Palestine under the auspices of the British mandate. The British now faced their very basic dilemma. How could the two components of the Balfour Declaration co-exist? That is, how could they combine between the recognition of the right of the Jews to a national home in Palestine, on the one hand, without prejudice to the rights of the non-Jews in Palestine, on the other? How could the creation of a Jewish national home in Palestine not negatively affect the rights of the Arabs in Palestine? The British dilemma had no simple solution.

The Arab Rebellion (1936–1939)

http://commons.wikimedia.org/wiki/File%3APalest_against_british.gif

Izz ad-Din al-Qassam

http://commons.wikimedia.org/wiki/File%3AIzz_ad-Din_al-Qassam.jpg

Well before the outbreak of the Arab Rebellion, there were those on the Arab side in Palestine who believed that there had to be a resort to force. Petitions and requests of the British would no longer suffice.

The leading figure behind the idea of armed rebellion against the Zionists and the British was a Muslim preacher originally from Syria, Izz ad-Din al-Qassam. In the 1930s he was active in Haifa in northern Palestine and it was he who preached for *jihad*, religious war, against the Zionists and the British. Qassam became an iconic figure in Palestinian history both among secular Palestinian nationalists, like in the Fatah movement, or Islamist Palestinians, as in

Hamas. Qassam is revered by all as the founding father of the armed struggle of the Palestinians against the Zionist enterprise. (The "Qassam" rockets, often fired from Gaza into Israel, were named after him.)

There was much disappointment amongst the Palestinians in the early 1930s, not only with the increasing Jewish population but with British policy as well. The British did not carry out the Passfield White Paper and backed down because of Zionist opposition. With the early manifestations of armed rebellion, Izz ad-Din al-Qassam was killed by the British in a clash in November 1935. His death was a major national event of mourning amongst the Arabs of Palestine and it was against this background of rising militancy that the Arab Rebellion broke out in early 1936.

Spontaneous riots began in April 1936, followed by a general strike that was declared amongst the Arabs in Palestine. This was the most widespread and significant Arab opposition that had been expressed to the Zionist enterprise until then and the Jews in Palestine were shocked once again by the ferocity of Arab resistance. The Zionists were seen as an extension of British Imperialism and as Baruch Kimmerling and Joel Migdal have written, the Arabs in Palestine shared an ideology "that totally negated any Jewish political right over the country."[6] Arab resistance was based on Islamic religious opposition and nationalist motivation. On the one hand, there were armed bands of men fighting against the British and against the Jews. At the same time, there was also a social movement to impose stricter religious observance amongst the Muslim population of Palestine, such as the wearing of the veil by women.

The rebellion continued for three years until 1939. The general strike that was initiated in April 1936 only lasted for a few months and was largely ineffective. The strike actually hurt the Arab population more than the Jews. The Jews as a result of the general strike became more economically

Jaffa Port

http://commons.wikimedia.org/wiki/File%3AJaffa_(before_1899).jpg

Building the Tel Aviv Port

http://www.namal.co.il/namal-history.aspx

6. Baruch Kimmerling and Joel Migdal, *Palestinians; The Making of a People* (New York: Free Press, 1993), p. 98.

independent and less reliant on the cooperation of the Arab population in Palestine. The building of a port in Tel Aviv was a good example. The port that the Jews in Palestine used most frequently, particularly in the Tel Aviv area, was the Arab port of Jaffa. But because of the strike, this was no longer possible, and the Jews had to build a port of their own. The port was symbolic of what was happening as a result of the rebellion. The Arabs suffered greatly from the economic loss of the strike and from the continued rebellion, whereas on the Jewish side, political and economic autonomy were steadily enhanced.

Considerable weaknesses were exposed in the Arab community in Palestine. Internal dissension racked the great families of Palestine who were organized in political alliances on a family basis: The Husseinis, those who supported the leader of Arab Palestine, Hajj Amin al-Husseini, and the Nashashibis, who were their opponents. There were other rivalries between different cities, between city and village and between Muslims and Christians. Arab society in Palestine was deeply divided.

The peasants of Palestine were the backbone of the Arab Rebellion. But the peasants were not only fighting against the Jews and the British. They were also fighting a war based on Islamic religious convictions and class motivation. The rebellion took place, for the main part, in the rural inland of Palestine, but there were no Jews there. This was also very much part of a class struggle of the peasants against the city, against the landowners and the money lenders in the Palestinian Arab community who were their social rivals and class enemies.[7] In its later years, the rebellion increasingly turned on its own. The armed bands carried out attacks and extortion of people of wealth and, at times, also against Christians. These attacks by the armed bands, led to the counter organization of other armed bands to protect those who were being attacked by them. The result was a mini civil war among the Arabs of Palestine which had a debilitating internal effect on the Palestinians, as the conflict with the Zionists continued unabated.

When the Arab Rebellion began in 1936, the Arabs in Palestine formed a leadership committee which was called the Arab Higher Committee, headed by the Mufti, Hajj Amin al-Husseini. After the killing of a senior British official by an Arab gunman in the summer of 1937, the Arab Higher Committee was outlawed, and the leadership was forced

The Arab Higher Committee

http://commons.wikimedia.org/wiki/File%3AArab_Higher_Committee1b.jpg

7. Baruch Kimmerling and Joel Migdal, *Palestinians*, p. 113.

into exile from Palestine shortly thereafter. This created a serious disadvantage for the Palestinians in their struggle against the Zionists. The leadership of the national movement, for decades thereafter, was forced to remain outside the country and to attempt to control affairs from a distance, while the Zionist leadership remained in the country all along.

The rebellion, however, was conducive to the formation of a national identity and it was an expression of the gradual progression of Palestinian nationalism. As Kimmerling and Migdal have written, "the revolt helped to create a nation — even while crippling its social and political basis."[8] The crippling of the social and political basis of the Palestinian community by internal dissension and conflict was an attrition of the Palestinians that lasted until 1948. In 1948 they entered the battlefield for a war with the Jews when they were in a state of collective exhaustion.

Exiled from Palestine, Hajj Amin al-Husseini maintained his leadership position by physically eliminating his competitors in Palestine. This only caused greater internal dissension and conflict and deepened the fragmentation amongst the Palestinians in their struggle with the Zionists. In the Arab Rebellion, more Arabs were killed by other Arabs than Jews and British combined. The rebellion, by revealing the political and social weaknesses of Palestinian society, pushed the Palestinians to rely ever more on outsiders. Arab volunteers from outside Palestine fought for the Palestinians in the Arab Rebellion, just as the Arab states intervened in Palestine in 1948, eventually leading to a situation in which the Palestinians, because of increasing Arab intervention on their behalf, gradually lost control of their own destiny.

Arab external intervention also served to create the complicated reality in the Arab Rebellion and again in 1948, in which different commanders competed for authority amongst the Palestinian Arabs. There was no clear hierarchy of command and organization as there was on the Jewish side. Generally speaking, the Palestinian national movement from the 1930s onwards vacillated between two extremes: self-reliance, on the one hand, and dependence on the external Arabs, on the other. During the 1930s and the 1940s, self-reliance was steadily declining, as the Arabs of Palestine became ever more dependent on the good, or the ill will, of their Arab brethren.

In the Jewish community in Palestine, the *Yishuv*, the Arab Rebellion led to the expansion of the Jewish self-defense force, known as the Haganah. The expansion of the Jewish forces was conducted with British permission. The British, after all, were very pleased to have more Jewish military forces with whom to cooperate in the suppression of the Arab Rebellion. Jewish auxiliary forces were therefore established not only with British permission but sometimes

8. Baruch Kimmerling and Joel Migdal, *Palestinians*, p. 123.

even under British command, such as the Field Companies or the Special Night Squads that were established by a British Officer, Orde Wingate. Jewish forces began to assume a more regular army style, rather than an underground organization, and Jewish military forces also developed their intelligence capabilities. Generally speaking, Jewish military potential in Palestine was augmented significantly.

"The Field Companies"

http://commons.wikimedia.org/wiki/File%3AYasur.jpg

"Special Night Squads"

https://upload.wikimedia.org/wikipedia/he/5/53/Night_squad.jpeg

No Jewish settlements were abandoned during the Arab Rebellion. In fact, many more were built. The building of settlements was continued with the idea of partition in mind, that is, the building of new settlements in contiguous blocks that would allow eventually for the partition of Palestine into two states. The fact that a port was built in Tel Aviv was an indication of the developing transport capabilities of the Jewish community in Palestine, as the *Yishuv* became more autonomous in just about every respect. Jews and Arabs became more physically separate as two distinct communities living apart were developing in Palestine.

The rebellion clearly had its limits and the Arab strike had much of a boomerang effect on the Arab community. The Arabs were weakened by the strike, economically and socially, and even more so by their general internal divisions and it was they and not the Jews who arrived exhausted to the decisive battle in 1948.

Lord Peel

http://images.npg.org.uk/800_800/8/4/mw160884.jpg

Shortly after the rebellion broke out, the British, as they usually did in circumstances such as these, appointed a commission of inquiry, headed by Lord Peel, and thus known as the Peel Commission. It investigated the situation in Palestine and in July 1937 published one of the most impressive pieces of scholarship ever written on the problem of Palestine. The Peel Report observed that the rebellion had proved that in Palestine there were ***two*** national movements. This was a radical departure from British policy as defined by the Balfour Declaration, which had only recognized Jewish national rights.

The Arab Rebellion may have had many failures, but it also had a number of important achievements. One of these, most importantly, was to convince the British and the Zionists, that there was, indeed, an Arab national movement in Palestine that could not be ignored.

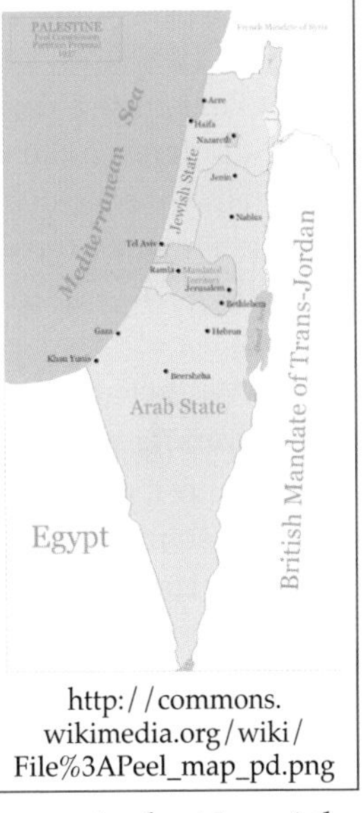

http://commons.wikimedia.org/wiki/File%3APeel_map_pd.png

The recognition that there were two national movements drove the British towards the logic of partition. If there were two national movements in Palestine, it made sense to create two states by dividing Palestine into a Jewish state and an Arab state. When the Report was published in July 1937, it pointed to partition as the logical solution to the Palestine question.

The Jews were given a state that included the coastal plain and the Galilee, some 20 percent of the territory of Palestine, and the rest was given to the Arabs of Palestine. Jerusalem was not included in either the Jewish state or the Arab state, but was to be included in an area that would still be run by the British mandate. The Arab state that was to be created in Palestine would not be independent but would be annexed to the state of Trans-Jordan and thus Trans-Jordan would become an Arab state that would encompass both sides of the Jordan River. Since there was a large Arab population within the boundaries of this Jewish state, particularly in the Galilee, the Peel Report came up with the idea of transferring the Arabs of the Galilee, some voluntarily and others by coercion, to the Arab state.

Emir Abdullah I of Trans-Jordan

http://commons.wikimedia.org/wiki File: Kingabdullahbinhussein.jpg

Arab opposition to the Peel Report was complete with one exception. The Emir Abdullah of Trans-Jordan who stood to acquire the Arab part of Palestine came out in support of the plan. But no other Arabs did. As for the Jews, they rather grudgingly accepted the British decision to give them some 20 percent of Palestine, which was, on the one hand, a historical recognition of the idea of Jewish statehood, but in only 20 percent of Western Palestine, on the other. Many on the Jewish side favored rejection. But in the end, the majority of the Jews went along with the partition idea, most of them believing that this would be a basis for further discussion with the British when the time came. The expansion of the borders, therefore, might come later.

But the British withdrew the idea in 1938. The winds of war were blowing in Europe, and there was a need to placate the Arabs. The Arabs were a much more useful ally for the British than the Jews, who only had their problems to offer. In early 1939, with no agreement in sight between the Jews and the Arabs in Palestine, and as the Arab Rebellion was grinding to an end, the British convened a conference in London at the palace at St. James. At the St. James Conference the Jews and the Arabs (from neighboring Arab states too) deliberated inconclusively for weeks on end. In the end, the British issued a White Paper of their own. This was the British statement of policy of May 1939, which, in essence, represented the final British abandonment of the Zionist project.

1939 White Paper

PALESTINE

Statement of Policy

http://cojs.org/wp-content/uploads/2008/11/White_Paper_of_1939.jpg

The White Paper included three main points. First, Jewish immigration to Palestine would be restricted to 75,000 in the next five years, at a rate of 15,000 a year. Jewish immigration thereafter, that is, from 1944 onwards, could only continue with Arab consent. Arab consent for Jewish immigration was unthinkable and would in fact mean that there would be no more Jewish immigration to Palestine.

Second, land sales were also restricted to those areas where the Jews were already predominant. Third, Palestine was to become independent in 10 years-time. If Jewish immigration would only continue at 15,000 a year until 1944, and Palestine would become independent in 1949, Palestine would be an independent Arab state, in which the Jews would be consigned to a permanent minority status. That meant, in practice, the end of the Zionist idea. The British also considered the future independent state possibly being part of a greater Arab Federation. There would, therefore, be neither a Jewish state nor an Arab state, but Palestine would be part of an Arab Federation. In such a greater Arab state, the Jewish minority would be even more inconsequential.

The timing of the White Paper in May 1939 was particularly unfortunate. The plight of the Jews in Europe was worsening from day to day. The White Paper was widely condemned by the opposition in Britain. It was also rejected by the League of Nations as the non-fulfillment of the commitments of the British mandate over Palestine. Britain's argument was that the Jewish national home already existed and that they had honestly fulfilled their commitments completely. There were half a million Jews in Palestine, many Jewish settlements and a vibrant Jewish community with its political institutions and organizations. For the Zionists, this was a tragically unacceptable disappointment. For them it was the ultimate betrayal and abandonment by the British of the Zionist enterprise.

Jews in Palestine protest against the 1939 White Paper

http://www.myjewishlearning.com/article/british-white-paper-of-1939/

The Arab Rebellion in Palestine also forced the Zionists into the realization that what they had ahead of them was a clash between ideology and reality. The project, contrary to their hopes, was not one of peace, but conflict. Armed conflict with the Arabs would eventually become inevitable. There were some on the Jewish side who now questioned the very right of the Zionists to carry on settling in Palestine and to continue with the project, if this was what it entailed. There were those who thought the idea of Jewish statehood should be abandoned. For the majority of the Zionists, however, that was not the conclusion. Their decision was to prepare for the fight that was certainly to come. There was no choice but to face up to this reality and it was the new generation of youth born in Palestine who would have to follow and execute this policy of confrontation. Active defense was the homeland style of Jewish self-help as opposed to the Jews of the diaspora who were helpless in facing their enemies.

The White Paper and its abandonment of the Zionist project meant that cooperation with Britain was no longer possible. The Zionist project as one of evolution and gradualism made no sense anymore. Time was running out. The predicament of the Jews in Europe was only getting worse and British support had come to an end. An evolutionary process would no longer suffice, and had to be replaced by a revolutionary process, which meant that eventually, there would have to be an armed confrontation with the Arabs in Palestine and perhaps, the neighboring Arabs too. War was not to be initiated. It was an option to be chosen only after all other options had been exhausted, and when it was imposed by the other side.[9] The Jews, therefore, at the end of the Arab Rebellion, had to prepare for partition and for possible war. Partition would not

9. Anita Shapira, *Land and Power*, pp. 270–276.

bring peace, they knew. Despite their willingness to concede on territory, they realized that armed confrontation would be unavoidable.

The Impact of the Second World War on Palestine

The outbreak of the Second World War changed the situation in the Middle East in general and in Palestine, in particular. The role of the Jews and the Arabs in the Second World War was radically different. This, of course, had an impact on the images and public standing of the Arabs and the Jews in the aftermath of the war in the eyes of the international community.

On the Arab side, there was considerable support for the Germans and their allies. The Mufti, Hajj Amin al-Husseini, was in exile and spent part of the war in Berlin in support of the German war effort. The cooperation between the Mufti and the Germans led to the de-legitimization of the Palestinian leadership in the aftermath of the war and it had a very damaging effect on the popularity, the prestige and the international stature of the Palestinian cause when the Second World War came to an end.

"Come, Help Victory"

http://web.nli.org.il/sites/NLI/Hebrew/digitallibrary/gallery/pearls/treasures/_w/05_jpg.jpg

On the other hand, the Jews of Palestine naturally supported the allied war effort against the Germans. Ben-Gurion, the leader of the Jewish Community in Palestine, who became Israel's first Prime Minister, made a subsequently famous statement at the beginning of the war when he declared that the Jews in Palestine would fight with the British, as if there were no White Paper, and they would fight against the White Paper, as if there were no war with Germany.

Jewish Volunteers Marching in Jerusalem

http://www.holylandtimeline.org/2014/02/the-jewish-infantry-brigade-group.html

There was a large flow of some 36,000 Jewish volunteers from Palestine for service in the British army. This was, no doubt, in service of the allied cause, but it was also an investment in the future, gaining military experience for the struggles in Palestine that were bound to come. New common interests linked the British and the Jews in Palestine, despite the White Paper, because of the need to

http://he.wikipedia.org/wiki/%D7%A7%D7%95%D7%91%D7%A5:Palmach.jpg

The Jewish Brigade

https://en.wikipedia.org/wiki/Jewish_Brigade

pursue the war effort. The British were supportive of the creation of new Jewish military forces, particularly the *Palmach,* an elite commando force that was established in cooperation with the British authorities in 1941 and was to become the spearhead of the Israeli military forces in the 1948 War. It took a few years until the Jews managed to establish a brigade of Jewish soldiers in the British Army. They had sought to do so since the beginning of the war, but only by late 1944 did this Jewish Brigade actually come into being, managing to gain significant military experience in the latter part of the war.

In the meantime, a Zionist conference at the Biltmore Hotel in New York in May 1942, had deliberated the Zionist demands in Palestine and came to a decision calling for the establishment of Palestine as a Jewish Commonwealth. This decision was understood at the time to imply a Jewish state in only part of Palestine, that is, the acceptance of the idea of partition. The fact that the conference took place in New York was indicative of a new reality, the centrality of US Jewry and of the US as a great power. The war in Europe contributed to the emergence of the United States as an unequalled great power, and the destruction of the Jews in Europe shifted the center of Jewish life in the diaspora from Europe to the United States as well.

These were also years of growing power and self-assurance of the *Yishuv.* The population had grown from some 85,000 in 1920 to 560,000 by the time the Second World War came to an end. The war years provided an opportunity for the impressive expansion of the industrial and agricultural base of the *Yishuv.*

When the war was over, the Jewish community in Palestine was ready to confront the British. In 1936, the Zionist leader Chaim Weizmann had spoken of a world divided into two parts, one part where the Jews could not live, and the other part to which the Jews could not go. After that came the disenfranchisement, the ghettoization and the industrialized mass murder of two thirds of Europe's 9 million Jews. The Jews were now desperate more than ever to establish their state. For the Arabs, it was politically imperative to detach the question of Palestine from its European context, that is, to separate the discussion of Palestine from the Jewish predicament in Europe. The Arabs, therefore, argued that the Holocaust and its aftermath was a Christian European problem that should not be converted into the problem of the Arabs of Palestine.

The Holocaust in Europe

http://commons.wikimedia.org/wiki/File%3AChild_survivors_of_Auschwitz.jpeg

But the Arabs were fighting a lost cause. The international community was not on their side, and the linkage between the European context and Palestine created a reality in which the Arabs could not possibly win the fight for world public opinion.

The British had difficulties of their own. Britain was economically devastated by the war and it had vital interests in the control of Middle Eastern oil and in friendship with the Arabs. Britain was, therefore, supportive of the creation of the Arab League in 1944 and generally unwilling to confront the Arabs on any issue, including the issue of Palestine. Britain sought to preserve its regional influence in the Middle East through a series of alliances with the newly independent Arab states, and as ready as the Jews were to confront them, the British were equally hostile to Jewish aspirations in Palestine. The British severely limited Jewish immigration, were opposed to the idea of partition, and were generally unfavorable

The Arab League (1944)

http://commons.wikimedia.org/wiki/File%3AFlag_of_the_Arab_League.svg

towards the Jews in Palestine. In Britain after the Second World War, there were many who had come to the conclusion that the Balfour Declaration had not been well thought out from the very beginning, and they had little patience with its consequences.

President Harry S. Truman (in office 1945–1953)

https://commons.wikimedia.org/wiki/Harry_S._Truman#/media/File:Harry_S._Truman.jpg

The British also had to contend with the changing international circumstances. There were new superpowers that had come to the fore after the Second World War. The United States and the Soviet Union were now, by far, the dominant powers in the international community, as the old colonial powers, Britain and France, were in rapid decline. The US administration of President Harry Truman and the Jewish community of the United States were deeply troubled by the fate of the Jewish displaced persons in Europe, the survivors of the Holocaust. They were extremely disturbed by the extent of the Holocaust, as they became increasingly aware of it, and by what they had failed to do about it in real time.

The survivors suffered from appalling conditions in Europe and they were in a situation of unbearable desperation. The US, therefore, strongly supported the urgent immigration of 100,000 Jews to Palestine. But immigration on such a scale to Palestine was antithetical to British policy. The British believed that in order to allow for the immigration of 100,000 Jews to Palestine, they would have to deploy large military forces in Palestine to put down Arab resistance that was bound to follow. The British could not afford these forces, neither economically nor politically.

In Palestine itself, the balance of power was changing too, and not in favor of the Arabs. Because of the stand taken by the Mufti during the war, his international legitimacy was failing. He remained in exile and his followers were still using force against their rivals to prevent effective competition. The Arab community lacked functioning institutions and increasing intervention by external Arab players and rivalries between them within Palestine only made matters worse.

On the other hand, there was growing international sympathy for the Jewish cause. The Jewish community was relatively cohesive in comparison to its Palestinian rivals, and the advancement of its political organizations continued apace after the war. This was characterized by more efficient military organization, the development of industry, and the self-taxation of the Jewish community to cover the expenses of the building of their society. External Jewish support was on the increase too, coming particularly from the United States, but also from other affluent Jewish communities in the Western democracies.

In 1946, an Anglo-American committee of inquiry came to Palestine to study the situation. Just the very existence of this Anglo-American committee was worthy of special note. Until the Second World War, commissions of inquiry were sent by the British themselves. But after the war, the British were no longer the single masters of Palestine and were not in a position to send a commission of inquiry just on their own. It had to be together with the Americans as the British could not operate in Palestine without the cooperation of the US, and, worse still, the British and the Americans did not agree on the question of Palestine.

The Arab testimony given to the Anglo-American committee of inquiry, in March 1946, was as it had always been. The Arabs rejected the Balfour Declaration and the British mandate, demanded an end to Jewish immigration, and the establishment of an independent, majoritarian Arab state. The Zionist demand, on the other hand, was for Jewish statehood and nothing less than statehood, after the Holocaust. These positions, of course, were mutually exclusive. As Chaim Weizmann, the Zionist leader, said to the committee of inquiry, the problem of Palestine was not between right and wrong, but between a greater and lesser injustice. Interestingly, Weizmann observed, the implementation of the idea of Jewish statehood in Palestine would cause injustice to the Arabs of Palestine, so he admitted. But, he argued, the non-creation of a Jewish state would be a much greater injustice to the Jewish people, and to the question of justice generally speaking.

Chaim Weizmann at Anglo-American Committe

http://commons.wikimedia.org/wiki/File%3AChaim_Weizmann_at_Anglo-American_Committee.jpg

Representatives of the committee did not only study the question of Palestine in Palestine. Taking the European context into account, some also visited displaced persons camps in Europe. As a result of this meeting with the remnants of the Holocaust, the committee's report emphasized the Jewish plight in Europe, arguing that there was no place for these refugees, except in Palestine. The US immediately endorsed the findings of the committee, arousing British fury.

In the meantime the Jews in Palestine rose in rebellion against the British, making the British position all the more difficult. Jewish underground forces engaged in very effective military operations against British installations throughout Palestine, such as the bombing of all the bridges crossing into Palestine by the self-defense organization of the Jews in Palestine, the Haganah, in June 1946. The right-wing underground, the Irgun, carried out a constant policy of revenge and retaliation against the British which included the bombing of the King David Hotel in July 1946, causing dozens of deaths, amongst the British and amongst innocent bystanders, Jewish and Arab too. The choosing of the target, the King David Hotel, was because it served as the headquarters of the British administration in Palestine. In their policy of revenge against the British in Palestine, the Irgun also kidnapped and hanged two British soldiers in July 1947, in retaliation for the hanging of Irgun fighters by the British.

The Yarmuk Bridge after being destroyed in the "Night of the Bridges" June 1946

wikimedia.org/wikipedia/he/c/ca/YarmukBridge19461.jpg

King David Hotel Bombing July 1946

http://commons.wikimedia.org/wiki/File%3AKD_1946.JPG

Illegal immigration to Palestine was used by the Jews in Palestine as a tool to embarrass the British. For the Jews, this was a life or death struggle for statehood and for free immigration for the survivors of the Holocaust. It was not only the genuine effort to bring Jews to Palestine, but also, in so doing, to undermine the British. By shipping refugees to Palestine who would then be stopped by the British navy,

An injured illegal immigrant taken off the Haganah Ship "Exodus" by British Soldiers

http://commons.wikimedia.org/wiki/File%3APikiWiki_Israel_20690_The_Palmach.jpg

deported to internment camps in Cyprus or in some cases sent back to Europe, even to Germany, the British were forced into an untenable position. Preventing immigration to Palestine, by taking these poor survivors of the Holocaust and sending them back to Europe, the British faced negative publicity that was devastating.

Adding to the complete deadlock between Jews and Arabs, the combination of the rebellion in Palestine and the illegal immigration had a most damaging effect on British policy. In February 1947, the British decided to give up the issue of Palestine, turn it over to the UN and let the international community decide. It is interesting to point out that the British decision to turn the question of Palestine over to the UN coincided with the British decision to leave India. The idea of a British presence in Palestine from the very beginning was connected to British control of the routes to India. Thus, if the British in February 1947 had made up their minds to leave India, then Palestine had lost much of its original importance.

In summarizing the British historical role in Palestine one may ask whether the British mandate was the backbone of the Zionist endeavor or did the British essentially betray the Zionist cause? The answer to these questions is not straightforward. One could argue that had it not been for British support for the Zionist enterprise for twenty years prior to the issue of the White Paper of 1939, Israel might never have come into being. But at the same time, the White Paper of 1939 was indeed the betrayal of the Zionist cause. One could make both contentions, and both would be correct.

Partition and the First Phase of War (1947–1948)

In May 1947, the UN established the UN Special Committee on Palestine. They too studied the question of Palestine, and the majority of the committee suggested partition. The Jews were elated. They would have their state. But the Arabs who saw the partition as unjust, threatened war.

What was surprising but critically important for the Zionist cause in this particular phase was the change in the Soviet position. The Soviet Union came out in support of partition and the creation of a state for the Jews in Palestine. The main motivation for the Soviet stance was the calculation that a state for the Jews in Palestine would mean the final withdrawal of the British from one of their important Middle Eastern assets. Such Cold War considerations were uppermost in Soviet thinking, considerably more than the aspirations of the Jews.

The Soviet Union was supportive of the Zionist project not only through the decision at the United Nations. Czechoslovakia, no doubt in coordination with the Soviet Union, made critical arms supplies to the Jews in the 1948 War. These timely supplies were one of the reasons that paved the way for the Jewish victory.

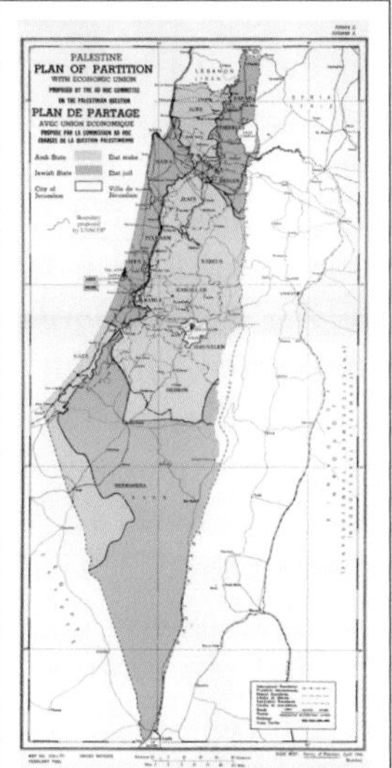

http://commons.wikimedia.org/wiki/File%3AUN_Palestine_Partition_Versions_1947.jpg

On 29 November 1947, two-thirds of the General Assembly of United Nations voted in favor of partition, that is, for the creation of a Jewish and an Arab state in Palestine. The Jews received 55 percent of Palestine (the green areas on the map) and the Arabs only 45 percent. Jerusalem was neither in the Arab state nor in the Jewish state, but designated as a separate zone to be under UN control.

The Jews, who were but one-third of the population in Palestine received 55 percent of the land, while the Arabs, who were two-thirds of the population in Palestine, obtained only 45 percent. The logic of that decision can only be found in the European context, that is, the consideration for the Jewish predicament in Europe. The international community at the time was urgently looking for a solution for the Jewish refugees in Europe, and the settlement of these Jewish refugees in Palestine seemed to be the obvious and the right thing to do (not to mention the reluctance of other countries to accept these Jewish refugees themselves).

One of the provisions of the partition resolution, was a demand of the British for an early evacuation of a port area that would allow for rapid Jewish immigration. It was clear that the United Nations, or the majority of it, bearing the Jewish predicament in Europe in mind, thought it just and necessary that most of the territory in Palestine be accorded to the Jews, to facilitate the massive expected Jewish immigration, which did indeed follow. Therefore the Negev, the southern part of Palestine, which was not given to the Jews in the 1937 partition, was accorded to the Jewish state in the 1947 partition. At the time, the United Nations was a predominantly European, Western and Christian body, and for that kind of United Nations, a nation-state for the Jews after the Holocaust seemed to be the right thing to do.

The immediate aftermath of the Partition Resolution of November 1947 was the first phase of war in Palestine, the civil war between the Jews and the Arabs of the country, which lasted from December 1947 until May 1948. The second phase, which began in May 1948, was no longer a civil war between the Jews and the Arabs of Palestine, but a regular war between the Israeli army, as established in independent Israel, and the invading armies of the neighboring

Arab states. The Arabs rejected partition. For them, it was the case of an injustice that was totally unacceptable. Therefore the Arabs went to war against this UN Resolution with the objective of scuttling its implementation. In the first phase of the war, some external Arab forces also participated, though not the regular armies of the Arab states. An Arab army of volunteers known as the Arab Liberation Army, which had a few thousand fighters, entered Palestine to join the local Arabs in their fight against the Jewish community. The first phase of the war was the fight for the main roads of Palestine, which was essentially the fight for the control of the territory accorded to the Jews in the partition. The Jews were in a most vulnerable situation as it was extremely difficult for them to control the roads of Palestine when there were significant Arab populations interspersed between the disparate Jewish populated areas of the country.

The Fight for the Roads

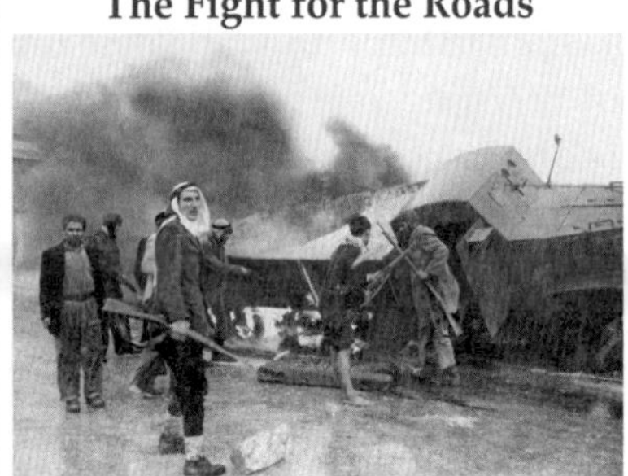

Arab irregulars, along with a burnt truck on the way to Jerusalem
http://commons.wikimedia.org/wiki/File%3AUN_Palestine_Partition_Versions_1947.jpg

By March 1948, with the great difficulty of maintaining control of the roads, it looked as though the Jews were on the verge of defeat. In March the United States suggested that the idea of partition be abandoned and that a UN trusteeship be imposed on Palestine. Partition, they thought, was not working. These were very undesirable developments from the Jewish point of view. If there was to be no partition, there would be no state for the Jewish people. The British, in the meantime, were proceeding with the withdrawal of their forces from Palestine. On the Jewish side, there was a dire situation of panic. Jerusalem with its Jewish population of 100,000 was under siege, completely cut off from the rest of the Jewish community in Palestine. The policy of sending convoys along the roads of Palestine to link up the different Jewish sectors was ineffective as it was very easy for Arab irregulars at any given point on the way to cut off Jewish traffic from one place to another. The Jewish side had to change tactics and this called for the implementation of new plans.

The most important of these was the implementation of an offensive plan known as Plan D. Plan D was implemented in April of 1948 in an offensive effort by organized regular forces to gain effective control of all the territory of the Jewish state. That meant the conquest of Arab towns and villages that were inside the borders of the Jewish state, and some beyond as well. Jewish forces had never taken Arab towns or villages in the struggle for Palestine until that point.

The implementation of Plan D gave rise to very important questions, such as what was to be done with the Arab population in these villages and towns that were conquered by Jewish forces? According to the plan, the Arab population was to remain in place unless they resisted the Jewish occupation. If they resisted, it was permissible to forcibly remove them. Plan D, once implemented, allowed for the, albeit temporary, opening of the road to Jerusalem and for the conquest of territory that enabled the Jews to prepare effectively for the expected invasion of the Arab regular armies.

This was the turning point of the war. It was this transition from the defensive to the offensive by the Jewish forces and the very effective use of Jewish military capabilities — the ability to wage concentrated offensives — that were much harder for the Arabs to resist. Essentially, in the battles of April, the Jews won the fight for the approaches to Jerusalem. Jerusalem's Jewish population was linked up to the rest of the Jewish community in Palestine and the siege was ended, though not yet entirely.

In these battles there were some unprecedented clashes of extreme violence between the Jews and the Arabs in Palestine. One of these was the infamous battle, in April, in the village of Deir Yassin just outside Jerusalem, where Jewish forces of the right-wing underground of the Irgun, carried out a massacre of the Arabs in the village.

For this massacre, revenge was taken on the Jews at least twice. Once, in the massacre in April of a convoy of doctors and nurses going from one side of Jerusalem to the Hadassah Hospital on the other side of the city, when about 80 doctors and nurses were murdered by Arabs. A month later, the Jewish settlement area of the Etzion bloc was overrun by Arab forces and some 130 of the Jewish defenders, who were taken prisoner, were massacred by their captors.

Palestinian Refugees in 1948

http://commons.wikimedia.org/wiki/File%3APalestinian_refugees.jpg

There was an initial exaggeration of the losses at Deir Yassin and it was said that more than 200 Arabs had been killed there. In fact, the numbers were far lower, around 100. But the report on Deir Yassin that was made in the Arab media at the time exaggerated the losses deliberately in an effort to convince the Arab population to stand up and fight, lest they meet this horrific fate if they elected to submit to the Jews. However, this propaganda effort had quite the opposite effect. It actually precipitated panic and massive flight, becoming one of the turning points in the war and in the creation and the acceleration of the Palestinian refugee problem.

But it was the fight for the breakthrough to Jerusalem and incidents like Deir Yassin and the creation of the Arab refugee problem that increased the popular pressure on the Arab governments to intervene in the war. Under the pressure of war, Palestinian Arab society was on the verge of collapse. The leadership was still outside the country, and as Arab society continued to falter, so the Jews continued to organize the government and the machinery of the state that they were about to declare. The Jews had unquestionably won this part of the war.

Israel declared its independence on 14 May 1948, as the British mandate came to an end and as the last of British soldiers left Palestine forever.

Declaration of State of Israel
May 14, 1948

http://commons.wikimedia.org/wiki/File%3ADeclaration_of_State_of_Israel_1948_2.jpg

The Second Phase of the 1948 War

The second phase of the war was the invasion of Palestine by the neighboring Arab states. Initially, the Arab states were hesitant to intervene, and they hoped that just by the threat of invasion, they would elicit international pressure to prevent partition. When they did invade in the end, in mid-May of 1948, it was not with all their forces either. The Arab states, for the most part, had to leave some of their forces at home to keep the peace in their own countries and to defend the regimes that were in power. But the Arab invasion, all the same, was a serious threat to the Israelis, and the military leadership initially feared possible defeat. The fear of defeat, even a repetition of the Holocaust, was not beyond the imagination of the Jewish leadership, and therefore the motivation to fight and to win at all costs.

As the war progressed, the Jewish side doing rather well, sought possible territorial expansion and in some cases, even to push out the Arab population. The objectives of the different Arab states in the war were, in theory at least, united in the objective of preventing the creation of a Jewish state in Palestine.

But between the different Arab invading armies, there was very little cooperation and coordination and they all had their own separate agendas. The Jordanians, for example, operated under severe British constraints. They had an army that was commanded by British officers, and the Jordanians also had a measure of moderation in their position towards the Jewish state. Essentially, they restricted themselves to taking over as much of the Arab state of Palestine as they possibly could without actually invading the Jewish state. The Iraqis had their own ideas about taking Haifa and taking control of the pipeline that led oil from Iraq to the port of Haifa at that time. As for the Egyptians, they were interested in blocking the other Arabs, that is, the Hashemites, the kingdoms of Iraq and Jordan, from doing too well in Palestine, at the expense of the Palestinians.

The Oil Pipeline from Iraq to Haifa

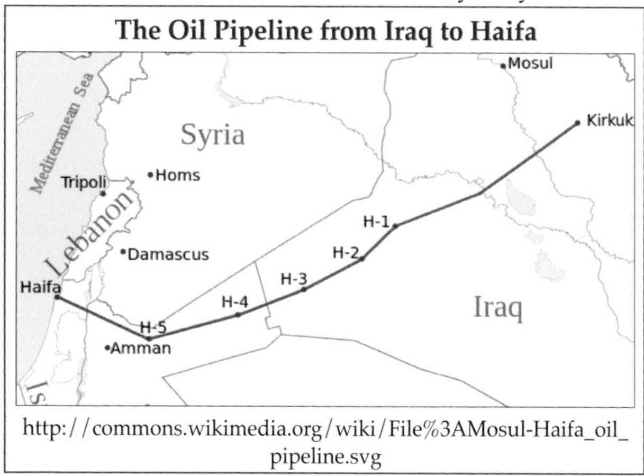

http://commons.wikimedia.org/wiki/File%3AMosul-Haifa_oil_pipeline.svg

The Israelis argued that the war in 1948 was an instance of the few against the many, that is, the few Israelis had fought against the many Arabs, and even so emerged victorious in a heroic struggle. There were 40 million Arabs in the surrounding Arab states, versus only 650,000 Jews in Palestine. Unquestionably, the Jews were the few fighting against the many. But in the field, the military forces arrayed against one another, were more or less equal in number when the war began, but the Arabs had an initial advantage in equipment, armor and air power. On the other hand, Israel had prepared and organized for the war, while the Arabs had not. Israel had a unity of purpose, while the Arabs had disparate objectives. As the war progressed, the numbers of men and equipment changed in Israel's favor in all spheres.

The first round of war took place between mid-May and mid-June, after which the first truce was introduced. There was another round of fighting for 10 days in July and by then, the Israelis were much stronger. After the first truce, the Israeli forces increased as did those on the Arab side, to about 50–60,000 each. But the Israelis were now better equipped than before, having succeeded in introducing into Israel equipment that they had purchased before the creation of the state and that was now brought into the country. By the end of the war, the Israelis actually outnumbered the Arabs in men and materiel, with the Israelis eventually fielding a force of over 100,000 men when the war came to its conclusion. The second truce lasted from 19 July until 15 October. The later campaigns of the war that were fought in the north and the south in late 1948 brought the war to an end with the expulsion of most of the Arab forces from Palestine.

The fate of Jerusalem was a question of great importance in and of itself. In the fighting between the Israeli forces and the forces of the Jordanian army in Jerusalem, the Israelis lost control of the Jewish Quarter in the old city of Jerusalem. They also failed to hold on to the Wailing Wall. Israeli military thinkers had to contend with two different kinds of considerations: the strategic versus the religious and the symbolic. It is clear, that in the manner in which the Israeli leadership conducted the war over Jerusalem, it was the strategic that was uppermost in their minds rather than the religious. The most important element in the struggle for Jerusalem was to maintain the Jewish population of 100,000 safely under Israeli control. Jewish holy sites were not the most important objectives that the Israelis had in mind. Actually, as the war progressed and Israel seemed to be doing better as time went by, the Israelis had the capacity to take all of the city from the late summer of 1948. Even though they could, they decided not to. It was preferable from the Israeli point of view, so the prime minister at the time, David Ben-Gurion thought, to have the city partitioned between the Jordanians, on the one hand, and the Israelis, on the other. The UN Partition Resolution was to have Jerusalem internationalized. The fear of the Israelis was that if they took the whole city, they would end up with nothing. There would be unmanageable international pressure on Israel to abandon all parts of Jerusalem in favor of internationalization. Whereas, if the city was shared between the Israelis and the Jordanians, the international community would acquiesce in this partition between Jews, on the one hand, and Arabs, on the other.

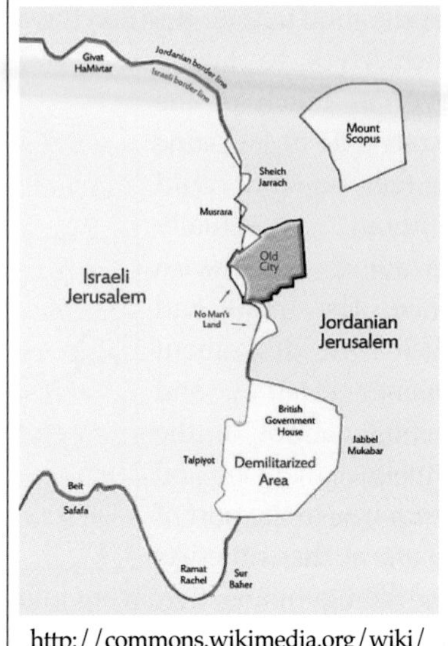

http://commons.wikimedia.org/wiki/File%3ASplit_Jerusalem_map_English.jpg

Competing Narratives of 1948

There are conflicting narratives of the War of 1948. The parties, of course, tell very different stories and there is an abyss that separates them. On the one hand, from the Zionist point of view, the war was part of the great heroic project of Zionism, in self-defense against the horrific fate of the Jews, in defiance of the Jewish historical predicament and suffering in Europe. This was a glorious victory obtained at a very heavy price. Literally, it meant the rising of the Jews from the ashes of the Holocaust, from the destruction of the Jewish people in Europe, to Jewish national liberation, statehood and sovereignty. This, in the Jewish mind, was the epitome of historical justice for the most oppressed of peoples.

For the Palestinians it was the complete opposite. This was not self-defense but net aggression from the first Zionist settler in Palestine. For the Palestinians, this was no victory, but the defeat and the dispersal of their people, the loss of their homeland, and refugeedom. This traumatic series of events was the formative historical experience of the Palestinian people. It was the very core of the Palestinian national identity, which was formed around this shattering experience of defeat and the uprooting of the Palestinians. There was an extremely profound and powerful sense of historical injustice that united Palestinians in their vision of 1948. From their point of view, the war and its consequences were the ultimate evil.

So what was 1948? Israel's War of Independence or the creation of the Palestinian refugee problem? It depends from which side of the equation one looks at that question.

Who was responsible for what happened in 1948? Was it the Arabs who assumed the major share of responsibility for the end result because it was they who launched the war with the object of eliminating the Israeli state? In the areas of Palestine that came under Arab conquest during the war, in what became the West Bank and the Gaza Strip after the War of 1948, not one single Jew was left in either one of them.

Or was the responsibility mainly that of the Israelis, whose military activities drove the Palestinians out? There is a new group of Israeli historians, who are known collectively as the "New Historians", who have for the last 25 years or so been rewriting the history of Israel in a somewhat more critical view of Israel's past. The most important of these historians on the refugee question is an Israeli by the name of Benny Morris, and his account of the causes of the refugee problem is probably the most reliable.

The New Historians

Prof. Benny Morris
http://commons.wikimedia.org/wiki/File%3ABenny_morris.jpg

There are many questions. Was the refugee problem caused by the flight of the Palestinians themselves, as the Israeli official view was for very many years, or was it a result, as the Arabs would argue, of a deliberate policy of expulsion carried out by the Israelis? What was more relevant to the discussion of this question, Israeli military actions, or the social disintegration of the Palestinian community? Were Palestinians in a mindset of flight because of their fear of conquest, because of the fact that the leadership had already left, that the upper classes were leaving and that the society was in a state of panic, or was it because of the actions of Israel? Did the Israelis have a grand design, to push out the Palestinian population, or did the refugee issue simply develop out of the exigencies of war?

It would be fair to say that the refugee problem had many causes. First of all there was the inter-mix of populations. The proximity of the populations to each other in a situation of war certainly encouraged the losing side to depart, and in most cases this happened to be the Arabs. Palestinian society was on the verge of collapse and disintegration. There was a relatively low level of nationalist conviction and cohesion in a society that was still largely illiterate. Under the pressure of war there was a certain psychosis of flight on the Palestinian side, provoked by the fear of war and the fear of Jewish rule.

But there were also numerous cases of expulsion. Benny Morris, the most reliable of the new historians, asserts that there was no deliberate policy or grand design, but there was a mindset on the Israeli side that did allow for expulsion to take place in various cases when certain officers pushed for it. There can be no question that the Israeli policy of non-return was accepted by the Israeli government during and after the war, and that the return of refugees was subsequently prevented by all Israeli governments.

But in the negotiations between Israel and the Arab states after the War of 1948, Israel did make an offer for the return of 100,000 refugees to Israel, provided the Arab States agreed to make full peace with Israel and to resettle the rest of the refugees in the Arab countries. That offer was not accepted by the Arabs, and Israel has not repeated it ever since.

Plan D in the Arab argumentation is cited as the evidence of an Israeli grand design to expel the Arabs. In Plan D there was an allowance for Jewish commanders to expel the population in cases of resistance. But as explained by the Israelis this was a permission to officers in some cases to expel certain populations in the name of local security needs, and not an overall plan to expel the Arab population from Palestine.

Plan D, the Israelis would argue, was a military plan designed to obtain effective control of the territory of the Jewish state prior to the expected invasion of the Arab states. There could be no effective resistance to the invasion if the Jews were not in firm control of the territory that was accorded to them by the UN. Not a grand design, the Israelis would argue, but the result of war and its consequences.

The debate on historical responsibility touches upon other issues such as the use of terminology about the war. The Palestinians refer to the war of 1948 as the "Catastrophe", or *al-Nakba* in Arabic. *Nakba* in Arabic is a natural catastrophe, like an earthquake or a tsunami, and it has been used to describe the results of 1948 in a way that does not ascribe any responsibility to the Palestinians or to the Arabs at all.

Some on the Arab side have criticized this usage, most notably, the Syrian Sadiq al-Azm. He criticized the use of the term *al-Nakba* by arguing that it carried to a certain degree an apologetic logic, along with "an evasion of responsibility and accountability, since whomever is struck by a disaster is not considered responsible for it, or its occurrence..."[10]

According to this general Arab understanding of the meaning of *al-Nakba*, it was Israel that was responsible for what had happened, and the Arabs, despite the fact that it was they who launched the war, did not share responsibility for its consequences. Israel was required by the Arab side in the negotiations that were held on the Palestinian question to admit its responsibility for the refugee problem without the Arab side admitting any responsibility of its own.

Palestinian Refugee Camp
Syria 1948

http://commons.wikimedia.org/wiki/File%3AMan_see_school_nakba.jpg

This essentially was asking the Israelis to admit that their country was born in sin. In exchange for recognition of their existence, the Israelis were expected to concede that they might not have such a right to exist in the first place. The Israelis, needless to say, were very unlikely to do so. As opposed to the Arab argument, the Israelis contended that the Arab side bore considerable responsibility, maybe not all the responsibility, but a large share of it, because of their rejection of partition and their decision to go to war.

The events of 1948 have become the core of the collective memory of the Palestinian people, and the most important facet of their particular historical sense of collective identity that distinguishes the Palestinians from other Arab peoples. The events of 1948 also came to mean the Palestinian loss of control of their destiny. The conflict now became what was known for very many years as the Arab-Israeli conflict. The major players in the conflict from the Arab invasion in 1948 were the Arab states, not the Palestinians. The armistice agreements that Israel signed at the end of the war in the early months of 1949 were only with

10. Sadiq al-Azm, *Self-Criticism After the Defeat* (London: Saqi Books, 2011), p. 40.

the Arab states, Egypt, Lebanon, Jordan, and Syria. The Palestinians ceased to be an autonomous player in Middle Eastern politics. In later years they were to return, but in the early years after the war of 1948, they were pushed to the sidelines. After 1948, there was no territory called Palestine, which no longer existed as a geographical unit on the map. It had become either Israel, the West Bank area of Jordan, or the Gaza Strip under an Egyptian military regime.

In the broader perspective of Israel and the Arabs the meaning of defeat was of greater consequence than just the recent conflict between Israel and the Arab states. The defeat was seen in the wider context of the struggle between the Middle East and the West that had been going on for the last two centuries. It was in this struggle between the Middle East and the West that the Middle East was defeated again by what was seen as a representative of the hostile West. Israel had also upset the traditional political order. In the traditional Muslim order the Jews were a tolerated minority under the rule of the Muslim majority. The creation of the State of Israel turned this order on its head by establishing a state with a Jewish majority in which the Muslims had become the tolerated minority. The Arabs refused to accept the new reality and spoke with a loud voice on the "second round" that was bound to come. In the much vaunted "second round" the Arabs would defeat the Israelis, or so they believed and hoped.

As for the statistics of the 1948 war, the most acceptable figure for Palestinian refugees was in the vicinity of 700,000. The number of Jewish refugees from the Arab countries was more or less the same, if not slightly higher. Israeli losses were massive on any scale. Some 6,000 Israelis were killed in the War of 1948, one percent of their population of just over 600,000. That was a huge loss, far greater than many other nations have paid in their respective wars. The Israelis saw their sacrifice initially as the unavoidable price of liberation, not expecting to have to fight repeated wars against the Palestinians and the Arabs thereafter.

The Palestinians lost approximately 8,000 people, a very high number too, although slightly less proportionately to the Israelis. The other Arab armies lost approximately 4,000 men.

There is a Jewish and Israeli contention, that the Jewish refugees from the Arab countries and the Arab refugees from Palestine were a kind of exchange of population between Israel and the Arab States. But there was no real symmetry between these two refugee questions. On the Arab side, the Palestinian refugees were generally not integrated into the Arab countries (Jordan was the exception to this rule). The acceptance of the Palestinian refugees by the Arab countries and their incorporation and naturalization in these countries, would have meant the final acquiescence and acceptance by the Arabs of the results of the 1948 War. And that the Arabs were not prepared to do. On the other hand, the acceptance by Israel of the Jewish refugees from the Arab countries was the fulfillment of the Zionist dream. These two issues were not really comparable.

In December 1948, the United Nations General Assembly passed a resolution that dealt in part with the refugee question and with what the Palestinians refer to as their "right of return." This was General Assembly Resolution 194, which the Palestinians interpret as an endorsement of the unqualified "right of return" of the Palestinian refugees to their former homes in Israel. However, a strict analysis of the text shows that this interpretation is questionable.

Resolution 194 states as follows:

> It "*resolves* that the refugees wishing to return to their homes and live at peace with their neighbors should be permitted to do so at the earliest practicable date, and that compensation should be paid for the property of those choosing not to return and for loss of or damage to property which, under principles of international law or in equity, should be made good by the Governments or authorities responsible;..." [11]

"*Resolves* that the refugees wishing to return"; that is, according to the resolution there were refugees who wished to return and there were those who did not. It was not an automatic assumption that all refugees indeed wished to return. Moreover, there was a condition imposed on those who wished to return, that they should "live at peace with their neighbors". Thus, it was not an unqualified right to return either.

This return had to be "permitted". Permitted, one may ask, by whom? This could only have meant permitted by the Israeli government, which was in control of the territories concerned. Therefore, no return was possible without Israel's agreement and permission, as the sovereign state in those territories to which the refugees, in part or in whole, may seek to return.

This should be done at the earliest "practicable date"; that is, the date would have to be agreed and practical. That could be at any time in the future. It is interesting to note that compensation that was to be paid, should be made good by the "Governments or authorities" responsible. That is, Israel alone was not responsible for the problem. There were various governments and "authorities", which presumably referred to the Palestinians, who were all responsible for this question. The resolution, therefore, did not endorse the unconditional, unfettered right of Palestinian refugee return to Israel.

In the vote on this resolution in 1948, all the Arab states who were members of the UN at the time voted against it. The Resolution was indeed insufficient

11. Laura Zittrain Eisenberg and Neil Caplan, *Negotiating Arab-Israeli Peace: Patterns, Problems, Possibilities* (Indiana University Press, 2010), Appendix B: Documents Online, Document 10, UN General Assembly Resolution 194, 11 December 1948.

from the Arab point of view and the interpretation given later by the Palestinians to Resolution 194 did not actually correspond with the original text.

The refugee issue is still unresolved, and remains perhaps the major stumbling block to an agreement that will finally put an end to the conflict between Israel and the Palestinians.

Key Sources and Suggested Further Reading

- Al-Azm, Sadiq, *Self-Criticism After the Defeat* (London: Saqi Books, 2011).
- Khalaf, Issa, *Politics in Palestine: Arab Factionalism and Social Disintegration, 1939-1948* (Albany: State University of New York Press, 1991).
- Khalidi, Rashid, *Palestinian Identity: The Construction of Modern National Consciousness* (New York: Columbia University Press, 1997).
- Khalidi, Rashid, *The Iron Cage: The Story of the Palestinian Struggle for Statehood* (Boston: Beacon Press, 2006).
- Kimmerling, Baruch and Joel Migdal, *The Palestinian People: A History* (Cambridge, MA: Harvard University Press, 2003).
- Masalha, Nur, *The Politics of Denial: Israel and the Palestinian Refugee Problem* (London: Pluto Press, 2003).
- Morris, Benny, *The Birth of the Palestinian Refugee Problem, 1947-1949* (Cambridge University Press, 1989).
- Morris, Benny, *Righteous Victims: A History of the Zionist-Arab Conflict, 1881-1999* (New York: Knopf, 1999).
- Morris, Benny, *The Birth of the Palestinian Refugee Problem Revisited* (Cambridge University Press, 2004).
- Muslih, Muhammad, *The Origins of Palestinian Nationalism* (New York: Columbia University Press, 1988).
- Rogan, Eugene and Avi Shlaim (Eds.), *The War for Palestine: Rewriting the History of 1948* (Cambridge University Press, 2001).
- Shapira, Anita, *Land and Power: The Zionist Resort to Force, 1881-1948* (Stanford University Press, 1992).
- Shapira, Anita, *Israel: A History* (Waltham, MA: Brandeis University Press, 2012).
- Vital, David, *The Origins of Zionism* (Oxford University Press, 1990).

Chapter Seven

Escalation and De-Escalation of the Arab-Israeli Conflict (I)

Israel's Security Doctrine

The Armistice Agreements that brought the 1948 War to an end did not lead to peace. After the Israeli victory, the Arabs called for what was to be a "second round." It was against this background of non-peace and Arab agitation for renewed conflict that Israel developed its security doctrine.

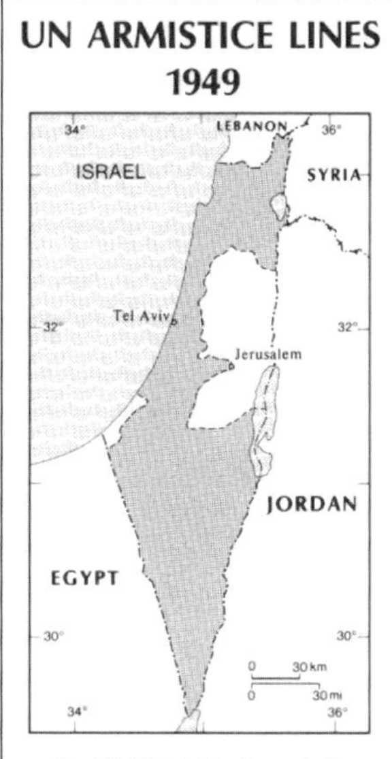

By UN [Public domain], via Wikimedia Commons

The security doctrine was developed for a very small country (about the size of New Jersey) with a rather small population and it distinguished between two kinds of security: basic security and current security. Basic security was that which referred to the very existence of Israel as the nation-state of the Jewish people. Current security was the dealing with the day-to-day affairs of keeping the Israeli people safe on a regular basis.

It was with these two kinds of security in mind that the Israeli military was structured and the security doctrine was developed. Israel had a small population of less than two million people in the years immediately after the war (which grew gradually to three million by 1970 and eventually reaching eight million in 2015). This relatively small population had to deal with an array of Arab countries that had a population which was many times larger. With such a small population, it would be impossible for Israel to establish a large standing army to defend the country.

Israel, therefore, established its military forces on the basis of a reserve army. Men were required to serve in the reserves for a long period of time (twenty years and more) after their regular service, which ranged from two to three years (for men and somewhat less for women) during Israel's history. Standard military service was required from the age of 18, after which men entered the reserve army, which became the major component of Israel's land forces.

Reservists were called up regularly for training for a few weeks a year and at times of emergency to participate in the defense of the country.

A key principle in Israel's security doctrine was the need to take the war to the enemy. Being a very small country with borders that were in close proximity to the major centers of population, Israel could not afford to fight a land war on its own territory. That could be far too costly and destructive for the country's long term survivability. It, therefore, became an Israeli principle of warfare to fight its enemies outside of its own territory and not to allow the Arab states to seize the initiative by launching an invasion into Israel's confined space.

This required the promotion of two other key principles: deterrence and preemption. Deterrence meant the development of military might that would suffice to deter the Arab states from attacking Israel, recognizing that war with Israel would be too costly. If deterrence did not work, and there was a serious chance that one or more of the Arab states were about to attack Israel (which required a massive investment in intelligence for early warning), it would be essential for Israel to preempt, that is, to launch a preemptive war rather than have the Arabs start the war by attacking Israel first.

In addition to these principles, because of Israel's small size and small population, wars could not be of long duration. Israel could not mobilize a high proportion of its male population to fight wars of long duration. The economy could not possibly withstand such long periods of absence of most of the younger men from their jobs while on active duty. Wars, therefore, had to be brief and brought to a rapid and decisive conclusion.

Border Problems

The Middle East of the late 1940s and the early 1950s experienced a trend of radicalization in some of the Arab states, as we have seen in the coups in Syria in 1949, and the officer regime that rose to power in Egypt in 1952. The most moderate of Arab rulers, King Abdullah of Jordan, was assassinated in 1951. In

Border Problems

https://he.wikipedia.org

these troubling circumstances Israel was also completely boycotted by the Arab states and was in a state of more or less siege.

In the early years after 1948, Israel had a variety of border problems too. These border problems resulted mainly from the fact that hundreds and thousands of people a year would attempt to cross the border into Israel, sometimes for peaceful purposes and other times for armed attacks against Israeli civilians or soldiers. There were large refugee populations on Israel's borders, in the West Bank or the Gaza Strip, and very often refugees would cross the border back into Israel to retrieve their property, in most cases, or alternatively, in fewer cases, to attack and kill Israelis. The border situation was relatively unstable in the early years after the 1948 War and the state had much difficulty in establishing a sense of security for the people who lived in the border zones.

In May of 1950, the three great Western powers, that is the United States, Britain and France, issued what became known as the Tripartite Declaration which recognized and guaranteed the borders of the Middle Eastern states as they existed at that time. This was an indirect guarantee for the borders that Israel had established after the War of 1948. The three Western powers similarly guaranteed that they would see to it that the arms race and the balance of power between Israel and the Arabs would be maintained in equilibrium.

In the early 1950s, the US and Britain had plans for regional security in the Middle East, along the lines of the NATO pact that had been established in Europe, that would allow for the creation of defense pacts with the Arab countries against Soviet influence in the region. For that purpose they needed an Egyptian-Israeli deal. The Western powers were convinced that if they could establish peace between Israel and Egypt it would be a lot easier to arrange regional defense pacts against the Soviet Union.

The Western powers failed to realize at the time that the Arab states were disinterested, for the most part, in any pact against the Soviet Union. They did not see the Soviet Union as an enemy and were unwilling to engage in such anti-Soviet defense arrangements. This was true particularly of Egypt. Nor did the Western powers take sufficiently into consideration the extent of Arab hostility towards Israel and the unwillingness of the Arab states, and again of Egypt in particular, to come to terms with Israel.

Nevertheless these Western powers proposed that Israel should possibly cede parts of the Negev desert to allow for a land connection between Egypt and Jordan. Such an Israeli concession, they believed, might pave the way for a peace agreement between Israel and Egypt, the most important of Arab states.

But President Abd al-Nasser of Egypt not only wanted parts of the Negev, and possibly even all of it, he also demanded a free choice for the Palestinian refugees on the question of whether to return to Israel or not. These, however, were conditions that were unacceptable to Israel. Israel's two main guiding principles after the War of 1948 were to preserve both the geographic and the demographic status quo. Israel would not budge on the two issues of borders or refugees.

Talk about Israel giving up parts of the Negev reduced Israel's willingness to consider international guarantees. After all, the Western powers had ensured Israel's boundaries in 1950, and just a few years later they were trying to convince Israel to give up parts of the Negev. Such disappointments for Israel had long-term effects on the manner in which Israel understood its place in the region and its capacity to rely on international guarantees for its defense.

The Negev

By CIA (CIA-WF) [Public domain], via Wikimedia Commons

Neither Israel nor Egypt really believed that they could have achieved a deal in 1955 when the Western powers were thinking of such an agreement between Israel and Egypt. Both Egypt and Israel firmly believed that the other side was actually looking for a fight. As a result, Israel's Prime Minister, David Ben-Gurion, and the Chief of Staff at the time, Moshe Dayan, were already beginning to think of the need to preempt a possible Egyptian attack.

David Ben-Gurion
Prime Minister

Fritz Cohen [Public domain], via Wikimedia Commons

Nasser was very popular in the Arab world, and he was unquestionably the most popular and charismatic leader in the Arab world of the 1950s and perhaps in the Arab world of the 20th century in its entirety. Israel was greatly concerned with the development of Egyptian power. There was tension on the borders with Jordan and Egypt

Moshe Dayan
Chief of Staff, Israeli Defense Forces (1953–1958)

http://www.nrg.co.il/images/archive/300x225/1/215/070.jpg

because of the constant infiltrations coming from both of these countries into Israel. As a result of the infiltrations, whether it was for civilian purposes or for attacks on Israelis, they resulted in Israeli acts of retaliation against Jordan and Egypt, in an effort to compel the Arabs to accept the finality of the boundaries that had been created in 1948.

Nasser and his Pan-Arab Popularity

Not credited ([1] at Bibliotheca Alexandrina) [Public domain], via Wikimedia Commons

The Countdown to the Suez War of 1956

The tension between Israel and the neighboring Arab states, Jordan and Egypt in particular, led eventually to the signing of an arms deal between Egypt and Czechoslovakia. Czechoslovakia, essentially a front for the Soviet Union, signed a large arms deal with Egypt in September of 1955 that changed the balance of power between Israel and Egypt. The deal was extremely troubling from the Israeli point of view. Egypt with its hostile intentions towards Israel, so the Israelis firmly believed, was arming itself with the most modern of Soviet weaponry in terms of both air power and armor.

The Soviet Union had made a major political and diplomatic coup by connecting with Egypt

US President Dwight D. Eisenhower (1953–1961)

By White House ([1]) [Public domain], via Wikimedia Commons

Eisenhower and Nasser

http://www.haaretz.com/polopoly_fs/1.538405.1375021313!/image/2364666977.jpg_gen/derivatives/landscape_640/2364666977.jpg

and thereby neutralizing any US plans for a possible alliance with the Western powers against the Soviet Union. For Abd al-Nasser, the arms deal with the Soviet Union was of great symbolic and historical importance. Arms from the Soviet Union meant the ultimate liberation of Egypt from more than 150 years of subservience and dependence on the West.

Israel was now in a difficult spot and it turned to the United States in an effort to obtain arms that would balance the Soviet deal with Egypt. But the United States turned Israel down. Israel in the 1950s was not the ally of the United States that it became in later years. The United States in the 1950s tended to see Israel as much more of a liability than an asset and supporting Israel, so the US feared, would push the Arabs ever further into the embrace of the Soviet Union.

The French in Algeria

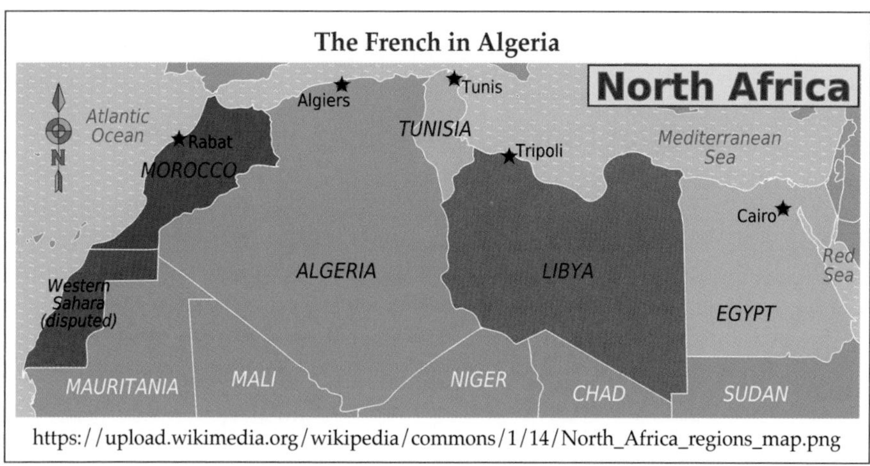

https://upload.wikimedia.org/wikipedia/commons/1/14/North_Africa_regions_map.png

Israel had to look for other options and it turned to France. In the mid-1950s Israel and France had common interests in respect to Egypt and Abd al-Nasser. In these years the French were fighting to suppress the Algerian War of Liberation. The Algerians, in their fight to liberate themselves from the imperial control of France, were strongly supported by Abd al-Nasser. The Egyptian President was consequently seen by the French as a mortal enemy, just as he was seen by the Israelis. As the escalation along the border with Egypt continued, Ben-Gurion's fear only increased that Nasser would attack Israel first. In the late months of 1956, there were serious French-Israeli discussions about a joint military operation against their common foe, Egypt of Abd al-Nasser.

At the same time, in the second half of 1956, Nasser was seen by the US to be moving firmly into the Soviet camp. On 19 July 1956 the United States announced its refusal to supply Egypt with aid for the building of the Aswan Dam. The Aswan Dam, as already mentioned (in Chapter Five), was seen by the Egyptians as a panacea for the ills of the Egyptian economy and a jumpstart for Egypt's modernization. Nasser retaliated a week later by nationalizing the British-French Suez Canal Company.

The Aswan Dam

One of the largest embankment dams in the world. Inaugurated in 1971

By NASA [Public domain], via Wikimedia Commons

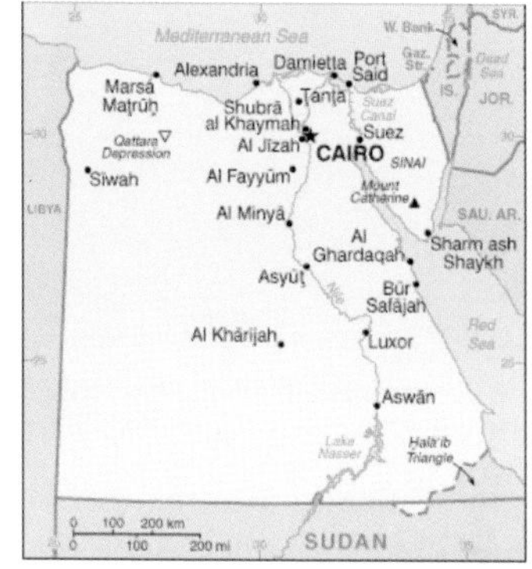

By user: Wolfman (Own work) [Public domain], via Wikimedia Commons

This was the background for the French-British-Israeli collusion in October 1956 to attack Egypt. Each of the players had their own various reasons for doing so. The British sought to restore their control of the Suez Canal and, at the same time, through war against Egypt to depose Abd al-Nasser. The French similarly wanted to rid themselves of Abd al-Nasser, but mainly to force Egypt to cease its intervention in Algeria. Israel aimed to secure its border with Egypt and the Gaza Strip and by inflicting a military defeat on the Egyptians to enhance Israel's long-term security.

Thus, the forces came together for what was known as the Sinai Campaign (or the Suez War) at the end of October 1956. Israel launched a land operation in the Sinai Peninsula, and the French and the British launched an assault in the Canal Zone. But these two military operations were not conducted simultaneously. First, it was the Israelis who attacked in the Sinai Peninsula

The Suez Canal

http://www.wonderfulnature.ru/photo/Suez_channel/5.jpg

The Sinai Campaign, 1956

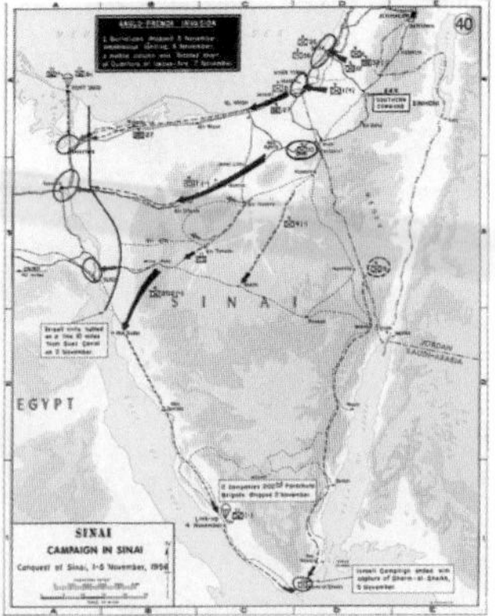

http://commons.wikimedia.org/wiki/File:1956_Suez_war_-_conquest_of_Sinai.jpg

and within four days, they had occupied the entire area.

The Anglo-French military campaign, which started a few days later, started late after various delays and turned into a political, military and diplomatic fiasco. By starting late they caught no-one by surprise and they were faced immediately with strident US and Soviet condemnation, just as both super-powers had strongly condemned the Israelis for attacking Egypt. The US believed that the attack by Israel, and then by the French and the British a few days later, would only push the Egyptians and other Arabs more firmly into the camp of the Soviet Union. US and Soviet pressure was mounted on the British, the French and the Israelis to withdraw their forces immediately. The British and the French never fully reoccupied the Canal Zone and they were compelled to end their operation before achieving its military objectives. The US, which was most effective in its pressure, similarly coerced the Israelis to withdraw completely from Sinai, by March 1957.

The Straits of Tiran

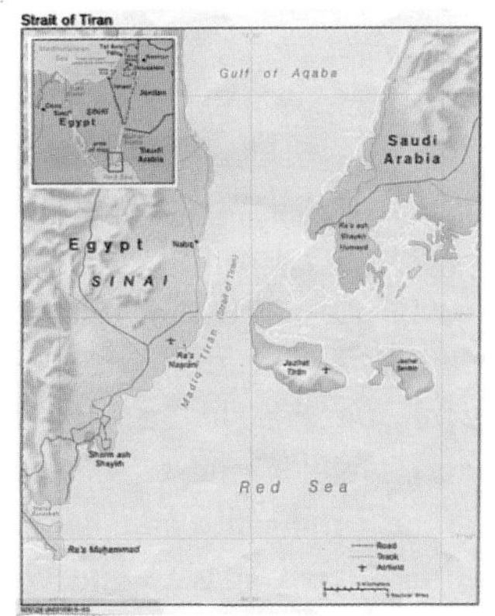

By "The following maps were produced by the U.S. Central Intelligence Agency, unless otherwise indicated." [Public domain], via Wikimedia Commons

Israel withdrew from the Sinai Peninsula in exchange for a US guarantee for the freedom of navigation in the Straits of Tiran, that is, the sea lane leading to the Israeli port of Eilat, hitherto blocked by the Egyptians to Israeli shipping. Another Israeli political gain from the Sinai Campaign was the establishment of a UN Emergency Force (UNEF) along its border with Egypt (on the Egyptian side) to keep the peace between the two countries.

For Britain and France, the Suez fiasco was the end of an era. Their historical influence in the Middle East had come to a humiliating end.

As for Egypt, though defeated militarily by Israel, Abd al-Nasser had won politically at least in the sense that he had defeated the British and the French military effort and he had also remained in power as opposed to the wishes of those who had attacked him. Nasser emerged from the Suez Campaign unquestionably as the leader of the Arab world. There was widespread support and even adulation in Egypt and in the Arab world as a whole for the Nasserist formula of Arab unity, Arab socialism (the centralized structure of the economy) and cold war reliance on the Soviet Union. It was widely believed that these were the three critical components of Arab power, prestige and prosperity that would finally liberate the Arabs from all vestiges of imperialist influence, and, in the end, defeat Israel too.

Israel, having cooperated in the 1956 war with France and Britain, only reinforced its image as a tool of imperialism in the eyes of the Arabs. That did not make peacemaking with the Arab states any easier. But Israel's victory did bring an end, for the most part, to the border problems that had previously existed between Israel and Egypt, and even between Israel and Jordan. Israel's victory in the battlefield seriously undermined the rather simplistic Arab thinking about a "second round." After Suez, Arab thinking about the conflict became much more complex. It was now firmly understood by Abd al-Nasser and by other Arabs that the struggle with Israel was not simply about a "second round" in which the Arabs would defeat Israel. The struggle with Israel was a long term affair. It would take generations. Israel was a powerful country and here to stay, or so it seemed.

After the 1956–1957 crisis, Israel had what one may call its "ten good years," until the war of 1967. Israel, compared to other periods in its history, enjoyed relative quiet on its borders. The boundaries had solidified, as had ideological positions. The Arabs did not accept Israel by any means, but the borders, for the most part, were quiet.

The understanding of the Arabs that the war with Israel was a conflict for generations required an entirely new strategic approach. If this was indeed going to be a struggle for decades, the Arabs could not afford to allow the Palestinian issue to be forgotten in the meantime. Until such time as the Arabs could deal with Israel effectively and emerge victorious, the claim of the Palestinian people to the territory of Palestine had to be preserved. The Arabs, therefore, could not allow the Palestinian people to disappear and for Palestinian specificity to be absorbed into the overall identity of the Arab nation.

The Revival of the Palestinian Entity

The long-term conflict with Israel required what became known in Arabic as the "Revival of the Palestinian Entity" *(ihya al-kiyan al-Filastini)*. It had to be made clear that there was, in fact, an Arab people who were Palestinians by definition, and who were politically and historically associated specifically with the territory of Palestine.

In the immediate aftermath of the 1948 War, the two banks of the Jordan River, the East Bank and the West Bank, were united under Jordan. Jordan sought to incorporate the Palestinians, who were now a two-thirds majority, into the kingdom. Jordan had no interest in the preservation of the Palestinian identity. On the contrary, the Jordanians sought to absorb the Palestinian identity into Jordan, and therefore the territory west of the river was designated as the "West Bank." After all, had the Jordanians wished to preserve the Palestinian identity, they could have called the West Bank, Palestine, which is what it was. But the Jordanians deliberately ceased using the term Palestine and employed the term "West Bank" as a way of erasing the Palestinian identity of the territory.

Two Banks of the Jordan River

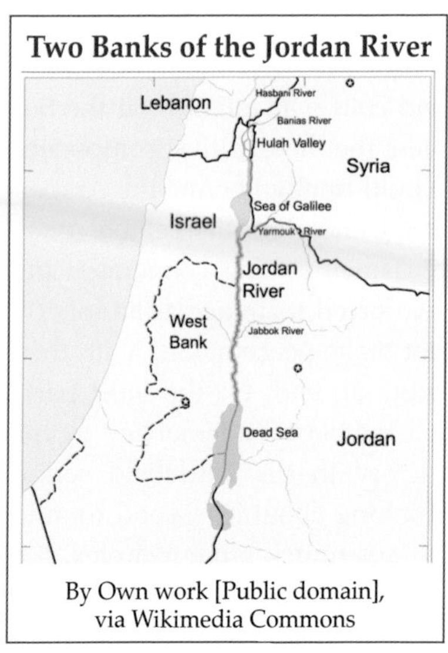

By Own work [Public domain], via Wikimedia Commons

Therefore, in the late 1950s after Suez, the thinking of Abd al-Nasser and other Arabs in favor of the revival of the Palestinian entity was totally opposed to Jordanian interests. Needless to say, this was not what the Israelis wanted either. It would have been preferable for both the Jordanians and the Israelis for the Palestinians to be absorbed into the various Arab countries, as part and parcel of the overall Arab nation, and for the specific Palestinian claim to Palestine to recede into the past.

Nasser and his Vision

By Louse at en.wikipedia (Transferred from en.wikipedia) [Public domain], via Wikimedia Commons

The Palestinians were great admirers of Abd al-Nasser's formula, and they really did believe in the Arab revolution that would be led by Nasser towards liberation. They were the most loyal of Arabs to Abd al-Nasser and his vision. But after the Suez War, there was a growing realization amongst some Palestinians that Abd al-Nasser may not be able to deliver Palestine, after all. Despite all the fanfare of victory, they knew that Abd al-Nasser had been defeated by the Israelis.

If the conflict with Israel was destined to be a long-term commitment, like Nasser they believed that it was critical to preserve the Palestinian entity and identity, but these Palestinians also sought to create a Palestinian political organization that would be independent of the Arab states. For Abd al-Nasser and for the Palestinians it was important to make it clear to all and sundry that the Palestinian issue was a political matter, an issue of a people and their right to self-determination in their own homeland of Palestine. The Palestinian question was not just a refugee problem, an issue of individuals who needed some kind of humanitarian solution. This was not about providing housing and jobs for the refugees, it was about the national rights of the Palestinians and their right to return to their homeland.

The Establishment of the PLO, 1964

Ahmad al-Shuqayri
http://www.ovguide.com/ahmad-shukeiri-9202a8c04000641f800000000015ece1

Against this background, two trends emerged in the Arab world. One was an autonomous clandestine Palestinian effort, to organize politically for an independent Palestinian struggle. The other was the public pan-Arab effort to revive the Palestinian identity, through the meetings, deliberations and decisions of the Arab League.

The discussions of the Palestinian issue in the Arab League culminated in May 1964 with the establishment of the Palestine Liberation Organization (PLO). The PLO was established under the chairmanship of Ahmad al-Shuqayri, as a result of a decision that was made by the Arab League.

For Abd al-Nasser, the establishment of the PLO was a means to control the Palestinian question. Abd al-Nasser was not interested in the Palestinians waging their conflict with Israel independently, which could possibly drag the Egyptians into a war with Israel at a time not of their own choosing. For Abd al-Nasser, the creation of the PLO was not intended to allow the Palestinians independent decision-making, but rather to control the revival of the Palestinian entity under Nasser's own watchful eye.

The Jordanians, oddly enough, agreed to this decision of the Arab League that led to the formation of the PLO, even though they had been opposed to the revival of the Palestinian entity from the very beginning. The inaugural meeting of the PLO, in May 1964, was actually held in Arab Jerusalem, which was part of Jordan at that time.

The Jordanians, just like Abd al-Nasser, believed that if they allowed for the PLO to be established, they would be able to control its development. Jordan's acquiescence was also a means for the Jordanians to accede to the Arab consensus and to make their peace with Abd al-Nasser, rather than having to confront him all the time, in a contest in which Nasser invariably had the upper hand.

But once the PLO was established, it made immediate demands of Jordan. The great majority of the Palestinian people, whom the PLO wished to represent, were Jordanian citizens living in the West Bank and on the other side of the river, on the East Bank. The PLO had to operate in Jordan to effectively represent the Palestinian people. It could not have a viable representative character, if it did not operate freely amongst the great majority of the Palestinians, who were Jordanian citizens.

The PLO therefore required of Jordan to allow it to collect taxes from the Palestinians in Jordan, and to conscript Palestinians for the Palestine Liberation Army (PLA), which the PLO established at that time. The PLO also demanded the political mobilization of the Palestinians in the West Bank on behalf of the organization, and even to arm the Palestinian villages on the front line facing Israel.

All of these demands were totally unacceptable to the Jordanians. For the PLO, Jordan was an indispensable base of operations. But for the Jordanians, the PLO's demands meant the erosion and eventual undoing of Jordanian sovereignty. The PLO was essentially asking the Jordanians to agree to the establishment of a kind of Palestinian independent political entity within the framework of the Jordanian state. To this the Jordanians, needless to say, would not agree.

The Establishment of Fatah

In the meantime, the clandestine organization of the Palestinians was conducted autonomously by Palestinians, not within the framework of the Arab League and not within the framework of the PLO either. This was the creation of independent Palestinian organizations of which the most important and most lasting was Fatah. Young Palestinians, like Yasser Arafat, had begun to organize as students in Cairo in the early 1950s,

The Fatah Emblem

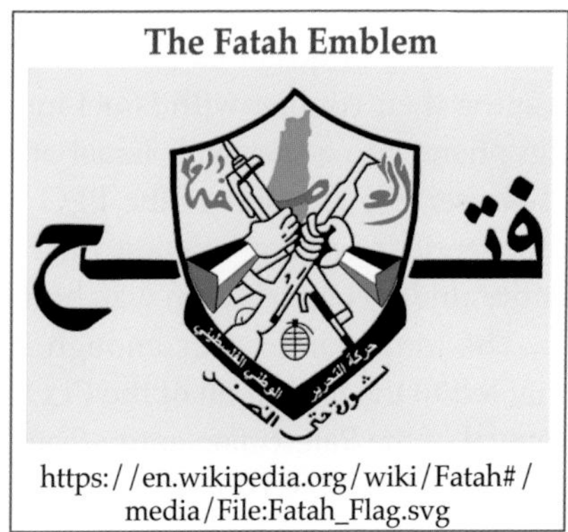

https://en.wikipedia.org/wiki/Fatah#/media/File:Fatah_Flag.svg

where they organized the General Union of Palestinian Students (GUPS). It was they who, after the Suez War and the realization of Abd al-Nasser's limitations, resolved to organize independent Palestinian armed struggle against Israel. Fatah was established in the Gulf in the late 1950s by Arafat and others, who became the founding fathers of the renewed Palestine national movement.

The Armed Struggle

http://www.telesurtv.net/english/multimedia/The-Anniversary-of-the-Palestine-Liberation-Organization-20150527-0057.html

In 1961, as already noted, the union between Egypt and Syria, the United Arab Republic (UAR), broke up. This was a great disappointment for the Palestinians. After all, Arab unity was supposed to be the vehicle of liberation. The breakup of the UAR was another indication for the Palestinians of the need to enhance their own self-reliance. They could not trust the Arab states to liberate Palestine for them. This disappointment with the Arab states required political and organizational autonomy. It pushed the Palestinians to ensure what they called their "independence of decision" *(istiqlal al-qarar)*. Fatah and likeminded organizations would not intervene in the affairs of the Arab states, and they did not have any particular social or revolutionary ideology, but they did believe very strongly in the need to establish a Palestinian organization that would decide for the Palestinians, independently of the Arab states, on the waging of their struggle.

The struggle had to be an armed struggle and they drew their inspiration from the Algerian model. In 1962 the Algerians emerged victorious in their war of liberation and forced the French to leave Algeria. The Palestinians believed that just as the Algerians had succeeded by armed struggle to force the French out of Algeria, so the Palestinians would push the Israelis out of Palestine.

There were many small organizations like Fatah in the late 1950s and early 1960s, but most had no firm organizational structure, and they did not last. Fatah did last but, as noted above, it was not initially part of the PLO and it operated independently. Fatah created strong connections with the radical Ba'thi regime in Syria, which allowed Fatah to conduct operations from Syria against Israel, but even more so, it allowed Fatah to use Syrian territory to infiltrate Jordan and to attack Israel from the West Bank.

The first armed operation by Fatah against Israel was conducted in January 1965 against the Israeli National Water Carrier. The water carrier was a great national enterprise of much ideological consequence in Israel. The completion of the water carrier in Israel, very much like the Aswan Dam in Egypt, was seen by Israelis as a great moment in the modernization and the progress of the Zionist enterprise. It was, therefore, not by chance that Fatah chose to attack the water carrier in its first operation. The operation failed and it was not important militarily, but symbolically it was the launching by Fatah of the renewed armed struggle against Israel.

Fatah's 1st Operation

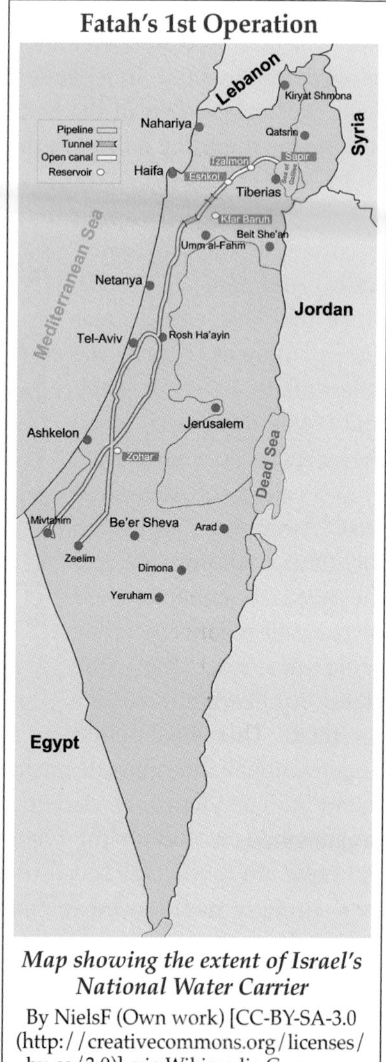

Map showing the extent of Israel's National Water Carrier

By NielsF (Own work) [CC-BY-SA-3.0 (http://creativecommons.org/licenses/by-sa/3.0)], via Wikimedia Commons

The armed struggle by Fatah put pressure on Shuqayri of the PLO to agitate for gains in the negotiations with Jordan to establish an effective base for the PLO in Jordanian territory. But just as before the talks ended in failure. By late 1965, the relations between Jordan and the PLO had broken down altogether. In early 1966, the Jordanian government, instead of negotiating with Shuqayri and cooperating with the PLO, was busy arresting all the supporters of the PLO in Jordan. In the summer of 1966, King Hussein of Jordan broke off all relations with Shuqayri and the PLO, and the two parties were now in all-out confrontation.

Hussein argued that "Jordan is Palestine and Palestine is Jordan." Jordan had essentially inherited Palestine and Jordan, therefore, represented Palestine. If Jordan represented Palestine and the Palestinians, any other Palestinian organization to represent the Palestinians was superfluous, so the Jordanians argued. Such contentions, of course, did not convince the Palestinians and more Fatah operations from the West Bank continued against Israeli targets.

These provoked repeated Israeli reprisals and the most important and significant of them was a massive Israeli retaliatory action taken against the

The Samu' Operation, November 1966

https://www.ovguide.com/samu-incident-9202a8c04000641f80 0000000577ff60

village of Samu' in the Hebron hills in November 1966. The Samu' operation came in the wake of the killing of a number of Israeli soldiers by a mine planted by Fatah in Israeli territory, and it had long term unintended consequences. Israeli forces took control of the village of Samu' in broad daylight and demolished 41 buildings, clearly demonstrating the incapacity of the Jordanians to defend the people of the West Bank. The PLO and the Arab states waged a huge propaganda assault against Jordan, arguing that the Jordanians, in their dismissive attitude towards Palestine and the PLO, were not taking an aggressive enough position towards Israel. The Palestinian population of the West Bank, rose in a kind of mini-uprising against the Jordanian government for about two weeks after the Samu' operation.

By NordNordWest [CC-BY-SA-3.0 (http://creativecommons.org/licenses/by-sa/3.0)], via Wikimedia Commons (modified)

The operation conducted by the Israelis in Samu' was intended to convince the Jordanians to take a firmer hand in controlling Fatah operations that were coming out of Jordan. Hussein, however, understood the Samu' attack, an unusually large-scale Israeli military operation conducted in broad daylight, as Israeli preparation for the eventual conquest of the West Bank. That is not what it was, but that is how Hussein understood the operation, and his assessment influenced Jordanian decisions in the future, as we will see.

In the meantime, matters were taking a turn for the worse on the border between Israel and Syria as well. After the Samu' operation, two main issues continued to sour relations between Israel and Syria and to create a serious deterioration in the security situation along the border between the two countries. The one was that the Syrians continued to allow Fatah to carry out operations from their territory against Israel. The other was the Syrian scheme to divert the sources of the Jordan River in order to interrupt and actually defeat Israel's irrigation plans. The National Water Carrier that the Israelis had built depended on water that was coming from the Sea of Galilee, which received its water from the Jordan River, and by diverting the tributaries of the Jordan River, the Syrians sought to deny Israel its water resources. Israel naturally would not stand for that, and as a result, the security situation along the border between Israel and Syria deteriorated constantly. Thus was laid the groundwork for the tensions that eventually led to the outbreak of all-out war in June 1967.

The Deterioration to War in June 1967

The Arab League Summit of 1964

https://en.wikipedia.org/wiki/1964_Arab_League_summit_(Cairo)#/media/File:Arab_League_Summit,_1964.jpg

In January 1964, the first Arab Summit conference was held in Cairo under the auspices of Abd al-Nasser. It adopted three important decisions. The first was to establish an organization that would represent the Palestinians, which eventually led to the creation of the PLO. The second was to establish a United Arab Command that would conduct the war against Israel in the future, and the third was to divert the sources of the Jordan River.

These decisions, which looked rather belligerent, were actually intended to postpone war. But in fact, unintentionally, they eventually provoked the war of June 1967. The resolutions to form a representative Palestinian organization, to establish a unified Arab command and to divert the tributaries of the Jordan, were designed to keep the conflict on a low controllable flame, but not to initiate all-out war. But keeping the conflict on a low controllable flame was much easier said than done.

In May 1967, due to the deteriorating situation along the border between Israel and Syria, Israel's Chief of Staff, Yitzhak Rabin, warned Syria publicly that if the situation continued to deteriorate, Israel would eventually have to take military action, which might lead to the toppling of the Syrian regime.

Shortly after Rabin's warning, the Soviet Union, for reasons that remain unknown to this very day, passed on false intelligence to Egypt that the Israelis were concentrating forces along the border with Syria with the intention of launching an attack. It was this coalescence of events that led to the crisis of May 1967 that eventually resulted in the June War. Following up on the information given to Egypt by the Soviet Union, Nasser sent his army into the Sinai Peninsula in a demonstrative show of force, in broad daylight and in front of the television cameras, to publicly threaten Israel not to attack Syria.

Yitzhak Rabin

http://images1.ynet.co.il/PicServer2/03072003/333166/yitzhak-rabin_h.jpg

The Civil War in Yemen, 1962–1970

Royalists led by Muhammad al-Badr

See page for author [Public domain], via Wikimedia Commons

Abd al-Nasser and the leader of the revolutionaries Abdullah as-Sallal

By Not credited ([1] at Bibliotheca Alexandrina) [Public domain], via Wikimedia Commons

This was a very surprising move taken by Egypt, considering the fact that significant Egyptian forces had been tied up in Yemen since 1962. In 1962, a civil war broke out in Yemen between the "revolutionaries" and the "royalists" as they were known, and Abd al-Nasser intervened with his forces on behalf of the "revolutionaries." The Egyptian intervention caused a major rupture between Egypt and Saudi Arabia that supported the "royalists." The Egyptian involvement in Yemen eventually turned into a quagmire akin to "Egypt's Vietnam," giving rise to the assessment in Israel that war with Egypt was most unlikely as long as Egyptian forces were deployed in Yemen.

All the same, in May 1967 Nasser moved his forces into Sinai and bellicose statements emanating from Cairo and Damascus, threatening Israel's impending demise, created new tensions between Israel and the Arab states. Israel mobilized its reserves setting in motion a series of miscalculations by all the players, leading to the war that no one had really planned for nor intended.

As already noted, it remains unclear why the Soviets passed on this incorrect information to Abd al-Nasser. Moreover, Abd al-Nasser checked the Soviet information and discovered very shortly after he had already sent his forces into Sinai that the Israelis had not concentrated troops to attack Syria, as the Soviets had informed him. Even though Abd al-Nasser now knew the truth, having moved his forces into Sinai in such a demonstrative fashion, he could hardly turn back without losing face. The Egyptian forces remained in Sinai and the old enemies of Abd al-Nasser, the Jordanians and the Saudis, who had always been ridiculed and humiliated by Nasser, now found their opportunity to taunt and ridicule him. The Jordanians and the Saudis waged a propaganda campaign against Egypt, arguing all along that the Egyptian forces in Sinai were just for show and that Egypt had no intention of really going to war with Israel. Egypt, they said, was hiding behind the apron of the UN Emergency Forces in Sinai and unless Abd al-Nasser removed the UN forces, it was clear that he was no more than bluff and bluster.[1]

Against the background of this humiliating critique, on 17 May Abd al-Nasser ordered the UN forces to leave the Sinai Peninsula, and they complied with his instructions. On the same day, Egyptian MIG aircraft flew over Israel's nuclear facility in Dimona.[2] The Israelis got the distinct impression that war might be imminent.

Levi Eshkol
Prime Minister of Israel
1963–1969

By KLUGER ZOLTAN ([1]) [Public domain], via Wikimedia Commons

The Israelis radiated what looked like fear and panic. Israel's Prime Minister and Minister of Defense, Levi Eshkol, was not a man of military experience. He was Israel's former Minister of Finance and he lacked the charisma of Ben-Gurion, his predecessor. Generally the Israeli public had little confidence in Eshkol's ability to lead Israel in such a serious crisis situation. The public were rushing to the supermarkets to stock up and the Israelis began to revive memories of the Holocaust. There were fears amongst the population of massive numbers of casualties that would be inflicted by attacks of Egypt's Air Force on Israeli cities.

1. Samir Mutawi, *Jordan in the 1967 War* (Cambridge University Press, 1987), pp. 83–86.
2. Avner Cohen, "Cairo, Dimona, and the June 1967 War," *Middle East Journal*, Vol. 50, No. 2 (Spring 1996), p. 201.

On 22 May, with the UN forces no longer in Sinai, Abd al-Nasser closed the Straits of Tiran to Israeli shipping. By closing the Straits Nasser was knowingly testing the Israelis who had declared unequivocally that such a closure would be a cause for war. Nasser did so, again very much against the background of the Jordanian and Saudi propaganda that was designed to humiliate him. After his expulsion of the UN forces from Sinai, the Jordanians and the Saudis had pressured Abd al-Nasser to close the Straits of Tiran to prove his seriousness to confront Israel and Nasser eventually caved in.[3] By deciding to close the Straits, Nasser had thrown down the gauntlet. War with Israel was a certainty, sooner or later.

Israel turned to the United States, which had given Israel a commitment to uphold the freedom of navigation in the Straits of Tiran after Israel's withdrawal from Sinai in 1957 (see above). But, this commitment came to nothing and the United States was unable to organize any kind of international naval force that would open the Straits of Tiran. Israel sought US guidance and support, but the US position, as communicated by President Lyndon Johnson to the Israeli government was that "Israel will not be alone, unless it decides to go it alone. We cannot imagine that it will make this decision."[4] The Israelis were left with an acute sense of isolation.

As the crisis escalated, Prime Minister Eshkol decided to deliver a speech to the nation at the end of May. Eshkol's speech turned into a political disaster. It was delivered live over the radio. But it was a stammering and stuttering delivery, as Eshkol found difficulty in reading certain corrections that had been made in the text of his speech. The speech conveyed the image of a government and a leadership at a loss. Domestic political pressure on Eshkol mounted to broaden the government as the confidence of the people in Eshkol as the leader in this crisis sank to an all-time low. The public pressure was to bring Moshe Dayan, the famous former chief of staff of the Suez Campaign of 1956, into the cabinet as Minister of Defense, instead of Eshkol.

Eventually, Eshkol succumbed to the pressure, and Dayan was brought in as Minister of Defense, and a broad national unity government was formed by also including the representatives of the political right, Menachem Begin, and others from his party who had never been part of any Israeli coalition. In the longer term this proved to be a new legitimization of the political right in Israeli politics. In the immediate short term it created a government that had a much more hawkish predisposition.

---

3. Mutawi, *ibid.*
4. Michael Oren, *Six Days of War; June 1967 and the Making of the Modern Middle East* (Oxford University Press, 2002), p. 157.

Dayan and Begin Enter the Coalition Government of Eshkol

Moshe Dayan

By Anefo/Croes, R.C. (Gahetna in het nationaal archief) [CC-BY-SA-3.0-nl (http://creativecommons.org/licenses/by-sa/3.0/nl/deed.en)], via Wikimedia Commons

Menachem Begin

By MSGT DENHAM [Public domain], via Wikimedia Commons

By the beginning of June, greater pressure was also coming from within the military command for Israel to strike first. The new cabinet and the pressure coming from within the military gave further support to the view that Israel needed to preempt. Indeed, war was initiated by Israel with a surprise air attack on the Egyptian Air Force and other Arab air forces on the morning of 5 June 1967. The air attack caught the Arab air forces completely by surprise. It was a phenomenal success militarily, and from the moment the air attack was over, it was clear that Israel was on the road to winning the war.

After the attack on the Arab air forces and the opening of the ground war on the Egyptian front, war also began on the Jordanian front. The fighting was initiated by the Jordanians, whose forces were under Egyptian command according to the rules of the United Arab Command and a defense pact concluded between King Hussein and Abd al-Nasser just a few days before. However, when the fighting began on the Jordanian front, the Israelis were reluctant to open a war on two fronts at the same time. The Israelis, therefore, sent a message to Jordan through the UN observers in Jerusalem to halt their fire, promising not to attack the Jordanians, if they complied with Israel's request. But Hussein, under the impact of Samu' and the belief that the Samu' operation in November 1966 was conducted by Israel as a kind of practice run for the occupation of the West Bank, was convinced that whether he joined the war against Israel or not, Israel would eventually attack Jordan on the West Bank

The Jordanian Front

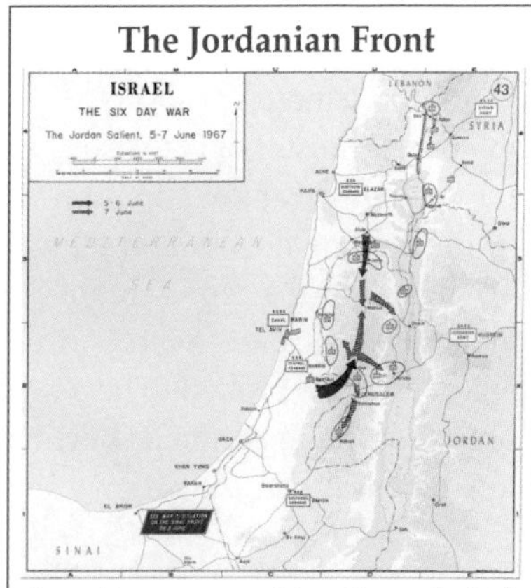

http://commons.wikimedia.org/wiki/File:1967_Six_Day_War_-_The_Jordan_salient.jpg

front. The Jordanians turned down the Israeli offer and opened fire along the entire front with Israel, leading the Israelis eventually to embark on a full scale attack against the Jordanian forces in Jerusalem and the West Bank. Within a few days, the Israelis soundly defeated both the Egyptian and the Jordanian armies.

The Syrians in the meantime had done very little on their front other than some incidents of minor warfare against the Israelis. But considering the role of the Syrians in the deterioration to crisis and war, the Israelis were in no mood to allow the Syrians to escape scot-free after so many years of conflict. Exploiting the momentum of success, the Israelis opened the front against Syria and within a few more days defeated the Syrians and occupied the Golan Heights as well.

Within six days in June of 1967, the Israelis had inflicted a stunning defeat on the Arabs. As stunning as the results of the war were to the Arabs so they were to the Israelis, who had hardly expected such a quick and comprehensive victory.

UN Resolution 242

The international community, by and large, regarded the Israeli campaign as a war of self-defense and Israel was strongly supported by international opinion in June 1967. Since the war was seen as an act of self-defense, Resolution 242 which was passed by the United Nations Security Council in November 1967, and which set the groundwork for the Arab-Israeli peace process after the war, was most understanding of Israel's needs.

Israel was not required by the Security Council resolution to immediately or unconditionally withdraw its forces from the territories it had occupied. On the contrary, Israel was required to withdraw, but on condition that the Arab states made peace. The resolution begins with an emphasis on the "inadmissibility of the acquisition of territory by war." That is, Israel ought to withdraw, but that requirement was linked immediately to the "need to work for a just and lasting peace in which every State in the area," that is, Israel too, could "live in security." The resolution also affirmed that the fulfillment of the UN Charter principles required the establishment of a "just and lasting peace" in the Middle East which should include the application of both of the following principles:

> First was the withdrawal of Israeli armed forces "from territories occupied in the recent conflict." Note the absence of the definite article "the" from territories, not from <u>the</u> territories, therefore not from <u>all</u> the territories, leaving room for negotiations on border changes.
>
> Second was the "termination of all claims or states of belligerency, and respect for and acknowledgement of the sovereignty, territorial integrity

and political independence of every State in the area, and their right to live in peace, within secure and recognized boundaries free from threats or acts of force."[5]

The resolution took Israeli security considerations into account and it made the fulfillment of peace with Israel a condition for Israel's withdrawal from territories that were taken in the war. Thus was born the "land for peace" formula that governed the Arab-Israeli peace process for decades to come.

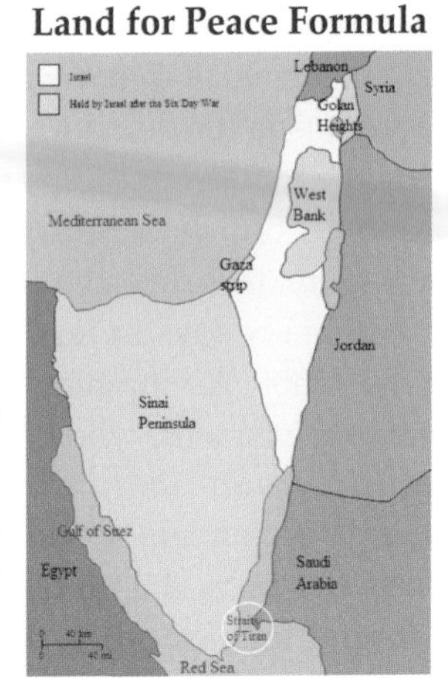

By User:Ling.Nut derivative work: Rafy (Six_Day_War_Terrritories.png) [CC-BY-SA-3.0 (http://creativecommons.org/licenses/by-sa/3.0)], via Wikimedia Commons

For the Palestinians, Resolution 242 was woefully inadequate. The resolution, passed in November 1967, was negotiated long before the Palestinians, through the PLO and the other Palestinian organizations, had made their mark on Middle Eastern politics. The resolution did not even mention the Palestinians. It was conceived as the basis for a negotiated agreement between Israel and the neighboring Arab states, and on the West Bank this meant an agreement between Israel and Jordan, and not the Palestinians. Ignored by the resolution, the Palestinians tended to regard it as insufficient and undesirable.

Israeli Euphoria

The war of 1967 had a profound psychological impact on the Israelis. The Israelis, who had entered the war with much trepidation and fear of possible defeat and destruction, were overcome after the war by the euphoria and hubris of their stunning victory. Some offered religious interpretations of heavenly deliverance of the Israelis from their enemies, which also facilitated the most significant conquest of the Jewish holy places in Jerusalem and in Judea and Samaria, that is, the West Bank, which was the territorial core of biblical Israel.

These new conquests had enormous historical and symbolic significance for Israel. While Israel was willing to think of parting with the territories it had taken from Syria and Egypt immediately after the war, it was not nearly as

5. Laura Zittrain Eisenberg and Neil Caplan, *Negotiating Arab-Israeli Peace; Patterns, Problems, Possibilities* (Indiana University Press, 2010), Appendix B: Documents Online, Document 19, UN Security Council Resolution 242, 22 November 1967.

Israeli soldiers celebrating at the Wailing Wall upon victory
http://www.jpost.com/Opinion/Op-Ed-Contributors/The-myths-of-1967-and-todays-realities

enthusiastic about withdrawing from the West Bank and Gaza, part and parcel of historical Eretz Israel. In the Israeli domestic debate, people were divided along new lines that did not even exist before 1967, that is, between those who believed in rational security arguments for drawing the country's borders, versus those who spoke in terms of religious belief and God-given rights.

Israelis digging trenches in preparation for the war
ארכיון שדה ורבורג [CC-BY-2.5 (http://creativecommons.org/licenses/by/2.5)], via Wikimedia Commons

Thus began a new contest of values within Israel, the domestic fight over Israel's soul. Was Israel to be governed by secular, humanist or religio-nationalist values? What was the struggle for Israel all about? Was it classical Zionism and Jewish self-determination, that is, a secular concept of Jewish nationalism? Or was it about the liberation of the historical homeland in the name of God and religious deliverance? As this internal Israeli debate continued to unfold for nearly half a century, Israeli governments successively "decided not to decide" on the ultimate fate of the West Bank and Gaza.

The West Bank or Judea and Samaria

By Ramiy (https://en.wikipedia.org/wiki/Yesha_Council#/media/File:Israel_judea_and_samaria_dist.png)

In the meantime, there was the beginning of settlement activity in the West Bank, some with government approval and some without. This too was an example of the indecision and the legal ambiguity that accompanied settlements in the West Bank. Often established illegally, in the end they were tolerated or supported by the various Israeli governments.

The Post-1967 Era — Some Critical Changes

The 1967 War had extensive, unprecedented regional effect. It deflated pan-Arabism as a force in the region. If the 1950s and the 1960s were the years of Abd al-Nasser's great charismatic, messianic leadership of the Arabs, pan-Arabism was crushed in 1967 and exposed as no more than an empty vessel.

If in the 1950s and the 1960s, the "revolutionaries," that is, the officer regimes and the republics, were arrayed in the domestic Arab debate against the so called "reactionaries," the monarchies and the pro-Western regimes, nothing was left of this dichotomy after 1967. The "revolutionaries" and the "reactionaries" had been defeated by Israel just as easily, and there was no more justification for the sharp, antagonistic distinctions between them.

Jordan, which had been in control of the West Bank since 1948, now lost the West Bank to Israel. The process whereby the Jordanians were "Jordanizing" the Palestinians now came to an abrupt end. The Jordanians, without the control of the West Bank, could no longer manipulate Palestinian politics as they had done before. With the West Bank under Israeli occupation, the Palestinians re-emerged in the post-1967 era as autonomous players, as they had never been since 1948.

The Israelis were governed to a large degree by a euphoric sense of invincibility, and this would take its toll on Israel a few years later, in the 1973 War that cost the Israelis dearly.

The 1967 War gave birth to Resolution 242 and it is important to note, first of all, that the Resolution called for Israel to withdraw from territories occupied, but only in exchange for peace. Secondly, the fact that Arab states like Egypt and Jordan, accepted Resolution 242, which included the requirement of making peace with Israel, was an important departure of these Arab states from their traditional attitude towards Israel. This was the very beginning of the willingness of countries like Egypt and Jordan to make their peace with Israel.

The Israelis were struck by indecision after 1967, except for the decision to unify Jerusalem as the capital of Israel, that is, to annex the Arab part of Jerusalem. As for the rest of the occupied territories, the decision was neither to annex, nor to withdraw. This was also the beginning of the domestic fight over Israel's soul, or over what Zionism was really all about? That debate is still raging in Israel, with a great deal of passion, almost 50 years after the war.

The Palestinian Struggle from Jordan

After the loss of the West Bank the Palestinians continued their armed struggle against Israel from Jordan, but now from the other side of the river on the East

Bank. After the June War the Jordanians were struggling to recover from their defeat and Hussein was reluctant to pick a fight with the armed Palestinian organizations. After all, if Hussein sought to represent the Palestinians in a negotiation with Israel over the West Bank, he could hardly go about it by fighting the Palestinians and their deployment in Jordan. But this deployment in Jordan gradually morphed into a kind of "state-within-a-state" and came to threaten the stability of the regime.

Immediately after the war, Fatah and similar organizations tried to take root in the West Bank and to conduct a guerrilla war against Israel from the occupied territories. But the Israeli security services were too efficient, and Fatah and the others were compelled to move out of the West Bank and take up new positions on the other side of the river. It was from the East Bank of Jordan that Fatah and other Palestinian organizations continued to wage their struggle against Israel and thereby also provoking Israeli retaliation.

A major operation was conducted by the Israelis in March 1968 on the village of Karameh in the southern Jordan Valley where Fatah had established a base of operations. The Karameh operation became a symbol in Palestinian historiography of the effective armed struggle of the Palestinians, which had ended in spectacular victory against Israel.

Jordanian Memorial for Karameh

https://upload.wikimedia.org/wikipedia/commons/f/f0/Memorial_to_Jordanian_soldiers_(Karameh,_Jordan).jpg

In the battle of Karameh there was a major confrontation between Israeli forces that had penetrated into Jordanian territory, and Jordanian forces and it was actually Jordanian armor and artillery that inflicted heavy losses on the Israeli forces that had crossed into Jordan.

But in the Palestinian narrative the Jordanians were completely left out. The Israeli difficulties in the battlefield, in an operation which ended with only limited success and many Israeli casualties, were described by the Palestinians as an Israeli defeat inflicted upon them by the Palestinian fighters.

Karameh was portrayed as a great Palestinian victory. Moreover, it was not only the victory of the Palestinian fighters, but the victory of their concept of popular armed struggle. The Palestinian popular armed struggle was poised to defeat Israel, in a way that the Arab regular armies could not. The Arab regular armies were defeated by Israel just a few months before, but the Palestinians were now able to achieve victory, just like the Algerians had against the French, or the Viet Cong against the United States in Vietnam.

The symbolism of Karameh, though militarily far less successful than portrayed by the Palestinians, paved the way for the volunteering of many, many thousands of young Palestinian men in Jordan to join the Palestinian fighting organizations. Karameh also paved the way for the takeover of the PLO by the Palestinian fighting organizations. During 1968–1969, the takeover of the PLO by Fatah and the other Palestinian fighting organizations was completed and the PLO was converted from a bureaucratic organization as it had been under Shuqayri into an umbrella organization of Palestinian fighting organizations. Since Fatah was the largest organization within the PLO, Yasser Arafat, the leader of Fatah, now also became the chairman of the PLO.

Yasser Arafat

By Tibor Végh (Arafat.jpg) [CC-BY-3.0 (http://creativecommons.org/licenses/by/3.0)], via Wikimedia Commons

After Karameh the Israelis continued to fight against the Palestinian presence in the Jordan Valley, and the Palestinian forces were gradually forced by Israeli heavy fire out of the valley further away from the frontier with Israel and deeper into Jordanian territory. The Palestinian forces began to take over Palestinian refugee camps in the interior and especially in the main cities of Jordan, particularly in Amman. They proceeded to erode the sovereignty of the Jordanian state by the creation of entire territories within Jordan, completely controlled by the Palestinian organizations, that were out of bounds to the Jordanian authorities, and to which even King Hussein was not admitted.

The Rogers Initiative, July 1970

https://en.wikipedia.org/wiki/William_P._Rogers

In the summer of 1970 the United States launched a peace initiative between Israel and the Arab states based on Resolution 242. This was known as the Rogers Initiative, named after the US Secretary of State at the time. A US initiative based on Resolution 242 meant an Israeli-Jordanian negotiation over the future of the West Bank and a parallel negotiation between Egypt and Israel over the Sinai Peninsula.

"Black September" 1970 and its Aftermath

For the Palestinian organizations the initiative posed a threat of marginalization and exclusion and Jordan had to be prevented from joining this US led process. It was, therefore, a decision of the Palestinians at this time to challenge the Jordanian regime by force to prevent it from entering a peace process that might resolve the Palestinian question in a manner ideologically unacceptable to them.

Jordan, however, by the summer of 1970, enjoyed unquestionable military superiority. But the Palestinians underestimated the Jordanians, and overestimated the measure of popular support for themselves, including within the ranks of the Jordanian army. They also expected meaningful Arab support from the Iraqi forces that were stationed in Jordan at the time, and help from Syria too.

The inevitable clash came in September 1970 between the Jordanian and Palestinian forces, in what became known by the Palestinians as "Black September," the defeat of their fighting organizations at the hands of the Jordanian military. While the Iraqis stood aside, the Syrians invaded Jordanian territory in order to help the Palestinians in their fight against the Jordanians.

The Jordanians, facing the internal struggle with the Palestinians buttressed by the external support coming from Syria, appealed to the United States for assistance. Turning to the United States for assistance in these circumstances really meant a Jordanian indirect approach to Israel. Israel did indeed take action to assist the Jordanians in defeating the Syrians first, and then the Palestinians. The Israelis mobilized large reserve forces very publicly and Israeli aircraft overflew the Syrian forces that had invaded Jordanian territory, thereby threatening to intervene themselves. The Syrians consequently refrained from using their air power in the battle against Jordan and limited the extent of their incursion. The Jordanians held off the Syrians and in the end delivered a crushing defeat to the Palestinian forces in Jordan.

For Jordan "Black September" meant the securing of the state and the regime. Jordan was now stable and secure with no Palestinian "state-within-a-state." For the PLO, on the other hand, this was a defeat of historical proportions. As Yezid Sayigh has written, it "represented the defeat of the strategy of people's war [...], and posed a fundamental challenge to their [the Palestinians'] professed aims, political programs and organizational structure."[6] The loss of the Jordanian base of operations to fight against Israel meant that the armed struggle, as the sole means for the liberation of Palestine, as the PLO had originally believed, was no longer a viable strategy, if it had ever been one.

---

6. Yezid Sayigh, *Armed Struggle and the Search for State: The Palestinian National Movement, 1949-1993* (Oxford: Clarendon Press, 1997), p. 280.

Palestinian Fighters in Lebanon

http://gotc-se.org/images/SOUTH_OF_LEBANON_January_Report_Updated%5B1%5D_html_m5a38e5c8.jpg

The PLO was now severely restricted in its room for maneuver. Expelled from Jordan, they expanded their base in Lebanon. But Lebanon was a poor second best alternative. It was nowhere near as effective as the Jordanian base for the waging of the struggle against Israel. Lebanon was not, and would never be, the area of decision of the Palestinian question. Jordan and the West Bank were the area of decision of the Palestinian question as that is where the great majority of the Palestinian people were located.

Lebanon was home to but a small minority of the Palestinian people and had no direct contact with the West Bank. Lebanon, therefore, was a distant second best alternative for an autonomous base of operations, but it was the last they had.

By mid-1973 the PLO had established another "state-within-a-state" in Lebanon which they used for their operations against Israel. In October of that year, as the PLO continued to build up its forces in Lebanon, Israel and the Arabs went to war again. Following the October War of 1973 (for details see Chapter Eight) the PLO had to take its 1970 defeat in Jordan and the post-1973 regional equation into account in the reformulation of its overall strategy vis-á-vis Israel.

The October War led to a resumption of the Middle East peace process on the basis of Resolution 242. The PLO now faced the serious danger of a peace process between Israel and its neighbors on the basis of Resolution 242 that would exclude the PLO and the Palestinians. After their defeat in Jordan and fully recognizing that Israel could not be defeated by an independent Palestinian war of liberation, the Palestinians were forced to adopt a new strategy. In the summer of 1974, the PLO published what was called the "Strategy of Phases."

The "Strategy of Phases" spoke of the PLO's willingness to use all means of struggle against Israel and "all means" meant not only military means, but diplomatic means as well. It also meant that the PLO was not about to liberate all of Palestine in one fell swoop. That, they also realized, was not possible. Liberation would be in phases and the PLO would establish a Palestinian authority in any territory that Israel withdrew from. The intention was to legitimize the PLO as a negotiating partner in the peace process. Doing so would enable the PLO to retrieve any Palestinian territories that Israel would withdraw from and thereby prevent the Jordanians from retrieving the West Bank, which would mean the end of the Palestinian struggle, as the PLO defined it. The "Strategy of Phases," however, would require a significant change in the regional balance of power. After all, Israel would not willingly cooperate in its dismantlement in stages.

The "Strategy of Phases" gave rise to a very active debate within the PLO between the radicals and the more moderate factions. The fear of the radicals was that if the balance of power would not change sufficiently, the "Strategy of Phases" would eventually lock the PLO into an agreement with Israel that would not bring about the complete liberation of Palestine.

The historical evolution proved the radicals to be right. The balance of power did not change sufficiently for the implementation of the "Strategy of Phases" and, in later years, the PLO was forced to come to terms with Israel (see below in Chapter Eight). But having accepted the "Strategy of Phases," and having agreed in principle to also use diplomatic means in the struggle with Israel, the PLO was finally recognized by the Arab League, at its Summit meeting in Rabat in October 1974, as the "sole legitimate representative of the Palestinian people." If nothing else, as the "sole legitimate representative of the Palestinian people," the PLO had succeeded, at least in theory, in finally disqualifying Jordan as a legitimate negotiator on behalf of the Palestinians.

The War of Attrition 1968–1970

In the aftermath of the June War of 1967, a War of Attrition was fought between Israel and the Egyptians across the Suez Canal for two years, from 1968 until 1970, as artillery barrages raged across the canal-zone, with the Egyptians and the Israelis trading blows on a regular basis. In these artillery exchanges the Israelis were at a distinct disadvantage. The Egyptians had far more artillery pieces than the Israelis, and very soon the Israelis began to resort to their superior air power to compensate for their disadvantage on the ground. This led to Israeli air-strikes deep inside Egyptian territory in the Nile Valley and on targets throughout the Egyptian interior. The deep penetration raids by Israel led eventually to direct Soviet intervention in the defense of Egypt, and even to dogfights between Israeli and Russian pilots in the skies of Egypt.

This War of Attrition had a profound impact on Egypt and the Egyptian people. This was the first time ever that the war with Israel was really felt by the Egyptian people on their home front. This was not a war fought in the distant deserts of the Sinai Peninsula in 1956 and 1967 or the Negev in Israel of 1948. The ravages of war were brought very immediately to the recognition of the Egyptian people.

In Egypt there were the first inklings of criticism of Egypt's role in the war with Israel. Some began to ask for how much longer should Egypt be the "blood bank" of the Arabs. Why should Egypt alone be paying this heavy price for the struggle of the Arabs against Israel? With the acceptance of the Rogers Initiative, in the summer of 1970, the Egyptians and the Israelis agreed to a cease-fire that put an end to the War of Attrition, as the parties also agreed to start negotiations for a peaceful settlement, on the basis of Resolution 242.

This apparent willingness of the parties to negotiate did not bring about any agreement. The Egyptians suggested a partial settlement between Israel and Egypt in 1971, whereby Israel would withdraw from the Suez Canal and from parts of the Sinai Peninsula, as part of a process that would eventually lead to peace between Israel and Egypt, based on Israel's complete withdrawal from all of the Sinai Peninsula, back to the 1967 boundaries.

The Egyptian initiative was not well received in Israel. There was serious discussion within the Israeli government on the pros and cons of the Egyptian initiative, but the Israelis were very reluctant to commit themselves to complete withdrawal and were not quite sure what kind of peace was on offer from Anwar Sadat, the new president of Egypt after the death of Abd al-Nasser in September 1970.

Anwar Sadat
President of Egypt
1970–1981

By The Central Intelligence Agency (Egyptian President Anwar Sadat) [Public domain], via Wikimedia Commons

Sadat spoke of 1971 as his year of decision; that is, if he could not achieve a settlement with Israel by peace, Egypt would turn towards the option of war. But after 1971 passed uneventfully, the Israelis, in their rather arrogant and euphoric post-1967 mood, did not take the Egyptian threat of war very seriously.

In July 1972, Sadat expelled the Soviet advisers from Egypt. This was actually an effort by the Egyptians to pave the way for war with Israel. Sadat believed that the Soviet presence in Egypt may constrain Egypt's freedom of decision, but the Israelis, and the Americans too, understood the expulsion of the Soviet advisers from Egypt in quite the opposite fashion. They believed that the removal of the Soviet advisers, many of whom were advisers for Egypt's air defenses, actually reduced the chances of Egypt going to war.

In early 1973, Egypt made movements towards an opening of relations with the United States and the expanding of diplomatic contacts with the Americans, further reinforcing the belief that Egypt's direction was not towards war. For the Egyptians, however, the indecision of no war and no peace was insufferable and there was ever-mounting pressure in Egypt to take action to change the status quo.

During 1973, there was joint Egyptian-Syrian planning for war against Israel. Egypt and Syria had come to the conclusion that they could cooperate in going to war with Israel, even though they had very divergent political objectives. Egypt wanted to initiate war with Israel in order to shake up the regional situation to allow for the unfreezing of the diplomatic front and to have the war reopen an opportunity for meaningful negotiations with Israel.

The Syrians, on the other hand, had no mind for engineering diplomatic breakthroughs. They sought to retrieve their territory from Israel by war, and if successful, maybe even to penetrate Israeli territory. It was not diplomacy that they preferred. In the planning of Egypt and Syria for war against Israel the Jordanians were not involved. The Jordanians were not trusted by the Egyptians and the Syrians. It was feared that if they knew about the war plans, they might leak them to the Americans or even to the Israelis. When war broke out in October 1973, Jordan decided to stay out and did not participate, except indirectly, by sending forces to help the Syrians face the Israelis on the Golan.

The October War of 1973, between Israel, Egypt and Syria, would radically change the situation that had existed between Israel and the Arabs since the War of 1967.

Key Sources and Suggested Further Reading

- Gorenberg, Gershom, *The Accidental Empire: Israel and the Birth of the Settlements, 1967-1977* (New York: Times Books, 2006).
- Heikal, Mohamed, *The Road to Ramadan* (New York: Ballantine, 1975).
- Khalidi, Rashid, *The Iron Cage: The Story of the Palestinian Struggle for Statehood* (Boston: Beacon Press, 2006).
- Morris, Benny, *Righteous Victims: A History of the Zionist-Arab Conflict, 1881-1999* (New York: Knopf, 1999).
- Mutawi, Samir, *Jordan in the 1967 War* (Cambridge University Press, 1987).
- Oren, Michael, *Six Days of War: June 1967 and the Making of the Modern Middle East* (Oxford University Press, 2002).
- Rabinovich, Itamar, *Waging Peace: Israel and the Arabs, 1948-2003* (Princeton University Press, 2004).
- Sayigh, Yezid, *Armed Struggle and the Search for State: The Palestinian National Movement, 1949-1993* (Oxford: Clarendon Press, 1997).
- Sela, Avraham, *The Decline of the Arab-Israeli Conflict: Middle East Politics and the Quest for Regional Order* (Albany: State University of New York Press, 1998).
- Shlaim, Avi, *The Iron Wall: Israel and the Arab World* (New York: Norton, 2000).
- Susser, Asher, *Israel, Jordan and Palestine: The Two-State Imperative* (Waltham, MA: Brandeis University Press, 2012).

Chapter Eight

Escalation and De-Escalation of the Arab-Israeli Conflict (II)

The October Surprise

On 6 October 1973, Egypt and Syria launched a surprise attack on Israel. In the October War, known also as the Yom Kippur War because of its outbreak on the holiest of holy days on the Jewish calendar, Syria and Egypt caught Israel completely unprepared. The Israelis operated under the assumption, the so-called "preconception," that the Arab states would not attack Israel, unless they had an answer to Israel's supremacy in air power. The belief was that the Arabs could not win a war against Israel in such circumstances, and therefore, they would not launch a war that they were bound to lose.

Above and beyond this "preconception," the Israelis were also deluded by the deliberately crafted deception that was conducted by Egypt and Syria in misleading Israel into the comfortable belief that war was not in the offing. Preparations for war were disguised as maneuvers time and again, and the Israelis were lulled into a sense of security that the situation of no war and no peace would continue.

When the Israelis discovered at the very last moment that war was about to begin within a matter of hours, they decided not to preempt, as they might have done in previous years. The Israeli decision not to preempt was motivated by a number of different calculations. One was that Israel was bound to be condemned internationally as the aggressor if it were to attack the Egyptians and the Syrians, seemingly without any obvious reason. Another was the confidence and the arrogance of the post-1967 era that allowed the Israelis to believe that they could easily

Why Israel Did Not Preempt:

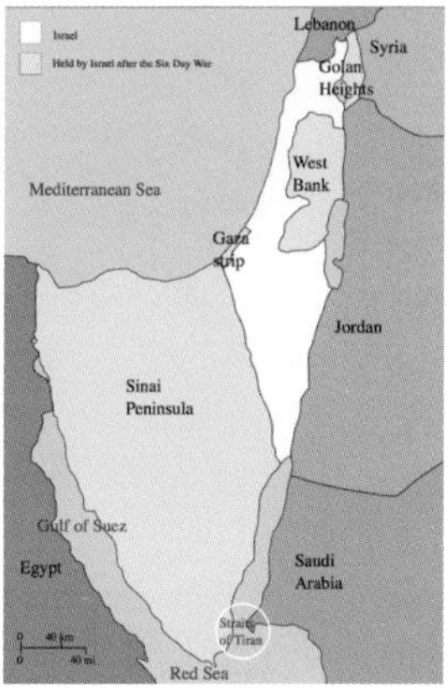

- **international condemnation**
- **the self-confidence**
- **the buffer of Sinai**

By User:Ling.Nut derivative work: Rafy (Six_Day_War_Terrritories.png) [CC-BY-SA-3.0 (http://creativecommons.org/licenses/by-sa/3.0)], via Wikimedia Commons

manage and repel any Arab attack. It would not take much to stop the Syrians in their tracks or to push the Egyptians back over the Suez Canal if they dared to cross. Yet another explanation was that preemption which was essential when Israel was small and vulnerable in its pre-1967 borders was no longer necessary. The wide buffer of the Sinai Peninsula, between the Suez Canal and Israel's major cities, made Israel much safer, and it could take the risk of not pre-empting.

Egyptian Army Crossing the Suez Canal

http://chronikler.com/wp-content/uploads/2013/10/Badr-6oct-war.jpg

In the first few days of the war the Arabs enjoyed unprecedented military success. On both the Egyptian and Syrian fronts, overwhelming Arab forces smashed through the Israeli lines that were only sparsely defended. On the Egyptian front, two entire Egyptian armies, the Second Army on the northern section of the Suez Canal, and the Third Army on the southern section, crossed the canal, broke through the Israeli positions and established themselves on the Israeli side of the Suez Canal. On the Syrian front, in the northern sector of the Golan, the Israelis stood fast, but very quickly, the Syrians broke through the Israeli lines in the southern sector and almost reached the Israeli Sea of Galilee.

The Golan Heights Campaign

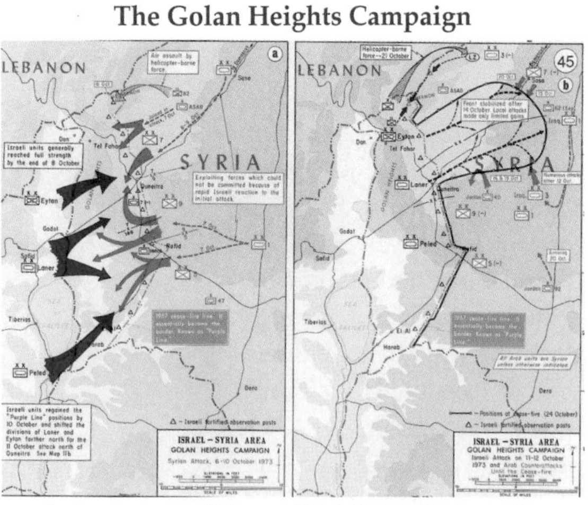

By Department of History, U.S. Military Academy. See Department Maps page. (Department of History, U.S. Military Academy) [Public domain], via Wikimedia Commons

The Egyptians had limited objectives. They sought to create a new political situation as a result of a successful military operation that would force Israel back to the negotiating table to talk seriously about withdrawal from Sinai. The Syrians, however, did not have diplomacy in mind, and sought to recover the Golan Heights and maybe even to break into Israeli territory in the Galilee by force. The Syrians and the Egyptians had divergent objectives and the Egyptians were actually cooperating with the Syrians to achieve an objective that the Syrians did not share.

Israeli Tanks Crossing the Suez Canal

By Israel Defense Forces from Israel (Israeli Tanks Cross the Suez Canal) [CC-BY-SA-2.0 (http://creativecommons.org/licenses/by-sa/2.0)], via Wikimedia Commons

Even though the Israelis were caught completely by surprise, it did not take very long for them to turn the tables in the war. First on the Syrian front, where after a few days they began to push the Syrians out of the Golan Heights completely, and in the northern sector of the Golan, to punch their way deeply into Syrian territory to within just 40 kilometers from Damascus.

On the Egyptian front, after about ten days of intensive fighting, the Israelis were in a position to cross the canal onto the Egyptian side, to successfully encircle the Egyptian Third Army, and to advance to within just 101 kilometers from Cairo. When it appeared as if the Israelis were about to establish yet another victory, the superpowers, the US and the Soviet Union, intervened jointly to bring about a cease fire. In accordance with UN Security Council Resolution 338 of 22 October 1973, the war was brought to an end. Fighting continued for another day or two, but the war was essentially over. Israel had suffered massive losses. Some 2600 men were killed and hundreds of Israeli soldiers were taken prisoner by the Syrians and the Egyptians. The Israeli people were shocked out of the euphoric mood they had enjoyed since 1967, which was rapidly replaced by a profound sense of loss and despair.

Encircling of the Egyptian 3rd Army

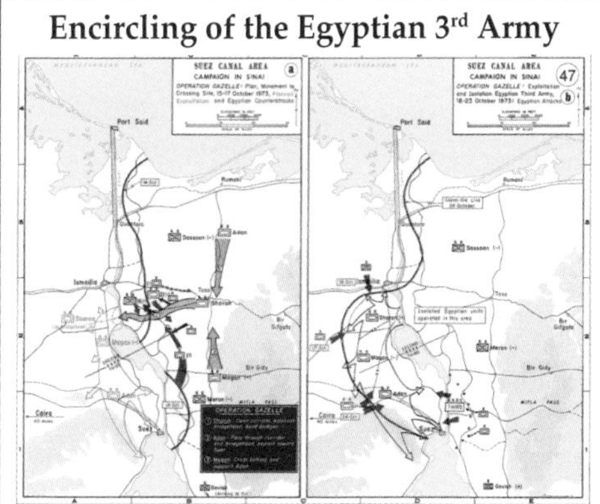

http://commons.wikimedia.org/wiki/File:1973_sinai_war_maps2.jpg

A new regional equilibrium was established after the October War. Israel, Egypt and Syria were now much more acutely aware of their respective limitations and were, therefore, willing to engage in agreements that would make war between them a lot less likely.

Agreements for Separation of Forces

The first agreement after the war was for the separation of forces in the Canal Zone that was signed between Israel and Egypt in January 1974. Israel withdrew its forces from the Egyptian side of the canal, allowing a certain limited presence of Egyptian forces on the Israeli side of the canal, with a buffer zone of separation between the forces of the two sides. The parties also exchanged prisoners and Egypt agreed to work towards the reopening of the Suez Canal and the creation of a much more peaceful reality between Egypt and Israel in the Suez Canal Zone, making the resumption of war far less likely.

Negotiations between Israel and Syria were considerably more difficult. But they too ended with a separation of forces agreement between Syria and Israel in May 1974. The Israelis withdrew from the territory they had taken from Syria in the recent war and moved back more or less to the lines that had existed after the war of June 1967, allowing the Syrians a minor symbolic gain which made little difference on the ground. As with Egypt, the agreement included a buffer zone between the parties and an exchange of prisoners. Since May 1974, that is, for more than forty years, the separation of forces agreement between Israel and Syria has remained in force governing the relations between the two countries.

There was no separation of forces on the Jordanian front. The Jordanians did not fight along their front, and only sent a limited force to fight on the Syrian front. There was ostensibly no need for a separation of forces agreement as nothing had changed on this front. But the Jordanians sought a separation of forces with Israel, even though there had been no war between them. The Jordanians had political objectives and sought a way to induce Israel to withdraw from the Jordan Valley, to create a situation that would suggest that Israel was beginning to withdraw from the West Bank as part of a broader agreement that would eventually be signed with Jordan. If Israel and

***Jordan Valley*: From the Sea of Galilee in the North to the Dead Sea in the South**

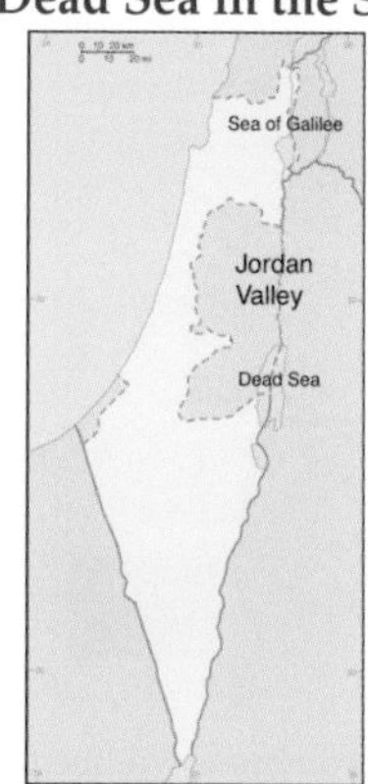

By someone from CIA, cleaned by myself [Public domain], via Wikimedia Commons

Jordan could come to a separation of forces agreement, the Jordanians surmised, this could isolate the PLO and make Arab recognition of the PLO much less likely, as it would give the impression that Israel was about to give back the West Bank to Jordan.

But such an agreement did not come to fruition. The Israelis regarded the Jordan Valley as an absolutely essential area for their security, and the Israeli government was unwilling to begin a process that would lead to Israel's withdrawal from the West Bank. There was no separation of forces between Israel and Jordan and the way was paved, by that non-agreement, for the recognition of the PLO by the Arab states as the "sole legitimate representative of the Palestinian people" and for Jordan's loss. (See also above, Chapter Seven)

In September 1975 Israel and Egypt came to yet another agreement which included further withdrawal by Israel from territories in Sinai, in exchange for what was essentially a non-belligerency agreement between the two countries. The agreement included a large UN-patrolled buffer zone some 30–40 kilometers wide between limited forces of the parties. The Egyptians, by signing this agreement with Israel, were taking a much more significant step towards abandoning the conflict with Israel entirely and the accord, therefore, was an important stepping stone towards what eventually became the Israeli-Egyptian peace treaty.

The Egyptian-Israeli Peace Treaty

The agreements for the separation of forces between Israel and Egypt and between Israel and Syria were achieved through the "step by step" diplomacy of US Secretary of State Henry Kissinger. In early 1977, a new administration came into office in the United States, and Jimmy Carter became President. The Carter administration had a different approach to the idea of Arab-Israeli peace. Instead of the "step by step" diplomacy of Kissinger, which was based on the view that a comprehensive settlement was not yet possible, the Carter administration sought to achieve a comprehensive settlement of the Arab-Israeli conflict.

US President Jimmy Carter (in office 1977–1981)

By Department of Defense. Department of the Navy. Naval Photographic Center [Public domain], via Wikimedia Commons

The Americans sought to reconvene the Geneva Conference which had been convened once after the October War, in December of 1973. For the Americans the Geneva Conference was a suitable forum where the Arab states and the Soviet Union would participate in the achievement of a comprehensive settlement of the Arab-Israeli conflict. Israel, however, had serious reservations about the international conference and a comprehensive settlement. The Israelis believed that an international conference, where all the Arab states involved in the conflict, together with the Soviet Union and possibly the PLO too, would be negotiating with Israel simultaneously would make the achievement of an agreement with the Arabs much more difficult. With this understanding, Israel was on a collision course with the Carter administration.

Henry Kissinger
US Secretary of State (1973–1977)

Kissinger with Egyptian President Sadat
By United States Information Agency [Public domain], via Wikimedia Commons

David Hume Kennerly [Public domain], via Wikimedia Commons

But it was not only Israel that differed with Carter on the attitude towards a comprehensive settlement. This was also true of President Anwar Sadat of Egypt. Sadat, like the Israelis, was not interested in Soviet participation, did not like the idea of an international conference, and did not want to negotiate with Israel in tandem with the other Arab states. Strangely enough, the US position on comprehensive peace and the Soviet role was closer to the more radical position of the Syrians than it was to the positions of the Israelis and the Egyptians. The Syrians sought an international conference and a joint Arab delegation that would negotiate with Israel, not so much to make peace with Israel, but to block Egypt from making a separate agreement, which the Syrians correctly believed was Egypt's real objective.

The PLO also supported the idea of an international conference, not so much to negotiate a peace agreement with Israel, but to bolster its position as the sole representative of the Palestinians and to block the Jordanians from making an agreement with Israel over the West Bank at the PLO's expense.

In Israel, there were major and unexpected political changes shortly after Carter entered the White House. In May 1977, the Israeli political right led by Menachem Begin and the Likud party won the general elections in Israel for the first time ever. Begin sought a deal with Egypt. As a believer in greater Eretz Israel, that is, in all of historical Palestine, as part of the Jewish political patrimony, Begin wanted a separate deal with Egypt, which would not require a withdrawal from the West Bank nor the need to address other related issues that he did not want to tackle.

May 1977 Israeli Legislative Elections: Likud Victory under Menachem Begin

By USAF personnel (http://www.dodmedia.osd.mil/) [Public domain], via Wikimedia Commons

President Sadat of Egypt and Peace with Israel

http://commons.wikimedia.org/wiki/File:Sadat_Camp_David.jpg

A certain Israeli-Egyptian common interest existed. Both Israel and Egypt were impatient with the efforts to reconvene an international conference that neither of them really wanted as the forum for negotiations. Sadat was keen on an initiative of his own that would enable Egypt to finally achieve the real objective of the October War, that is, a process in which Egypt would regain all the territory it had lost to Israel in 1967. Sadat's sense of urgency became even more acute as the socio-economic situation in Egypt deteriorated further in early 1977. There were food riots in Egypt as a result of the cancellation of subsidies on basic foodstuffs, which made it all the more important for Egypt to look for an exit from the costly Arab-Israeli conflict.

In August 1977 Prime Minister Begin met with Romanian President Nicolae Ceausescu and told him of his desire to make peace with Egypt. Ceausescu passed the message on to Sadat, but the main secret channel between Israel and Egypt was King Hasan of Morocco. In mid-September Moshe Dayan, the

Foreign Minister in Menachem Begin's cabinet, and Hasan Tohamy, an Egyptian Deputy Prime Minister, held secret talks in Morocco on a possible peace agreement between the two countries.

Shortly thereafter, on 1 October, US Secretary of State Cyrus Vance and his Soviet counterpart, Andrei Gromyko, issued a joint statement on the convening of an international conference to achieve Arab-Israeli peace. The joint statement caught Israel and Egypt off guard and angered both Sadat and Begin, being in contrast to what both the Israelis and the Egyptians really wanted. The US, on the other hand, was convinced that without Soviet participation and without Syrian and PLO involvement, there could be no comprehensive agreement. Egypt and Israel, however, were equally convinced that with Soviet, Syrian and PLO participation there would be no deal with anyone at all.

Cyrus Vance – Andrei Gromyko
Joint Statement on an international conference October 1977

By White House Staff Photographer [Public domain], via Wikimedia Commons

The time had come for a bold new departure. It was against this background that Sadat came to the extraordinary conclusion that he should take the brave and unprecedented decision to make a visit to Jerusalem and speak to the Israelis directly, in their own parliament. Thus, Sadat arrived in Jerusalem in November 1977 on his historic groundbreaking visit to Israel, recognizing Israel, and making this extraordinary gesture of goodwill and peace with the Jewish State.

But when Sadat appeared before the Israeli parliament, in the Knesset in Jerusalem, he made it clear that he had not come to Israel for a separate deal. There had to be an agreement not only between Israel and the Egyptians, based on complete Israeli withdrawal from the Sinai Peninsula, but Israel also had to make concessions to the Palestinians. It was important for Sadat, though driven by Egyptian interests, not to appear to be abandoning the Palestinians. Sadat, therefore, also demanded an independent Palestinian state; a complete Israeli withdrawal from the West Bank and Gaza; and an Israeli agreement to divide Jerusalem into two: the Arab part, as the capital of the Palestinian state, and the Jewish part, as the capital of Israel. In exchange for his dramatic recognition of Israel, Sadat expected similarly dramatic concessions from the Israeli side. But that is not exactly what happened.

The Israeli cabinet was divided. Prime Minister Begin was more reluctant to agree to the complete withdrawal of Israel from the Sinai Peninsula than were the Foreign and Defense Ministers, Moshe Dayan and Ezer Weizmann. Begin's hesitation and concern for Israel's long term security and his reluctance to commit to complete withdrawal almost scuttled the initiative.

Sadat's Visit to Israel, November 1977

http://42796r1ctbz645bo223zkcdl.wpengine.netdna-cdn.com/wp-content/uploads/2011/11/sadat.jpg

The fear of possibly missing this historic opportunity induced President Jimmy Carter to convene a conference in September 1978 of Israel, Egypt and the United States to bring about a final agreement and avert the failure of the Sadat initiative to Israel. The US role in achieving agreement between Israel and the Egyptians was critical. The parties could accept American ideas more readily than they could accept ideas from each other. Israel finally agreed to withdraw fully from the Sinai Peninsula, including from the settlements it had established, and from the airfields it had built there as well. The United States agreed to rebuild the airfields that Israel had abandoned in Egypt in Israeli territory, with considerable US financial and technical assistance. The United States also promised an aid package to Egypt. Egypt in turn agreed to supply Israel with oil and the final treaty was signed in March 1979, establishing full peaceful relations between Egypt and Israel.

The agreement between Israel and Egypt that was achieved at Camp David did not only relate to Egyptian-Israeli relations. There was also a Palestinian section dealing with the creation of autonomy for the people of the West Bank and Gaza. It is important to note that there was no binding linkage between the implementation of the Palestinian section

The Camp David Accords

https://upload.wikimedia.org/wikipedia/commons/a/a0/Camp_David,_Menachem_Begin,_Anwar_Sadat,_1978.jpg

and the implementation of the Israeli-Egyptian section. The failure to achieve agreement on the implementation on the Palestinian section, therefore, did not automatically lead to a breakdown on the Israeli-Egyptian front.

The autonomy talks went nowhere, mainly because there were no Palestinians who were willing to take part in them. Autonomy in the West Bank and Gaza was insufficient for the PLO or for any of the Palestinians who resided in the West Bank and Gaza itself. Despite the fact that the autonomy talks did not take off, the treaty between Israel and Egypt held. Begin had essentially succeeded in trading Sinai for the maintenance of Israeli control over all of Eretz Israel.

Sadat and Begin

By Leffler, Warren K., photographer. Work for hire made for U.S. News and World Report [Public domain], via Wikimedia Commons

Peace with Egypt had great historical meaning. It dramatically altered the regional balance of power in Israel's favor. Egypt had now finally departed from the Arab order of battle. The Arab states were no longer capable of waging war against Israel. Without Egypt, neither Syria nor any other Arab state or group of states could go to war with Israel. In fact, since the October War of 1973, Israel has not fought any further wars with any of the Arab states, although the active conflict with the Palestinians continued.

The PLO and the 1982 Israeli Invasion of Lebanon

In June 1982 Israel invaded Lebanon in order to put an end to the PLO's military presence there. For the PLO their Lebanese haven was an essential asset to be preserved at all costs. It had no practical substitute from where to wage its confrontation with Israel. The PLO in Lebanon began to build a much more significant military force and it was against this background that Israel decided to go to war against the PLO. The Israeli objective was to expel the PLO from Lebanon and to install Bashir al-Jumayyil, the leader of the Maronite Christian Phalange militia and political party, as the president of Lebanon, and thereby to re-establish Maronite Christian supremacy in the country.

The domestic Lebanese part of the Israeli plan ended in failure (as already noted in Chapter Five). But Israel did succeed in evicting the PLO forces from Lebanon. This PLO loss had great historical significance. Losing the Lebanese haven meant that the PLO had lost much of its political independence. It could not wage the armed struggle effectively against Israel from distant Arab states that had no border with Israel.

The Israeli Objective

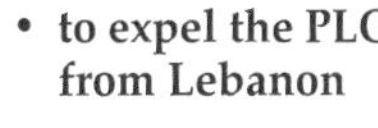

- **to expel the PLO from Lebanon**

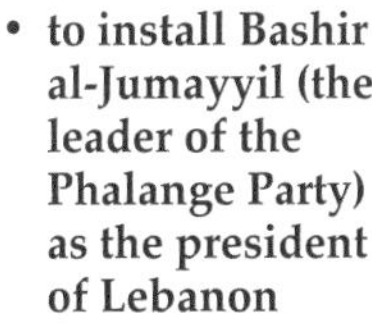

- **to install Bashir al-Jumayyil (the leader of the Phalange Party) as the president of Lebanon**

Bashir al-Jumayyil

https://en.wikipedia.org/wiki/Bachir_Gemayel#/media/File:Bachir_While_Giving_A_Speech.jpg

Moreover, the center of gravity of Palestinian politics after the PLO's defeat in Lebanon began to shift from the Palestinian diaspora, that is, outside of Palestine, into the West Bank and Gaza. The West Bank and Gaza henceforth became the active core of the Palestinian political endeavor.

The Reagan Initiative, September 1982

(in office 1981–1989)

- **A plan for Palestinian autonomy linked to Jordan**
- **Opposed to Palestinian state and to Israeli control or annexation**

http://listproducer.com/2014/02/ronald-reagan-was-a-list-maker/

Immediately after the PLO's defeat in Lebanon, the United States under President Reagan, offered an initiative of its own in September 1982, for Palestinian autonomy in the West Bank and Gaza, linked in a confederation with Jordan. The American plan was equally opposed to an independent Palestinian state and to Israeli control or annexation of the West Bank and Gaza. But Israel was not interested in Palestinian or Jordanian control of any kind in the West Bank and Gaza. Israel's idea of forcing the PLO out of Lebanon in 1982 was designed to give Israel a free hand in the West Bank and Gaza, and not to pave the way for a negotiation with Jordan and the Palestinians to concede these territories.

The PLO and Jordan, in the aftermath of the Reagan Initiative of 1982, engaged in a negotiation of their own to see if they could come to a common stand in reference to the US plan and to perhaps involve themselves jointly in a negotiation with Israel. But the PLO and Jordan failed to come to an agreement on the Reagan plan.

The mid-1980s were a twilight zone for the PLO. These were years of regional and international decline. The PLO was losing ground, having lost its autonomous base of operations in Lebanon, and as the focus of Palestinian political developments shifted inwards, into the West Bank and Gaza.

The First Palestinian Intifada

Palestinian politics were now going through a critical period of change. This was the culmination of a process that had actually begun in September 1970, when the PLO lost its base in Jordan. Having lost the base in Jordan, the conduct of the armed struggle became considerably more difficult. The loss of the autonomous base of operations in Lebanon contributed further to the PLO's regional decline. In the meantime the West Bank and Gaza were influenced by a combustible combination of economic difficulties, political stagnation and the strengthening of the Israeli hold. Opposition to Israel was intensifying amongst the younger generation that was agitating for change in the West Bank and Gaza.

The new younger generation of Palestinians had two different political representations, one was secular nationalist, supportive of the PLO generally speaking, and the other was the ever increasing strength of the Islamists in the Palestinian national movement.

The Palestinian Intifada

By Sven Nackstrand, Getty Images Israel

In December 1987, the people in the West Bank and Gaza spontaneously rose in a civilian uprising against the Israeli occupation. The civilian uprising had great political impact, far exceeding the effect and political influence of the armed struggle that the PLO had waged against Israel for decades. The armed struggle had a certain built-in weakness. While it put the Palestinian issue high up on the international agenda, it was also seen by many important players in the international community as terrorism and, therefore, illegitimate. Conversely, the Palestinian civilian uprising in the West Bank and Gaza was unarmed and it was the Israelis, the armed occupiers, who were on the defensive, facing the censure and de-legitimization of the international community.

It became ever more difficult for Israel to maintain its control over the West Bank and Gaza. Politically, militarily, diplomatically, it was becoming a much more costly enterprise for Israel as a result of the Palestinian uprising in the West Bank and Gaza. The uprising, known by its Arabic term, *Intifada,* also created new political realities for the Palestinians. If in previous years, the people in the West Bank and Gaza had been the passive bystanders to the conflict that was waged by the fighters of the PLO, who were spilling their blood for the Palestinians in the West Bank and Gaza, the *Intifada* put the shoe very much on the other foot. It was now the Palestinians in the West Bank and Gaza who were leading the struggle against Israel and it was the PLO fighters in the diaspora who became the passive bystanders in the struggle waged by the people inside the occupied territories. For the PLO to maintain its leadership position, it had to change its political priorities. The PLO had to make new decisions that would transform the great effort of the uprising in the West Bank and Gaza into meaningful political gain.

The uprising was not against the PLO, but actually in support of it. Nevertheless, the PLO now needed to listen to the voices coming from inside the West Bank and Gaza, especially from those who were its active supporters. The people in the West Bank and Gaza wanted a partnership with the PLO leadership outside. They did not wish to replace the PLO by any means. They recognized the legitimacy and the leadership of the PLO, but they wanted a share of equals in the decision-making process. This was a civil society that had developed under the Israeli occupation with an active and relatively free press, with a series of universities, and a long string of NGOs that gave civil society in the West Bank and Gaza a sense of real political power and influence.

In November 1988, the Palestine National Council (PNC), the quasi parliamentary body of the PLO, convened to make new decisions. With the *Intifada* in mind, and pressure for change coming from within the West Bank and Gaza, the PLO initiated a new historical departure. The PNC accepted two UN resolutions that the Palestinians had never accepted in the past. The PLO now accepted Resolution 242, as well as the Partition Resolution of 1947. The resolutions were accepted with various reservations that made their interpretation a rather difficult and tortuous exercise. All the same, the PLO had made decisions that were an important first step towards the acceptance of a two-state solution.

The albeit qualified acceptance by the PLO of Resolution 242 and the Partition Resolution of 1947 paved the way for a much greater measure of international recognition of the PLO, including the willingness of the United States to engage with the PLO. But that willingness did not last for very long. In the Gulf War of 1990–91, when Saddam Hussein invaded Kuwait and the United States went to war against Iraq, Yasser Arafat, the Chairman of the PLO, took the side of Saddam Hussein. Having done that, he disqualified himself in the eyes of the Americans as a legitimate representative of the Palestinians.

Arafat at the PNC, 1988

By AFP, Getty Images Israel

When the United States initiated an international conference at Madrid in October 1991 as the forum for the resumption of negotiations between Israel and its Arab neighbors, the PLO was not directly represented. The Madrid representation formula for the Palestinians accepted Palestinians from the West Bank and Gaza in the framework of a joint Jordanian-Palestinian delegation. This was a very unwelcome formula from the PLO's point of view. The PLO therefore made it clear from the very beginning of the Madrid process of late 1991 that it would

The PLO and the Iraqi Invasion of Kuwait

By Getty Images Israel

By Jheijmans at en.wikipedia [Public domain], via Wikimedia Commons

Madrid Peace Conference, (October 30th–November 1st 1991)

By Pool Apesteguy/Merillon/Simon, Getty Images Israel

not allow the Palestinian representatives from the West Bank and Gaza to speak for the Palestinian people. The Palestinians in the joint Jordanian-Palestinian delegation could do very little in the Madrid negotiations without prior approval from the PLO itself.

The Oslo Accords

By Vince Musi / The White House [Public domain], via Wikimedia Commons

Eventually, the PLO re-established itself fully as the sole negotiator on behalf of the Palestinians without any qualification by joining Israel in what became the "Oslo Surprise." The agreement between Israel and the PLO allowed the PLO to eclipse the insider leadership from the West Bank and Gaza and to fully reassert its representative status. By negotiating directly with Israel, the PLO was not only eclipsing the internal leadership in the West Bank and Gaza, it was also trying to bypass the Islamist challenge which had emerged in Palestinian politics in the years of PLO decline.

For considerable time, there had been a very strong and impressive showing for the Palestinian Islamist movements in the student unions of the various universities in the West Bank and Gaza. In the *Intifada* in 1987, Hamas emerged as the leading Islamist organization amongst the Palestinians. The Hamas leadership became a serious contender with the PLO for the leadership of the Palestinian people. It was far less clear, as Hamas emerged as a competitor over the leadership with the PLO, who exactly the "sole" legitimate representative of the Palestinian people really was.

While contending with the insider leadership and the competition with Hamas, the PLO also had to contend with the results of Jordan's decision to disengage from the West Bank in the summer of 1988. King Hussein realized that his efforts to maintain a hold on the future of the Palestinians were not making much headway. During the *Intifada*, there was considerable expression of anti-Jordanian sentiment, which led the Jordanians to finally decide to disengage formally from the West Bank. What the Jordanians were saying to the Israelis by disengaging was not that the Jordanians were disinterested in the future of Palestine and they were not asking to be ignored. The Jordanians were suggesting that in order to settle the Palestinian question, the Israelis must also speak to the PLO, and not just to the Jordanians. By pressuring the Israelis to talk to the PLO, the Jordanians were also challenging the PLO to deliver. By walking away from the West Bank, the Jordanians were putting the PLO to the test. Could the PLO negotiate with the Israelis and actually bring about real change on the ground? The PLO had to prove to the Palestinians in the West Bank and Gaza that it was indeed capable of delivering a political solution to their predicament.

The Oslo Accords — The Motivations of the Parties

In addition to Jordan's challenge to the PLO to deliver, there was a series of other immediate causes that brought the PLO to the negotiating table with Israel. First of all was Arafat's perception of time. Things were changing in the Middle East and in the world at large that created an unusual sense of urgency for the PLO and for Arafat as the organization's leader. In the early 1990s the Soviet Union, the great supporter of the PLO for decades, collapsed. There were no longer two superpowers, but only one and it was the United States of America, Israel's greatest ally. The balance of power, therefore, was shifting most uncomfortably, strategically and historically, against the PLO.

The collapse of the Soviet Union led to other changes as well. The most critical from the Palestinian point of view, was the massive immigration of Soviet Jews to Israel. The numbers that were first spoken of were in the hundreds of thousands but in later years, during the decade of the 1990s, as many as one million Soviet Jews immigrated to Israel. The massive immigration was cause for real fear amongst Palestinians that the numbers game was no longer working in their favor. The possibility that hundreds of thousands of Soviet immigrants would be settled in the West Bank added to the PLO's sense of urgency that something had to be done.

The Immigration of Soviet Jews to Israel

By Esaias Baitel, Getty Images Israel

In early 1991 Iraq was resoundingly defeated by the United States as it was forced out of Kuwait, that it had invaded just a few months earlier, in the summer of 1990. The destruction of the Iraqi military was another serious change in the balance of power in the Middle East. For Arafat and the PLO, Iraq was a strategic hinterland that no longer existed.

The *Intifada*, the Palestinian uprising in the West Bank and Gaza that had begun in 1987, which had given so much added impetus to the Palestinian national endeavor, was losing steam by the early 1990s. There was an urgent need to address the priorities of the insider constituency, the people in the West Bank and Gaza, and to transform the *Intifada* from an effective expression of opposition to the Israeli occupation into a tool for real political gain.

To all of the above one must add the financial bankruptcy of the PLO. After Iraq's invasion of Kuwait, Arafat made the mistake of supporting Saddam Hussein. By doing so, he aroused the hostility and the anger of the PLO's traditional bankrollers: Saudi Arabia, Kuwait and other Gulf States. Their financial backing was suddenly withdrawn, putting the PLO into dire financial straits.

Within the PLO, even radicals like Faruq al-Qaddumi, the Head of the PLO's Political Department, spoke of the danger for the PLO if it did not engage in some kind of political negotiation with Israel. It might find itself on the trash heap of history, he and others warned. There was also the constant fear that if the PLO did not take the initiative, the pro-PLO leadership inside the West Bank and Gaza may create an alternative leadership of its own to challenge or even replace the PLO. Though this was not a realistic fear, it was a fear all the same.

The Rise of Hamas

Hamas Demonstration in Gaza, 1993
By Esaias Baitel, Getty Images Israel

Moreover, inside the West Bank and Gaza, other political changes were taking place that were not in the PLO's best interest. The most important of these was the rise of Hamas, the Palestinian Islamist movement, which had gained in strength during the *Intifada* and was becoming a serious challenge to the PLO's leadership.

For all these reasons, the PLO was moving towards a direction of greater willingness to negotiate with Israel.

Israel also had its own reasons to meet the PLO at the table. Israel under Yitzhak Rabin, the Prime Minister as of the Labor victory in early 1992, saw its place in the region in the center of concentric circles, which required a strategy of peace. Rabin's analysis was as follows: Israel needed peace with the Arab states that were on its borders, that is, Egypt, Syria, Lebanon, Jordan and the Palestinians. This would create an inner circle of peace that would keep the more radical states in the outer circle, like Iran and Iraq, at bay, at an arm's length from Israel, without the provocation of the Arab-Israeli conflict to have them interfere in Israel's affairs. Rabin seriously believed in the urgent need for progress in the peace process with Israel's neighbors that did not have peace with Israel yet, and key amongst these were, of course, the Palestinians.

Rabin's analysis of the Palestinian *Intifada* was another contributing factor. The *Intifada* was a drain on Israel's resources, financially and politically. It seriously damaged Israel's international standing and it brought Rabin to the conclusion that this was the time to do Israel's level best to bring an end to the occupation. The Madrid Process that had begun in late 1991 under the auspices of the United States was not going anywhere in terms of the negotiations with the other Arab players, particularly the Palestinians. Israel, like the PLO, had an interest in the early 1990s in a historical breakthrough.

The Content of the Oslo Accords

The historical breakthrough came in the summer of 1993 with the final success of secret negotiations in the Norwegian capital of Oslo. These were the famous Oslo Accords. The agreement between Israel and the PLO, most significantly, on mutual recognition was a historical breakthrough in and of itself. The agreement included a variety of other details of no less importance. Israel was to withdraw, firstly from the towns of Gaza and Jericho as part of a multi-phased withdrawal from the occupied territories. This phased approach was intended to test the goodwill of both sides and to serve as a confidence building measure. There was to be a transitional phase of five years, at the end of which the Israelis and the Palestinians would come to an agreement on all the outstanding issues that had been left for final status negotiations.

The Oslo Accords called for the immediate establishment of the Palestinian Authority that would take control of those areas that Israel gradually withdrew from in the West Bank and Gaza. The Palestinian Authority would also be responsible for security in these areas. Though the Accords did not specifically refer to the creation of a Palestinian state, these steps were essentially the Palestinian state in the making.

The establishment of the Palestinian Authority required the election of two critical institutions of this Palestinian state in the making: the presidency and the legislative assembly. The creation of these two elected institutions of the Palestinian Authority in the West Bank and Gaza was similarly a move of great historical consequence. The president and the legislative assembly of the Palestinian Authority were elected only by the people of the West Bank and Gaza and not by Palestinians who lived in the Palestinian diaspora, who were not residents of the West Bank and Gaza. This creation of the Palestinian Authority and its elected institutions essentially meant the narrowing down of the Palestinian question to the West Bank and Gaza. That, at least, was the meaning as the Israelis understood it.

The first elections were held in 1996 and Hamas, the Palestinian Islamist opposition, which totally rejected the Oslo Accords, refused to take part because the elections were, so Hamas argued, under the illegitimate auspices of these Accords.

1996 Palestinian Elections: The Non-Participation of Hamas

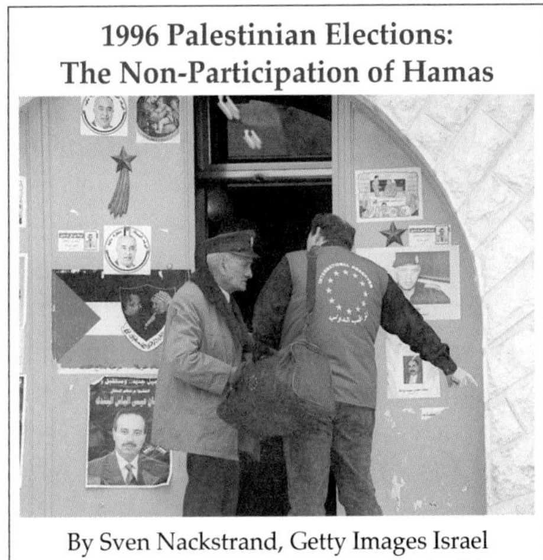

By Sven Nackstrand, Getty Images Israel

The final status issues that were to be negotiated and agreed by the end of the transition period were the following: Territory, which meant settlements and borders, that is, determining the fate of the Israeli settlements in the West Bank and Gaza and the final borders between the future Palestinian state and the State of Israel; Jerusalem, which was supposed to be not only the capital of Israel, but, as far as the Palestinians were concerned, the Arab part of the city was to be the capital of the future State of Palestine. Final status negotiations would have to deal with this future division of the city; Security, which related to the security arrangements that would exist between this Palestinian state of the future and the State of Israel; and Refugees, perhaps the most difficult and explosive of all issues, which was to discuss the fate of the millions of Palestinian refugees from the 1948 War (a few hundred thousand in 1948, but whose numbers had now swelled to millions) and to determine their future, whether to have a right to return to Israel or to the State of Palestine or some other solution to their predicament.

Though they did not specifically refer to a Palestinian state, the Oslo Accords certainly included a state-building dynamic and the Accords clearly meant statehood. Indeed, Palestinian opponents of the Oslo Accords were especially critical of precisely that point. They argued that the PLO had signed an agreement which was not about peace, but rather capitulation to Israel. In Arabic, the criticism was made to rhyme, "*la salam illa istislam*," which meant "not peace but capitulation." The PLO, so the critics argued, had accepted the idea of statehood in part of Palestine in preference to the historical objectives of liberation (of all of Palestine) and return (of the refugees). The PLO had conceded the notions of liberation and return in exchange for a little state alongside Israel. Indeed, the Oslo dynamic was prioritizing statehood in the West Bank and Gaza.

Aside from the Palestinian opponents, there were the Israeli opponents from the ideological/political right and the religious right, who at times were one and the same, and who fiercely opposed the idea of withdrawal from the West Bank and Gaza which were integral parts of historical Eretz Israel. From their viewpoint, these territories could never be conceded, neither to the Palestinians nor to anyone else. Conceding them to the PLO of all people was, so they argued, especially dangerous. These were not reliable allies of Israel in the future. They could not be trusted to keep the peace and were not to be Israel's partners in a negotiation over these territories, which was illegitimate from the outset anyway.

There were, therefore, two destructive efforts of the oppositions from both the Palestinian and the Israeli side that severely undermined the capacity of the parties to actually implement the Oslo Accords. On the one hand, there was the terrorism conducted by the Palestinian opponents of the agreements, who sought to bring down the agreements by eroding confidence in their execution. From the Israeli side, there were the Jewish opponents, who continued to settle in the West Bank and Gaza, with, and mainly without, the approval of Israeli governments. These actions from both sides had the effect of emptying the Oslo process of any real content for both major constituencies. Neither side was really able or willing to reign in their more radical opponents, who supported terrorism on the Palestinian side or the settler movement on the Israeli side.

If a transition period of five years was supposed to contribute to confidence building, it did not. There was no real sense of partnership and no real sense of trust. The settlements, on the one hand, and the suicide bombings, on the other, turned into confidence destroying measures that outweighed any effort of serious confidence building. For the Israelis, Oslo was equated with

Suicide Bombings and Settlements

By STR, Getty Images Israel

By Menahem Kahana, Getty Images Israel

insecurity. For the Palestinians, it was equated with expanding settlements. The transitional and phased process, therefore, instead of giving time to the parties to build the agreement, gave time to the opponents to destroy it. In November 1995 Yitzhak Rabin, the Prime Minister who led Israel into Oslo, was assassinated by a religious opponent of his policy. Rabin was succeeded by a government that was far less enthusiastic about Oslo. The Oslo Accords, henceforth, faced insurmountable difficulties of implementation.

The Assassination of Yitzhak Rabin (1995)

By AFP, Getty Images Israel

The Jordanian-Israeli Peace Treaty

All the same, the agreement between Israel and the PLO paved the way for a peace agreement between Israel and Jordan. Israel and Jordan had been "the best of enemies"[1] for decades. Though hostility between the two countries was hardly ever extreme, the Jordanians could never sign a separate peace agreement with Israel unless the Palestinians had done something of the kind ahead of them. Indeed, in the Madrid process, Jordan and Israel had already agreed on an agenda for a peace treaty in October 1992, well before the Israeli-PLO agreement. But the Jordanians would not go ahead with their agenda and turn it into a peace treaty until the PLO had made its move, so as not to have the Jordanians accused of making deals with Israel behind the backs of the Palestinians.

There were also other reasons why the Jordanians moved towards peace with Israel at this particular juncture. After the 1990–1991 Gulf War Jordan had certain urgent strategic needs. During the Gulf War Jordan had refused to side with the United States against Iraq. Jordan did not support the Iraqi invasion of Kuwait, but it refused to cooperate with the United States in the war against Iraq.

Jordan's position was a function of King Hussein's understanding of his Arab legitimacy. It was also part of Jordan's regard for Iraq as a potential

1. Uri Bar-Joseph, *The Best of Enemies; Israel and Transjordan in the War of 1948* (London: Frank Cass, 1987).

strategic hinterland for Jordan in its relations with Israel. After not supporting the US effort against Saddam Hussein, US relations with Jordan deteriorated rapidly. The US was furious with the Jordanians for their lack of cooperation. Following Saddam's defeat by the Americans, Jordan desperately needed to move back into the US-Israeli orbit of strategic understanding. Therefore, making peace with Israel was part of the Jordanian effort not only to come to a strategic understanding with Israel as the Israelis moved ahead on Palestine, but also to come to an understanding with Israel that would pave the way for improved Jordanian-US relations.

The Jordanian-Israeli Peace Treaty, 1994

Hussein, Clinton and Rabin
By David Rubinger, Getty Images Israel

The peace treaty between Jordan and Israel was unique. It was very different from the peace treaty between Israel and Egypt or from the relationship that developed between Israel and the Palestinians, or what might have been a peace treaty with Syria one day. The treaty between Israel and Jordan did not include any bilateral security arrangements. Jordan and Israel were never the worst of enemies and it was not really a peace treaty to put their hostility aside, but more about arranging the relationship between the two of them and a variety of third parties.

One of the most important elements of the Israeli-Jordanian peace treaty had to do with Israel and Iraq. Iraq was a much more dangerous enemy to Israel than were the Jordanians. By coming to an agreement with Jordan that would not allow the stationing of any potentially hostile foreign forces in Jordan, as part of the treaty, Israel ensured that Jordan would remain a stable buffer against Iraq.

For the Jordanians the peace treaty was important to allay Jordan's concerns about the Palestinians. The Jordanians over the years had developed a fear of those in Israel, and possibly elsewhere too, who believed in the transformation of Jordan into the state of the Palestinian people, that is, those who argued that "Jordan was Palestine." To guarantee themselves against that possibility, the Jordanians had a clause included in the agreement with Israel that would prevent the involuntary movement of population from one country to the other. That is, Israel would not allow the expulsion of Palestinians from the West Bank or from Israel proper to Jordan. Israel would recognize Jordan as the state of the

Jordanian people, and would not consider any kind of support in the future for the idea that "Jordan was Palestine."

The Geopolitical Centrality of Jordan

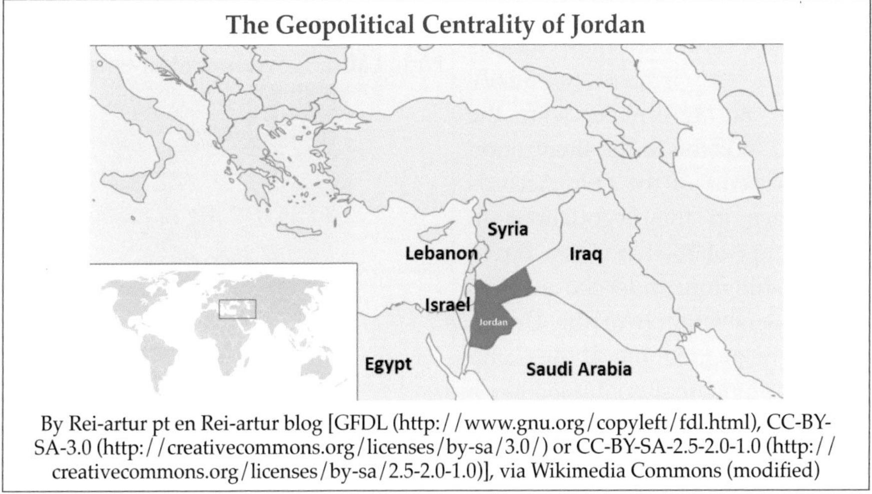

By Rei-artur pt en Rei-artur blog [GFDL (http://www.gnu.org/copyleft/fdl.html), CC-BY-SA-3.0 (http://creativecommons.org/licenses/by-sa/3.0/) or CC-BY-SA-2.5-2.0-1.0 (http://creativecommons.org/licenses/by-sa/2.5-2.0-1.0)], via Wikimedia Commons (modified)

The Jordanians had great expectations from the peace treaty with Israel. They believed that it was one of a series of agreements with Israel that would lead to the stabilization of the region. Israel and the Palestinians, so the Jordanians believed, were on the way to the creation of a two-state solution. The region, as a result, would be stabilized, and Jordan, at long last, between Iraq, on the one hand, and Israel and Palestine, on the other, would enjoy long term stability.

Jordan also harbored the expectation that the relationship with Israel would rapidly improve the kingdom's struggling economy, and that Jordan, thanks to peace with Israel, would extricate itself from its economic distress. But that was an unrealistic expectation from the outset and it did not materialize. The Jordanians, after a number of years, though they kept the peace treaty with Israel, were deeply disappointed by its real results.

Most important for the Jordanians was that the Israelis and the Palestinians would come to a stable agreement. The Jordanians believed a stable agreement between Israel and the Palestinians would secure Jordan from the most undesirable consequences of an Israeli-Palestinian conflagration. The Jordanians constantly feared that if there ever were to be a major Israeli-Palestinian confrontation, it would be the Jordanians who would suffer most. The fact that Israel and the Palestinians never managed to complete their negotiations, as expected after Oslo, was a constant source of great concern and anxiety for the Jordanians.

The Failure of the Israeli-Palestinian Talks at Camp David 2000

New Labor Government in Israel, 1999

Ehud Barak

By Robert D. Ward source photo: Ehud_Barak_and_Robert_M._Gates_at_the_Pentagon,_11-2009.JPG: Robert D. Ward derivative work: Ladislav Faigl [Public domain], via Wikimedia Commons

One of the last and most serious efforts of the Israelis to finally conclude an agreement with the PLO and to come to the finalization of all elements of the Oslo Accords took place in the negotiations in the summer of 2000 at Camp David near Washington, under the auspices of President Clinton of the United States. The negotiations at the Camp David summit that continued for a few months thereafter, until early 2001, took place between the newly elected Labor government in Israel, headed by Prime Minister Ehud Barak, who came into office in July 1999, and the PLO headed by Yasser Arafat.

Briefly after his election, Barak tried to achieve an agreement with Syria, momentarily putting the Palestinians on the back burner. The negotiations with Syria were not productive and Barak returned to the Palestinian track.

There was a sense of urgency on the Israeli side that time was of the essence, and that a dramatic move, like the Camp David summit, was essential as long as President Clinton was still in office, to finally conclude a historical agreement between Israel and the PLO and the Palestinian people. Ehud Barak, therefore, came to Camp David with a territorial offer, more generous than any Israeli government had made to the Palestinians ever. Though the proposal was very far-reaching in the Israeli mind, from the Palestinian point of view it fell far short. The difference in perceptions stemmed from the very different points of departure that the Israelis and the Palestinians started from in their negotiations at Camp David.

The Israelis offered initially to withdraw from about 80 percent of the West Bank. This was a lot more than the Israelis had offered the Palestinians at any time before, but was far less than the Palestinians expected and what they regarded as the bare minimum. The Palestinians expected Israel to withdraw from all of the West Bank and not from 80 percent of it. From the Israeli point of view, this was a Palestinian "all or nothing" approach and an unwillingness to compromise.

From the Palestinian point of view, however, things were seen very differently. The Palestinians argued that Israel already had 78 percent of historical Palestine, that is, Israel within the boundaries that existed until 1967. The West Bank and Gaza were barely the remaining 22 percent of Palestine, and over that minimum the Palestinians were unwilling to concede. The Israeli point of departure was in 1967. The Palestinians, however, were coming from 1948. The parties were not operating in the same political time zone and this made agreement very difficult indeed.

If one major problem was on the territorial issue, another was on Jerusalem. It was understood by the parties at Camp David that Jerusalem would be divided. From the Israeli point of view, this was a very significant break from the past and from the Israeli traditional position, as it had been since 1967, that all of Jerusalem should be Israel's undivided capital. The Israelis were willing to concede and the Palestinians agreed that, in principle, the city of Jerusalem ought to be divided on an ethnic basis, that is, Jewish residential areas would remain part of the State of Israel and Arab-Palestinian residential areas would become part of the future State of Palestine.

The problem that proved to be intractable, however, was the issue of the holy sites on Temple Mount *(al-haram al-sharif)*, those that were for the Jewish people the holiest of holy sites, and those that were the third holiest place for the Muslims after Mecca and Medina, the Dome of the Rock and the Al-Aqsa Mosque. The Jewish sites were the Wailing (or Western) Wall and the holy remains of the Second Temple beneath the Muslim holy places on the Mount. The parties were unable to agree on how the Mount ought to be divided, if divided at all. From the Palestinian point of view the *Haram* (Temple Mount) had to be under Palestinian-Muslim sovereignty. But that was unacceptable to the Israelis, who regarded the area as the most important of holy places to the Jewish people. The issue of sovereignty over the Mount remained unresolved.

The Dome of the Rock and the Wailing Wall

By Peter Mulligan [CC-BY-2.0 (http://creativecommons.org/licenses/by/2.0)], via Wikimedia Commons

Perhaps even more difficult than Temple Mount was the issue of Palestinian refugees and the question of their "right of return." The Israelis would not accept the "right of return" of Palestinian refugees to Israel proper. That, in the Israeli mind, would irreparably undermine the Jewish character of the Israeli state as the nation state of the Jewish people. The refugee problem, the Israelis argued, was a result of the 1948 war, for which they, the Israelis, were only partly responsible. The solution to the problem, therefore, could not be entirely at their expense.

The Palestinians argued that for the "right of return" to be truly meaningful it could not be the Israelis to decide on who returned to Israel. The "right of return" would not really be a "right," the Palestinians argued, unless the Palestinian refugees had a free choice on whether to return to Israel or not. The gap between free Palestinian choice to return to Israel if they so desired, and the Israeli emphasis on the right of sovereign states to admit only whom they accepted, was unbridgeable. With positions such as these, failure on this issue was inevitable.

There was a major difference between the inter-state conflict between Israel and the Arab states, and the conflict between Israel and the Palestinians. In the conflict between Israel and the Arab states, there was one set of issues that related to the war of 1967, and its consequences. In the negotiations between Israel and Egypt, Syria or Jordan, the issues that Israel had to deal with were the territorial matters arising from its conquests in 1967. Peace with Egypt, for example, was possible if and when Israel gave the territory captured in 1967 back to Egypt and the Egyptian people, and likewise with the other states.

But between Israel and Palestine, there were two sets of issues, the 1967 questions and the 1948 issues, and the latter were more complicated, more demanding, and far more difficult for the Israelis to address than those of 1967. The 1967 issues were those that related, as we have seen in the Oslo Accords, to the territory of the West Bank and Gaza and to Jerusalem. These were matters on which Israel could concede, in principal, without eroding the nature of the Israeli state as the nation-state of the Jewish people.

But Israel cannot address the 1948 questions without touching upon its very essence. The 1948 questions are two. One is the right of the Palestinian refugees to return to Israel proper, and the other is the question of the collective political rights of the Palestinian people, who are citizens of the State of Israel itself. It is these two issues that belong to the 1948 set of questions that Israel cannot address without opening the existential debate on Israel's very being as the nation-state of the Jewish people. The 1967 issues, as difficult as they may be, were far easier to address than those of 1948. The 1948 questions were not part of the inter-state agenda, but they were at the very core of the Israeli-Palestinian negotiation, and that made all the difference in seeking to end the conflict.

A presently unbridgeable clash of narratives also encumbered the Israeli-Palestinian negotiation. If for the Israelis the creation of their state was an act of heroic Jewish self-defense in defiance of their miserable past, from the Palestinian point of view, it was never an act of self-defense, but an act of aggression from the very beginning of Jewish settlement in Palestine. If in the Israeli view, the creation of the State of Israel was the epitome of historical justice for the most oppressed of all peoples, from the Palestinian point of view, the creation of Israel was the height of injustice. These were not narratives that diverged somewhat, they were miles apart.

The being of the Palestinian people, the nature of Palestinian-ness and their collective identity have been well-described by the American-Palestinian academic Beshara Doumani. In Doumani's words, being Palestinian was based on "the shared memories of the traumatic uprooting of their society and the experiences of being dispossessed, displaced, and stateless." It was these factors that were to "come to define 'Palestinian-ness.'"[2] It was very difficult for Israelis to come to terms with Palestinian-ness defined in such terms, and it was equally difficult for Palestinians defined in such terms to come to terms with Israel.

The failure of the talks at Camp David in the summer of 2000 and the failure of the Oslo process gave way to the Second *Intifada*, the second uprising of the Palestinians against the continued Israeli occupation. The Second *Intifada* was very different from the first. It was not an unarmed civilian uprising of mass-demonstrations by men and women and young boys and girls against the Israelis. The Second *Intifada* was the *Intifada* of the suicide bombers, the most vicious, violent and bloody confrontation between Israelis and Palestinians ever since 1948.

The campaign of suicide bombings and other incidents of the Second *Intifada* took over one thousand Israeli lives, and many more Palestinian lives in Israeli retaliation, in the next few years. If the bombings were intended to soften Israeli positions, they achieved quite the opposite. The bombings took place in Israel's major cities, in Jerusalem, Tel Aviv, Haifa, Beersheba, and the other towns of Israel. Whether intended or not by the Palestinian side, the Israelis understood the bombings in their cities not as part of a struggle for a state in the West Bank and Gaza, and not as a fight to end the occupation, but as a challenge to the very existence of the State of Israel. Israeli positions towards the Palestinians became ever-more recalcitrant.

The suicide bombings also gave rise to the old problematique of armed struggle and terrorism. By using this kind of armed struggle, the Palestinians again delegitimized their own movement by actions that were deliberately designed to take civilian lives, exposing them once more, in Israel and beyond, to the condemnation as terrorists. The end result was the Israeli reoccupation of

2. Beshara Doumani, "Palestine versus the Palestinians? The Iron Laws and the Ironies of a People Denied," *Journal of Palestine Studies*, Vol. 36, No. 4 (Summer 2007), p. 52.

the West Bank, and for the meantime, an end to any serious Palestinian-Israeli negotiations.

Between late March and early May 2002, Israeli forces conducted a massive military campaign in the West Bank known as "Defensive Shield," during which they temporarily reoccupied densely populated urban areas from which they had withdrawn during the Oslo process. "Defensive Shield" and the subsequent construction of a security barrier between the West Bank and Israel brought the bombings to an end.

Israel's Unilateral Disengagement from Gaza

Ariel Sharon (1928–2014)

Helene C. Stikkel [Public domain], via Wikimedia Commons

In Israel, despite the failed negotiations, the recognition still prevailed that the continued occupation of millions of Palestinians against their will was most undesirable from the Israeli long term historical perspective. After the failure of the Oslo process, the Prime Minister of Israel, as of March 2001, was the leader of the Likud, Ariel Sharon, a person with a strong right wing bent in his original political make-up. Strangely enough, it was Sharon of all people who, as Prime Minister, changed his mind completely. It was Sharon who came to the conclusion that the occupation was so damaging to Israel in the long run that even without an agreement with the Palestinians, it was preferable for Israel to withdraw. Sharon, therefore, decided on the unilateral withdrawal of Israel from the entire Gaza Strip including the dismantling of all the Israeli settlements in that area.

The unilateral disengagement of Israel from Gaza was carried out in the summer of 2005, arousing much domestic debate and disagreement in Israel, essentially focusing on the tension between the different needs of "current security" and "basic security."

There were many who argued that the disengagement from Gaza was a grave mistake. In terms of Israel's current security, it did not improve the situation, quite the contrary. Israel withdrew from Gaza, but Gaza was eventually taken over by Hamas in 2007. For years, Israel has been exposed to the escalating rocketry of Hamas against Israeli towns near Gaza and further afield. Many in Israel, probably a majority, would argue, therefore, that the disengagement from Gaza was wrong-headed.

Others contend, in the name of Israel's basic security, the long term preservation of Israel as the nation-state of the Jewish people, that withdrawing from Gaza and thereby having 1.7 million less Palestinians under Israeli control was a critical long term contribution to Israeli security and survivability even if, in the short term, it did cause current security problems.

Removing Settlers – The Israeli Withdrawal from Gaza

http://www.ynet.co.il/PicServer2/24012010/2509981/TK720968-wa.jpg

The failure of the peace process between Israel and the PLO led to the ever-increasing power and influence of Hamas, the Islamist opposition, in Palestinian society. The rising stature of Hamas begged the question of who really spoke for the Palestinians. If Israel was expected to negotiate with the PLO, could the PLO deliver on an agreement that it signed, considering the rising influence of Hamas? The PLO's greatest asset that it had ever obtained was its recognition by the Arabs, and thereafter by the international community, and even Israel, as "the sole legitimate representative of the Palestinian people." But especially after Hamas's impressive victory in the Palestinian elections of 2006, the question arose with ever greater frequency and urgency, who really spoke for the Palestinian people?

Summation: The Causes of the Oslo Failure

In seeking the causes of the Oslo failure, first and foremost would be the gap between the 1967 and the 1948 files. As difficult as the 1967 questions were between Israel and the Palestinians, the 1948 questions were virtually insoluble. As already noted in the discussion of Resolution 242 (see above in Chapter Seven) it remained the basis for the negotiating process between Israel and the Palestinians, even though the resolution never satisfied the Palestinians on the questions of 1948. Resolution 242 was specifically designed to relate solely to the 1967 questions, and not to the issues of 1948.

The Israelis came to Camp David 2000 with the idea of a trade-off. Israel would concede generously, as they thought, on the 1967 questions in the hope that the Palestinians would agree, in exchange, to close the file of 1948.

The Rise of Hamas

The leader of Hamas Ismail Haniya
By Abid Katib, Getty Images Israel

But the Palestinians were not willing to do so. As a result, the tension between the 1967 issues and the 1948 questions remained the major reason for the failure of the Israelis and the Palestinians to agree to an end of conflict.

After the negotiations had failed in 2000, instead of the narrowing down of the question of Palestine to its 1967 dimensions, as the Oslo dynamic had initially suggested, the Palestinians began to refocus on the centrality of the 1948 questions and, above all, on the "right of return." Instead of being placed on the back burner, the "right of return" was placed back at the top of the Palestinian agenda. It became much harder, therefore, for Israelis and Palestinians to agree to an "end of conflict." In order to "end the conflict," the Palestinians would only naturally demand that all problems, as of "the beginning," ought to be satisfactorily addressed and resolved, and that meant a resolution of the refugee problem that Israel could not accept.

The last round of serious negotiations between the Israelis and the Palestinians was held between Prime Minister Ehud Olmert and President Mahmud Abbas in 2008. During these negotiations, there was an important narrowing of the gaps on the 1967 questions, on certain territorial issues and even on Jerusalem, but not on the questions of 1948.

Abbas–Olmert Talks, 2008

Ehud Olmert, Condoleezza Rice and Mahmud Abbas
By Matty Stern (U.S. Embassy, Tel Aviv) [Public domain], via Wikimedia Commons

On the questions of 1948, the differences not only remained intact, but were even exacerbated. Olmert offered the Palestinians the return of 5,000 refugees to Israel over five years, that is, a thousand refugees a year for five years. That was a far cry even from the positions the Palestinians suggested in private, which they were never willing to repeat in public. Privately, the Palestinians had suggested the return to Israel of 100 to 150 thousand refugees, which was 20 to 30 times more than Olmert's proposal. But these were numbers that in public they were not willing to repeat. When the figures were publicized by Wikileaks, the Palestinian negotiators denied these offers had ever been made.

Furthermore, both sides had intrusive perceptions of the two-state solution. The Palestinian idea of the refugee solution intruded into Israel's territory, by demanding the return of Palestinian refugees to Israel proper. From the Israeli point of view, if there should be a return of Palestinian refugees, it ought to be to the State of Palestine and not to the State of Israel. Having refugees return to the State of Israel made no sense from the Israeli point of view. This, the Israelis would argue, was an unacceptable intrusion of the Palestinian state into the State of Israel.

The Palestinians made a similar argument in reference to Israel's security demands. These required an Israeli military presence and various forms of control of the territory of the Palestinian state and its airspace. The Palestinians argued that the way in which the Israelis understood security was an intrusion into their territory and an undermining of their sovereignty. Both sides agreed in principle to the two-state solution, but each had perceptions of the two states that intruded into the territory of the other, making the respective concepts of two states mutually unpalatable.

Lastly, a general historical observation about Israel's place in the Middle East. The environment in which Israel has been operating since 1948 has changed dramatically, as borne out by the events of the last few years, the so called "Arab Spring," and its aftermath (see below in Chapter Nine). Recent events have exposed the great weakness of the Arab states, whereas, Israel in its early years was most concerned with how to deal with ever increasing Arab power. Israel's present-day concerns are very different from those which its founding fathers had predicted. It is not Arab strength that Israel has to grapple with, but rather Arab weakness, maybe less threatening, but in some ways harder to contend with effectively.

Key Sources and Suggested Further Reading

- Gorenberg, Gershom, *The Accidental Empire: Israel and the Birth of the Settlements, 1967-1977* (New York: Times Books, 2006).
- Heikal, Mohamed, *The Road to Ramadan* (New York: Ballantine, 1975).
- Khalidi, Rashid, *Under Siege: PLO Decision Making During the 1982 War* (New York: Columbia University Press, 1986).
- Khalidi, Rashid, *The Iron Cage: The Story of the Palestinian Struggle for Statehood* (Boston: Beacon Press, 2006).
- Morris, Benny, *Righteous Victims: A History of the Zionist-Arab Conflict, 1881-1999* (New York: Knopf, 1999).
- Mutawi, Samir, *Jordan in the 1967 War* (Cambridge University Press, 1987).
- Oren, Michael, *Six Days of War: June 1967 and the Making of the Modern Middle East* (Oxford University Press, 2002).
- Quant, William, *Camp David: Peacemaking and Politics* (Washington, DC: The Brookings Institution, 1986).
- Rabinovich, Itamar, *Waging Peace: Israel and the Arabs, 1948-2003* (Princeton University Press, 2004).
- Sayigh, Yezid, *Armed Struggle and the Search for State: The Palestinian National Movement, 1949-1993* (Oxford: Clarendon Press, 1997).
- Schiff, Ze'ev and Ehud Yaari, *Israel's Lebanon War* (New York: Simon and Schuster, 1984).
- Sela, Avraham, *The Decline of the Arab-Israeli Conflict: Middle East Politics and the Quest for Regional Order* (Albany: State University of New York Press, 1998).
- Shlaim, Avi, *The Iron Wall: Israel and the Arab World* (New York: Norton, 2000).
- Stein, Kenneth, *Heroic Diplomacy: Sadat, Kissinger, Carter, Begin, and the Quest for Arab-Israeli Peace* (New York: Routledge, 1999).
- Susser, Asher, *On Both Banks of the Jordan: A Political Biography of Wasfi al-Tall* (London: Frank Cass, 1994).
- Susser, Asher, *Israel, Jordan and Palestine: The Two-State Imperative* (Waltham, MA: Brandeis University Press, 2012).

Chapter Nine

Middle Eastern Stateness, Islamic Revival and the "Arab Spring"

The Post-1967 Middle East: The Victory of State Interest

The Arab failure in the 1967 war with Israel was the beginning of a new era. The defeat was not just a defeat in the battlefield, but a monumental failure of pan-Arabism to achieve the power, the prestige and the prosperity that it had promised the Arabs. Pan-Arabism appeared to be an empty vessel and the vacuum it left behind was filled by two simultaneous, but essentially contradictory trends: The entrenchment of the territorial state; and the rise of political Islam, which generally posed a serious challenge to the secular concept of the territorial state.

The defeat of 1967 accelerated the decline of the pan-Arab movement which had actually begun a few years before with the break-up of the United Arab Republic in 1961, for example.

In the new post-1967 era the old dichotomy of "progressive" and "reactionary" Arab regimes, as they were referred to before 1967, had become completely irrelevant. Both the "progressives" and the "reactionaries," were defeated equally by Israel.

Now was the time for the salience of the narrow state interest — *raison d'état* as the French call it. With pan-Arabism in decline, it only made sense to begin to emphasize the narrow state interest, rather than the collective Arab imperative, that had proved disappointing.

Egypt, like in so many other earlier and later instances, was the leading actor in the new trend. The War of Attrition that Egypt fought for two years against Israel after the 1967 War was another costly war for Egypt and its people. The price of war with Israel was felt immediately for the first time in the very heart of their own country, in the Nile Valley and the delta, urging the Egyptians to think more about their own self-interest.

After succeeding Abd al-Nasser in 1970, President Anwar Sadat, in one of his first major decisions, restored "Egypt" to the name of the country, changing the name from the United Arab Republic to the Arab Republic of Egypt. In Arabic it became *Gumhuriyyat Misr al-Arabiyya*, and the order was important.

Misr (Egypt) came first and *Arabiyya* (Arab) came second. This was not about semantics, but the reorientation of Egyptian politics and policies. This was an "Egypt First" policy and it was in the service of Egypt's state interest that Sadat first went to war with Israel and then chose to make peace with it, without any particular reference to the wishes of the Arab collective.

Of all the Arab states, Egypt of the Nile was the most self-evident, natural, territorial state. Egypt was a separate, clearly-defined political entity with a relatively homogeneous population, and Egyptians had an authentic collective sense of belonging to the Egyptian state well before the advent of pan-Arabism. Egyptianism had emerged in the latter part of the 19th century, well before pan-Arabism became a household term throughout the Arab world in the 20th century.

The territorialist trend was less obvious in other countries. Nevertheless, there too, as artificial as these countries may have been, similar territorialist trends were encouraged or enforced by the various regimes.

In Ba'thi **Iraq**, from 1968 until 2003, also known as Saddam's "Republic of Fear,"[1] until Saddam Hussein was overthrown by the US invasion, ethnic or sectarian minorities, such as the Kurds and the Shi'is (although the latter were a minority in the political, and not the numerical sense) were all crushed into submission by the institutions of violence controlled by the Iraqi Ba'th Party.

The Swords of Qadisiyya in Baghdad

https://upload.wikimedia.org/wikipedia/commons/9/97/Swords_of_Qādisīyah_(7112414819).jpg

Cohesion in the name of Iraqi-Arab nationalism and Iraqi leadership of the Arab world was not attractive or especially convincing for either Kurds, who were not Arabs, or Shi'is for whom Arab nationalism was just another version of Sunni domination. Neither of these communities could truly identify with Arab nationalism, which was not an effective formula for Iraqi cohesion.

But neither was Iraqi-ness, which was an illusory concept thrust upon the public from above. The Ba'th and Saddam, through state sponsorship of historical theories, the arts and archaeology endeavored to foster a sense of national Iraqi pride and uniqueness through the creation of an intimate relationship between the people and the territorial pre-Islamic history of Babylonian Iraq. Iraqi artists,

1. Samir al-Khalil (Kan'an Makiya), *Republic of Fear; The Inside Story of Saddam's Iraq* (New York: Pantheon, 1990).

poets, novelists, and playwrights were all encouraged by Saddam to derive their inspiration from the civilizations and cultures that flourished in ancient Mesopotamia (Iraq), from remote antiquity to the modern age, anchored in Iraq's pre-Islamic, Babylonian past.[2] But these Babylonian-Iraqi manipulations could not paper over the predominant sectarian identities that continued to prevail in Iraq.

The occupation of Kuwait by Iraq in 1990 was intended to serve the narrow strategic interests of the Iraqi state, despite the justifications that were ostensibly based on pan-Arabism. All the Arab states favored the preservation of the old state order and the restoration of independent Kuwait that had been overrun by Saddam Hussein. The Arab States, for the most part, supported the US in its war against Iraq, to dislodge the Iraqi forces from Kuwait and to reestablish Kuwaiti independence and thereby to recreate the former territorial state order, despite its colonial origins. In the heyday of pan-Arabism it would have been unimaginable for a war to be waged by the United States against an Arab state, with most of the other Arab states cheering for the US on the sidelines.

Iraqi Occupation of Kuwait, 1990

http://en.wikipedia.org/wiki/File:Kuwait-Iraq_barrier.png

Kurdistan Regional Government:
Part of the new Iraqi federal structure, but quasi-independent

By Zirguezi (http://krg.org/services/print_material.asp) [Public domain], via Wikimedia Commons

Clearly the decline of pan-Arabism meant greater Arab acquiescence in the territorial state and the regional state order. But in countries like Iraq, territorialism was also strictly sectarian. Irrespective of whether the regime was more or less pan-Arab, or more or less territorial or even Islamist, the modern trappings of the Ba'thi regime were a mere pretext for sectarian Sunni domination of Iraqi society. The real political foundations of

2. Amatzia Baram, "Territorial Nationalism in the Middle East," *Middle Eastern Studies*, Vol. 26, No. 4 (October 1990), pp. 425–426.

the regime had nothing to do with Saddam's invented historical manipulations of Babylonian Iraq.

However, the iron-fisted grip of Saddam in Iraq began to weaken after Iraq's expulsion from Kuwait by the US in early 1991. Kurdish and Shi'ite uprisings of the spring of 1991 were suppressed, but the regime could not prevent the de facto autonomy that was established with US support in the Kurdish region. After the overthrow of Saddam by the US military invasion in 2003, the Kurdish Regional Government, though part of the new Iraqi federal structure, developed into a quasi-independent state in all but name, and achieved a level of stability and prosperity far above the rest of the country.

The toppling of Saddam was in fact the overthrow of the Sunnis, who had been in control of Iraq for more than a millennium from the early days of the Muslim Caliphates to the Ottomans, and then in the British-constructed state of Iraq. The new post-Ba'thi Iraq was no longer defined as an Arab state but as a more decentralized Arab-Kurdish federation. The Kurds took their separate course, but the Arabs of Iraq remained deeply divided between Sunnis and Shi'is. The US invasion of Iraq "swept away this comforting fantasy" of a non-sectarian society. "For the first time in the modern history of Iraq, the Sunni Arabs were forced to confront the loss of their ascendant power *as a community*."[3] The empowerment of the Shi'ite majority was an insufferable defeat for the Sunnis, who have essentially refused ever since to acquiesce in the new reality. Sunni disaffection is at the root of the on again, off again violent struggle, if not to say civil war in Iraq ever since the US invasion, which has claimed the lives of many thousands on both sides.

Despite all the conflicting subnational and supranational identities, some sense of Iraqi-ness and identification with the state has coalesced over the almost 100 years since Iraq was founded. This sense of Iraqi-ness has not been entirely erased from the consciousness of Iraqis despite the profound religious and sectarian cleavages. Thus the Shi'ites of Iraq have shown no inclination to wed their Arab state to the Iranian state of their Persian co-religionists, and ethnic tensions between Persians and Arab Iraqis are part of the Iraqi-Iranian reality.

Another example of developing stateness was that of **Syria**. In Syria there remained the bitter taste of Arab union that had not worked between Syria and Egypt between 1958 and 1961. There was a strong desire in Syria, despite all the flair and fanfare about Arab unity and Arab nationalism, to protect the country's independence.

3. Ali Allawi, *The Occupation of Iraq; Winning the War, Losing the Peace* (New Haven: Yale University Press, 2007), p.135. Emphasis in source.

From the mid-1970s, the uniform fabric of Ba'th pan-Arab ideology in Syria started to show shades of territorial Syrian and pan-Syrian nationalism. Hafiz al-Asad, like Saddam Hussein, had reached the conclusion, that since it was not realistic to expect complete Arab unity to be achieved any time soon, it was essential to satisfy the popular need for a more permanent political base of identification than a Syrian entity that was deemed illegitimate by pan-Arab Ba'thi doctrine, and as such, necessarily temporary.

While Hafiz al-Asad officially remained faithful to the party's long term vision of Arab unity, the Syrian leadership searched for a formula that would bridge the gap between party ideals of Arab unity and political reality. As Egypt had shifted away from the conflict with Israel, Syria was desperately in need of a new strategic alignment that would encompass Lebanon, Jordan and the Palestinians, and enable the Syrians to establish some form of parity with Israel.

The old motif of "Greater Syria" was given a new lease on life by the Ba'thi regime in service of Syria's *raison d'état*. In later years, it did not disappear, it actually became part of Ba'thi political thinking together with a more traditional pan-Arabism that was coupled with notions of a more narrowly defined territorial nationalism based on Syria's existing borders. Thus, the archeological finds of the Roman era in Syria gave a great boost to a Syrian sense of national pride, and were presented as evidence of the pre-Islamic historical greatness of Syria. There was no effort to present these finds as part of the Arab heritage but rather as a chapter of Syria's great past.[4]

Occupation of large parts of Lebanon in 1976 by Syria and the inter-state arrangement between these two states did not bring about any change in the boundaries. Syria continued to preserve the border between Syria and Lebanon, even though it was rejected by Ba'thi ideology as artificial and illegitimate. "Greater Syria" became a question of strategic need rather than ideological conviction. Syria had become a regional player in its own right. It was a stable and powerful country, and though it remained the fountainhead and beating heart of Arabism in theory, the real emphasis was on Syrian state interest above all else.

Jordan and the Palestinians have also experienced an evolution of their respective versions of stateness and territorial identity, each as a reflection of their own particular circumstances.

Palestinian-ness was unique, created in the crucible of 1948 and the defeat by Israel, the *Nakba*. The Arab states were generally "in search of a usable past"[5] to provide a measure of historical content to their rather artificial territorial

4. Baram, "Territorial Nationalism," pp. 435–437.
5. Emmanuel Sivan, "The Arab Nation-State: In Search of a Usable Past," *Middle East Review*, Vol. 19, No. 3 (Spring 1987).

entities. For the Palestinians, however, their formative history was all about the *loss* of territory. It was this sense of *loss* that created the backbone of their cohesive collective memory. It was the loss of Palestine that ultimately gave the Palestinians their sense of territorial identity.

As for Jordanian-ness, it was defined against the ultimate Palestinian "other," especially after the civil war between the Jordanians and the PLO in September 1970. Since September 1970 there has been a deliberate promotion in Jordan of a particular Jordanian identity based on a common past, albeit evoking a measure of historical invention. The Jordanian identity was portrayed as having existed as far back as Ottoman times in the mid-19th century. Though this contention had little or no foundation, it became part and parcel of the Jordanian national narrative all the same. It followed, therefore, that the foundation of the monarchy was based on the self-determination of the Jordanians who were an existent people in the 1920s, and not on a colonial fiat, as was the case in fact. Jordan was described as a wellspring of civilization ever since the Roman conquests, through the ancient Nabateans and the Muslim conquests of the seventh century, all of which were appropriated as integral parts of Jordanian history. Jordanian-ness was also founded on the unique tribal-monarchical compact, the special association between the tribes and the monarchy as the core and linchpin of Jordan's national identity.

Jordan's relative cohesion in comparison to the other Arab states of the Fertile Crescent has also contributed to its surprisingly long-term stability. No less of an artificial creation than its neighbors, and many would argue even considerably more so, Jordan has had a much more stable political record, which was related to Jordan's character as a homogeneous society in religious-sectarian terms. Well over 90 percent of Jordan's citizens are Sunni Muslim Arabs. Jordan has a very small Christian minority, mainly Orthodox.

Since 1948, Jordan has become increasingly Palestinian, and Palestinians presently constitute a majority of just over 50 percent in Jordan of the East Bank alone, that is, not taking into account the West Bank territory occupied by Israel since 1967. But as tense as relations are between Jordanians and Palestinians, there is more that unites them than divides between them. Palestinians like their Jordanian compatriots are Sunni Muslims for the most part, with a similarly small Christian minority, also mainly Orthodox. The nationalist distinctions between them are latter-day 20th century creations which are skin-deep in comparison to the far more profound sectarian fault lines in other countries, such as between Sunnis and Shi'is, the origins of which are to be found in the seventh century.

Tribalism amongst Jordan's East Bankers is a strong and relevant social marker. But tribalism in Jordan has actually been mobilized far more in the service of the state than against it. In fact, the Jordanian state has become the political patrimony of the Jordanian tribes. They have no other and they will fight to defend their own. Therefore, in Jordan the promotion of a collective Jordanian identity was not just a top-down exercise like in Iraq, but a bottom-up one too, whereby the tribes have actively adopted the Jordanian identity as their own to the extent that they have become the main standard bearers of Jordanianism. For more than a decade, Abdullah II, who has been in power since 1999, has promoted the idea of "Jordan First," a good example of the uninhibited design to advance territorial identity.

The Islamic Revival

The disappointment with Arab nationalism that set the stage for a new emphasis on territorial identities and their deliberate promotion in some of the Arab states was also the impetus for the revival of Islamic politics, a contradictory phenomenon in many ways to the advance of territorialism.

Abd al-Nasser's defeat in 1967 was a humiliating revelation that the Nasserist panacea was no more than an illusion. The uneven process of development and modernization produced a socio-economic malaise in the Arab countries, characterized by rapid population growth and massive urbanization, which all contributed to the poverty and distress of masses of people who were easily attracted to the message of political Islam.

As James Piscatori observed, "most rural migrants [to the Arab cities] quickly became the urban poor, victims of their own hope, swallowed by the very process which they believed would liberate them."[6] This pervasive sense of despair, dislocation and disillusionment was a key factor in the return to religion. Migration from the countryside generally served to spread rural attitudes in the cities, particularly the greater emphasis on religious tradition. Amongst other classes too, religious instincts ran deep, and this was especially true after the secular ideologies like Nasserism and Ba'thism had failed so miserably to deliver.

The ideological underpinnings of the Islamist trend were related, first and foremost, to the opposition to secularist modernization, secular nationalism and territorialism. The Islamists were not opposed to modernity and nationalism, but to their secular and secularizing thrust. The Islamists sought a version of modernity wrapped in the preservation of traditional identities, norms and values, and, above all, to base society on Islamic law, the Shari'a.

6. James Piscatori, *Islam in a World of Nation States* (Cambridge University Press, 1986), p. 27.

Since the late 19th century, as Piscatori has pointed out,[7] there were three main theories that came to explain the relative weakness of Muslim societies in comparison to the West.

One was that the decline was a consequence of deviation from true Islam. True Islam correctly interpreted did not conflict with Western ideas of rationalism and science. These were the arguments of the Islamic reformers of the late 19th century, like Jamal al-Din al-Afghani and Muhammad Abduh, discussed at length in Chapter Two.

A second explanation was that the relative weakness of the Muslim world was the fault of Islam itself, which was an obstacle to change and revival. This was the attitude of the secularists like Kemal Atatürk, the founding father of the secular Republic of Turkey.

Hasan al-Banna (1906–1949) founded the Muslim Brethren in 1928

See page for author [Public domain], via Wikimedia Commons

The third school were those who argued that the retreat of the Muslim world was actually because of its intoxication with the West. The Muslims had gone too far in the process of Westernization, as Hasan al-Banna, the founding father of the Muslim Brethren (1928), or the revolutionaries in Iran would argue. In their view, the Islamic modernists had failed because they themselves were too Western-oriented, seeking to establish Islamic justifications for Western-inspired reform. These new critics of Westernization thought in terms of a return to the idea of Islamic self-sufficiency, that which the modernists like Afghani and Abduh had begun to doubt. "Islam is the solution," claimed Hasan al-Banna and the Muslim Brethren.

Sayyid Qutb (1906–1966)

http: / / ar.wikipedia.org / w / index.php?title=ملف:سيد_قطب_الشاذلي.jpg&filetimestamp=20120823171243&

The key ideologue of the Muslim Brethren in Egypt was Sayyid Qutb (1906–1966).

7. Piscatori, *Islam in a World of Nation States*, pp. 22–24.

Qutb, who was hanged for "treason" by the Nasserite regime in Egypt, wrote considerably more than Hasan al-Banna, and it was he who became the main ideologue of the Muslim Brethren in the second part of the 20th century. Qutb expanded on the theme of the "new *Jahiliyya*," a term that was originally coined by the Pakistani Muslim thinker, Abu al-A'la Mawdudi, (1903 to 1979).

Abu al-A'la Mawdudi (1903–1979)

By DiLeeF (Own work) [CC-BY-SA-3.0 (http://creativecommons.org/licenses/by-sa/3.0)], via Wikimedia Commons

Mawdudi developed the concept of a "*Jahili* society," which was a society that did not live according to the Shari'a. The *Jahiliyya* was the period of barbarism and ignorance, according to the Muslim belief, that preceded the advent of Islam. Therefore, societies that were described in the present as "*Jahili* societies" were societies that were un-Islamic, societies that were not governed by the Shari'a. The "new *Jahiliyya*" was about the present, not the past that preceded the advent of Islam. *Jahiliyya*, according to Mawdudi and followed by Qutb, was not a period in history but a condition, a state of affairs which could apply to the present as well. There could be no coalescence and compromise with Western thought and Western culture ought to be rejected because of its secular, permissive and materialistic ways.

Qutb went through a process of radicalization during his prolonged imprisonment before his execution by the Nasserite regime. In his more radical thought Qutb justified *jihad*, holy war, and revolution, to overthrow the "infidel regimes" that did not implement the Shari'a. Qutb was imprisoned for his beliefs and hanged in 1966.

According to James Gelvin, the new radical Islamists were "able to counterpose their own brand of 'cultural authenticity' as represented by Islam, to the 'imported' secular nationalist creeds, which, they argued, brought nothing but oppression, economic stagnation, and defeat to the region."[8]

The new radical Islamists railed against the marginalization of religion in politics, law and society. They dismissed and disagreed with what they called the "cult of the nation-state" and its leadership which was nothing less than a form of heresy; that is, the cult and the belief in the leadership of the state rather than the belief in religion and God.

8. James Gelvin, *The Modern Middle East: A History* (Oxford University Press, 2011), p. 315.

The state monopoly over education was unacceptable because it eroded Islamic values and the mass media that were controlled by the state allowed permissiveness and generally un-Islamic behavior. Countries like Egypt and others were exposed to the Western economy and globalization, leading to corruption and to a consumer society that began to look like the permissive societies of the West that they referred to derisively as "Coca-Cola societies." The real enemy, they argued, was the "infidel regime" from within that had to be removed, even before the pursuit of the struggle against Israel.

Islamic Revival in Egypt, Syria and Iraq

The new radical Islamists had an ever increasing influence on the Islamization of Arab societies in the latter part of the 20th century. In **Egypt**, for example, while President Sadat promoted Egypt's *raison d'état* and territorial identity, in the process of de-Nasserization, that is, the weakening of the Nasserite institutions that challenged Sadat's leadership in his early years, Sadat also allowed for a greater measure of freedom for the Islamists. The Islamists were particularly active in the universities where they became, in their own mind, the vanguard of the *umma.* They were the vanguard of the Islamic community, which they would Islamize first in the universities and thereafter in society as a whole.[9]

When they appeared to be gaining too much ground, the Islamists were suppressed by Sadat and it was this suppression of the Islamists that eventually led to the assassination of Sadat in October 1981. Those who murdered Sadat, members of the Islamic Jihad organization, proclaimed the killing of Sadat to be the killing of Pharaoh, the Egyptian ruler of pre-Islamic times. Sadat's original sin was his governing of Egypt as a pre-Islamic, *jahili*, and un-Islamic state, and for that he deserved to die.

Husni Mubarak (in office 1981–2011)

By White House photo by Eric Draper. [Public domain], via Wikimedia Commons

Sadat was succeeded by President Husni Mubarak, who allowed for a somewhat greater measure of political pluralism. In practice, this meant that the government acquiesced in the erosion of the secularizing foundations of the Egyptian Republic. Under Abd al-Nasser,

9. Gilles Kepel, *Muslim Extremism in Egypt; The Prophet and Pharaoh* (Berkeley: University of California Press, 1986), pp. 144–153.

Shari'a courts were abolished and were accorded no role at all, even with respect to matters of personal status. This went much further than many other Muslim countries. Under Mubarak, however, the regime permitted the Islamists to file charges in the secular courts based on the Shari'a. Thus, the courts were regularly employed by Islamist lawyers to sue secular intellectuals, writers, professors, artists and journalists and to have them convicted for the purely religious crimes of blasphemy or apostasy.

Egyptian society from the late 1980s onwards showed ever-more external signs of religiosity. The construction of new mosques was rampant. People of all classes flocked in great numbers to Friday prayers. The *hijab*, the veil or scarf that covered the head and shoulders, was worn by over 80 percent of women. The consumption of religious literature was constantly on the rise, while movie-going, alcohol consumption and the patronage of bars and nightclubs all declined.

Islamists controlled the teachers training college where they trained future teachers who would disseminate Islamization in the classroom. In the late 1980s, the Ministry of Education promoted greater religiosity in the schools through a revised curriculum, and religious sentiments and ideas were said to dominate the schools. The mainstream print and electronic media in Egypt were likewise deeply influenced by Islamization. The mostly state-owned press shifted towards conservative religiosity and self-censorship, abandoning much of the secular liberal content of the 1950s and the 1960s.

Official religious publications were decidedly anti-secular, and national radio and television promoted a religious sensibility by increasing the number of Islamic-oriented programs. As Asef Bayat has noted, Islamic sentiment thus "eroded nationalism's secular expression."[10] In state schools Islamic religious education was part of the Arabic language and history curriculum, which were compulsory subjects for non-Muslims too. School textbooks tended to represent Egypt as a Muslim society and sometimes included specifically anti-Christian texts, and the curriculum required students to recognize the supremacy of Islam and the special relationship between Islam and the State of Egypt.

The Islamization of society was therefore having a negative impact on Egyptian social cohesion and on relations between Muslims and non-Muslims. The situation of the Coptic Christian minority became steadily more precarious as they were exposed to increasing levels of intolerance and violence. The regime had consciously acquiesced in the transformation of Egypt, allowing it to become what Asef Bayat has described as a "seculareligious" state.[11]

10. Asef Bayat, *Making Islam Democratic; Social Movements and the Post-Islamic Turn* (Stanford University Press, 2007), p. 165.
11. Bayat, *Making Islam Democratic*, pp. 48, 173.

In **Syria**, the religious factor in politics was intimately related to the sectarian structure of Syrian society. Just like in Iraq, Syria under the Ba'th party had always been deeply influenced by sectarian politics. Ever since the rise to power of the Ba'th in 1963, Alawi sectarian solidarity played an important role in regime stability, a fact never openly admitted by the men in power, but a fact all the same.

Ba'thi secularism was a vehicle for sectarian domination by the Alawi minority, just like it was for the Sunni minority in Iraq. The systemic marginalization of religion was a blessing for the Alawis, whose heterodox faith was a political and social liability. Therefore, from its inception in 1963, the Ba'thi regime was avowedly secular, and even radically so, during the rule of the so called neo-Ba'th from 1966 to 1970.

Under Hafiz al-Asad, who came to power in 1970, the Ba'th changed course. After rising to the presidency, Asad, the first Alawi president, sought to enhance the religious legitimacy of the Alawis. In 1973, he reinstated the clause in the constitution requiring the head of state to be a Muslim, a clause that the neo-Ba'this had previously removed in 1969.

Asad simultaneously managed to get the leading Lebanese Shi'ite cleric, Musa al-Sadr, to recognize the Alawis as orthodox Shi'is, and thus as Muslims constitutionally eligible for the presidency in Syria. From then onwards, the link between the regime in Syria and the Shi'is in Lebanon has been particularly strong. Needless to say, many in the Sunni majority community of Syria continued to resent the Alawis.

After having crushed the Sunni opposition as expressed by the Muslim Brethren in 1982, President Asad adopted a more conciliatory attitude towards the Brethren accompanied in the 1990s by a greater measure of tolerance toward religion in general. The process set in motion by Hafiz al-Asad having the Alawis accepted as Shi'is was accelerated under Bashar, his son. Bashar as president of Syria developed a more sustained program of Shi'ization, with the help of Iran, as a means of legitimizing both the Alawi community and the regime in the eyes of the Sunni majority. Hundreds of Alawis were sent to Iran for religious training while Iranian men of religion toured Syria to preach on Shi'ite religion to Alawi

Bashar al-Asad
In power since 2000

communities, as the regime sought to rid itself of its former ultra-secularist, anti-religious image.

The Syrian mass media diligently presented Hafiz al-Asad to the Syrian public and the world at large as a bona fide Muslim. Bashar, like Hafiz before him, made a deliberate effort to portray himself not only as a Muslim, but as a devout one. Furthermore, since the 1990s, religious schools have been opened all over the country. Religious literature was readily available and was sold to the general public in far greater quantities than books on other subjects. The number of students studying Shari'a in the university was constantly on the rise. Popular religious programs, just as in other Arab countries, were broadcast on national television. Syrian society, especially its Sunni component, was becoming more observant, at least if judged by participation in prayer or the adoption of the Islamic dress code.[12]

All of the above did nothing to abolish the sectarian fault lines. On the contrary, many in the Sunni majority community continued to regard the Alawis as socially inferior heretics, whose political dominance was unbearable. When the "Arab Spring" erupted in Syria, it did not take long for it to develop into an all-out sectarian civil war.

Even in **Iraq** under Saddam Hussein, the regime went through an Islamizing phase. Shi'ite opposition to the essentially Sunni regime was always ruthlessly suppressed. After Saddam Hussein's final rise to power in 1979, along with his effort to forge an Iraqi sense of national consciousness drawing on Iraq's supposed pre-Islamic, Babylonian past, Saddam was not averse to exploiting political Islam when he felt that such a shift might better serve his purpose.

Saddam Hussein
Became President in 1979

By INA (Iraqi News Agency) (Dar al-Ma'mun) [Public domain or Public domain], via Wikimedia Commons

Thus while cracking down on Shi'ite political movements, outlawing the Shi'ite opposition party *al-Da'wa* and arresting and executing Shi'ite leaders, the regime changed gears in its political language. Saddam even claimed direct descent from Ali Bin Abi Talib, revered by the Shi'ites as the rightful successor to the Prophet. The employment of Islamic themes for regime legitimization increased consistently from a toeing of the Islamic line for most of the war with Iran in 1980s to deliberate Islamic flag

12. Eyal Zisser, *Commanding Syria: Bashar al-Asad and the First Years in Power* (London: I.B. Tauris, 2007), pp. 48–58.

waving in the 1990s. During the war with Shi'ite Iran, hundreds of thousands of Iraqi Shi'ites fought shoulder to shoulder with their Sunni compatriots partly out of loyalty to the State of Iraq and to their own Iraqi-ness, partly out of intimidation by the state's ruthless organs of suppression.

The war, however, also made it increasingly clear to the regime just how effectively the Iranians had made religion into a mobilizing force, as opposed to the weakness of Ba'thi ideology in emotionally motivating Iraqis. This further encouraged the process of Islamization, which peaked on the eve of the Gulf War in early 1991, when the words of *Allahu Akbar* (God is great) were embroidered on the Iraqi flag.[13]

But these efforts were obviously artificial and got nowhere in bridging the sectarian divide between Sunnis and Shi'is in Iraq. After Saddam's overthrow by the US in 2003, the country rapidly degenerated into sectarian strife between Sunnis and Shi'is, which has yet to come to an end, more than a decade later.

Islamism in Jordan, Algeria and Palestine

Jordan, like other Arab states, has also experienced its chapter of Islamic revival. But Jordan, like all other Arab states, has a uniqueness of its own. Jordan has a religiously homogeneous population, like Egypt, and well over 90 percent of its people are Sunni Muslim speakers of the Arabic language. There is but a small minority of Arab Christians, mostly Orthodox.

Much is usually said, justifiably, about the cleavage between original Jordanians and Jordanians of Palestinian origin, but not enough attention is paid to the fact that the great majority of both Jordanians and Palestinians are Sunni Muslims, a collective cultural and religious identity that has bound them together for centuries and is more significant than their distinct but relatively new and more shallow modern national identities.

Though the monarchy in Jordan and the Islamists were clearly on opposite sides of the ideological divide, they had not always been so. In fact, the Muslim Brethren and the Jordanian regime had been long-standing political allies in the confrontation with the Nasserists and the Ba'thi secular Arab nationalists, throughout the 1950s and the 1960s. The Muslim Brethren also stood by the regime in 1970 in its war against the PLO, whose ranks included Marxist factions that also happened to be led by Christians.

There was, therefore, no residue of bad blood between the Jordanian regime and the Islamists, as there was in countries like Egypt, Syria and Algeria. Moreover, the Hashemites were not a religiously illegitimate minority, like the

13. Ofra Bengio, *Saddam's Word; Political Discourse in Iraq* (New York: Oxford University Press, 1998), pp. 80, 176–191.

Alawis in Syria. On the contrary, the monarchy regularly emphasized its noble Islamic ancestry, as descendants of the Prophet, who was himself of the House of Hashim.

Moreover, the Muslim Brethren and their political party, the Islamic Action Front (IAF), were no match in any competition with the Jordanian political establishment. The Islamists won some 40 percent of the seats in Jordan's 1989 relatively free parliamentary elections, an amazing feat and a sign of the changing times. The feat of 1989, however, was never repeated. The regime has used every available means, from new legislation to repression and fraud, to insure that no similar outcome would ever be obtained again by the Islamists.

Algeria was another example of Islamist electoral success. In December 1991, the first multi-party elections were held in Algeria since its independence in 1962. After the first round of the elections, it was clear that the Islamists were on the road to victory. The military intervened and cancelled the elections leading to the outbreak of a bloody civil war which lasted for ten years and claimed between 40,000 to 100,000 lives before the Islamists were finally subdued.

Palestine was yet another case, though the Palestinian example was extraordinary in the Arab world. The Palestinian Authority was not a fully sovereign entity, it was not a state and did not have the means of repression that other Arab states possessed and, therefore, lacked a forceful enough counterweight to the Islamic trend.

In the elections for the Palestinian Legislative Council in 2006, Hamas, the Islamist Palestinian group, emerged victorious in both the West Bank and Gaza. Fatah, essentially supported by Israel, the US and other Western governments, would not come to terms with Hamas on how to proceed with the implementation of the election results.

In June 2007, Hamas took over the Gaza Strip by force. The Palestinian Authority (PA), dominated by Fatah, remained in control of the West Bank, ruling through the instrument of a declared state of emergency. The West Bank under the PA, and Gaza under Hamas, have since developed as two separate political entities and all attempts at reconciliation have failed thus far.

2006 Palestinian Elections: The Victory of Hamas

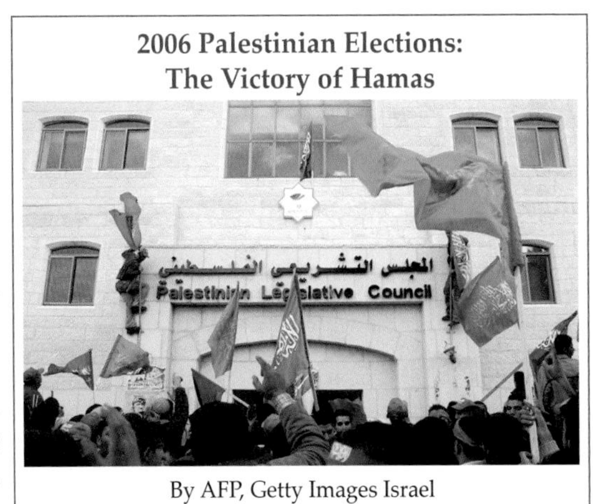

By AFP, Getty Images Israel

Secularism in Check

Hamas Takeover of Gaza, June 2007

By CIA (CIA-WF) [Public domain], via Wikimedia Commons

The fact that Islamist movements had risen to preeminence in Algeria and in Palestine — the lands of the FLN (the Front de Liberation Nationale) and the PLO, the two prototypical, ostensibly secular, national liberation movements of the 20th century Middle East — was another dramatic illustration of the secularist retreat.[14]

Throughout the Middle East, since the late 1980s, when fair and free elections have been held, the Islamists have either won outright or performed very well. This was also the case in Egypt and Tunisia in the "Arab Spring," and in Turkey in all elections since the mid-1990s, except for one.

The formerly prevalent assumption on the part of the secularizing Middle Eastern regimes, that the process of secularization was one of inevitable progression that would eventually extend to all Middle Eastern societies has been proven wrong.

The notion of secularization championed by these Middle Eastern regimes was drawn from the European experience of state formation and modernization, and based on the idea of secularization expounded upon in the works of the trinity of social theory, Durkheim, Marx, and Weber, in which the decline of religious belief was "scientifically" forecasted. State secularism in the 20th century Middle East, however, failed to produce secular societies. Though organized religion did decline, new religious movements with mass followings emerged.

In one of his earliest works over four decades ago, Bernard Lewis wrote that "the introduction of the secular heresy of nationalism, of collective self-worship, is the best founded and least mentioned of the many grievances of the Middle East against the West."[15] After a period in which secular nationalism assumed the dominant political role in Middle Eastern societies, its ideological offspring, the secularization of politics in society, was now being seriously challenged.

---

14. Steven Humphreys, *Between Memory and Desire: The Middle East in a Troubled Age* (Berkeley: University of California Press, 1999), p. 195.
15. Bernard Lewis, *The Middle East and the West* (New York: Harper Torchbook, 1966), p. 70.

While the secular nationalists sought to nationalize Islam and demote it to just one of various components of the national identity, for the Islamists, religion was the cohesive element of society. While they did not reject nationalism, they sought to Islamize the nation and the state.

Thus, the difference was essentially between those who wished to nationalize Islam and those who sought to Islamize nationalism. The nationalists were usually not so secular as to completely reject religion, while the Islamists were usually not so radical as to completely reject nationalism. But the two camps clearly had different centers of gravity.

Hamas and the PLO were good examples of these differences. The charter of Hamas, the Islamic Resistance Movement in Palestine, accepted nationalism as part and parcel of its religious ideology. But it proclaimed Palestine to be an Islamic trust or endowment, *waqf*, and condemned the PLO for having accepted the idea of a secular state. Secularism was in total contradiction to religious thought, as Hamas would have it. The Islamic character of Palestine was part of the Palestinian people's religious belief, the charter said. Once the PLO accepted Islam as a way of life, Hamas would serve as its soldiers, so the charter proclaimed.

The "Arab Spring": Between Modernity and Tradition

It was against this background of political struggle between forces more oriented towards tradition and others more oriented towards modernity that one should seek to analyze the new regional phenomenon that came to be known as the "Arab Spring."

Various basic paradigms have been used to explain the "Arab Spring." The most common was the democracy-autocracy dichotomy, seeking to explain the "Arab Spring" as a struggle between the forces of autocracy and those of democracy. An alternative, and preferable, paradigm would be to explain the events in terms of the ongoing struggle over the last two centuries between the forces of modernity and tradition. The "Arab Spring" has exposed the salience of neo-traditionalist political forces, in the form of political Islam, sectarianism and tribalism and it is these that have been far more demonstratively relevant in the "Arab Spring" than the democracy-autocracy confrontation.

After all, if we look at the Egyptian example, where it was clearly a clash between the Muslim Brethren and the military, neither of these were the epitome of democracy. These were essentially two autocratic forces: the Muslim Brethren, far more representative of the neo-traditionalist forces, versus the military, as more representative of the forces of modernity.

The forces of neo-traditionalism were not opposed to modernity and have been deeply affected by it. Political Islam was unquestionably a product of the modern world. But it was also most disturbed by the secularizing thrust of modernity and nationalism. They sought in their various ways to channel modernity and nationalism through a traditionalist mold that would allow for modernization and nationalist identity, while preserving critical traditional or neo-traditional values, rather than abandoning, marginalizing or suppressing them in the name of secular nationalism or modernity. These sets of values related to religion and to the observance of religious law, or to the preservation of sectarian and/or tribal identities, with their attendant traditions, customs and values.

As for the socio-economic background to the "Arab Spring," a wealth of analysis and information can be gleaned from the UN Arab Human Development Reports that have been published regularly since the early 2000s. These reports have pointed to three deficits from which the Arab world tends to suffer: The deficit in political freedom; the deficit in first world education systems; and the deficit in gender equality. The combination of these three have created economies, with poor productivity, largely because of low levels of female participation in the workforce, coupled with high rates of population growth. Poorly performing economies with high rates of population growth were a recipe for profound socio-economic crisis that many Arab states had to cope with.

In these societies an entire generation of young people between the ages of 18 to 30 had nothing to wait for, no expectation for a job in the near future, or even for the possibility of getting married and having a real life any time soon. An entire younger generation was completely disenchanted with the present and entirely hopeless for the future that awaited them. James Gelvin has referred to this age group as those, who after childhood and boyhood reached this age of 18 to 30, the age of "waithood," as they waited in hopeless anticipation for something to turn up that may give them a life.[16] It was this sense of exasperation and hopelessness that was at the root of the outburst of the "Arab Spring," more than any sudden inspiration for democratization against authoritarianism.

"Spring" has been used very widely to describe the phenomenon of the uprisings throughout the Arab world. But "spring" was a misnomer. "Spring" had a European connotation and its origins were in the Spring of Nations in 1848, the Prague Spring of 1968, or the Spring of Nations in Eastern Europe after the fall of communism in the late 1980s. This was a "spring" that ushered in secular democratic governments, for the most part, on the ruins of various

16. James Gelvin, *The Arab Uprisings: What Everyone Needs to Know* (New York and Oxford: Oxford University Press, 2012), pp. 18–22.

authoritarian regimes. But there has not been such a democratic outcome in the Middle Eastern countries. In the Middle East (with the partial exception of Tunisia — see below) the neo-traditional forces of Islamism and sectarian or tribal politics and widespread extreme political violence and civil war have proved to be far more pervasive than the promotion of democratic regimes.

How could the depiction of the events and the implied expectations have been so far off? Just as there was an emphasis on this flawed European analogy, there was a similarly extraordinary focus on technology and the new social media of Facebook and Twitter in explaining the explosion of the "Arab Spring." Thus, the revolutions in the Arab world were given a universal character, that is, similar to other parts of the world with no cognizance of any Middle Eastern specificity, or attempt to seriously consider any recognition of the potential "otherness of the other."

There was a tendency on the part of scholars in the West, strangely enough, usually ideological multiculturalists, to underrate or even to ignore the cultural input of the "other" as a valid explanatory and analytical tool and to obfuscate the importance of religion as a factor in people's behavior in the Middle East, even though it was fairly obvious that religion was a key marker of identity in Muslim societies.

Culture matters. That is **not** to make the case for Middle Eastern exceptionalism, but only to say that culture matters in all cultures, including in the Middle East, just as it matters in other regions of the world and in other cultures. Though scholars have been urged by some to be careful not to throw out the political culture baby with the bath water, many have done so, and many still do.

The apparent reluctance to deal with culture has a lot to do with the extraordinary impact of Edward Said's *Orientalism,* and Said's rejection of the Orientalist emphasis on culture. In *Orientalism,* Said made the point of dismissing the "notion that there are geographical spaces with indigenous radically 'different' inhabitants who can be defined on the basis of some religion, culture, or racial essence proper to that geographical space."[17]

As others have pointed out, this results in the proclivity to "explain events as if these were generic phenomena inextricably linked to paradigms of a universal nature [...] Such universal paradigms attempt to explain widely divergent historical developments as if differences in culture, time, and place, had no vital bearing on historical outcomes."[18]

---

17. Edward Said, *Orientalism* (New York: Vintage Books, 1979), p. 322.
18. Jacob Lassner and S. Ilan Troen, *Jews and Muslims in the Arab World: Haunted by Pasts Real and Imagined* (Lanham, MD: Rowman and Littlefield, 2007), p. xi.

Thus, there was this politically correct tendency to ignore the undercurrents of political culture and to focus on the more superficial, readily apparent globalized features of universalism such as Facebook and Twitter, instead of the more profound and less immediately recognizable political and social trends of Middle Eastern societies, as they have evolved over the last 200 years. The focus, therefore, of those who spoke of the "Arab Spring" was on the westernized secular democrats and not the Islamists; but it was the Islamists and not the miniscule minority of secular democrats, who actually rose to the fore and won the elections or launched sectarian civil wars at the expense of the virtually non-existent secular democrats.

There were those who said that perhaps "Arab Awakening" would have been a more suitable term than "Arab Spring." "Arab Awakening" was intriguing but not original. It was 100 years old. "Arab Awakening" was the name that was given to the Arab nationalist awakening in the early years of the 20th century, on the eve of, and during the First World War (see above Chapter Three).

But there was a major difference between the "Arab Awakening" then and now. The "Arab Awakening" of the early 20th century was essentially secular. It was about Arab nationalism and, thus, about defining people in accordance with the language they spoke, Arabic, and not by their religion, Muslim or otherwise. But that was hardly the case now, when secularism was actually very much in retreat, for a number of reasons.

The attraction of secularism in the late 19th and much of the 20th centuries in the Middle East was in emulation of the West that was at the height of its power and expansion. But the West of recent decades was far less impressive, and seemingly in economic and political decline in both the United States and Europe. It was presently a far less appealing example to follow than it was in the earlier part of the 20th century.

Another great secular model to follow was that of the Soviet Union in the middle of the 20th century. The Soviet Union was an amazing example of a weak and underdeveloped country, which in the space of one generation, between the two world wars, turned into a superpower. For the Arabs, who were in an urgent quest for power, prestige and prosperity, the Soviet model looked ideal. But the Soviet model collapsed in the Soviet Union itself, and there was nothing much left to admire.

Perhaps most important of all, was the failure of Arabism. Pan-Arabism was not only a movement for the unity of the Arab people, it was, at least in theory, a secular ideology. Arabism was the platform for the secularization of Arab politics and society. Its political failure, therefore, also meant the failure of this platform of secularization, as well as the general undermining of the regional stature of the Arab states.

The decline of the Arab states meant the ascendance of the non-Arab countries, Turkey and Iran, and Israel to a lesser degree, as regional superpowers. Neither Turkey of the Islamists nor Iran of the Ayatollahs were models for secular emulation by other Muslim states. Turkey and Iran, much like the Ottoman and Persian Empires of the 19th century, met in the territory of present day Iraq, in their respective spheres of influence. Turkey was influential in northern Iraq, and Iran in much of the rest of the country. These were not just spheres of influence between the two rising powers, Turkey and Iran, but the spheres of influence of Sunna and Shi'a, Turkey being the most powerful of the Sunni states, and Iran the leader of the Shi'ites in the region.

In the formation of Middle Eastern alliances these days, it was not the pro-American states against the pro-Soviet states, which was obviously an anachronism irrelevant to the present. Neither was it the monarchies versus the republics, which was equally out of date. The states of the Middle East now tended to form alliances on the basis of their religious/sectarian affiliation, Sunnis versus Shi'is.

The Island of Bahrain was a case in point. Bahrain was a country with a Shi'ite majority ruled by a Sunni minority. In the early months of the "Arab Spring" in February 2011, it was essentially the Shi'ite majority that rose in rebellion against the Sunni minority.

Bahrain

By Hégésippe Cormier aka Hégésippe [GFDL (http://www.gnu.org/copyleft/fdl.html), CC-BY-SA-3.0 (http://creativecommons.org/licenses/by-sa/3.0/)], via Wikimedia Commons

The transformation of Bahrain into a Shi'ite dominated state would have been most unwelcome to Saudi Arabia and the other countries of the Gulf. For them such a change in Bahrain meant the creation of a staging ground for Iranian influence, an Iranian platform of subversion adjacent to the coast of Saudi Arabia and the other Gulf States. Saudi Arabia and its Gulf allies invaded Bahrain in March 2011 and put down the Shi'ite rebellion, to prevent Iran from making strategic gain so close to home.

The "Arab Spring": Egypt, Tunisia, Syria, Jordan, Yemen and Libya

If between states, relations were governed by the sectarian/religious fault line, this was all the more so within the various states of the Middle East. The neo-traditionalist forces of Islamism, sectarianism and tribalism could be readily identified in every single example of the "Arab Spring." Egypt, Tunisia, Syria, Iraq, Bahrain, Libya and Yemen are all examples of this resurgence of the neo-traditionalist forces of Islamism, sectarianism or tribalism.

In **Egypt**, after the overthrow of President Mubarak in February 2011, the Muslim Brethren and other Islamists won in all the various elections and referendums that were held by wide margins, with the exception of the presidency, where the candidate of the Muslim Brethren, Muhammad Mursi, barely scraped through with a very narrow victory.

Mursi's term in office was disappointing to many, if not most Egyptians. Mursi's almost dictatorial ways toward the Islamization of the state, his inept governance, the rapidly declining economy and the chaotic breakdown of law and order led millions of Egyptians back to the streets in June 2013 to demand his removal. After just a year at the helm, Mursi was brought down by a military coup that had very widespread popular support. The main forces in Egyptian politics were clearly the Islamists, on the one hand, and the military, on the other. The secular democrats were in short supply and the big question was, of course, could there possibly be a democracy in Egypt without legions of democrats.

The rise to power of the Muslim Brethren, the political prominence of the even more radical Salafis, and the general chaotic decline of law and order exposed the Copts in Egypt to rising sectarian violence against individuals, churches and other institutions. In the mass demonstrations that preceded the military coup that unseated President Mursi in July 2013, Copts were noticeably present. Moreover, Nagib Sawiris, the Copt multimillionaire and media mogul, was by his own admission, instrumental in financing the movement that led to the struggle that brought Mursi down. After the coup, the dispossessed Islamists singled out the Copts as targets for their anger and frustration. Copts faced a new wave of violence amidst accusations that they had conspired with the secularists and the military to unseat the legitimate and freely elected government of Egypt.

In Egypt and in other Arab states, like Syria and Iraq, where there were serious sectarian tensions, it was often the Christians who found themselves in the crossfire. In recent years there has been a considerable increase in the emigration of Christians from the Middle East to other places.

In **Tunisia**, where the "Arab Spring" had begun, after the overthrow of the ruling dictatorship of Zayn al-Abidin Bin Ali, it was the Islamists of the *Nahda* (Awakening) party who emerged victorious in the first free elections. A coalition government led by the Islamists was formed in early 2012. The Tunisian experience of Islamist government also proved disappointing. No one had miracle solutions for the profound socio-economic problems facing these countries.

Arab Spring in Tunisia

Zayn al-Abidin Bin Ali
Par R. D. Ward (original uploader was Profburp at fr.wikipedia) [Public domain], via Wikimedia Commons

In Tunisia in early 2013 there were two political assassinations of liberal politicians and other forms of political violence initiated by Islamic radicals. Liberals accused the Islamists in power of not doing enough to restrain the extremists who sought to push the country too far and too fast towards more radical Islamization.

Tunisia remained deeply divided between Islamists and secularists, a division which was reinforced by regional fault lines too, the northern and eastern more urbanized coastal areas serving as the heartland of the secularists, while the rural hinterland and the south were more firmly in the hands of the Islamists.

Probably the most secular of all Arab states, in Tunisia the Islamists were more forthcoming in their willingness to compromise with their secular opponents. At the end of 2013, the Islamists and the secularists came to an agreement whereby *al-Nahda* would step down in favor of an independent caretaker government that would prepare the country for new elections. After a prolonged and very convoluted, but non-violent, negotiating process, a new constitution was finally ratified in January 2014. The constitution, seeking to balance between the country's Islamic identity and its democratic aspirations, was not free of internal contradictions. These might prove to be contentious in the future, but in the meantime they made agreement possible.

Beji Caid Essebsi
President of Tunisia since December 2014

https://upload.wikimedia.org/wikipedia/commons/thumb/2/25/Beji_Caid_el_Sebsi_at_the_37th_G8_Summit_in_Deauville_006.jpg

New elections for Tunisia's parliament took place in October 2014, followed at the end of the year by elections for the presidency.

In both elections the secularist alliance emerged victorious as the Islamists graciously accepted defeat. *Nida Tunis* (The Call of Tunisia), an alliance of a wide variety of secular groups, defeated the Islamist *al-Nahda* party in the parliamentary elections. In the presidential campaign *al-Nahda* chose not to run a candidate and the election was won by the 88 year old leader of *Nida Tunis*, Beji Caid Essebsi, a scion of the ancient regime. He provided a fatherly semblance of stability and continuity to Tunisia's, thus far, successful transition to pluralist democracy. Tunisia was, therefore, the encouraging exception to the rule in the post "Arab Spring" Middle East. Whether the new government had the wherewithal to address Tunisia's social and economic troubles still remained to be seen.

Syria of the "Arab Spring" was a story of sectarian politics. In Syria under Hafiz al-Asad domestic stability was secured from the early 1980s for the next 30 years. However, under his successor, Bashar al-Asad, beginning in June 2000, Syria was never as effectively governed, as it had been by Hafiz, his father. With the "Arab Spring" protests, beginning in March 2011, Syria progressively spun out of control with disastrous humanitarian consequences. What began as a minor protest by disgruntled peasants and workers in Syria's rural backwater soon mushroomed into a full-scale sectarian civil war, the end of which was nowhere in sight.

The opposition in Syria was composed mainly of representatives of the Sunni majority. But not all Sunnis were firmly allied with the opposition. The regime still enjoyed support among urban Sunnis who had largely remained neutral and uncommitted. A myriad of Sunni organizations made up the bulk of a very disparate opposition. In the meantime Syria was no longer the unitary state it once was. It might recover if Asad wins in the end, and it could disintegrate if he does not, with a variety of partial and decentralized options in between.

Map of Syria 2015

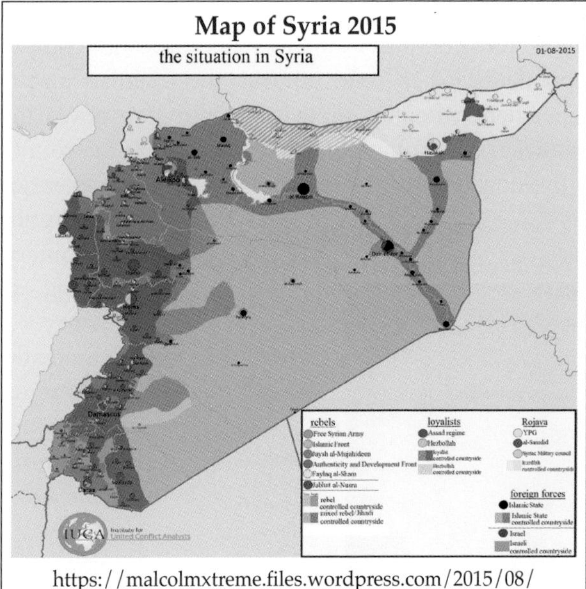

https://malcolmxtreme.files.wordpress.com/2015/08/syria-8-7-2015.jpg

By late 2014, three-and-a-half years into the civil war, the country was divided into a number of zones of control. The regime had lost control of the border area with Turkey, which was divided into two different zones, one in the northwest, controlled by the rebels, in which Aleppo was still contested territory, and the other in the northeast, controlled by Syria's long marginalized and newly assertive Kurds. The rebels also controlled much of the Jazira area in the east, including the towns of Raqqa and Dayr al-Zor. The regime still controlled the capital Damascus (although not entirely), important sections of the border area with Lebanon, and the northwestern coastal area, which was territory predominantly populated by the ruling Alawi minority.

In sum, the territorial identities that were cultivated by the regimes in Iraq and Syria have proved to have been very thin veneers. Behind the territorialist façade, the regimes in question were sectarian to the core. Just like the Tikriti group that ruled in Iraq, the Syrian Ba'thi regime was dominated, though obviously not exclusively, by the Asads and their allies from the Alawi community. The intimate cohesion of these minorities in power was a source of great stability and reliability as long as they lasted. But once the minorities lost their unbridled control, the sectarian genie was let out of the bottle. The oppressed and the oppressors changed places, as in Iraq, or fought it out inconclusively so far, as it was in Syria.

The weakening of the former authoritarian regimes in countries like Syria and Iraq did not usher in pluralist democracies but rather sectarian civil war and state disintegration. It was in this chaotic reality that a plethora of militias and armed groups have risen to fill the vacuum. Of these, **the ISIS phenomenon** is unquestionably the strongest, the largest and the most impressive, albeit in ways and means that many would regard as morally reprehensible, if not to say barbaric.

A word is in order about the confusion in the name of ISIS or ISIL. In Arabic, the name of the group was *al-Dawla al-Islamiyya fi al-Iraq wal-Sham*, that is, the "Islamic State in Iraq and al-Sham." Sham is Greater Syria (the lands of what are today Syria, Lebanon, Israel/Palestine and Jordan) alternatively translated into English as "Syria" (thus ISIS) or the "Levant" (thus ISIL).

In June 2014, ISIS declared the establishment of a Caliphate, under the self-proclaimed Caliph, Abu Bakr al-Baghdadi, in the territories under their control in northwestern Iraq and much of eastern Syria. The Caliphate was henceforth referred to simply as the Islamic State (IS), with its capital in the eastern Syrian city of Raqqa.

The origins of ISIS are to be found in post-Saddam Iraq. The empowerment of the Shi'is in Iraq led to the formation of various Sunni opposition groups, one of which was al-Qa'ida in Iraq, which subsequently transformed into the Islamic

State in Iraq. Exploiting the convulsions of the Syrian civil war, the Islamic State in Iraq expanded into Syria and formed the Islamic State in Iraq and al-Sham in April 2013. ISIS is thereby filling some of the Sunni void, fighting the Shi'ite dominated government in Iraq as well as its allies in the Alawi regime in Syria, while it goes about erasing the borders between Syria and Iraq, undoing the state structure that was established a century ago.

The expansion of ISIS resulted more from the weakness of its opponents than from its own intrinsic power. ISIS was not invincible and has also suffered serious setbacks and severe losses. Their future depended very much on the unpredictable determination and resilience of their very disparate collection of rivals such as the Asad regime and the Kurds in Syria, or the Shi'i majority and the Kurds in Iraq, all backed up, directly or indirectly, strangely enough, by both the US and a coalition of Sunni Arab states, on the one hand, and Shi'i Iran, on the other. They all have their different reasons for opposing Sunni extremists like ISIS.

In **Jordan** the "Arab Spring" initially emboldened the opposition. But the outcomes of the revolutions in countries like Egypt, and especially the bloodbath in Syria, were horrifying to most Jordanians. Even opponents of the monarchy in Jordan tend to see the Hashemite regime as the cohesive device that holds the country all together. The situation, therefore, in Jordan remained manageable, as long as the unswerving loyalty of the security establishment lasted. The capacity of the regime to continue muddling through will depend more on its ability to deal effectively with the economy than on any other single factor, including the pace of political reform.

Yemen and **Libya**, where tribalism was so deep-rooted and stateness so extremely low, were at the far end of the spectrum. After the removal of Muammar Qadhafi in Libya (August 2011) and of Ali Abdullah Saleh in Yemen (February 2012), both countries have degenerated into empty shells of formerly sovereign entities, as competing tribal militias jockeyed for position, often violently.

The Arab Spring in Libya: The Overthrow of Muammar Qadhafi in August 2011

By U.S. Navy photo by Mass Communication Specialist 2nd Class Jesse B. Awalt/Released [Public domain], via Wikimedia Commons

The Arab Spring in Yemen:
The Overthrow of President Ali Abdullah Saleh in February 2012

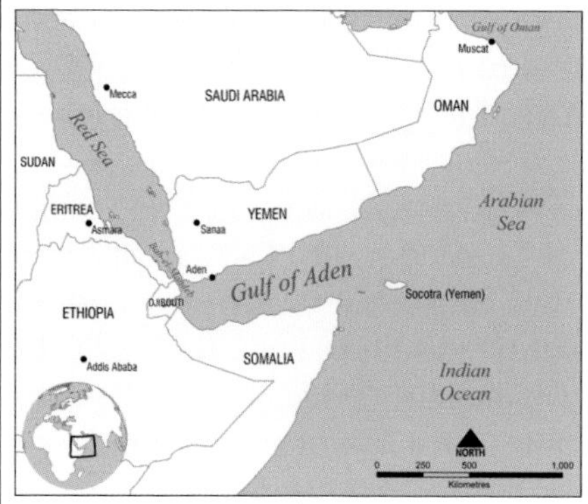

By NormanEinstein (Own work) [CC-BY-SA-3.0 (http://creativecommons.org/licenses/by-sa/3.0) or GFDL (http://www.gnu.org/copyleft/fdl.html)], via Wikimedia Commons

Kremlin.ru [CC-BY-3.0 (http://creativecommons.org/licenses/by/3.0)], via Wikimedia Commons

In Yemen, the tribal fault lines were reinforced by sectarian divisions between Sunnis and Shi'is, who were concentrated in the mountains in the northwest of the country and were about 40 percent of the overall population. Yemeni lawlessness and anarchy, already pervasive after years of ongoing tribal and sectarian conflict, a persistent presence of al-Qa'ida strongholds in the countryside, and other Islamist political opposition to the regime, hit rock bottom when Shi'i rebels, known as the Houthis, overran the capital of Sana'a in September 2014.

The Houthis, who have been in a state of active rebellion against the central government for over a decade, were named after their commander, Hussein Badr al-Din al-Houthi, who was killed by Yemeni government forces in 2004. The Houthis were Shi'is of the Zaydi branch of Shi'ism, that is an offshoot of the mainstream Shi'ism that is practiced in Iran, Iraq and Lebanon. But because of their Shi'ite faith the Houthis were widely suspected by their Sunni opponents as potential, or actual, allies of Iran. Their spectacular takeover of Sana'a turned the Yemeni government into even more of a powerless empty shell. Shortly thereafter the Houthis also took control of the port of Hudayda, just north of the strategically important Straits of Bab al-Mandab on the Yemeni coast, at the entrance to the Red Sea *en route* to the Suez Canal and Europe.

The Houthis were not expected to interfere with shipping in the straits, which would probably provoke a fierce international response. But just the fact that a force widely perceived to be close to Iran was located in such a strategically sensitive location, provided Iran with possible control, or at least leverage, over both the Straits of Hormuz at the exit from the Persian Gulf and Bab al-Mandab, a potentially significant boost for Iranian hegemonic design.

Yemen and Libya are extreme cases of countries that might fall apart. The chaos in Yemen might eventually lead to the reconstitution of the division of the country into North and South Yemen as had been the situation before the unification of the two in 1990.

https://commons.wikimedia.org/wiki/File:Map_of_traditional_provinces_of_Libye-en.svgorg/copyleft/fdl.html)], via Wikimedia Commons

Libya was very low in components of stateness. It had most ineffective state institutions, was torn asunder by tribal identities and also split between Tripolitania, Cyrenaica and Fezzan, those three territories that were thrust together in the creation of Libya by the Western allies in 1951. Its oil wealth was unequally distributed between the three provinces, very much in favor of Cyrenaica, another factor which may precipitate the dissolution of the state as warring tribes competed for control of the country's resources. According to some Jordanian ambassadors quoted in the Jordanian media, Libya remained "the tribal society it was in 1951" when it became independent. "As a political concept," they say, "Libya for many of its citizens remains limited to tribe, family, or province: The notion of a unified system of political checks and balances remains terra incognita." So these Jordanian ambassadors observed.[19]

Looking at the "Arab Spring" in perspective, Arabism and the Arab state have been challenged in recent years more than they have been for the entire century that has passed. Arab nationalism and the formation of the Arab state were the two most important processes that governed Arab politics for much of the 20th century. Arabism failed for the most part, and the Arab state at the beginning of the 21st century is being challenged in terms of its cohesion and integrity perhaps more than at any time since the Arab state system was formed a century ago.

The Non-Arab Countries

Iran and Turkey had long traditions of independent statehood that went back for centuries. They also had their own specific linguistic identities. But here

19. Musa Keilani in *JordanTimes*, 20 March 2011.

too, in both cases, secular nationalism has given ground, albeit in very different forms, to Islamic revival. As opposed to various Arab states, although they also had their domestic difficulties, there was, as of yet, no serious challenge to the territorial integrity or national identity of either of these two countries.

The Republic of Turkey: From the Second World War to the Present

Kemal Atatürk, the founding father of the new secular Turkish Republic, died in 1938. Since his passing from the scene, his secularist Kemalist vision was gradually eroded. Beginning with democratization and multi-party politics introduced after the Second World War, religion gradually reestablished a high profile in Turkish society and political life.

In 1950, the new Democrat Party won the elections, in part thanks to its policies in favor of expanding the role of religion in education and in society in general, in reaction to the secularist policies of the Kemalist elite. In 1960, after ten years of the Democrat Party in power, which included an exhibition of both social disorder and strong authoritarian tendencies in limiting the freedom of action of the opposition, the army intervened in what was to be the first of three such military coups in Turkey. The military regarded itself as the ultimate guardian of the secular order, and its interventions in politics were ostensibly designed to uphold the principles of the Kemalist Republic.

Mustafa Kemal Atatürk
1881–1938

By Cemal Işıksel (1905-1989) [Public domain], via Wikimedia Commons

But after the return to power of the politicians, the trend of Islamic revival continued. The 1960s were a period of rising radicalism and political violence from both the extreme left and from the national and religious right, coming in the wake of rapid urbanization, expanding education and especially the growth of the universities. Political violence between left and right escalated severely in 1970 and 1971, and the army stepped in again in early 1971, and remained in power for two years until 1973.

In 1970, the National Order Party emerged as the first Islamist party in Turkey, but it was banned by the Constitutional Court for violating the secularist principles of the constitution. The banned National Order Party was succeeded by another Islamist party, the National Salvation Party, in 1972. These parties reflected the ever increasing role of religion in society and politics, which continued unabated during the 1970s as the National Salvation Party rapidly expanded its power base.

The Emergence of Islamist Parties in Turkey

Necmettin Erbakan, the founder of the first Islamist party in Turkey

Zest at the Turkish language Wikipedia [GFDL (http://www.gnu.org/copyleft/fdl.html), CC-BY-SA-3.0 (http://creativecommons.org/licenses/by-sa/3.0/) or CC-BY-SA-2.5-2.0-1.0 (http://creativecommons.org/licenses/by-sa/2.5-2.0-1.0)], via Wikimedia Commons

Towards the end of the decade, Turkey entered another period of domestic turbulence. The country faced economic difficulties in the wake of the international oil crisis. The politicians and the police force proved incapable of dealing with the political violence. Matters were made worse by the upsurge of guerrilla activity by the disaffected Kurdish minority in Turkey, and the Islamic revolution in Iran in 1979, which further encouraged the Islamists in Turkey. The National Salvation Party now had the self-assurance to openly call for the restoration of the Shari'a in Turkey. In 1980, the army intervened, staging the third and, thus far, last coup, remaining in power this time for three years until 1983.

Ever since the late 1940s, there has been a remarkable proliferation of religious schools known as the Imam Hatip Schools. These were schools ostensibly for prayer leaders (Imam) and preachers (Hatip), but were actually religious schools with a mixed curriculum of secular and religious subjects. They expanded from a handful in 1949 to about 1,000 in their peak during the 1990s.

The expansion of the Imam Hatip schools produced increasing numbers of graduates who joined the ranks of the party activists of Islamist political parties. Very much in contrast to the views of the Kemalist elite that regarded public education as the chief instrument for the transformation of the people into citizens committed to the principle of secularism, these schools expanded at a pace that was most disturbing to the secularists in Turkey. In the minds of the secularists, these schools, where students were infused with Islamist views, were the training grounds of the Islamist movement.

Ironically, the military, historically the ardent protector of the secular order, had itself contributed to the Islamic revival. After the 1980 coup, the army sought societal reform that would counterbalance the extreme ideologies of the Marxist left and the fascist right, both of which had disrupted Turkish politics. The alternative they presented came to be known as the "Turkish-Islamic synthesis," which meant a controlled Islamization process undertaken through the vehicle of state supervised religious education. The military now redefined the role of religion as a possible source of solidarity to cushion the tensions arising from the multiple ideologies between left and right. State sponsored Islam, it was thought, would serve as a barrier to the penetration of more radical Islamists. As a consequence, religion made some headway into parliament and personal religious devotion was considered normal, as religiosity became more publicly visible from the 1980s.

All the political parties were shut down by the army in 1980, and new parties were established in 1983, when military rule came to an end. The newly established Motherland Party, which was a heterogeneous coalition of liberal secularists and Islamists, dominated politics in the 1980s. They adopted a conciliatory stand towards religion, due in part to the rising influence of the Islamist Welfare Party which had replaced the National Salvation Party in 1983. In the December 1995 general elections, the Welfare Party emerged as the largest party, and joined, as senior partner, a coalition government with the True Path Party in early 1996.

Religious mystical orders became more active, and there was another huge increase in the number of Imam Hatip schools. The army, displeased by the growing Islamist influence now also represented in the ruling coalition, intervened again. Not by a coup on this occasion, but by what was seen as a post-modern military intervention. The army applied pressure on the government to dissolve the coalition and the government was indeed brought down in May 1997. The Welfare Party was soon banned by the Constitutional Court, a ruling induced by similar pressure from the military.

The Justice and Development Party (AKP) – Established in 2001

Party leader: Recep Tayyip Erdoğan

The banned Welfare Party was succeeded by the more liberal Justice and Development party, known by its Turkish acronym as the AKP that was established in 2001. These, albeit more moderate Islamists of the AKP, led by Recep Tayyip Erdoğan, came to power and won the elections three times in a row, in 2002, 2007 and again in 2011.

After his three successive terms as Prime Minister, Erdoğan ran for the Presidency in

August 2014 and won by a handsome margin. Ever since, Erdoğan has been systematically shifting power from the Prime Minister and the cabinet into the hands of the formerly mostly ceremonial Presidency in an obvious effort to further enhance his increasingly autocratic regime.

Under the AKP there has been a calculated marginalization of the military in Turkish politics. Hundreds of officers were imprisoned by the government on charges of having conspired against the AKP government. It was not clear whether the charges were well founded or possibly contrived to suppress legitimate opposition to the government. There were more imprisoned journalists in Turkey under the AKP than anywhere else. There are signs of growing opposition in the more secular liberal public and also in certain religious circles to the seemingly authoritarian ways of the AKP government of Erdoğan.

No other Muslim country had ever undergone a process of intensive state imposed secularization as had the Turkish Republic. But there too, secularization was being pushed back to the extent that in the eyes of some Turks a quiet counter revolution was underway. The Kemalist revolution had never really penetrated into the depths of the rural periphery. The rural folk, who had migrated in ever increasing numbers to Turkey's major cities, were still deeply attached to their traditional norms and values.

Instead of the cities bringing secular Kemalism to the villages, the Islamist periphery has brought religion back into the city. The population of Turkey has increased from 21 million in 1950 to 52 million in 1986 and to 75 million in 2012. Though Turkey has enjoyed impressive economic development, rapid population growth has been a constant socio-economic liability. Moreover, neoliberal policies have, as in other countries, led to widening gaps between rich and poor. Poverty was widespread in Turkey. Most of the students in the Imam Hatip schools come from poor rural families or from city-born children of migrants from the villages. It is they, too, who sought the comfort of the mystical religious orders. As Islam reasserts itself as a critical component of the Turkish identity, a much more positive view towards the Ottoman Islamic heritage is being encouraged, in comparison to the early days of the Turkish Republic.

For decades, the Turkish Republic was in bitter conflict with its Kurdish minority. For a while the AKP government adopted a more conciliatory attitude towards Turkey's Kurds. As Sunni Muslims, the Kurds were more easily assimilated into an Islamist Turkey than they were previously under the strict secular nationalist Turkishness from which they were essentially excluded. But the moderation did not last and conflict has resumed.

In the over 70 years since the death of Atatürk, Islamist political parties have become an ever more salient feature of Turkish politics. Though in stark contrast to the original secularist formulations of the Turkish Republic, the Islamists

Distribution of the Kurdish Population in Turkey

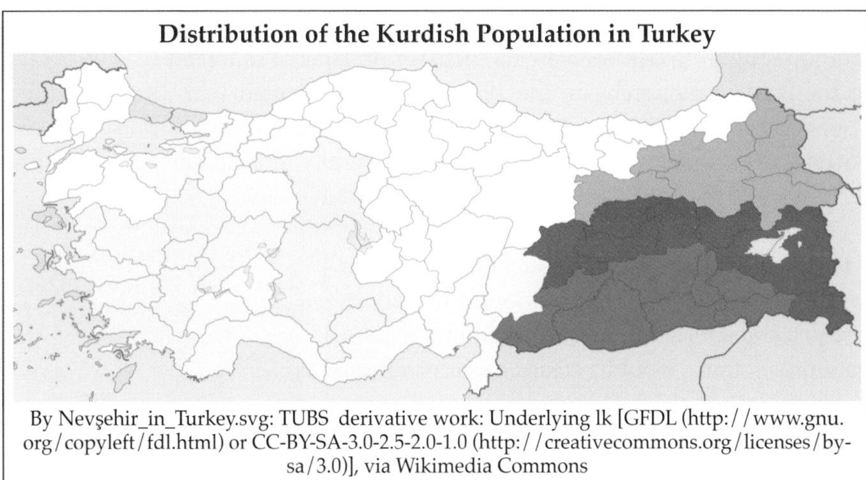

By Nevşehir_in_Turkey.svg: TUBS derivative work: Underlying lk [GFDL (http://www.gnu.org/copyleft/fdl.html) or CC-BY-SA-3.0-2.5-2.0-1.0 (http://creativecommons.org/licenses/by-sa/3.0)], via Wikimedia Commons

could not but eventually make their mark in the upper echelons of the political order.

There was, as a result, a growing sense of trepidation within the ranks of the secular center that the Islamist periphery will gradually erode the founding secularist principles of the republic and establish a new regime that would not pay homage to the Kemalist revolutionary heritage. There is significant and increasing opposition to the Islamist trend. Only time will tell who is to emerge victorious.

Iran: From the Pahlavi Dynasty to the Islamic Republic

In Iran, Islamic politics completely overthrew the monarchy that the Pahlavis had established in the 1920s. The name Pahlavi that the monarchy chose for

The Sassanid Empire From 3rd to 7th Century AD

By Getoryk (Own work) [CC-BY-SA-3.0 (http://creativecommons.org/licenses/by-sa/3.0)], via Wikimedia Commons

itself had Sassanid origins, taken from ancient pre-Islamic Persia. The monarchy thereby sought to demonstrate its secular non-Islamic character. The crowning of the Pahlavi monarchy in the 1920s was implemented with British indirect approval, contributing to the image of the regime from the outset as one buttressed by foreign support. This image generally reflected negatively on the legitimacy of the Pahlavis in the eyes of the Iranian people.

Riza Shah was deeply influenced by Kemal Atatürk of Turkey. Like in Turkey, he sought rapid modernization: The creation of a modern army, transportation and communication networks, that would create a centralized government, and the promotion of Iranian nationalism, based on the country's pre-Islamic Persian greatness.

The Coronation of Riza Shah Pahlavi (1926)

See page for author [Public domain], via Wikimedia Commons

In 1929, a law was passed on Western clothing, and in 1935 European hats were required too, taking a leaf out of the book of the Kemalist Republic.

But Iran was not well prepared for this kind of forced Westernization. Iran had been far less exposed to the West during the 19th century, when the Ottomans underwent their most intensive reforms. Consequently, the Iranians also had a less Westernized elite to implement the reforms, and a much stronger religious establishment to resist them.

Muhammad Riza Shah

See page for author [Public domain], via Wikimedia Commons

During the Second World War, important changes took place in Iran. Riza Shah was an admirer of Hitler in the 1930s, and during the war Iran was occupied by Soviet, US and British forces. The Allies forced Riza to abdicate and to have his son Muhammad Riza Shah succeed him in 1941.

After the War, anti-Western sentiment was very powerful in Iran, particularly in demanding the nationalization of the Anglo-Iranian Oil Company. One of the key figures leading the campaign was Muhammad Musaddeq, a prominent critic of the Shah's dictatorship. In March 1951, a nationalization bill was passed in parliament under Musaddeq's leadership. He became so popular and influential that the Shah had no choice but to appoint him Prime Minister.

Muhammad Musaddeq (1882–1967)

See page for author [Public domain], via Wikimedia Commons

Musaddeq remained in office for two years until 1953. Iranian oil in the meantime was boycotted by Western nations, leading to a major economic crisis in Iran, causing much local discontent. The Shah tried to dismiss Musaddeq in August 1953, but failed as Musaddeq simply refused to step down. Massive demonstrations in Musaddeq's favor forced the Shah to briefly flee the country as the monarchy seemed to be about to fall. The army supported the Shah and removed Musaddeq. The removal of Musaddeq was widely believed to have actually been engineered by the CIA, which was probably true in this particular case. The Shah returned from his brief exile to resume control. An international consortium was formed to manage the export of Iranian oil in agreement with the Iranian government. The crisis was over, but the price for this solution was in the image of the Shah, now seen as even more dependent than before on foreign support.

In January 1963, the Shah initiated what was called the "White Revolution." This included a moderate land reform, and economic and social reforms. An education corps was established to reduce illiteracy from 80 to 50 percent within a decade. There was an attempt, as part of the "White Revolution," to bureaucratize the *ulama* and to expand Western-style secular education. A health corps was formed to raise standards of public health.

Ayatollah Khomeini was forced into exile in late 1964

By نامعلوم (پایگاه اطلاع‌رسانی امام خمینی) [Public domain], via Wikimedia Commons

But the "White Revolution" had only limited success. The landed aristocracy and the *ulama* were never happy with these reforms. Ayatollah Khomeini was vocally critical of these secular Westernizing reforms and he was forced into exile as of late 1964.

The reforms did not do very much for the expanding rural population, which continued to swell the ranks of the urban poor. Urbanization and the growing disaffection of the urban poor in an inflationary economy with an ever-rising cost of living was a growing liability for the regime.

In 1971, the Shah initiated the celebrations commemorating 2,500 years of the Persian monarchy, starting with Cyrus the Great, that is, 1,200 years before the advent of Islam. In 1976, a new Persian calendar, also starting with Cyrus the Great, was introduced and later cancelled after protests by the religious authorities.

2,500-Year Celebrations of the Persian Monarchy, 1971

By Iran's government (http://www.ir-psri.com/pic/Photos/Photo36_1.jpg) [Public domain], via Wikimedia Commons

See page for author [Public domain], via Wikimedia Commons

The religious provocations, both in the celebrations of 1971 and the issue of the Persian calendar were typical of the relations between the Shah and the *ulama*, which were deteriorating constantly because of his emphasis on Iran's secular nature and its pre-Islamic past.

The extent of opposition was increased even further by the ineffective use of the oil wealth of the early 1970s and its social inequalities. Oil wealth led to widespread corruption, social injustice and waste. The unrestrained spending

The Iranian Revolution – Mass Mobilization

- Religious leaders objected to the regime's secularizing policies and extensive corruption
- Merchants and traders (the bazaaris) resented modernization schemes damaging to their interests and also suffered from the severe economic crisis
- Middle class intellectuals set the protest movement in motion
- Joined by the students
- And subsequently by the unstoppable masses of the urban poor mobilized by the appealing slogans of Khomeini and others in the religious leadership
- Finally organized labor joined in with paralyzing strikes and with the actions of the guerrilla groups of the opposition

Nikki R. Keddie, *Modern Iran: Roots and Results of Revolution* (New Haven: Yale University Press, 2003), pp. 222–233.

spree that started in 1973 with the beginning of the massive oil revenues, after the hike in prices by the oil producing countries, was terribly mismanaged and three years later came to a sudden halt, causing widespread unemployment and suffering, especially amongst the masses of the urban poor.

Protests began in mid-1977, and from early 1978, a cycle of rioting developed in which religious leaders and religious motifs became increasingly apparent. There was an effective alliance between the urban poor and the men of religion, led by Khomeini in exile, in their shared disaffection with the economic and political situation.

In the organized opposition, there was a key role for the network of mosques and religious associations in the mobilization of this revolution in the making. The Shah could repress political organizations, but he could not close down the mosques. It was through these that the recorded speeches of Khomeini were efficiently distributed to the masses leaving the regime at a loss. Khomeini's appeal to the urban masses was magnetic. He was adamant in his demand for the overthrow of the Pahlavis and the establishment of an Islamic republic.

Khomeini's Appeal to the Masses

By unknwon (http://www.nasr14.blogfa.com/8803.aspx) [Public domain], via Wikimedia Commons

The regime was indecisive, mixing between conciliation and repression. The usually coercive regime was restrained in its use of force. The President of the United States, Jimmy Carter, pressured the Iranian regime to be more diligent in its pursuit of human rights and therefore reduced the capacity of the regime to use coercive force against the opposition. The regime was in need of US support to preserve its deterrent image of outside protection, but such support was not forthcoming.

By the end of 1978, government began to break down, and Khomeini returned from exile in Paris on 1 February 1979. The regime of the Pahlavis fell ten days later. This was the first instance of a revolution of the masses in the Middle East, and it can be explained by the coalescence of four main destabilizing factors.

Khomeini Returns from Exile

Also uploaded by en:User:Sa.vakilian in en.wiki and by fa:User:Mrostam in fa.Wiki [GFDL (http://www.gnu.org/copyleft/fdl.html) or CC-BY-SA-3.0 (http://creativecommons.org/licenses/by-sa/3.0/)], via Wikimedia Commons

First, the massive disaffection and dislocation due to rapid population growth, urbanization and growing social divisions between the haves and the have-nots. The lower classes did not enjoy the oil wealth of Iran. Tehran had a population of 1 million in 1945 and 5 million in 1977. Iran's population was approximately 14 million in 1945, 40 million in 1980 and about 75 million in 2011.

The second factor was the revolutionizing of the men of religion by Khomeini (see further below).

The third was the failure of the regime to maximize its coercive potential.

And the fourth, the absence of the traditional external force in Iranian politics to act as a deterrent against the opposition.

There was a critical link between Shi'ism, Ayatollah Khomeini and the Revolution. The Revolution was characterized by a typically Shi'ite form of mobilization, invoking the Shi'ite historical narrative of suffering and oppression at the hands of their Sunni oppressors since the seventh century. This was the story of the struggle over the Caliphate in support of Ali, the Prophet's son-in-law and his descendants, his sons Hussein and Hasan, who were killed just like Ali before them by their Sunni opponents in the early years of Islam. These were the memories of the historically downtrodden underclass that were now exploited to great effect to mobilize opposition against the Shah, as if he were in the role of the oppressive Sunnis of old.

The Islamic Republic was established in accordance with the traditional principle of *wilayat al-faqih*, the guardianship of the jurisprudent. In comparison to the Sunni Islamists, a much greater emphasis was laid in the Shi'ite example on the personality of the ruler, whereas the Sunnis tended to place their emphasis on the implementation of religious law, the Shari'a.

Guardianship of the jurisprudent was given new meaning by Khomeini. Instead of the general, traditional responsibility of the jurisprudent for the needy in the community, such as minors, widows and orphans, this now became a reference to government by the jurisprudent. The men of religion in the Shi'ite tradition were always deeply involved in politics, but the majority view was that their role was to advise the ruler, and not to rule themselves. Government by the jurisprudent was, therefore, a new revolutionary interpretation introduced by Khomeini.

The new constitution defined Shi'ite Islam as the state religion. It also determined the formation of a Council of Religious Experts, whose task was to ensure that all legislation passed by the Iranian parliament was in accordance with religious law. In 1982, drastic changes were introduced into the legal system and all laws that were not in conformity with Islam were revoked.

Ayatollah Khamenei

By User:Seyedkhan [GFDL (http://www.gnu.org/copyleft/fdl.html) or CC-BY-SA-3.0-2.5-2.0-1.0 (http://creativecommons.org/licenses/by-sa/3.0)], via Wikimedia Commons

Iran of the revolution has been in existence for well over 30 years. When Khomeini died in 1989, the transition to his successor Ayatollah Ali Khamenei was smooth and uneventful. Iran withstood the onslaught of Iraq in eight years of war. It has developed its nuclear program and has established impressive regional influence in Iraq, Syria and Lebanon (through Hizballah).

The weakness of the Arabs has allowed for the shift of the center of gravity in Middle Eastern politics to the Gulf, and to Iran. The agreement between Iran and the great powers in November 2013 to negotiate Iran's nuclear program was an important recognition of and acquiescence in Iran's rising regional stature.

There are issues at home facing domestic criticism. The population has doubled since the Revolution and the economy has not been able to keep up with population growth. There are rumblings of dissent on corruption, repression and on national priorities. Many in Iran ask why more is not invested in domestic construction and development, rather than on Iran's foreign hegemonic design.

But perhaps most importantly, the regime of the Ayatollahs enjoyed an aura of legitimacy and authenticity that the Pahlavi monarchy, always tainted as an instrument for foreign influence, never had.

Key Sources and Suggested Further Reading

- Ayalon, Ami, *Egypt's Quest for Cultural Orientation* (Tel Aviv University: Moshe Dayan Center, Data and Analysis Series, June 1999).
- Ayubi, Nazih, *Political Islam: Religion and Politics in the Arab World* (London: Routledge, 1991).
- Ayubi, Nazih, *Overstating the Arab State: Politics and Society in the Middle East* (London: I.B. Tauris, 2008).
- Baram, Amatzia, "Territorial Nationalism in the Middle East," *Middle Eastern Studies*, Vol. 26, No. 4 (1990).
- Bayat, Asef, *Making Islam Democratic: Social Movements and the Post-Islamic Turn* (Stanford University Press, 2007).
- Ben-Dor, Gabriel, Ofra Bengio (Eds.), *Minorities and the State in the Arab World* (Boulder, CO: Lynne Rienner, 1999).
- Carkoglu, Ali and Ersin Kalaycioglu, *The Rising Tide of Conservatism in Turkey* (New York: Palgrave-Macmillan, 2009).
- Doumani, Beshara, "Palestine Versus the Palestinians? The Iron Laws and the Ironies of a People Denied," *Journal of Palestine Studies*, Vol. 36, No. 4 (Summer 2007).
- Esposito, John (Ed.), *Voices of Resurgent Islam* (Oxford University Press, 1983).
- Esposito, John, *Islam and Politics* (Syracuse University Press, 1984).
- Esposito, John and Azzam Tamimi (Eds.), *Islam and Secularism in the Middle East* (London: Hurst, 2002).
- Gelvin, James, *The Modern Middle East: A History* (Oxford University Press, 2011).
- Gelvin, James, *The Arab Uprisings: What Everyone Needs to Know* (Oxford University Press, 2012).

- Halliday, Fred, *Nation and Religion in the Middle East* (Boulder, CO: Lynne Rienner, 2000).
- Hashemi, Nader, *Islam, Secularism and Liberal Democracy: Toward a Democratic Theory for Muslim Societies* (Oxford University Press, 2009).
- Humphreys, Steven, *Between Memory and Desire: The Middle East in a Troubled Age* (Berkeley: University of California Press, 1999).
- Kepel, Gilles, *Muslim Extremism in Egypt: The Prophet and Pharaoh* (Berkeley: University of California Press, 1985).
- al-Khalil, Samir (Kanan Makiya), *Republic of Fear: The Inside Story of Saddam's Iraq* (New York: Pantheon, 1990).
- Lassner, Jacob and Ilan Troen, *Jews and Muslims in the Arab World: Haunted by Pasts Real and Imagined* (Lanham, MD: Rowman and Littlefield, 2007).
- Lewis, Bernard, *The Middle East and the West* (New York: Harper Torchbook, 1966).
- Lewis, Bernard, *What Went Wrong? Western Impact and Middle Eastern Response* (Oxford University Press, 2002).
- Litvak, Meir (Ed.), *Palestinian Collective Memory and National Identity* (New York: Palgrave Macmillan, 2009).
- Moaddel, Mansoor, *Islamic Modernism, Nationalism and Fundamentalism: Episode and Discourse* (University of Chicago Press, 2005).
- Nasr, Vali, *The Shia Revival: How Conflicts within Islam Will Shape the Future* (New York: W.W. Norton, 2006).
- Piscatori, James, *Islam in a World of Nation States* (Cambridge University Press, 1986).
- Piscatori, James (Ed.), *Islam in the Political Process* (Cambridge University Press, 1986).

- Ramadan, Tariq, *Islam and the Arab Awakening* (Oxford University Press, 2012).
- Qutb, Sayyid, *Milestones* (Damascus: Dar al-Ilm, 2007).
- Said, Edward, *Orientalism* (New York: Vintage Books, 1979).
- Salem, Paul, "The Rise and Fall of Secularism in the Arab World." *Middle East Policy*, Vol. 4, No. 3 (March 1996).
- Sayigh, Yezid, *Armed Struggle and the Search for State: The Palestinian National Movement, 1949-1993* (Oxford: Clarendon Press, 1997).
- Seale, Patrick, *Asad of Syria; The Struggle for the Middle East* (London: I.B. Tauris, 1988).
- Sivan, Emmanuel, *Radical Islam: Medieval Theology and Modern Politics* (New Haven: Yale University Press, 1990).
- Susser, Asher (Ed.), *Challenges to the Cohesion of the Arab State* (Moshe Dayan Center, Tel Aviv University, 2008).
- Susser, Asher, *The Rise of Hamas in Palestine and the Crisis of Secularism in the Arab World* (Crown Center for Middle East Studies, Brandeis University, 2010).
- Susser, Asher, *Israel, Jordan and Palestine; The Two-State Imperative* (Waltham, MA: Brandeis University Press, 2012).
- Susser, Asher, "The 'Arab Spring': Competing Analytical Paradigms," *Bustan, The Middle East Book Review*, No. 3 (2012).
- Vatikiotis, P. J., *Islam and the State* (London: Routledge, 1987).
- Yapp, Malcolm, *The Near East since the First World War* (London: Longman, 1991).
- Zisser, Eyal, *Commanding Syria: Bashar al-Asad and the First Years in Power* (London: I.B. Tauris, 2007).
- Zürcher, Erik, *Turkey: A Modern History* (London: I. B. Tauris, 2009).

Chapter Ten

Conclusion

In conclusion some key points:

1. The introduction of reform and new ideas in the 19th century, under the impact of Western expansion, and political, economic and ideological encroachment, had great influence on the manner in which the modern Middle East was shaped.
2. The reforms were imposed, for the most part, top down, often on an unwilling population, and their impact therefore, was not always as deep as it might have been.
3. In later years, at the end of the 19th century, the movement of Islamic reform made its impact as did the emergence of other modern ideas such as nationalism: Egyptian, Arab, Turkish and Iranian.
4. Much of the 20th century was the century of Arabism and the development of the Arab state, but the 20th century also saw the retreat and the failure of pan-Arabism as a crucial platform of secular politics. Society, as a result, was never really secularized.
5. Recent years have seen the resurgence of neo-traditionalist forces of political Islam, sectarianism and tribalism.
6. Another factor to be remembered is the growth of population and the massive urbanization, and, as a result, the widespread economic distress that characterizes many countries in the Middle East.
7. It is the combination of these factors that led to the outbreak of the so-called "Arab Spring" and the resurgence of the neo-traditionalist forces that have come to challenge the cohesion of the Arab state as it was formed almost a century ago.
8. The relative weakness of the Arab states has led to the rising influence, regionally speaking, of the non-Arab states in the Middle East: Turkey, Iran and Israel. Israel, as we have seen, finds itself in an Arab world far less powerful than the Arab world that its founding fathers had predicted. Israel is presently engaged far more with the difficulties that emerge from Arab weakness rather than those that arise from Arab power.[1]

1. See Asher Susser, "Israel's Place in a Changing Regional Order, 1948-2013," *Israel Studies*, Vol. 19, No. 2 (Summer 2014), pp. 218–238.

9. Recent years during the "Arab Spring" have shown a rather disappointing performance of the Islamists in power, undermining their own argument that "Islam is the solution."
10. Thus, coming to our final conclusion; the ongoing struggle between the forces of modernity and those of tradition, or neo-tradition, of the last 200 years is far from over. It will continue to govern politics and society in the Middle East for years to come. Which of the two will prevail in the end remains an open question.

Index

S